D0710621

MY FOURTH TIME, WE DROWNED

MY FOURTH TIME, WE DROWNED

SEEKING REFUGE ON THE WORLD'S DEADLIEST MIGRATION ROUTE

SALLY HAYDEN

MELVILLE HOUSE
BROOKLYN • LONDON

MY FOURTH TIME, WE DROWNED

First published in 2022 by Melville House
Copyright © Sally Hayden, 2021
All rights reserved.

Maps on pp. ix - x by Martin Brown

Melville House Publishing
46 John Street
Brooklyn, NY 11201
and
Melville House UK
Suite 2000
16/18 Woodford Road
London E7 0HA

mhpbooks.com
@melvillehouse

ISBN: 978-1-61219-945-0
ISBN: 978-1-61219-946-7 (eBook)

Library of Congress Control Number: 2021950244

Designed by Beste M. Doğan

Printed in the United States of America
1 3 5 7 9 10 8 6 4 2

A catalog record for this book is available from the Library of Congress

"I was caught by the Libyan coastguard
three times—first time from Qarabully, east Tripoli;
second time, Zawiya; third time, Zuwara.
And my fourth time, we drowned.
And the fifth time, I made it to safety."

—SOMALI REFUGEE NOW IN EUROPE

"The real damage is done by those millions
who want to 'survive.' The honest men who just want
to be left in peace. Those who don't
want their little lives disturbed by anything bigger
than themselves."

—SOPHIE SCHOLL, ANTI-NAZI POLITICAL ACTIVIST

"One day, I will reach Europe and we will meet. If it
doesn't happen I want you to write a book which tells
my story, because the world's people need to read
this story for their enjoyment."

—ERITREAN REFUGEE IN LIBYA

TABLE OF CONTENTS

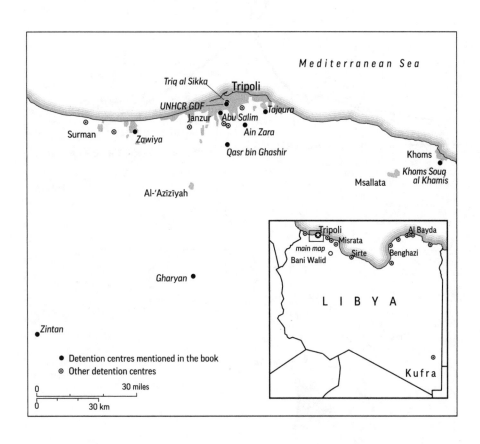

Mediterranean Sea

Triq al Sikka

Tripoli

UNHCR GDF

Janzur   Abu Salim

Surman   Tajoura

Zawiya   Ain Zara

Qasr bin Ghashir   Khoms

Msallata   Khoms Souq
al Khamis

Al-'Azīzīyah

Gharyan

Zintan

● Detention centres mentioned in the book
⊙ Other detention centres

30 miles

0

0   30 km

Tripoli   Al Bayda

main map   Misrata   Benghazi

Bani Walid   Sirte

L I B Y A

K u f r a

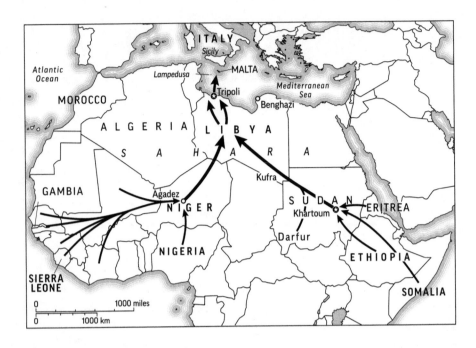

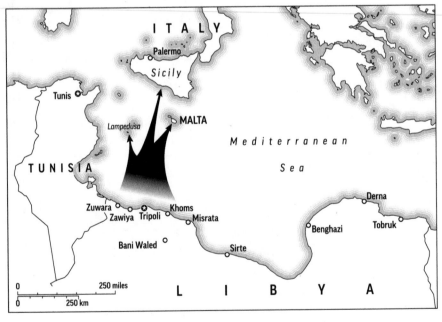

THIS SIM CARD IS OUR LIFE

On Sunday, August 26, 2018, I was browsing through Netflix, in a sublet room in north London, when I received a Facebook message. "Hi sister Sally, we need your help," it read. "We are under bad condition in Libya prison. If you have time, I will tell you all the story."

Of course, this did not make sense to me. How did someone thousands of miles away find my name? How did they have a working phone if they were locked up? I was skeptical, but I replied quickly to see what would come next.

"I'm so sorry to hear that," I wrote. "Yes, of course I have time, though unfortunately I can't do much to help." We exchanged WhatsApp numbers. The sender explained that his brother knew my journalism from Sudan, a neighboring North African country, and had traced my contact details on-line. He needed them because he was trapped in Ain Zara, a migrant deten-tion center in Libya's capital, Tripoli, alongside hundreds of other refugees. Conflict had broken out around them. Smoke rose above the walls outside. They were watching the city smolder and burn.

The Libyans in charge at Ain Zara, who had been abusing them for months, fled when the sounds of fighting grew nearer. It was never clear whether the guards—or the "police," as the refugees called them—left to escape or join in: many had sympathies with those fighting, while others were simply frightened or arrogant young men who signed up because they needed work, felt comfortable being armed, and had spotted the potential for extra profits through exploitation. There were still children and pregnant women inside the building. The refugee men, who had been locked in one big hall for months, broke down the separating door. They hoped the group would be safer if they were all together.

"We see bullets passing over us and heavy weapons in the street," my new contact typed, before sending me photos he said were from that day. One, taken through a window, showed vehicles with anti-aircraft guns visible outside the center's gates. Another was an image of himself: an emaciat-ed-looking 28-year-old sitting on the ground with three young children.

Everyone inside the building was unarmed and defenseless: stick thin after months with maybe a meal a day, sometimes nothing. Their bodies were scarred from torture and beatings, inflicted both by the guards who had just left and the smugglers who held them for months or years before they arrived in Ain Zara. The war raging outside had been coming for a long time, and these people needed help—any help, even if it was a journalist in a faraway country with little to offer.

"If there is any United Nations Refugee Agency or human rights organi-zations near you, contact them. Since yesterday we haven't eaten any food," messaged the man. "If you have a page post something on that about this situation." He said he came from Eritrea, a repressive country in the Horn of Africa where citizens are forced into unending military service by the ruling dictatorship. He had breached two borders, survived kidnapping by traffickers, and traveled nearly 3,000 kilometers to get to Libya.

Like everyone else with him, the man then tried to cross the Mediterranean Sea to reach Europe but was caught and incarcerated. Now they were in trouble. They had one phone between hundreds that the detainees had kept hidden for months. He said it was the phone a smuggler gave him to bring on board the rubber boat so they could call for rescue once it inevitably began to sink. The European Union was responsible for the situation they were now in—it was Europe that had forced them back.

I spent the next twenty-four hours doing all I could to verify his story.

I asked for photos of his surroundings, videos, selfies, GPS locations, and contact details for his family members. I knew people in Libya, and they confirmed there was conflict in the suburb they were in.

I called him numerous times.

As I requested more and more detail, the man I was speaking to told me how, before the fighting got bad, detainees had regularly been taken from the detention center and forced to work like slaves in the homes of wealthy Libyans. Women were raped, and Christians targeted for particular abuse—violently assaulted while their crucifixes were ripped from their necks. Some mornings, around 3:00 a.m., the armed Libyan guards would call hundreds of detainees out to be "counted," sadistically making them stand in the cold for hours. They probably were not aware, but this ordeal echoed *Appellplatz*, the early morning roll calls Nazis used to do in concentration camps—a grim ritual carried out with the aim of intimidating and humiliating prisoners.

Despite the UN saying its staff had regular access to the centers, that did not seem to be true. Many detainees who had fled war or dictatorships were never even registered as refugees. That meant there was no list of their names anywhere. They were terrified of being sold back to smugglers, who torture migrants until their families pay hefty ransoms. They were begging to be saved.

I had stumbled, inadvertently, on a human rights disaster of epic proportions.

––––––––

There were eight pregnant women and roughly twenty babies and toddlers among the Ain Zara group. As the man and I spoke on the phone, bombs exploded nearby, and I heard the sounds of shrieking.

"Now everyone is disturbed, it is becoming worse and worse . . . Look at the women and children, you can post this video for the European people to know."

Frantically, I searched for an answer. I contacted the UN and international aid organizations working in Libya, but they said it was too dangerous for their staff to act ("In Libya today, everybody is at risk, so not an easy situation," one aid worker responded, showing a callous pragmatism I was to encounter again and again). I emailed editors asking whether they would publish a report, but I was a freelancer, and—as often happens—replies were slow.

Feeling unmoored and useless, I began to post screenshots of my messages with the refugees on Twitter, where they were quickly shared, garnering tens of thousands of views, and then hundreds of thousands. Within months, their words would reach millions.

"There's no food, no water. The children are crying. We are suffering, especially the children. We haven't slept in two days. We are waiting for some miracle. Tell them the people are dying here."

Time stretched out for me, with sleepless nights and nerve-racking days measured in countless moments laden with danger. I barely left the sparse room I was renting, except when I was picked up by a taxi to do TV and radio interviews after BBC producers spotted my Twitter updates. Online, there was a cascade of retweets and likes and shares, but in Ain Zara nothing changed. The refugees would turn off the phone to conserve its battery, silence suddenly interrupted by a flurry of messages at any new development.

Eventually, buses arrived. Was this salvation? At first, we did not know if their drivers were Libyan authorities or smugglers (I would later learn there is not always much to distinguish the two). Armed men in uniform said they were taking the detainees to a different area, which was—at least at that moment—farther from the front line.

Then, about fifty hours after I received the first message, I watched through WhatsApp as the GPS location of the man's phone edged across the city. I used it to update the refugees on where they were. "To your left, you will see the University of Tripoli," I remember typing, and they responded excitedly when they spotted its modern facade. For many of the passengers on board, this was the first time they had seen the city in daylight.

The buses and their occupants reached another compound. Worried that they might have been transferred to a smuggler's den, my main contact asked me if it was a detention center under the control of Libya's Tripoli-based government. I, in turn, emailed my new UN sources, who told me yes, it was. Inside, there were already around seventy other detainees who had been moved from elsewhere. Staff with the UN's International Organization for Migration—wearing fluorescent, garishly branded jackets—turned up to hand out water. Those employees would later message me, too, telling me that things were under control.

Around midnight, the detained refugees were given cake and yogurt: their first food in days. "Get some sleep, it is enough for you too, you were with us the whole time," read my final messages from that night. "The guys are thanking you so much. They are saying 'give her some rest.' May God bless you."

––––––

What does your phone mean to you? Is it a way to chat to friends or swipe through dating apps? Do you take selfies, send voice notes or Snapchats? Is it a vital source of information? Has it saved your life?

What would it represent if you were incarcerated, its little screen your only window to the outside world? What would it be like to spend months or years in the same building without one? Could you share a phone with five hundred others? Would you risk being tortured to keep it or forego eating to buy data, knowing you would starve without food but could disappear forever if you had no way of sending a distress call?

What is it like to watch innocent people being shot through Facebook messenger? How would you feel listening to their faltering voices as they mentally and physically withered away? That's what I was going to discover.

Originally, I believed these first contacts in Libya were an anomaly, the isolated victims of an accidental oversight. Once these people were helped, I thought, my job would be done. I was wrong. Within days, more and more detained refugees began contacting me. They got my number from friends, or found what I had been posting online. They sent messages through Twitter and WhatsApp. Their stories were eerily similar.

I would learn that roughly six thousand people were being held indefinitely, at that time, in more than twenty so-called "official" migrant detention centers in Libya. These centers were ostensibly run by Libya's Department for Combatting Illegal Migration (DCIM), which was associated with the UN-backed Government of National Accord in Tripoli—one of two governments vying for power in the febrile North African country. In reality, the Tripoli government was weak, propped up by a collection of militias that operated with impunity.

The majority of those locked up had already tried to reach Europe but they had been caught on the Mediterranean Sea. I researched more and discovered that, in an effort to stop sea crossings, the EU had committed to spending close to 100 million euro on the Libyan coastguard.[1] Libyan sailors—many of whom were former smugglers—were encouraged to patrol the Mediterranean and intercept refugees' boats. This allowed the EU to circumnavigate international law, which says people cannot be returned to countries where their lives are in danger. Between 2017 and late 2021, more than eighty thousand men, women, and children were captured at sea and forced back to Libya. Most of them were then locked up for being in the country illegally, but there were no official charges, trials, or any way to contest their imprisonment.

Captives had seen friends escape detention centers only to be killed by militias that patrolled the streets. Others were shot trying to get away. They told me how tuberculosis ended lives and food deprivation left people lying motionless on the ground. They described detainees who stopped speaking after losing their minds through stress and hopelessness, rocking backwards and forwards, their arms tight around their knees. They sent me torture videos of tormented relatives held for ransom by merciless smugglers. They felt abandoned by the UN and cursed the EU for not recognizing that refugees are humans, too.

Throughout everything that happened, my contacts carefully hid their phones, begging friends elsewhere to top up their credit so they could connect to the internet and secretly charging the batteries on the rare occasions there was electricity. "This SIM card is our life," one man explained. Groups of tens or even hundreds of people would crowd around a phone to craft messages together, carefully deliberating how best to describe their situation. Each word they sent was a precious cry for help. Raising awareness of their plight might be the only thing giving them hope.

———

In the course of my reporting, I found many ways to confirm what I was told, and I am grateful to all the people who assisted me but cannot be identified. Over time, I developed many sources in each detention center. This book is based on interviews with hundreds of refugees and migrants who have found themselves stuck in Libya since the EU started funding interceptions in 2017. I also built up a large network of contacts among international and local humanitarian workers who wanted to talk but needed to go unnamed to continue their work. Much of what they said could not be published at the time due to security risks. Instead, my job became passing information between detained refugees and the aid organizations or UN agencies that were supposed to be assisting them. Unexpectedly, my geographic distance from Libya was exactly the reason that refugees trusted me to do this.

The first thing I always say to people who contact me is that I cannot help them directly. I am just a journalist; I don't have the power to do anything except report. I have been surprised by how many responses are positive. New sources say they understand but still want their stories told. They hope the rest of the world will realize they exist, that for now they are alive and worth saving.

For years after that first message came in August 2018, I messaged refugees and migrants in different Libyan detention centers every day.[2] I imagined the network of hidden phones, the connections between me and them, between them and their families or friends, like lifelines—arteries, pumping blood. I could not fathom the bravery of the people I spoke to. We talked about the dangers of going public, but if a source wanted to take that risk, I respected their choice. Some were beaten up or tortured on suspicion of sending information. Their phones were regularly confiscated.

Still now, I often receive videos, photos, or audio I cannot share. Missing people and evidence of atrocities accumulate in my phone's photo album in between pictures of autumn leaves or friends' babies. I set WhatsApp to save media automatically because detained refugees send me videos they cannot keep for safety reasons, and I do not want to risk them failing to download. I was getting so many messages at one stage that it was almost impossible to read them all.

These images are a sharp reminder of the world's growing disparities. People are more able to communicate than ever before, yet routes to safety are being shut down. Citizens in the West can look away, despite windows everywhere—phone screens, TV broadcasts, videos posted online—providing insight into our vast inequality. Anyone who does open their eyes may end up bearing witness to human rights abuses thousands of miles away without any ability to intervene.

This is not a story about me, but it is true that when I received those first messages, I could not have anticipated the personal ramifications of reporting on this crisis. The following years would see my life threatened in North Africa and my freedom on the line in Europe. I would travel across three continents chasing leads, spending weeks on a ship in the Mediterranean Sea and coming face to face with human smugglers accused of torturing people to death. I would uncover corruption, lies, and gross negligence and be denounced by government propaganda channels. My reporting would be referenced in human rights reports, legal challenges, and a submission to the International Criminal Court that called for EU officials to be charged with crimes against humanity.

I wrote this book because I wanted to document the consequences of European migration policies beginning from the point at which Europe becomes ethically culpable: when refugees are forcibly turned away. Until I began writing it, I did not realize how small a book can be. There is a lot I had to leave out, but I hope what is contained here goes some way towards documenting the scale of what we are responsible for. I ignored an initial suggestion by a literary agent to avoid naming detention centers because it could be too confusing for a reader. It felt important that the places where so many people suffered were identified. For length reasons, I was not able to include all the centers where I was in touch with detainees, but each had its own particular definition of hell.

Seventy years after the global refugee system began, we are locking people up for trying to seek safety. We force them out of sight and fortify systems that make it easy for us to forget about them. Some die in captivity, and others will be traumatized for life.

Sources in Libya tell me all the ways they are treated like animals. They have been flogged; sold; beaten; herded; crammed into halls, into small rooms, even into cages. They have come to despise each other's smells. Their minds slip away, denied the ability to think clearly for so long. They become malleable, forgetting their goals and values. They fret they will never trust again.

The hidden side of doing this sort of reporting is the time commitment. Mostly I am just chatting to people about themselves; their past lives; small, daily updates. Like the photos on my phone, their messages dart between the mundane and the nightmarish.

In italics throughout this book I have interspersed some of the thousands of messages I received from refugees in Libya, most of whom are not identified in the text. I wanted to include their voices, unfiltered.

This book will recount human stories, as well as giving some insight into the systemic issues destroying lives—negligence; corruption; apathy; inequality. It is not a comprehensive account of everything that is happening to people who try to reach Europe, or even to those who are caught by the Libyan coastguard—there are new abuses, new humiliations, every day— but I hope it plays some role in the quest for accountability.

A NOTE

Though no other factual details have been changed, some names have been altered to protect safety or privacy, and some messages lightly edited for clarity or to take out identifying information.

A portion of the proceeds from this book will be donated to refugee-supporting initiatives.

This book is dedicated to the men, women, and children who lost their lives in Libya and in the Mediterranean Sea; to their families, who suffered alongside them; and to the survivors, who will never forget.

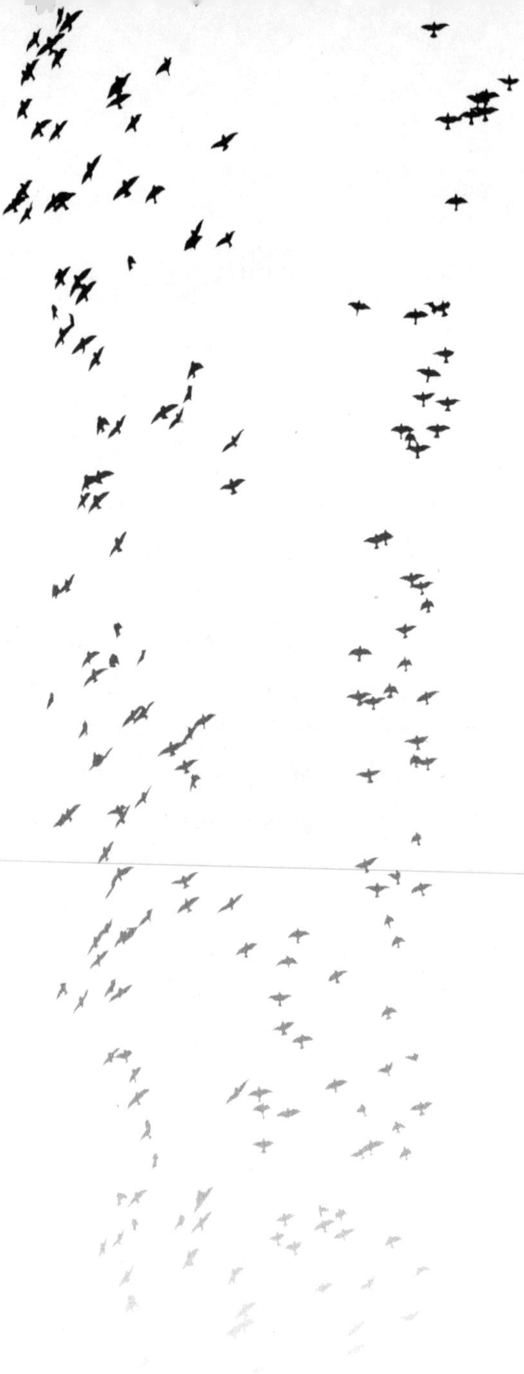

TIMELINE OF IMPORTANT EVENTS AND RELEVANT STATISTICS

2011	Revolution in Libya, dictator Muammar Gaddafi killed.
NOVEMBER 2015	The EU launches the Trust Fund for Africa, a multibillion pot of money aimed at stopping migration to Europe.[1]
FEBRUARY 2, 2017	Italy signs a Memorandum of Understanding with Libya agreeing to work with the Libyan coastguard "to stem the influx of illegal migrants." The EU pledges a sum of almost 100 million euro towards training and equipping the coastguard over the next few years.[2]
AUGUST–SEPTEMBER 2018	Intermilitia war breaks out in Tripoli.
AUGUST 30, 2018	Hundreds of refugees are relocated from Ain Zara detention center to Abu Salim.
OCTOBER 24, 2018	A Somali refugee sets himself on fire in Triq al Sikka detention center and dies of his injuries.
OCTOBER–NOVEMBER 2018	Medical care is halted during a tuberculosis outbreak in Triq al Sikka.

FEBRUARY 26, 2019 A protest in Triq al Sikka results in twenty-two people being taken underground and tortured.

MARCH 2019 The European Union declares the migration crisis "over" ahead of EU Parliament elections two months later. The EU ceases sea rescue patrols in the Central Mediterranean completely, though continues to fly planes and helicopters, which can spot refugee boats and direct the Libyan coastguard to them.

APRIL 4, 2019 Eastern general Khalifa Haftar orders his self-styled Libyan National Army to advance on Tripoli.

APRIL 23, 2019 Qasr bin Ghashir migrant detention center is attacked by fighters aligned with the Libyan National Army, and several detainees are killed.

JUNE 2019 A rare interagency UN visit to Zintan detention center confirms that twenty-two detainees have died there since the previous September.

JULY 2–3, 2019 Tajoura migrant detention center is bombed, and dozens of detainees killed.

MARCH 2020 The UN's International Organization for Migration says the death toll in the Mediterranean Sea has topped twenty thousand since 2014.[3]

JUNE 19, 2020 The EU Parliament passes a resolution to say "Black Lives Matter" in reaction to the murder of George Floyd, a 46-year-old American killed by police officers in the US.

JULY 2020 Pope Francis compares Libyan migrant detention centers to concentration camps.[4]

OCTOBER 2020 A ceasefire is signed between warring parties in Libya.

MARCH 2021   A new Libyan unity government is announced.

OCTOBER 2021   At least 5,000 refugees and migrants are rounded up in raids in Tripoli and detained indefinitely again. At least seven are killed during the raids or during a later escape.

OCTOBER 4, 2021   A fact-finding mission commissioned by the UN Human Rights Council finds there are "reasonable grounds to believe that acts of murder, enslavement, torture, imprisonment, rape, persecution and other inhumane acts committed against migrants" in Libya "form part of a systematic and widespread attack directed at this population, in furtherance of a state policy" which "may amount to crimes against humanity."

IMMIGRATION STATISTICS

SEA ARRIVALS TO ITALY[1]

2014	170,100
2015	153,842
2016	181,436
2017	119,369
2018	23,370
2019	11,471
2020	34,133
2021 (JANUARY–NOVEMBER 7)	55,895

NUMBER OF PEOPLE INTERCEPTED OR RESCUED BY THE LIBYAN COASTGUARD ON THE MEDITERRANEAN SEA

2017	19,452[2] (figure as of December 12, 2017)
2018	14,949[3]
2019	9,035[4]
2020	11,891[5]
2021 (JANUARY–NOVEMBER 27)	30,990[6]
TOTAL	86,317

PERCENTAGE OF PEOPLE WHO DIE
ATTEMPTING TO CROSS THE CENTRAL MEDITERRANEAN[7]

2017	1.98%	(one in every 51)
2018	2.86%	(one in every 35)
2019	4.78%	(one in every 21)

NUMBER OF PEOPLE WHO HAVE DROWNED IN THE
CENTRAL MEDITERRANEAN[8] (UNDERSTOOD TO BE AN UNDERESTIMATE)

2014	3,165
2015	3,149
2016	4,581
2017	2,853
2018	1,314
2019	1,262
2020	983
2021 (JANUARY–NOVEMBER 29)	1,303

MY FOURTH TIME, WE DROWNED

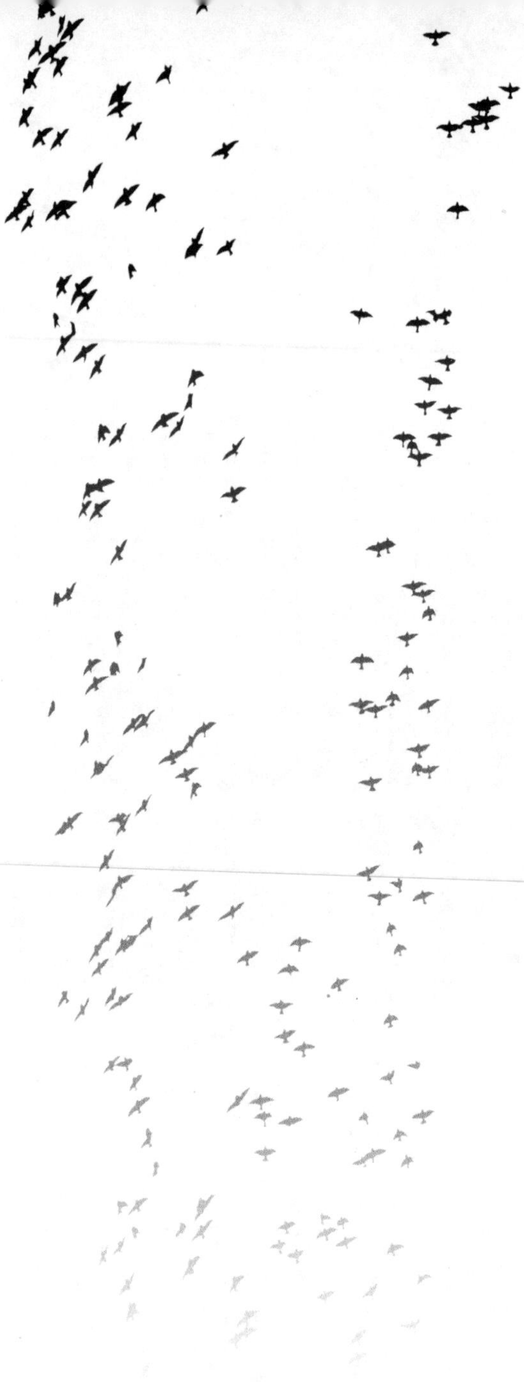

WHERE IT ENDS AND WHERE IT BEGINS

"I, being poor, have only my dreams;
I have spread my dreams under your feet;
Tread softly because you tread on my dreams."
–W. B. YEATS[1]

After ten hours at sea, Kaleb, a teenager from Eritrea, appealed to God for a sign. He was crouched in the middle of an overcrowded rubber boat, which was being thrown about by waves. His limbs were frozen still, apart from the occasional muscle spasm, and his fingertips had wrinkled. He could taste salt, though maybe this was not as much the spray as the sweat of unwashed bodies around him.

The sea was dark, the water cold. Some of the hundred people in the boat were crying softly, stomachs heaving as they retched from seasickness. Women would occasionally shout out, clutching their children as they beseechingly praised the Lord. Others had stopped making any sound at all. A passenger fainted, her weight on Kaleb. Around them, pooled seawater mixed with vomit. Every big wave was an insistent reminder that many of them could not swim.

Most of the men were perched sideways on the edge of the boat, with one foot in the water. They had taken off their shoes on the shore, or thrown them in the sea, so they were not weighed down and to avoid puncturing the rubber. The tired engine was another potential hazard: any leaking fuel combined with saltwater would cause vicious burns. Fed up or frightened, one man lit a cigarette, and others began to argue, begging him to put it out. They had one satellite phone on board, provided by the smugglers. Once they reached international waters, they dialed a number, as instructed, and asked for a rescue.

As Kaleb prayed, he heard a hum, and then a whirring. It was a small passenger plane, one he felt certain must have been sent by Europe. Its appearance signaled hope for the teenager and his fellow travelers. High above them, the plane began to circle. Its crew had spotted their dinghy, so small it looked almost invisible. The boat's white rubber merged with the Mediterranean Sea as it lurched, the souls upon it specks of dust. The Central Mediterranean was the deadliest migration route in the world.[2] All those lives, wildly adrift, could have easily disappeared without any trace. Did the plane's crew think about that?

Next, a helicopter arrived. It began to circle, too, before flying a slow path in another direction. "They are leading the way," Kaleb thought, anticipating a rescue ship ahead and European volunteers, their arms outstretched, ready to greet them. "It is taking us to where the safe boat is."

Though he was still so young, Kaleb had spent years getting to this point. But with success in sight, he was about to be thwarted. A message had been relayed.

The next people he saw were the EU-funded Libyan coastguard—rough, uniformed men who powered towards them on a motorized ship. Kaleb recognized their red, black, and green flag, though others wondered aloud if it was Turkish or Tunisian. The Libyans carried weapons and were prepared to use them. There was no resistance as they ordered the refugees off the rubber dinghy. People who had not moved their limbs in hours were suddenly thrashed into activity, each stiff and frigid body part starting rudely and painfully awake. Their thin bodies were forced down low onto the new boat's deck, and they cowered, surrounded by volatile men with weapons—a position they had been in many times before.

They had not realized they could be taken back to Libya, the country from which they were trying to escape. This, along with the role the plane and helicopter had played by illuminating their position for the interception, dawned on each refugee in turn. It was painful, but even more crushing than this European treachery was the death of a dream. This could have finally been their moment, their chance.

It was 2018, and Libya was a war zone where refugees and asylum seekers were locked up indefinitely without charge or trial. Kaleb's interception at sea marked the crushing culmination of all the time and more than $10,000 he had paid out while attempting to reach safety. His hopes were obliterated by hardening European migration policy at its most brutal.

On the journey back to North Africa, Kaleb's thoughts whirled. His family were fated to try and try, but they would never join the ranks of the world's privileged people: those who could flee a war by plane; those who had a passport or the documents needed to apply for university; those who did not fear a pounding on the door in the middle of the night, a gun in the face, and the understanding you would never be spoken of again. History was repeating itself. Kaleb's father had made a similar trip before him in 2012, after decades of obligatory, unending military service and a lengthy separation from his family. Already middle-aged, he had set out for Israel, taking an earlier migration route well-traveled by Eritreans. Instead of reaching his promised land, he died in Egypt's Sinai Desert—of hunger, lack of water, or sheer exhaustion, Kaleb never knew.

The small country of Eritrea, with its roughly six million people, is often referred to as the "North Korea of Africa" by the Western media.[3] It is one of the most secretive and brutal places on earth, where citizens experience their lack of freedom as something physical and stifling. On the Reporters Without Borders 2021 press freedom index, it was ranked as the least free state in the world, behind North Korea itself and other countries well known for oppressing and jailing journalists, like Iran, Egypt, and Syria.[4] Yet Kaleb's people were survivors and freedom fighters. They had battled for decades against European colonizers, as well as their much larger, oppressive neighbor Ethiopia, which was constantly trying to secure access to the Red Sea coast by bulldozing through the small state's independence.

Eritrea became an Italian colony in 1890. During the Second World War, the British defeated the Italians there and the UK took charge for the next decade. The US located a spy station in Eritrea after realizing it was possible to monitor nearly half the world's radio waves from its highlands.[5] The station was used to intercept information leading to the Normandy landings and again during the Korean War, with the US arguing that Eritrea should not be allowed to have the independence its people desperately desired because of its strategic location. In 1952, Eritrea, which is also bordered by Djibouti and Sudan, was subsumed by Ethiopia.

During a thirty-year-long war of independence, Eritrea's *tegadelti*— male and female freedom fighters—lived in trenches, sang revolutionary songs, and took classes on democracy as well as battle tactics. Around sixty-five thousand of them were killed before Eritrea achieved statehood in the early 1990s. Isaias Afwerki, a former liberation fighter, took control.[6] Like many other leaders across the African continent, he initially preached people power, even as he transitioned into an autocrat and refused to allow elections. Under him was an army of young slaves. After sovereignty came, Eritrea's education system was run by ex-independence fighters, with a command style system of management that funneled students into the army and national service indefinitely.[7]

Independence did not lead to freedom. By 2014, the UN Human Rights Council announced that around 6 percent of Eritrea's population had fled the country. The following year, thirty-nine thousand Eritreans crossed the Central Mediterranean to Italy—more than one quarter of all arrivals there by sea.[8] In 2016, the UN body said crimes against humanity had been committed in "a widespread and systematic manner"[9] across Eritrea, in military training camps, detention facilities, and elsewhere. People who were caught trying to escape described being incarcerated for years. Some prisons were underground, others, like one that survivors said included a roasting hot torture chamber for political detainees known as "the oven,"[10] were facilities specifically designed for interrogation.

"Crimes of enslavement, imprisonment, enforced disappearances, torture, persecution, rape, murder and other inhumane acts have been committed as part of a campaign to instill fear in, deter opposition from and ultimately to control the Eritrean civilian population," the UN report read.[11]

"Eritrea is an authoritarian state. There is no independent judiciary, no national assembly and there are no other democratic institutions," added Mike Smith, the chair of the Commission of Inquiry. "This has created a governance and rule of law vacuum, resulting in a climate of impunity for crimes against humanity to be perpetrated over a quarter of a century. These crimes are still occurring today."[12]

Kaleb's childhood memories are laced with his family. Sweet grandparents. Capital city Asmara, with its fading Italian colonial architecture. Cyclists everywhere, because it is almost impossible to import cars.

It is rare that journalists have been allowed inside Eritrea, and much of its population has no access to the internet. Even when a person does manage to get online, maybe in one of Asmara's few internet cafes, the connection is incredibly slow. In 2012, the UN's International Telecommunication Union called Eritrea the least technologically connected country on earth.[13] Citizens who escaped its borders had to come to terms not only with what they could see and hear in person—new landscapes, languages, and ways of life—but also everything they could now access online. The internet opened up their eyes to the rest of the world, to the full spectrum of human existence and previously inconceivable prospects, in a way that could feel both inspiring and crushingly overwhelming.

———

I had been fascinated by Eritrea for years. In August 2015, I was sent to Calais, in northern France, on an assignment for millennial-focused news outlet VICE, where I worked as a staff writer. On my first night there, I met Petros, a gaunt 27-year-old in a brown leather jacket who came from Keren, Eritrea's second largest city. We stood in a green field at the edge of a raised motorway, where refugees and migrants gathered at dusk. They were all planning to jump on trucks or trains headed towards the UK. There was a bonfire under the nearby trees where people of various nationalities warmed their hands and discussed their chances. A number were probably smugglers. In front of us, facing the lights of cars dashing by, a line of Eritreans knelt in prayer, asking God if this could be their night.

His story stayed with me. Petros was just three years old when his brother and uncle disappeared without a trace. At age nineteen, frustrated after reaching adulthood with no answers, he asked about the fate of his brother at a community meeting.

Security forces came for Petros in the night. He was blindfolded and spent the next nine months in prison, where he was beaten every day. When Petros needed to pee, he was handed a plastic bottle.

He described a land where people could be happy if only they had free will and did not keep going missing. His wife ended up in the UK after traveling abroad to work as a maid for an abusive family in Saudi Arabia; she escaped during a visit to Europe. Petros sold everything he could to join her. As he spoke, his voice wavered, yet contained a level of determination I would witness again and again in Eritreans I met. His descriptions even veered into pride. Petros wanted to tell me how beautiful his father's orange trees were, how rich the Eritrean landscapes, how wonderful their food and musicians, and how much he would miss everything he was leaving behind.

Six weeks later, in September 2015, I stood on the Simien Mountains along Eritrea's border with Ethiopia. I had hiked for days to get to a peak where I could see into Eritrea, accompanied by a kind Ethiopian guide and a local guard, a requirement for walking this rural terrain. The guard wore crocs, carried an AK-47, and spoke little English. He was supposed to keep us safe from "bandits" and sat out in the rain at night, his gun upright between his palms, keeping watch as we lit a fire for warmth before falling asleep in tents. As the sun rose, we walked by clumps of torch lilies, by child goatherds, baboons, and donkeys, looking out for the rare but prized walia ibex goats and copper-colored Ethiopian wolves. We passed through small villages, improbable in their remoteness. Locals—who came out to stare—were totally reliant on this soil. It felt like a place far from politics, though I later found out the Ethiopian government was forcibly relocating people from their villages as part of efforts to improve conservation and increase tourism.[14]

Eventually, on a mountaintop, my guide told me we would normally have been able to see Eritrea from where I stood, but there was too much fog. It seemed emblematic for such an inaccessible place. I stayed a while, gazing downwards and wondering at all that still was not clear to me.

———

By the time I stood looking into the blanket of fog over Eritrea, Kaleb had already left. When he was around ten years old, Kaleb's mother escaped so her son could be saved from the same system of enforced national labor his father was pulled into. She raised him and his younger siblings in Ethiopia's capital city, Addis Ababa, 1,200 kilometers away. Ethiopia and Eritrea were mired in a bloody border war, but that did not stop people from fleeing. By 2017, around 2,500 Eritreans were crossing the border into Ethiopia every month, joining the roughly 130,000 Eritreans already there.[15]

Ethiopia was like Eritrea in a lot of ways. The people were still *Habeshas*—a word commonly used to describe those born of both countries. They had similar cultures, including the traditional coffee ceremony, which involves rounds of *buna* or *bun* sipped in small, handleless cups, often accompanied by popcorn. The dominant religion was the same: Christian Orthodox.

Addis Ababa's streets were bustling with shops, stalls, and restaurants selling bitter injera flatbread, tej honey wine, and other staples. Churches blared out music and preaching as early as 5:00 a.m., as their congregations, draped in white scarves, trekked cobbled lanes to worship. Donkeys wove through roads packed with cars, while gangs of abandoned children sniffed glue to keep hunger pangs at bay, or begged for money. The altitude was high in Addis, which meant it was a good place for athletic training. In central Meskel Square, runners went through their laps at sunrise. They followed in the footsteps of Haile Gebrselassie, treading this crescent-shaped terrace of tracks.

Kaleb was not Ethiopian, though, he was Eritrean, and he was constantly reminded of it. As a child, his background occasionally came up as a joking insult during play fighting with friends. But when he matured, he realized the consequences were bigger than that.

Growing up, he had always been intelligent, with a fast smile and a knack for charming people, old and young. He was a quick student and loved reading. At his school, there were a lot of relatively affluent Ethiopian students. Kaleb might have been talented, but it was hard not to notice how limited his options were in comparison to his classmates. He was trapped in the same invisible cage as refugees all over the world—one where opportunities for work, for education, for travel are blocked because of a lack of documentation or a passport. "I wanted to have an identity there," he remembered.

This became especially clear when he won a scholarship to go to China in high school after getting a good score in English and mathematics in the national exams. The labyrinthine system to secure a refugee travel permit, mired with corruption, meant it would not be possible to go.

"Dreaming is not good sometimes. Me, I dream."

Kaleb had heard about the migration route towards Europe, which went by land through Sudan and Libya. He started gathering information, taking a sudden interest in the stories of people who had crossed the Mediterranean Sea. When someone mentioned a brother, aunt, or cousin in a European country, he would ask how they got there, never mentioning that he was considering the journey himself.

————

There is something otherworldly about the *Habesha* countries. Ethiopia and Eritrea have their own script and run on their own calendar, roughly seven years behind the Gregorian calendar used by much of the rest of the world. On New Year's Eve, celebrated in September, you must jump over a fire for good luck. Ethiopia's Christians long claimed that the Ark of the Covenant was kept in their northern highlands, where it was brought three thousand years by the Queen of Sheba's son, Menelik, though no one had laid eyes on it for decades, except for a single anointed guardian. The year is dotted with festivals—*Meskel, Irreecha, Kiddus Yohannes,* and *Genna.*

But these ancient beliefs, this magnificent culture, do not protect people from the harshness of life in a developing country and all its accompanying faults—corruption, poverty, nepotism, lack of opportunity. Kaleb tried one final time to go to China, contacting a new travel agent who also arranged educational scholarships. Again, his attempts proved futile. In the meantime, he would not, or could not, tell his mother about the new plan that was forming inside him. It hurt too much to think about her reaction; he knew it would break her heart.

Like most humans, Eritreans live a life underscored by quotes and sayings. *"Nab laeli ente temitka hgus aykit kewn eka"* ("If you look up, you will become unhappy") and *"Chamaka mare egreka"* ("Your shoe should be equal to your foot") were two the elderly would repeat, the message a pointed reminder of the dangers of ambition. Maybe Kaleb had made the ultimate mistake and dared to dream of more for himself, beyond years of scrabbling for food and money to get by. If he wanted a better life, he knew he had to take the next step alone.

In the end, Kaleb was certain of his decision. "If I didn't go quickly [I knew] it would be a hard life," he recalled. His friend knew a man who worked in Sudan, and they met him together. That was how they got their first contact for a smuggler and began their journey west.

SUDAN: THROUGH THE DESERT

"Sudan is a source, transit and destination country for
asylum seekers, refugees and economic migrants along the Eastern
Africa Migratory Route into North Africa and Europe. Trafficking,
kidnapping and smuggling of persons are major concerns."

—UN REFUGEE AGENCY AUDIT, 2018

Sudan was a necessary stop for East Africans en route to the Mediterranean Sea. There were the Eritreans running from slavery-like military service, though when you asked them about their motivations they usually said they were fleeing ignorance and searching for freedom. They were joined by Somalis escaping war or the Islamic terrorist group al-Shabaab, Ethiopians—often ethnic Oromos, a tribe repressed for decades—and Tigrayans, who were exhausted by ceaseless poverty and hoped to pass for Eritreans, with whom they shared a common language, to make claiming asylum easier. Then there were Sudanese who survived ethnic cleansing in Darfur, and South Sudanese who fled the catastrophic conflict that had dominated the short life of their country, the world's newest state. Most had a clear entitlement to international protection, though the irony of asylum law is that they must first illegally reach a safe place to be granted their right to live in it.

By 2018, the UN would say half a million Eritreans had fled their country—one tenth of its population.[1] But statistics alone could not convey the reality: the Eritrean exodus was an exodus of children. Teenagers, even pre-teens, wanted to get out before they reached their final year of high school, when they had to report for national service and lost any ability to make choices about their lives. While Kaleb's mother took him to Ethiopia so he did not have to go through this, many others on the migration route had experienced grueling military training at a very young age.

> *"They tried to put us in the military [in Eritrea] but we escaped. But the ones who didn't escape, they are still in the military. Almost everybody escaped, even the kids escape because they already know their brothers' future, what will happen in the future. That's why they try to escape when they are kids."*

In the most infamous training camp, Sawa, Eritrean teenagers rose before sunrise. They could be beaten if they underperformed at weapons classes or war simulations.[2] As part of their conditioning, they were sent on day-long hikes without any food or water, a resolve-building exercise former Sawa students told me prepared them to survive the migration routes they embarked upon later. Discipline was prized above all else. Women and girls were at risk of sexual violence by superiors.[3] Once, in Khartoum, I spoke to a young man who showed me a tattoo he had inflicted on himself with a needle and burning tire in Sawa. When I asked if it hurt, he said the pain was nothing compared to everything else he was going through at the time.

Though national service was originally supposed to last eighteen months, it could be unending. Eritreans would be assigned to another posting, and a life of effective slavery would begin. Young people knew their futures were being stolen from them. So they broke with the past, losing their innocence along with their homes. In Sudan, Eritreans became suspicious and untrusting, seeing potential spies or enemies everywhere. And they were right to be worried. A whole business had built up around harming them.

The journey from Addis Ababa to Khartoum cost Kaleb $1,200. First, he spent a full day on a bus north to Gondar, an Ethiopian city famed for its seventeenth century royal castles. He joined others, who were paying the same smuggler, to drive another 200 kilometers west to Metema, a border town. There, they left the vehicle they had been traveling in and walked for two hours, leaving Ethiopia behind. Kaleb's family believed he was staying with a cousin; it was only after he arrived in Sudan—in January 2017—that he called his mother and told her what he had done.

At the time, Sudan was littered with checkpoints and travel controls; it was a much less welcoming environment than Ethiopia had been. Kaleb traveled west to capital city Khartoum under the control of his smuggler. That man introduced them to another smuggler, who easily convinced the group that it was better to continue their journey rather than waiting around in Sudan. Kaleb was told it would cost $3,800 to cross the Mediterranean Sea. Rather than paying in advance, he was assured that he could call his family to ask for the money once he reached Libya. He would be in Europe within two weeks; at worst, one month, they promised.

———

Without knowing it, I was in Sudan a few months after Kaleb. I was endeavoring to figure out where hundreds of millions of euro in funding, earmarked by the EU with the aim of stopping migration from and through Sudan, were actually being spent.[4] I found a heavily controlled state with a prevalent air of tension where civilians suffered the crushing effects of US sanctions, imposed two decades before due to accusations that Sudan's regime was sponsoring terrorism.[5] Omar al-Bashir, who took control in a 1989 military coup, remained president, despite the issuance of an international arrest warrant by the International Criminal Court, which accused him of war crimes and crimes against humanity. The country was full of liberal, intelligent young people craving change, yet governed by leaders who imposed increasingly restrictive rules. In 2017, women could be whipped by public order police for wearing trousers.[6] It seemed impossible to walk outside without being harassed by Sudanese men or security officials. "In other countries, they say ladies first. In Sudan, men are always first," one male interviewee laughed before he walked up the stairs ahead of me for a meeting. Tourists were even barred from taking photos without approval from the Ministry of Information.

I wanted to get closer to Eritrea's western border, to find out what escapees expected as soon as they crossed it. I had written in advance to Sudan's Commission of Refugees asking for permission to travel there. A few days in sweltering Khartoum, and an hour drinking coffee with the Refugee Commissioner, ended in a stamped letter approving my visit. After a trip to the Ministry of Information, I also had a travel permit. A short flight east brought me to Kassala, a market town around 20 kilometers from Eritrea. Kassala lay in the shadow of the Taka Mountains, which rose like gray, crumbling sandcastles to the southeast and attracted Sudanese honeymooners because of a belief that a visit could boost fertility. Secret police were everywhere. I spent my first day making mandatory visits to security offices to let them know I had arrived. Still, an undercover official entered my hotel during the afternoon, when he knew I was out, and asked the receptionist for a scan of my passport and my UK home address.

A long drive in jeeps over mottled terrain ended at Shagarab refugee camp, where forty thousand refugees were passing whole lives in temporary tents and huts, waiting for Eritrea to be safe for them again. The camps were barely livable, even for those with money sent by relatives abroad that long-term residents used to set up businesses selling food and coffee, renting out pool tables, or charging for an afternoon watching TV in a shelter. Along with the daily grind of getting enough to eat or drink was the threat of sporadic abductions by local tribes or detention by security forces.[7] Refugees continuously told me the Eritrean regime had intelligence sources in the camps, making them feel extremely vulnerable.

With representatives from the UN Refugee Agency, the government, and Sudanese military intelligence all listening in to my interviews and taking notes, I visited a dormitory for unaccompanied Eritrean minors. They had the insecurity of youth: girls smiling shyly or looking worried; boys posing and laughing, though their thoughts seemed far away. The stories were breathtaking. Teenagers described planning their escapes together, meeting under a tree at the back of a garden at dusk to go over details while hiding everything from their parents. Those without money walked for weeks, while older, better-connected escapees might drive by car. They were unable to visualize what lay outside the repression they observed each day but dared to hope it could be better than the life stretching out before them.

How was this story so unknown internationally? These children knew they were risking everything. On the Eritrea-Sudan border, there was a shoot-to-kill policy. Even if they survived, they would likely never see their families again. Their relatives could be punished, locked up, or interrogated when their escape was discovered. They had to willfully ignore those repercussions. Thinking too much meant they would never get away.

One boy, who had crossed into Sudan weeks before, told me with pride that he knew how to craft traditional beds. He wanted to work, he kept repeating, but was still grappling with what it meant to now be in a foreign country with no family connections. A girl said she had been kidnapped by men from the Rashaida, an Arab tribe, while trailing siblings who had crossed the border before her. Their mother had already reached Europe, leaving six children behind in the hope they could be legally reunited with her by plane, thereby avoiding the treacherous journey through North Africa and across the sea. But this legal process had stalled, and the children were struggling. "She was raped," a Sudanese official told me when the girl finished speaking and was still within earshot.

Once they were out of Eritrea, escapees would start asking other refugees to connect them with people who could facilitate their travel onwards, or they would look for recommendations from friends and relatives who had already reached Europe. In Kassala, I visited a prison built by the British in colonial days where 150 convicted smugglers and traffickers were incarcerated. Hunched men sat in rows on the dusty ground. In his office, prison director Abdehkreem Hamid Muss proudly described the football matches they played, showing off trophies. He brought in men, saying they had agreed to talk to me, though, of course, a prisoner never speaks freely. The men mostly told me they had driven Eritreans towards Khartoum or agreed to accompany them on public transport. "There's no crime in what I did. It's not harming anyone," said a 57-year-old father of eight, who was sentenced to five years. "I don't know why the government imposes such harsh sentences. I was only doing it so I could feed my children."

"I didn't need the money," claimed a 35-year-old farmer with graying hair, who was serving a ten-year sentence. "Before 2011 we used to host Eritreans in our houses, allow them to call their families, give them clothes and food, but now no one will do that because of the government considering it human trade. The reasons are political, of course, especially from other governments, especially from the UN. Sudanese people have been helping Eritreans for a long time. They just come through, and then they leave. People should face the roots of the problem. Eritreans are very pressured, even children."

Most of the prisoners said they had been targeted by police because they were poor. It was my first step towards understanding that the most influential figures enabling North Africa's migration routes were not the main focus of law enforcement, despite constant European rhetoric about breaking down their business. Sudanese authorities wanted to be seen to crack down on smuggling, but any significant smuggler would never end up in prison: they likely already had strong ties to people in power or, at worst, had enough money to pay their way out. The low-level associates were the ones who suffered. Kassala locals confirmed this. The perception that actions were being taken was important politically and vital for attracting donor funds. It did not necessarily reflect the realities on the ground.

Back in Khartoum, I met more Eritreans. We'd duck into their houses, people cramming together to speak surreptitiously. They were worried about getting hassle from the police if they were seen with a journalist. We talked about smuggling. Older Ethiopians and Eritreans whispered about their children being abducted or stolen. In reality, young people could be kidnapped and sold to traffickers, but it was more likely they were convinced to leave on a "go now, pay later" scheme—with payments seemingly reserved until they saw results.

An Eritrean woman in her twenties told me her sister had already gone to Libya and she was desperate to follow. In Khartoum, she was harassed, sexually assaulted, and extorted for money by police almost every day while traveling to her low-paying job in a restaurant. As it was for many other refugees, she found it so painful and costly to stay still that her only real option was to keep moving. She needed a way out.

One hot day, I met Ismail Omer Teirab, the deputy chair of Sudan's National Committee to Combat Trafficking, which had been specifically mentioned in EU documents as a reason Sudan was worth supporting. The EU had allocated more than 200 million euro of migration-related funding to Sudan over the previous two years.[8] The bloc said the money went to projects "implemented by agencies of EU member states, international organizations, private sector entities, and NGOs" rather than going directly to the ruling regime. Despite this, there were allegations that equipment and other benefits were reaching a paramilitary group accused of war crimes in Darfur that was previously known as the Janjaweed but had been renamed the Rapid Support Forces (RSF). The Sudanese government had tasked the group with managing the western border with Libya. While the EU denied giving money directly to the RSF, the EU Trust Fund supplied the UN with millions of euro to train them, according to an investigation by German newspaper *Der Spiegel*.[9] Two years after my visit, the RSF was blamed for another massacre during popular protests against the Sudanese regime in which around 128 civilians were killed; its leader, Mohamed Hamdan Dagalo—known as "Hemeti"—would go on to become vice president of Sudan's transitional government following the ousting of Bashir.[10]

Back in 2017, Teirab claimed his work was hugely under-resourced and said he saw no benefit from EU money. Besides that, he had not even been granted permission to visit Sudan's refugee camps himself. He had no printer, and he asked me to reimburse his meager transport costs. Even if he had funding, he said, it would be almost impossible to fight the real enemy: smartphones, which acted as tiny windows into the greater world. Africans who could never have conceived of anything beyond their nearest town were now gaping at centers of wealth and the luxuries rich people enjoyed in the West. They began to comprehend how unfair the world was, and how difficult their lives were in comparison.

Teirab did not say it, but it occurred to me that smartphones had not just enabled Africans to see what life was like in Western countries. They were also seeing, laid clear, the corruption of their own politicians. There were big cars, expensive weddings, well-dressed relatives monied by association, all boasted about on the internet. With online access, it is easy to compare lives, and it is easier to become conscious of hypocrisy, too.

CHAPTER 3

LIBYA: THE TWENTY-FIRST CENTURY SLAVE TRADE

"There are pains on their body, but there are even pains on their heart, like seeing your wife raped in front of your eyes and seeing your little sister being raped by a Libyan; a wife watching her husband killed in front of her. I have seen twenty-nine people die in front of me."

—AN ERITREAN SMUGGLING VICTIM IN LIBYA

Sudan to Italy was what Kaleb called the "road of death." The first hurdle was a week-long drive across the Sahara Desert, lasting roughly 1,400 kilometers. There were no roads or tracks, just an expanse of sand so unending it felt like a movie set or a mental trick. There was little food or water, and the passengers sat packed together out the rear, exposed to the blistering sun. At any time, their Hilux jeeps could be attacked by other militias. Sometimes people died, and their bodies were abandoned. If anyone fell out, the drivers would not stop.

A mere thirty minutes into the journey, one man said he wanted to go back. He was not allowed to. "I don't forget him now," Kaleb said later. "I don't know if he's alive or dead." That removal of choice made it very clear: from then on they were cargo, objects to be bought or sold.

There was no clear demarcation along the Libyan border, but Kaleb knew they had crossed it when the group was transferred from armed Sudanese men to Libyans with lighter skin. After more driving, they reached Kufra, an oasis town and human smuggling hub, where they were deposited into a building. There were already hundreds of people inside, all waiting for their next connection. It was here that Kaleb got talking to Meri, a teenager from Eritrean capital Asmara. Kaleb asked him how the city was, suddenly longing for stories about the place where his grandparents still lived and his mother had escaped from. He was surprised by the kindness of this boy, who spoke readily and still managed to smile, despite their surroundings. They stayed in the same holding house for five days, but it would be a long time until they would meet again.

Then Kaleb was shifted onwards, farther inland. While traveling the next series of roads, their armed guards informed his group that they would need to pay an extra $1,000, on top of the money that had already been agreed. There was no way out of this, and the upcoming stop would be the worst so far. It was Bani Walid, a Libyan town and former Gaddafi stronghold migrants call the "Ghost City" because of the number of people who disappear there without a trace and the total lack of rule of law. Dotted around the outskirts of the town are compounds with warehouses inside them; up to three thousand people can be stored in each one.

In charge of all the armed men who shepherded them into buildings and trucks was an absent Eritrean man nicknamed Wedi Babu. Kaleb's relatives had known Wedi Babu personally, and he thought he could trust the smuggler, even though Wedi Babu was not in Libya himself. He was said to live a nice life in Dubai, directing his associates from a distance. His real name was Yasin, though no one I asked knew his surname.

Around five hundred people were held in a Bani Walid warehouse with Kaleb—women and men. They slept on carpet laid on soil. There were just four toilets, with negligible plumbing. Water tanks had to be driven in on trucks so they could shower, once a fortnight at most. Even when he got to wash, Kaleb did not always have soap. His body quickly became covered in infections, and his clothes were never clean. He tired of the constant noise. People chattered the whole day and night. There were so many of them packed together, and so many reasons not to sleep. They would fight over everything, even who controlled which tiny patch of ground. Kaleb felt that life had become ugly. He also felt fragile in comparison to many of his companions. The other Eritreans seemed hardier; some had already survived military training and stints in prison. Kaleb became sick and weak.

Shortly after he arrived, Kaleb was herded into a line to call his family for the first time. "I bought you," Kaleb was told before the call by one of the armed men guarding them. "For now, you are safe." The threat hung in the air. The call would only last a few precious minutes; no time for pleasantries. He had to explain to his mother where he was and that he had made a "deal," before telling her the amount of money she had to raise and the bank accounts she should deposit it into. Each detainee was given an individual code that their family could reference as they paid, so there was no confusion about which captive it was meant for. It was after the initial few calls that the beatings started.

Kaleb's family paid $5,000 within the first two months, but he stayed in that first warehouse for seven. Even when the transaction was done, the smugglers listed excuses as to why they postponed putting him in a boat: the sea was stormy; there was conflict in coastal city Sabratha. *"Inshallah bukra,"* the armed men would say when they were asked—"God willing, tomorrow." Kaleb waited as 5,000 kilometers away, in Dubai, Wedi Babu busied himself gambling. Detainees were told about his favored pastime by their guards. They heard this expensive habit meant Wedi Babu was running out of money, and they worried about what could happen if he hit rock bottom.

———

At this point, Libya was already known to be the home of a twenty-first century slave trade. As the fourth largest country on the African continent and with more than 90 percent made up of desert, Libya has a lot of space for illicit business to flourish. Human smuggling and trafficking have long been rife. In May 2017, months after Kaleb arrived there, the chief prosecutor at the International Criminal Court, Fatou Bensouda, called Libya "a marketplace for the trafficking of human beings." She told the UN Security Council that her office was collecting information about crimes against migrants and refugees there and was considering launching an official investigation to see who could be held accountable.[1] Later that year, CNN International released a report that shocked global audiences. Its journalists went undercover to film migrants being auctioned as slaves in Libya for as little as $400 each.[2] "This is a digger, a big strong man," a slave trader announced as part of his filmed sales pitch. The UN Security Council held a special emergency session in the aftermath and an African Union-EU task force was formed, but little came out of it.[3]

So the trade in humans carried on. When people are desperate they will recklessly avail of any opening, even turning themselves over to a system where they are bought and sold. Lighter-skinned Libyans have been known to refer to those with darker skin as *abed*, which translates as "slave." Refugees I spoke to who went through Libya said they grew accustomed to answering to it.

Different nationalities were charged varying amounts of money by smugglers. Somalis and Eritreans paid thousands of pounds, and sometimes even tens of thousands. They were followed by Ethiopians and Asians, particularly Bangladeshis,[4] while West Africans and Sudanese people paid less—maybe as low as $300. "Many traffickers look at Eritreans, Ethiopians, and Somalis with a dollar sign on them," said Mark Micallef, a Malta-based researcher who spent years studying smuggling routes. Those countries have large, well-connected diasporas made of people who, by the virtue of already living abroad, are more easily able to access and raise money, he noted.

It can also come down to luck. A Sudanese man in Libya told me that everyone who traveled with him paid at least $3,000, in various installments, but a Somali woman he knew paid a whopping $60,000. Prices were usually higher for girls or women because of family concerns about their safety and honor. Some smugglers gave the option to partially pay their ransom with sex.

Once the money was collected, it was transferred to a bank account in Dubai, or to Khartoum or Istanbul through the hawala system, an alternative financial exchange channel that exists outside normal banking and is difficult to trace. Some former captives even told me there were posters with the details for different bank accounts stuck to the walls around them in the area where they went to call their relatives.

––––––––

In Sweden, an Eritrean journalist and activist called Meron Estefanos adapted to a strange new reality: getting contacted regularly from smugglers' warehouses by people with no one else to turn to. Estefanos first began getting anguished calls in 2011 from Eritreans in Egypt's Sinai Desert, which was once part of the popular migration route to Israel.[5] On the phone, people would tell her they were being tortured and asked to pay up to $40,000 each. Over five years, Estefanos estimates one billion dollars' worth of ransoms were delivered by friends, family members, and supporters from the Eritrean diaspora towards securing releases there. As Libya became a more common route, she believes the money received by smugglers approached the same figures. "[Captives] are being extorted again and again," she said.

Estefanos paid and crowdfunded many ransom payments herself. Originally, she tried contacting human rights groups, UN agencies, celebrities, and anyone else she could think of, but slowly she realized that there would be no heroic rescues of the kind seen in movies with fair-skinned American hostages, and there would never be the same level of international interest. "We are black people," she told me. "The world doesn't care. We always say paying ransoms is not good. But hey, if your brother or your sister was in that situation, if your child was in that situation, which parent is going to say 'I'm not going to pay'?"

Eritreans in particular have a culture of helping, she explained. Yet no one's pockets were limitless. Again and again, she had to deal with the impossible question: How much financial value can you place on a life? "You don't think of that. You're hearing their voices," she mused, one of the many times I spoke to her about it. "You know they're suffering, these people, they're asking you to help them . . . It gives you kind of a peace of mind that you contributed one hundred dollars to save one life." Still, she worried about those who could not raise money, and asked herself whether each payment bolstered the amount demanded the next time.

In the highly unlikely scenario that authorities managed to close down smuggling routes through Libya, Estefanos expected the same patterns of captivity and ransom would develop or be exacerbated in other countries as migration routes simply shifted. "The smugglers are smart, so wherever there are a lot of refugees there will be a lot of smugglers," she said. "Migration never really stops, to be honest."

————

It was only when his family paid his ransom in full that Kaleb was allowed to venture outside the warehouse. The longer he stayed, the more Kaleb became acquainted with the workings of the big compound they were based inside. At least five notable smugglers operated there. Each had their own buildings, homes, and sometimes multiple warehouses for storing migrants. He learned that they were only about a twenty minute drive from Bani Walid town, but it felt like the depths of the desert. Police never call, but they must have known this cooperative existed.

Two of the smugglers sharing the compound were particularly infamous. Tewelde Goitom, nicknamed "Welid," was a small, stout man, known for the massive number of women and girls he raped. The other, Kidane Zekarias Habtemariam, was tall and bald and seemed to enjoy the pain he inflicted while beating his charges "like animals." These men lived like kings. "They feel powerful," Kaleb remembered. "They are among a bunch of poor people and everybody is under their control. [The captives] cannot go anywhere. They don't have anything—food, water, clothes—and [in contrast, the smugglers] have their own car that they only drive in the compound. They have a house, they have drink, they have everything."

In Kidane's warehouse, roughly nine hundred men, women, and children were packed together. There were three toilets. "You sleep overcrowded, it didn't have the capacity to hold that amount of people," recalled Aaron, an Eritrean who was held there between June 2017 and May 2018. "The temperature is very high; you have to suffocate. You drink water from the toilets and wash from the toilets. There are people dying because of starvation."

Upon arrival, Aaron was told he owed $10,000—much more than he expected. "Personally, I wouldn't have cared if they only smuggled. That's why we went to Libya," said the young man—who was nineteen when he first arrived in Bani Walid. "They raped virgin women. They beat people to death. They ransomed enormous amounts of money from each of us and in doing so they used all tools of torture . . . They starved people, and many died as a result."

"They call our parents to pay or kill us. That is ransom. They say if you are not paying we will kill or cut his body by dividing the whole body into pieces. Like a horror movie."

During his daily two-minute calls, Aaron's parents and siblings grasped for information on the other end of the line. Sometimes, people were tortured while on the phone. "They don't have to beat a lot, but a few severely," said Aaron, who described Kidane "displaying" grievously injured people to show others what could happen if they did not pay up quickly. "One guy was beaten with electricity wires. [Kidane] beat him to the point that he was at the verge of death. He beat him with his own hands. Fortunately, he survived."

"He said, 'I know how to make you pay,' . . . There was so much blood on
my clothes. I stayed there with punishment every day for two years."

Like Kaleb, Aaron was struck by how quickly humanity crumbled in
this environment. In time, he came to feel the people in the warehouse were
no longer human at all. They were more akin to "a herd of animals after you
slaughter them and want to sell them," he said. He experienced "beating,
starving, insanity," and, like so many others, he saw people die there.

————

Kidane and Welid were friends, united by their quest for money, their sadism,
and the enjoyment they got from toying with those under their control. Sometimes, they would hold football matches, each one handpicking a team from
their weak detainees. If one of their side missed a shot, the smugglers might
shoot towards their feet, missing but terrifying the players. The winning man
got to pick a girl from the other's captives, take her away, and rape her.[6]

"He does it to show power. He says, 'Even if God himself showed up, I
would beat him and take his money.' He said God accounts for only two
percent of his abilities. The other ninety-eight percent was him."

Sexual abuse was particularly common in Welid's warehouses. Former
detainees told me they personally knew several women who had babies as a
result of his rapes. He allegedly videotaped encounters, threatening to post
them online if the woman spoke out. One Eritrean remembered Welid's
guards carrying around a phone that was broadcasting live as he raped
someone—the guards encouraged everyone to watch it. Another time,
Welid spotted a detainee talking to a female friend and ordered him to have
sex with her immediately or suffer the consequences (the man refused and
was beaten). Some women had no choice but to pay their way towards Europe with sex. In other cases, Welid would refuse to let married women
proceed after they had paid, until they were raped by him. The smuggler

also selected a woman or girl to live in his house and cook for him; when he got tired of her, he would choose someone else.

Welid was erratic. The rumor was that he used to work in the Sinai Desert, between Egypt and Israel, where he sold the kidneys of migrants who tried to cross. In Libya, he occasionally subverted expectations by doing something kind, which kept everyone on edge. One evening, he drunkenly set off fireworks as refugees watched. A few times, he allowed couples to marry inside the warehouse, providing food for a celebration. Some of the couples were besotted with each other, calling their parents to ask permission and describe their new love; in other cases, the women agreed after calculating that marriage to one man meant they were less likely to be raped by others.

> "The warehouse could accommodate a maximum of about three thousand people. When we slept, there weren't even any rugs or mats on the floor. There were only four bathrooms. If you couldn't wait in line, you had to pee on your pants and wet yourself . . . Welid rapes countless women. He separates couples and rapes the women. He is also racist. He once said Somali people weren't people. He sent the Somalis to Italy while there was a storm in the Mediterranean. He did it to test if he can safely send his Eritrean customers. As faith would have it, the Eritreans got caught, while the Somalis got in to Europe. He fed us once a week. There was barely any water. Beatings were regular. I have been beaten for two years straight. My head is barely functional."

Welid had two warehouses, where refugees would stay for around a year on average. The most despairing might eventually try to kill themselves, but the compound was so packed that these attempts were generally spotted and stopped. A brave few tried to escape, but they were surrounded by snipers and concrete, and it was all but impossible. Beyond the concrete was endless desert, and they could hardly envisage what other dangers might lie out there, across a vast country they had barely seen anything of.

"When one of the sick girls was about to die, he told her she can't die before she gives him more money, while she was crying. He insisted she call her family to speed up the process. Then she died for lack of treatment and medication."

———

The sad truth of that time was that even those who managed to pay ransoms, while surviving the extremes of captivity, had an increasingly small chance of actually making it across the Mediterranean Sea. The refugees still had ideas of the continent as a bastion of human rights where they could live emancipated, happy lives. They did not know yet that huge amounts of money were being spent to make sure they would never get to experience it for themselves.

The EU's support for the Libyan coastguard had a significant impact on Libya's smuggling industry. People said the "sea was closed" after the coastguard began intercepting boats full of refugees. This information was passed through smuggling chains, and new refugees temporarily stopped making the journey to Bani Walid from Sudan. Cutting off the smugglers' money supply gave them a big incentive to further exploit those already under their control. Smugglers began to exchange hostages between themselves. Each time, a fresh ransom of thousands more dollars was demanded, irrespective of what had been paid before.

Eventually, it was Kaleb's turn. On New Year's Eve, the last day of 2017, his group were told they were now the property of someone else because their smuggler, Wedi Babu, had literally gambled them away in a Dubai casino. Four hundred people remained in the same compound, but they were no longer allowed to leave the warehouse, and the whole routine began again. Another $5,000 was the asking price for a chance at Europe, though in reality they now knew they were simply buying their lives.

———

Across Ethiopia, Eritrea, Somalia, and Sudan, there were families making public appeals, pleading with richer relatives, or going to markets and churches to beg for help so they could secure the release and further passage of relatives in Libya. They were selling possessions, land, and giving up heirlooms and other treasures. Mothers and wives sold their jewelry and borrowed money from family, especially those in the diaspora. "Our culture is good, they help each other," a father who made the journey through Libya told me, but the debts incurred could last long after a journey had succeeded, or ended in failure.

Increasingly, there was also another, more modern way to find the money: crowd-funding on social media.

For tens of thousands of African migrants and refugees who tried to escape war, dictatorships, or poverty by heading for Europe in the late 2010s, social media both directed the way and raised the cost. Technology became both a blessing and a curse: it could be a lifeline used for asking for help or a humiliation—the way oblivious friends and relatives could chance upon their abuse, suffering, and anguish in real time. It influenced migration in ways that had never been seen before, inflating the ransom prices even further.

I began to trawl the internet and found dozens of posts that included heart-wrenching photos of captives in Libya, along with the phone number of a family member to whom anyone, anywhere, could donate money. Facebook, WhatsApp, and Twitter were all being used to raise ransoms. This was another piece of evidence that the buying and selling of people in Libya was not hidden. Facebook was popular in Libya, as in much of North Africa, where it was a platform for both political debate and misinformation. It was used to sell weapons, while opponents who supported different sides of the various conflicts used it to offer their allies battlefield guidance and bombing coordinates.[7] But the obvious trading of people so contrasted with the filtered selfies and life status updates we are used to in Europe that it shocked me the most. This slave trade was playing out for everyone to see online.

In the photos I came across, captives had their faces pressed to hard ground or stared pleadingly at the camera. A woman was shown, her wrists and ankles chained together behind her back, rust-colored vomit or blood beside her face and an electrical prod lying by her side; it had more than 1,200 shares, along with 273 likes, hearts, and crying emojis—symbols that did not seem suitable for the horror that was on display. A shackled man hung from the ceiling, a gun pointed to his head by someone out of sight; that one had 418 likes, crying emojis, and angry emojis, 1,800 comments, and 3,900 shares. In another picture posted to Facebook, less graphic than the others but in some ways more sinister, a couple sat with their children, the asking price for their lives written in the text over their head: $4,400.

> *"They are burning them. There are no windows and air. They burn them with [dripping hot] plastic bags on their bodies. He told me he can't tell me the smuggler's name because the smuggler was with him when he needed to call me or my mum."*

WhatsApp audio messages were used, too. One, sent from Bani Walid, asked for $17,500 for each of a group of one hundred and fifty Somalis. A widely shared video showed a man jolting as he was tortured with molten plastic, before the camera zoomed in on his face—which served the joint purpose of confirming his identity for loved ones and giving them a close up of his grimaces and cries. Sometimes, messages were recorded by the smugglers themselves.

Mothers of captives set up WhatsApp groups to share information. In one case, each woman contributed ten dollars towards the release of a Somali orphan who had no one else to pay for him. "You see that always, mothers begging, my son is in Libya and I don't have the money to pay [for] him," Estefanos told me. "I used to save it, take a picture, but it's become our new normal; it's almost every day."

Victims and researchers told me people in Libya, Sudan, and northern

Niger had all used Facebook to raise ransom money, and that Eritreans, Ethiopians, and Somalis were the most likely to be held captive like this. "There were people [held] with me, when their family couldn't pay money, they posted on Facebook and they got help," said one former victim, who was held by smugglers for more than a year. "If you don't pay fast, [smugglers] force you to post your picture on Facebook. They give you a deadline to pay the money or tell you that they will kill you."

When I sent screengrabs to Facebook of the posts of tortured captives I had seen, asking whether they were aware this was happening, a spokesperson said they needed links before they could decide what to do. "This is a really sad and complex issue and one that we're aware of, which holds various consequences on all sides," the spokesperson emailed me. "Without specific links to the content it is difficult to fully assess the situation. However, we remain fully committed to working to understand the challenges and how we address these."[8]

I did not share links because I suspected Facebook might take the posts down. As a journalist, I decided it was not right for me to play a direct role in removing the chances these families had to raise the cash, disturbing as it was.

————

Human smuggling has always been a huge industry, with tentacles across North Africa that permeate institutions, security forces, criminal gangs, and government offices. Outside Bani Walid, there were other smugglers, perhaps even more fearsome. They worked along different routes, some specializing in West Africans instead. Smugglers usually went by single names —Abdusalem, Abdulaziz, Abdallah—and were each notorious for individual kinds of cruelty. Former captives sent me photos of injuries: burns or scars, damaged limbs, missing fingers. Of course, there was also the mental anguish, which could not be captured in a picture.

Some refugees told me they were almost sucked into the smuggling industry themselves. If a smuggler liked you, he might invite you to work with him. Women, money, weapons, drugs, extra food, a house—all of this was on the table. There could even be an promise of a free boat journey across the Mediterranean to Europe, once a new recruit had served their dues. These people were called *capos*, a word which means "boss" in Italian, the language of Eritrea's former colonizers. It was strangely similar to *Kapos*, the name for the World War Two concentration camp prisoners who worked with the Nazis to oppress others under them (in Libya's government-associated detention centers, later on, the same word was used for detainees who worked directly with the Libyan guards). Refugees did fall into that trap, excited to experience a level of control they had never felt in the hopeless situations they ran from, more than happy to forget they too had been human cargo days before. They pummeled fellow detainees, ordered them around, or supervised their tearful calls to their families, cutting the line after the allocated time. One Somali remembered a chaotic situation where he picked up a stray gun and shot wildly at a militia who attacked the compound he was imprisoned in, trying to protect children behind him. This action won the admiration of his smuggler, who he said offered him weapons and sex to stay.

There are many stories about what is essentially a small group of prominent smugglers. Among survivors, they can even sound like gossip, until you grapple with the horror of it. One man raped so many captives that a rival was said to have found and raped his young daughter to teach him a lesson. Others boasted about their connections to African governments or militia groups. They were proud of what they had become.

Later, Kaleb would remember a smuggler in an unusually reflective mood telling him: "All of this, it is blood money. Someday, someone's going to come after me." Kaleb wondered what would happen to them in the future. "For the smugglers who have gone this far, killed too many people, raped too many women, where can they go?" he asked himself.

In Bani Walid, deaths piled up. In 2018, medical organization Médecins Sans Frontières said they were delivering fifty body bags a month to a local charity that collected unidentified corpses dumped in the streets and had buried more than 730 people since the previous year.[9] Inside the smugglers' warehouses, too, tragedies were ever present, and the situation forced seemingly ordinary people to carry out extraordinary acts of bravery. One of these people was Abdi, who had been held for a year by a smuggler "worse than evil." For the first two months, captives were given macaroni twice a day. Then it was reduced to one portion. The lack of nutrition made Abdi's friend particularly weak. "He was not able to breathe well. He couldn't wake up from his bed, and he was doing feces where he was. After that, he died in my hands," Abdi later told me.

Abdi insisted on accompanying the smugglers to bury his friend. "I was hearing they just throw it away," he said about the bodies of those who perished. Dismissively, one smuggler told Abdi that his friend was not the only person who had died, and he had no right to go with them. "If you don't take me with you, it's better to kill me," Abdi replied. He slept with the body of his friend that night and escorted him the next day before digging his friend's grave himself.

"I am still young, but I also left friends in their graves in Bani Walid who were the same age as me and younger. The time of death is with God."

———

After more than a year with smugglers, Kaleb ended up in a truck hurtling towards the coast at night. He was one of around one hundred and eighty people packed into cargo containers, speeding in the care of a drunk driver. Some sixty kilometers southeast of Bani Walid, the overloaded vehicle hit a hole in the road, wobbling, swaying, and then toppling over. There was an earsplitting crash and a series of thumps. Nineteen people died, some of them children.[10] Afterwards, the driver handed a flask of whiskey around the survivors, showing something akin to remorse.

Two weeks later, those who were still alive gathered together again, and their ill-fated boat left land.

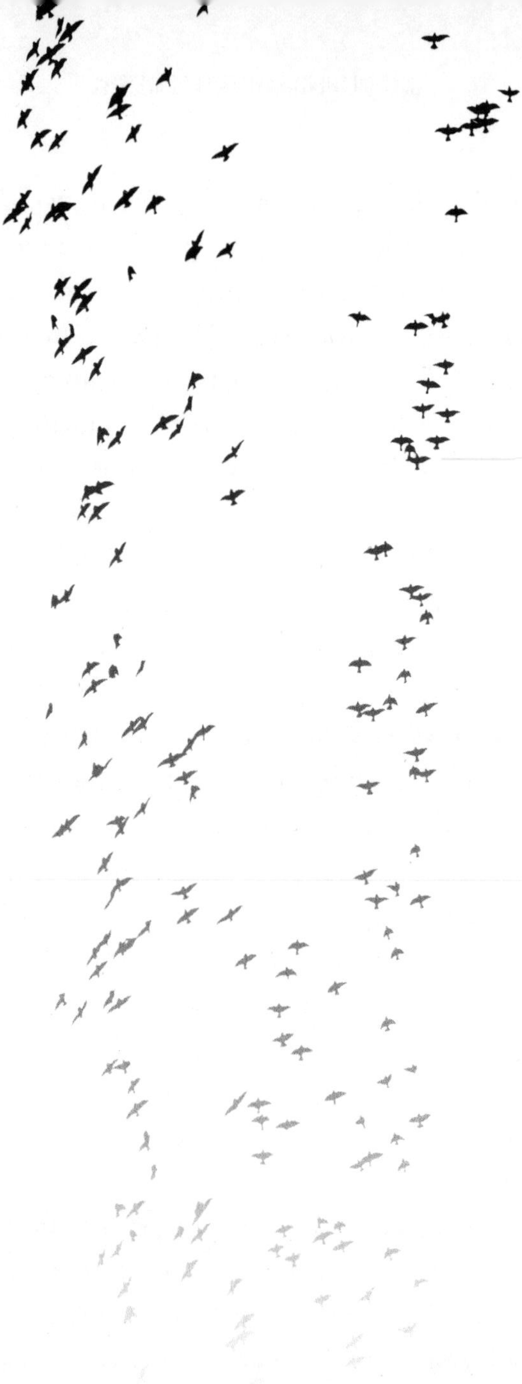

CHAPTER 4

AIN ZARA AND ABU SALIM: NEW LIFE AND NEW DEATH

"It's like this: you stay in the detention center for years. No resettlement, no evacuation. You try the sea. You get intercepted or you die. Only a small percentage reach their destiny."

—REFUGEE IN LIBYA

"Most people who go to sea die, or return to Libya, and few arrive to dream land. After the rubber boat moves in the sea, if the coastguard catches the boat they return people to refugee centers in Libya, and these centers are like hell. Or hell is better than these centers."

—REFUGEE IN ABU SALIM DETENTION CENTER

AIN ZARA DETENTION CENTER

Picture this. A building in southern Tripoli, Libya's capital city. The walls beige and plain from the outside, not as ominous looking as you might expect a place of torment to be. There was a compound, surrounded by walls. There were guards, whose uniforms sometimes changed without explanation. No one was certain where their loyalties outside this prison lay. It hardly mattered. The guards had ultimate power: life or death for hundreds of men, women, and children.

This was Ain Zara migrant detention center. Kaleb would try to cross the sea twice before he was taken here, the first time paying his way out of another detention center and complicit guards looking the other way as he escaped into the vehicle of a smuggler. On both occasions, the boat he was on was intercepted by the EU-backed Libyan coastguard. Now, his family's money had run out, and there was no escape anymore.

They had been locked up without charge or trial, indefinitely, with no end in sight. There were around twenty of these government-associated detention centers across western Libya, where refugees and migrants were taken after being caught at sea. Many were old factories or warehouses. They did not always have toilets or showers, and because they were being run by militias, there was no real distinction between civilian and military areas. Weapons and bombs were stored close to the sleeping bodies of the incarcerated.

Men and boys were separated from women, girls, and young children upon arrival. That meant there was always an air of anxiety in the locked men's hall, with husbands and brothers listening for screams from the women, which could signal an assault attempt. In Ain Zara, there were around two hundred women and girls, and twenty children under the age of five. The Libyans in charge were regularly violent towards the men and boys, too—everyone from the guards, to their drivers, to the cook was prone to lashing out at them. More than that, the guards were psychologically abusive, deliberately causing division. "They made us fight each other," Kaleb said. "Libyans try and make you fight each other because they know if you're united then you can achieve something. If they make you busy with [finding] food and inside [conflicts] you'll be fighting for food, for water, not concentrating on getting out and living a normal life."

The water taps might purposely only be turned on for ten minutes a day, causing scuffles between people hoping to drink or wash themselves. Refugees would steal jerrycans or buckets from others who seized them back again while they were sleeping. On the rare days aid agencies visited to distribute soap or clothes, the Libyan guards ordered the refugees into two lines. Then one line would be given priority, and the others would panic. Guards might insult the refugees, calling them "motherfuckers." Anyone who reacted would be taken away for punishment. Complaining led to provisions being withheld. "They would say you're fighting, we can't work," Kaleb said. If there were protests, during which detainees might refuse food, anyone accused of being a ringleader could also be locked up in an isolation area, chained, beaten with iron rods, and worn down for a week, before being deposited back in the larger group. Like smugglers, the guards seemed to enjoy violence.

The younger Libyan guards were clearly taking drugs, Kaleb thought, and they had been driven even crazier by the weapons they carried. "Every kid has [a gun]," he noticed. "They think smoking marijuana is a fashion. They take tramadol. Some take heroin. [Then] they come to us and think they are the boss."

"When they smoke and drink it's a problem, you know it. You see them in the daytime, if they are already a bit high they want to play. And we are a toy there for them. We are just a toy."

They were fed plain macaroni once or twice a day. When Kaleb was particularly hungry, he would steal food from the guards. One clumsy attempt meant he was caught and, as retribution, made to stand in the sun for three hours until he passed out.

Kaleb had already noticed his own behavior changing. A year and a half had passed since he left home. He stopped trusting anyone, even other refugees in the same position as him, and became more aggressive, despite knowing it put him in greater danger. For amusement, individual guards provoked detainees. If anyone retaliated, the guard would reappear with backup: masked men carrying metal rings to hit captives with. "Running was the best way to defend yourself, so people can protect you," Kaleb said.

If they were popular, other detainees formed a protective barrier around the person being targeted. Sometimes guards would shoot the ceiling in frustration, leaving everyone terrified that the bullet would ricochet back down.

Amid all this, they had one hope: the UN Refugee Agency—the global organization with a mandate to protect the world's refugees. It was simply known as "the organization" among Ain Zara's detainees. They would stay up all night, hearts beating with anxiety, if they thought UNHCR staff might come the next day. They had heard there was an opportunity for legal evacuation from Libya and resettlement to a Western country, where they would be safe. Before their journeys began, some of them had seen the agency's social media profiles filled with statements about the good work it was doing and photos showing its logo splashed across tents, boxes of food, and the jackets of staff.

Ain Zara's detainees wanted to be registered as asylum seekers or refugees in need of international protection, which would mean the UNHCR had a record that they existed. Without this, they worried they could be sold back to smugglers; sent to farms, construction sites, or military barracks as slave labor; or taken to the detention center's isolation room and never released. "Nobody knows how many [people] exactly [are] inside these detention centers. There is no registration mechanism," said an aid worker who visited Ain Zara around this time. When UNHCR staff did make an appearance at Ain Zara, detainees were disappointed at how little they interacted with the refugees, and their names were still not taken down. "The UNHCR listens to the soldiers and not us," Kaleb complained. By the time the war broke out in August 2018, less than one quarter of them had been registered.

During those early months, there were other visitors to Ain Zara, too. Once, a human rights organization even managed to get in. It was Kaleb's first time speaking to white people, and he had a misplaced idea that they could do something to help. He catalogued what was happening inside the center, aware the Libyan guards were listening. Later, Kaleb was thrashed and denied food. "We were new, we didn't know we couldn't say it," he recalled, but he learned his lesson. "After that I stopped talking to visitors, I didn't volunteer." He still hoped that single meeting would lead to change, but nothing improved.

> *"They are afraid of the Libyans . . . They give us shampoo, they say calm down, calm down. They are saying to us you are under the UN Refugee Agency, but the UNHCR doesn't even come here to register us."*

An Italian official came to see the center. Beforehand, the guards brought workers who trimmed trees and cleaned and sprayed antiseptic across the halls the refugees slept in. On the day itself, musicians arrived with big speakers and costumed dancers. Children were allowed outside to play. There was football, juice, and cake. A TV channel crew filmed the scene. "It looked like a place that is easy to live," Kaleb said. "This was fake." Afterwards, everything was removed again, and—because detainees had agreed to be interviewed by the visiting journalists about the poor conditions—they were locked inside a room for days with the water turned off. People were shouting by the time they were released, frantically calling out for aid, wondering if they had been totally forgotten.

There were also visits from medics. At first, it was the international charity Médecins Sans Frontières (MSF), or Doctors Without Borders, whose staff have a reputation for practicality and kindness. Twice a week, when MSF arrived, a negotiation would begin. MSF staff wanted the detainees to be allowed to leave their locked halls regularly so they could breathe fresh air. They began pushing for better food to be fed to the refugees, especially those with tuberculosis who needed vitamins and full stomachs to take their medication. The medics even asked for barefoot detainees to be given shoes, which Ain Zara's management opposed because it would make it easier for them to escape. Refugees remember Ain Zara's manager eventually losing his temper and banning MSF, though MSF say another charity was already scheduled to take over in providing assistance.

Other medical organizations came, but their staff were not as effective. Refugees began faking faints so they could be admitted to a hospital and get three meals a day. The guards quickly became suspicious of how regularly this was happening and started refusing to move anyone at all.

Libyan summers are sweltering, and as the temperature cranked up to 104 degrees Fahrenheit, Ain Zara's detainees began really fainting. They were weak from a lack of nutrition. At night, in cramped halls, they lay on their sides so their bodies did not touch—the heat was too much.

Stress caused many to turn in on themselves and avoid conversation. But the more curious would talk and talk. The most valuable asset in detention was information, but a lot of what they did was speculate. They did not know if anything had changed in their home countries; why they were locked up; how they might get out. A mix of nationalities merged that would never naturally come together: Sudanese, Somalis, Eritreans, Ethiopians, Ivorians, Nigerians, Nigeriens, a dozen Egyptians, and three Ghanaians. They began teaching each other about their cultures and sharing what they missed from home. They had disparate languages and habits, divergent ways of computing their thoughts and conducting themselves. They were brought together only by the shared ache of stolen months and years, and the understanding that their life before this meant nothing anymore.

"There are some racist people, there are some thieves, there are some good people, there are people who are more spiritual."

Athletes, artists, musicians, preachers, farmers, teachers, bakers, and dentists—they were all incarcerated as one, their lives reduced to waiting, begging, and scrabbling for their basic needs. Kaleb even met his first West Africans. "I thought West Africa was like the *National Geographic*, they don't wear clothes, they have no development, and always have war," Kaleb remembered wryly. Growing up in Ethiopia, he had been unaware the western part of his continent even had cities.

They might not have always understood each other, but they all knew why they were in Libya. "Do you live to die or die to live?" one man asked Kaleb, a question that became a mantra among them. The teenager had already seen death on this journey, and he knew the correct answer: "We die to live."

During the early months of their detention, those torturous early morning roll calls during which refugees were forced to stand outside and be counted were the only times couples were able to see each other. They would make eye contact and endeavor to smile, despite being separated into gender-specific rows. Gradually, the guards began to let husbands and wives meet; a few of the more sympathetic ones even let them spend a night together.

"[The roll calls] were to make people tired and to make people crazy. If refugees are strong and well fed, they will make problems for the police."

With cigarettes easier to procure than food, Kaleb had smoked heavily in the smugglers' warehouses, his hands, stomach, and brain keen for anything to occupy them. When he had boarded the rubber boat onto the sea, he threw his last cigarette packet in the water, declaring that he was giving up and would be healthier in Europe, because he would finally have a life worth growing old in. Now, back in captivity, he began to smoke again. It helped Kaleb stay sane, and the guards were more likely to distribute tobacco than food. That was just the way Libya was, he thought.

So it went on like this, through the summer of 2018, until intermilitia fighting erupted in Tripoli that August, leading to the Libyan guards abandoning the detention center and the detained refugees contacting me for the first time. Those five hundred men, women, and children were locked up in the middle of a raging conflict. In my head, I began to refer to this period as the first war, though of course it was not the first fighting Libya had seen, and it would not be the last. The refugees in Ain Zara would eventually come to say it was this conflict that freed them. Weeks later, after they spoke to me that initial time and hundreds of them were moved to Abu Salim detention center by Libyan authorities, the manager of Ain Zara tried to take them back, realizing he had lost valuable human cargo. It was too late.

ABU SALIM DETENTION CENTER

Their new neighborhood, Abu Salim, was traditionally a Gaddafi-supporting stronghold. It was the last part of Tripoli to fall during the 2011 revolution seven years earlier, a victory that had great symbolic value because the area was home to an infamous prison.

In the late 1980s and 1990s, Libyans would be taken to Abu Salim's prison after they were tortured underground.[1] Survivors said an inmate died every week from tuberculosis. They were always hungry, received no medical treatment, and had to rest in shifts because of the lack of physical space. A brutal massacre took place there in 1996 when around 1,200 inmates were shot to death after they protested for better conditions.

In his Pulitzer Prize-winning book *The Return*, Libyan writer Hisham Matar quotes a letter that his father—who later disappeared without a trace—had written to him from Abu Salim prison. "The cruelty of this place far exceeds all of what we have read of the fortress prison of Bastille. The cruelty is in everything, but I remain stronger than their tactics of oppression . . . My forehead does not know how to bow." In another letter, also from the mid-1990s, his father wrote: "At times a whole year will pass by without seeing the sun or being let out of this cell."[2]

The migrant detention center was in a different part of Abu Salim to that prison, but its newest arrivals were equally terrified entering it, and just as accustomed to cruelty. They were relieved to leave Ain Zara after days without security, food, or water, but when the buses stopped, they messaged to say the new center was dirtier and darker, with no bedding. Outside, fighting still raged.

"Listen [to] the screaming of the people. We are hearing the voice of heavy guns and a jet has passed above us."

Before this latest battle, Libyans in the capital city had dared to imagine elections, which were supposed to take place in the following months. The conflict between militias jostling for power shattered that hope, but there had really only been an illusion of stability all along. In Tripoli, the internationally recognized government was propped up by militias, aligned under the umbrella of the Libyan Government of National Accord. To outsiders, Prime Minister Fayez al-Serraj—with his serious stare framed by a gray mustache and sideburns—appeared to be in charge. But he ruled over fighters whose priorities and loyalty shifted as they competed for prestige, control, and resources.

The reasons behind the conflict were fairly incomprehensible to some detainees, who had little contact with the outside world, but I read as much as I could and shared it with them. News reports said it was sparked by fighters from the Seventh Brigade militia, also known as Kaniyat, becoming angry at the lavish lifestyles of some Tripoli militia commanders. The Seventh Brigade came from Tarhouna, a town 65 kilometers southeast of Tripoli. It launched an attack on two of the capital's largest armed groups, the Tripoli Revolutionaries' Brigades (TRB) and the Nawasi.[3]

"The children are crying because of hunger . . . The only way we can be safe is if they take us to a neighboring country . . . We are in a different hall to the ladies, if anything happens we can't even help them. We are afraid they may be sick and losing hope."

It was right after the refugees arrived at Abu Salim that the information games began. On August 30, the UN Refugee Agency released a statement saying around three hundred Eritrean, Ethiopian, and Somali nationals who had previously been in Ain Zara had been "evacuated" and taken "out of harm's way," which it was already clear was not true.[4] This group remained in danger, as did thousands of other refugees close to Tripoli's rapidly shifting front lines. MSF made this clear in their own statement, which came as the bout of fighting began to garner more attention and called for refugees to be taken out of the country instead.[5] "Transferring detainees from one detention center to another within the same conflict zone cannot be described as an evacuation and it is certainly not a solution," it read. "They should not be held captive simply because they were looking for safety or a better life. They should be immediately released and evacuated to a country where they will be safe." The treatment of Libya's refugees started attracting international attention. There was soon coverage by the *Washington Post*, the *Associated Press*, and *Voice of America*.[6]

"If they are going to take us out of the war, they should take us out of Libya."

Within days, the Libyan guards in Abu Salim ran away, too, afraid that they would be attacked.[7] Disputes between UN agencies meant the refugees had nothing to eat. More than four days passed before a meal of chicken and rice arrived.[8] Another two days went by, this time without water, too.[9]

UNHCR's spokespeople were still saying they had "regular" access to the detention centers, but that did not seem to be true.[10] (They would later tell me, "We do have regular access, but it doesn't mean that we have access to all at the same time."[11]) Outside Libya, this conveyed a false impression that things were under control, when in truth detained refugees continued to be in grave danger. It also meant there was an illusion of oversight. Speaking anonymously, UNHCR staff, uncomfortable with how things were developing, told me they were worried the agency would pull out of the country completely. On September 2, UNHCR's high commissioner, Filippo Grandi, added fire to those rumors. "I am extremely concerned by the escalation of violence in Libya, which endangers thousands of lives," he tweeted. "Unless fighting ends, we may have to suspend work for refugees and migrants stranded in Libya, and for Libyan displaced people. Months of efforts would be wasted."[12]

Still, the refugees' pleas were reaching people of importance. On September 12, a group of European parliamentarians wrote to Grandi asking for registration for the detainees in Abu Salim.[13] In the meantime, the detainees made me their own list, putting together hundreds of names, ages, and the UN case number given to the minority who had previously been registered elsewhere. I could not believe how young they all were: fifteen, seventeen, sixteen, twenty-three, two, three—there were so many teenagers and children.[14] Though they were getting little food and water, my contacts there felt energized now, and began deliberating what other pleas they could release to raise awareness of their plight.

"When we are registered UNHCR will know us, where we are, how many people we are. It is important for us. Maybe they'll think of us."

"You are our hope to make the world know about us, to know our suffering in the hell country, Libya."

The sounds of humans hating each other rumbled outside Abu Salim one night, a week after the refugees were moved there, as another piece of news came through. Through furtive phone calls, they found out that a man called Tesfu, whom many of them knew from the Bani Walid warehouses, had been killed in another government-associated detention center. Tesfu was one of a group that organized a rare protest against their indefinite imprisonment and living conditions while asking for legal evacuation.[15] As a punishment, the ringleaders were taken away and forced to labor together, until one day Tesfu refused. Guards dragged him off, only returning his weak body when it had begun to shut down. Tesfu managed to tell friends he had been electrocuted. Around thirty minutes later, he died in their arms.

As Abu Salim's detainees started to wail, setting off the communal mourning that was the only way they could process this news, one of the pregnant women, Helen, went into labor. Without other options, women pulled plastic bags on their hands to help, as men prayed and panicked about whether assistance would come.[16] There was a hum of anxiety throughout the big hall. Aware that there was no medical worker available if anything went wrong, detainees prayed for the baby's safe delivery. "It was the traditional way. But God was there with us," one remembered later.

The infant's first breaths were those of the incarcerated, her deliverance praised by people who were waiting for their own. Like them, she would go without sunlight and nourishment; she symbolized desperation, but also hope. After coming into the world, she remained locked up: just another of the thousands of refugees and migrants trapped in indefinite detention in a war-torn country without a stable government, and one of roughly 640 children who were being held in "official" government-run Libyan detention centers at that time.

"Surprise. The pregnant woman I told you about has born a child."

The backstory of the young parents of this girl was a reminder that love could blossom in the most unlikely places, even along an unpredictable and chaotic migration route that sporadically tore people apart. Helen escaped Eritrea in 2016 and made her way to Khartoum. Also in the city, though she did not know it, was Birhan, another Eritrean, who worked in a bakery. Both of them wanted to reach Europe.

In January 2017, they ended up in the same vehicle crossing the Sahara Desert and arriving in a smuggler's warehouse. The man who transported them announced it would cost $6,000 to get in a boat, so Helen phoned relatives, well aware that if she could not raise the money she would be brutally tortured. They would stay in that warehouse for a year.

Birhan had no one to come to his aid. The smugglers beat him daily. "He broke my arm, he broke my head, he broke everything in my body," Birhan recalled, referring to his smuggler. "He knew I didn't have anything. He was not happy, he was so angry, he was so mad." Birhan was even shot in the leg at one point.

Helen's brother and other relatives pooled together and raised the money she needed, but by this stage she had fallen in love with Birhan. More than that, she was two months pregnant. He told Helen to go on ahead of him, to get their baby to safety. The couple separated, but Helen was not sent to the sea; the gang who took her claimed they had problems reaching the coast. Confusingly, the chief smuggler seemed to tire of beating Birhan and put him on a boat instead. He stayed at sea for sixteen hours before he was intercepted and brought back to Tariq al Matar detention center in Tripoli, then relocated to Ain Zara.

Helen remained with the smugglers. Her pregnancy meant she was sick every day. Birhan procured a phone to contact her captors, who demanded 600 dinars to have her sent to Tripoli. She arrived at Ain Zara by car, six months pregnant, her stomach protruding. At the gate, she explained who she was, angering Ain Zara's manager, who threatened to send Birhan to the police station. In the end, Helen was allowed inside. Birhan was present as their first child was born.

———

Weeks later, I used a press briefing with Natalia Kanem, the Executive Director of the UN Populations Fund (UNFPA), to tell her how Helen had given birth. UNFPA is a UN agency focused on reproductive health and the rights of mothers and pregnant women that operates in more than 150 countries. I described the plastic bags used as gloves, hundreds of refugees bent in prayer, and the echoes of war outside. This was a woman turned back from the sea under EU policy, I said. This baby could have been born in Europe.

Kanem listened carefully. She said women should not be forced to give birth in detention centers and should have privacy, no matter where they were. "Any pregnant woman deserves her full human rights and dignity, and it does not matter whether you're a refugee," Kanem said. "I believe the concern for the life of the mother and her newborn is something enshrined in the common will, which the definition of human rights represents."

Helen knew her baby was far from any concept of human rights. "I just want to get my baby in a perfect place, a good place, and live as a normal person," she told me through WhatsApp from Abu Salim. Birhan echoed this. "My plan was just to escape [Eritrea], but now I have a wife and child to worry about," he said. "I just want to work and have a normal, proper family."

For Helen and Birhan, their current surroundings now presented as a list of all the ways their child was in danger. A baby was a burden, the complication that could prevent their escape, but also their biggest motivation for getting out of there.

———

I was being contacted more and more. I would stay up late messaging detained refugees and wake up early to send appeals and information to humanitarian agencies. I had contacts in four detention centers; then five; then six—it would eventually climb to nine official centers. I also heard from refugees still in the grips of smugglers, and escapees living a precarious life in various parts of Libya—some working for a pittance on farms or factories, others hiding in cities, constantly terrified of being rearrested. I was asked to share what they were going through on Al Jazeera, BBC World Service, and BBC TV. The intermilitia conflict would last until the end of September 2018, by which time at least 115 people had been killed, and thousands displaced from their homes.[17]

For the detained refugees, there was crushing repetition: medical emergencies, days without food and water, and worries about a militia attack or the guards coming back to beat them. In parts of the city, other refugees were "released": a poisoned chalice, as they were thrown out of detention with no idea where they were or where to go. Some ran straight into bullets. Others submitted to traffickers. We still do not know how many people died. And trying to cross the sea was increasingly futile: one in five migrants and refugees who attempted to leave Libya in September 2018 died or disappeared, while only one in ten actually made it to Europe.[18]

———

During that first month of communication, I traveled a lot for other work. I went from London to Uganda to Tunisia, where I was invited to accept first prize in the European Union's Migration Media Awards for an investigation I co-authored with a Syrian colleague, Ziad Ghandour. We had spent months looking into what happened to Syrian refugees who left Europe to go home—a project that culminated with me traveling across Syria for ten days. On the last night there, I managed to evade my regime-assigned minder and meet a refugee who had voluntarily traveled back to Damascus from Germany to be present while his mother underwent a life-saving operation. Sami had been arrested in the airport, crammed into a cell with other returnees, and tortured. He was sent to the front lines to fight against ISIS, where much of his battalion was killed by a suicide bomber. His experience disproved what was being said by European far-right groups, who wrongly claimed the parts of Syria controlled by Bashar al-Assad were safe for refugees to return to.

This report was the reason I ended up in an expensive hotel in Tunis, and at a ceremony in the Carthage Acropolium, a 130-year-old Roman Catholic cathedral, with EU politicians who praised our "sumptuous surroundings" over wine and canapés. On screens behind the mostly white crowd flashed images of black and brown refugees. I was anxious because I had no internet connection. We were close to Libya, only hundreds of miles from Abu Salim, and I wanted to know that everyone there was okay. By then, I was used to communicating with them constantly.

*"We were sent you because we need the world to know the true
life of Libya."*

The ceremony was in the evening. Though politicians spoke at length, journalists were not allowed to say anything as they accepted their awards. It felt like we were props. I had drafted words in my iPhone notes that I posted on Twitter instead.

"Thank you so much for this award," I wrote. "At the same time I found out we won it, a few weeks ago, I was messaging terrified refugee detainees who are just a few hundred miles away, in Tripoli. Tens of thousands have been locked up there indefinitely, in the middle of a war zone, after being forced back to Libya because of EU policy. Men, women, pregnant women, and children are being starved, tortured, forced to work, raped, kidnapped by militias, or victims of a range of other abuses. I promised the detainees in Abu Salim detention center in Tripoli that I'd mention them tonight."

The only bright spot in my trip to Tunisia was a visit to MSF's Tunis office. Staff who had seen the chain of messages from refugees in Libya that I was posting on Twitter, along with the accompanying newspaper reporting, took me out for coffee. Despite everything I had done to verify the information, I told them I was still second-guessing myself, wondering if the messages could be a hoax. If things were this bad, why was it not big news internationally? They assured me I was not imagining it, that the detention centers were real and the accounts of suffering were true. This made me wonder how much the European politicians I had met in Tunisia knew. Why were they not considering the consequences of their policies, and what could I do to make them listen?

LIBYA: ESCAPE TO HELL

"Overall, the international agenda in the North of Africa region
tends to be more focused on migration management and development than
humanitarian assistance and peace-building."
—A REVIEW OF THE EUROPEAN UNION TRUST FUND FOR AFRICA, 2021[1]

"The suffering of migrants detained in Libya is an outrage
to the conscience of humanity."
—ZEID RA'AD AL HUSSEIN, FORMER UN HUMAN RIGHTS CHIEF, 2017[2]

In mid-2011, the world watched on TV as Libya's rebels rode into Tripoli's Green Square, tearing down or shooting at pictures of Muammar Gaddafi, the eccentric, Botoxed, and barbaric dictator who had ruled Libya since the 1960s. It was the climax of a popular revolution that would change the country's history forever, one that had inspired civilians from all walks of life to take up arms and call for freedom. For decades, protests had been banned and criticism was not tolerated. Now, people thronged the streets greeting their liberators. The mood was loud and joyous.

As the rebels celebrated, Gaddafi's weapons stores were raided and his guns dispersed. The young fighters were men and boys, many of whom had only recently been students. They set off celebratory gunfire—civilians were even killed by these hails of bullets, which had to return to ground eventually.[3] Were those early deaths—Libyans killing Libyans—a symbol of what was to come?

Violence was well-known in Libya. Older citizens grew up watching Gaddafi-ordered executions broadcast on the television while hearing stories of Italian colonial abuses that had taken place long before.[4] Boys learned how to use Kalashnikovs in school and even wore military uniforms.[5] Cruelty was an invisible undercurrent, an everyday threat. In the years after revolution, Libyans described the Gaddafi regime as one that permeated all parts of their lives, leaving nothing secure and nowhere unrestricted, even the family home. Informers were everywhere, and their leader's tastes were fickle: musical instruments were burned; history books banned.[6] And then there was Gaddafi himself: a hypocrite, a man who preached religion while drinking, taking drugs, and raping countless female subordinates.[7] His will was the country's command.

In February 2011, shortly after the uprising began, Gaddafi threatened to hunt down revolutionaries and "purify" Libya "inch by inch, house by house, home by home, alleyway by alleyway, person by person."[8] His son, Saif al-Islam, warned there would be "rivers of blood" if protests did not stop because the regime would "fight until the last man, the last woman, the last bullet."[9] In the end, Gaddafi's own killing, in October 20, 2011, was as brutal as anything that had gone before it. The 69-year-old was discovered in a drainpipe and sodomized with a bayonet before being shot. Afterwards, the former dictator's corpse was displayed in a shopping center freezer, so there could be no doubt that his rule had ended.[10]

What came next might have been Gaddafi's revenge. Throughout his reign, Gaddafi had promoted and empowered armed militias, frightened that a too-strong army could lead a coup to oust him at any time. After his death, these militia groups carved up power and territory. They had shifting goals and loyalties, which meant that building a state on top of militias was like building a city on sand.

These days, many critics condemn NATO for getting involved in Libya and carrying out air strikes. ("We came, we saw, he died," then-US Secretary of State Hillary Clinton said at the time about Gaddafi, with a gleeful shrug and a laugh,[11] her delight contrasting with former US President Barack Obama's sentiment later on, when he was said to privately describe the intervention as a "shit show."[12]) Other commentators say the country was destined for catastrophic upheaval before NATO got involved, and the air strikes saved lives—though Libyans should have been given much more assistance by the international community in the years that followed. These were long-oppressed people with minimal experience of democracy. According to journalistic accounts of the time, the US believed Europe would take the lead in rebuilding, while Europe thought the UN would be central.[13] Yet the UN brought in no peacekeepers or military observers, and, until mid-2012, the UN Support Mission in Libya (UNSMIL), a political mission set up the previous year, had no one with expertise in reforming security institutions.[14]

In an attempt to ensure security, Libya's transitional government began to pay militias as early as December 2011, creating a further lure for young men to join them.[15] The militias were armed groups with varying levels of order that had organized and formed during the revolution and were loyal to different commanders, cities, religious agendas, or tribes. Libya was still wealthy from oil, blessed with what Reuters correspondent Ulf Laessing called "an embarrassment of riches,"[16] and billions of dollars were potentially on the table.[17] Weapons were everywhere, too. In Gaddafi's first decade in power, the self-styled "Brother Leader" spent $22 billion on weapons—which worked out at an annual expenditure of around $890 for each Libyan citizen.[18] The collapse of the Gaddafi regime led to Libya being described as the "Tesco" of the illegal arms trade by British intelligence.[19] Post-revolution, having a gun became a type of insurance, and joining a militia was a way to protect yourself, your family, and your life savings. Landlords became fighters to protect their properties. For teenage boys, it could be more like schoolyard behavior: they wanted to secure roles as the bullies rather than the bullied.

In the beginning, journalists multiplied as well. In the year after Gadd-afi was ousted, the number of Libyan TV stations increased tenfold. Information is power, and, after so much censorship, locals say it was exciting to see fresh media outlets springing up. But the dangers of speaking freely quickly became clear, and by 2012, Libyan journalists recounted being told by their managers to keep their reporting away from the "world of militias" and human rights.[20] Instead of one regime to fear, there were many.

In the early 1990s, Gaddafi published his own collection of essays and short stories called *Escape to Hell*.[21] The book was typical of the erratic dictator—rambling and often incoherent, buoyed by the extreme levels of self-belief that had propelled his control of Libya across four decades. The "Hell" of his title was the city: living there, rather than in a village with your kinsmen, is a form of being buried alive, he said. Since his death, the word "hell" has come to epitomize Libya as a whole for refugees and migrants, but also for many Libyans.

———

When the Arab Spring swept across the Middle East, I was twenty-one, in my final year of a law undergraduate degree in Dublin. Along with my core legal requirements, I took an elective in Middle Eastern politics. As young Arabs courageously challenged autocracies that had made them miserable for as long as they could remember, I sat at the back of a tiered lecture hall in an Irish university arts building, looking at photos of the uprisings on a PowerPoint below. I remember our professor looking confused, saying it was the first time since he started teaching this class that his syllabus did not seem fully relevant anymore. The rule book was being torn up, and he had no idea what would happen in the region by the end of the semester, let alone the following decade.

Three years after Libya's revolution began, in early 2014, I was an anxious and eager-to-please intern in CNN International's London bureau. Every second day, I worked on the eponymous news show hosted by the legendary British-Iranian journalist Christiane Amanpour. Fetching interviewees from the lobby in Great Marlborough Street, bringing them to makeup, lodging them comfortably in the small green room, and getting them tea or coffee was part of my job. We had guests like former US Secretary of State Madeleine Albright and then-Tanzanian president Jakaya Kikwete. I even made hot chocolate for the Tanzanian president's bodyguard.

On a particular afternoon in March, I remember Libyan Prime Minister Ali Zeidan arriving for an interview. The former diplomat had originally defected in India, becoming a Gaddafi opponent for the next thirty years. In 2012, he was elected to lead the new Libya, post-revolution, by a narrow margin. He threatened to cut off payments to militias while attempting to rebuild Libya's army. In October 2013, Zeidan was briefly kidnapped: he told the nation, in a televised address, that it was a coup attempt.[22]

Five months later, he had been ousted and fled the country, but when I met him, weeks after this abrupt departure, he seemed convinced that he would soon be reinstated as prime minister. He requested tea, and I remember how dejected he seemed in person. On screen though, he sounded defiant. "The situation requires a few arrangements, and I will go back there," he told Christiane on air. "There are forces from within the army—legitimate forces—in the country that will protect me. And I am supported by a segment of the population that will be behind me." He decried "weakness" in the security agencies and the intelligence groups. "The intelligence apparatus was destroyed after the revolution . . . There are people who wanted the security apparatus to be weak."[23]

In the end, Zeidan did not return to Libya. He moved to Germany, with reports saying he was too shaken by the militias to risk his life anymore (the next time he traveled back to Libya, in 2017, he was kidnapped and released once again).[24] In Zeidan's absence, Libya was effectively split between two opposing governments: one in Tripoli, in the west, and one in Tobruk, in the east. The following year, there were three governments, none of which seemed capable of actually governing.[25]

One of the key reasons the EU was pushing for a national government to be established in Libya was because it wanted to stop migrants from arriving across the sea. In May 2015, as the so-called "European migration crisis" was at its height, EU foreign policy chief Federica Mogherini told the UN Security Council that the EU was politically, logistically, and financially supporting Libya in that process, which was being led by the UN. "We all know also very well that the vast majority of human trafficking and smuggling in these months is happening in Libya, or rather, through Libya," she said. "As long as there is not a unity government that can exercise its legitimate authority over the entire territory of the country and its land and sea borders, the situation is likely to continue this way."[26]

That year, the Government of National Accord (GNA) was formed, following a UN-brokered peace agreement. It began to operate in Tripoli from 2016 and was led by Prime Minister Fayez al-Serraj, but it still only ruled over a minority of the country.[27] In Libya, true power was wielded through money and guns, not government.

Migration has long been a key factor when it comes to international decision-making on Libya. Gaddafi himself used it as a bargaining chip, threatening that Europe would turn "black" unless he was given billions of dollars a year to stop Africans crossing the Mediterranean Sea to Italy.[28] "We don't know what will happen, what will be the reaction of the white and Christian Europeans faced with this influx of starving and ignorant Africans," he said in 2010, standing next to former Italian Prime Minister Silvio Berlusconi in Rome. "We don't know if Europe will remain an advanced and united continent or if it will be destroyed, as happened with the barbarian invasions."[29] (The Libyan president took time on the same Italy trip to hire hundreds of Italian female models so he could preach the benefits of Islam to them.[30])

Gaddafi promoted himself as the African "King of Kings" and had gone through phases of encouraging hundreds of thousands of Africans from across the continent to come and work in Libya.[31] He even used Africans from other nations as mercenaries when suppressing and killing his own citizens. Chadians and Sudanese were among those extrajudicially executed in retaliation attacks by rebels during the revolution, with international journalists discovering their bodies after they had been shot through the heads, their hands tied behind their backs.[32]

When deciding whether to support Gaddafi's ousting in Libya, migration was a major consideration for European powers. "Do we want a situation where a failed, pariah state festers on Europe's southern border, potentially threatening our security, pushing people across the Mediterranean and creating a more dangerous and uncertain world for Britain and for all our allies, as well as for the people of Libya?" asked UK Prime Minister David Cameron while making the case for intervention in Libya in 2011, after the Arab Spring had already begun.[33] Of course, that's close to what transpired anyway.

———

In the years after the revolution, a Libyan coastguard was recruited, but few of them had sailing experience.[34] The EU Integrated Border Management Assistance Mission in Libya (EUBAM), which was initially set up in 2013, struggled to have any impact in encouraging Libyans to secure their own borders. That same year, US public radio NPR reported that dozens of migrants caught by a Libyan militia were being held in cages in Tripoli's zoo, which was both horrific and showed how haphazard any anti-migration effort was.[35]

From 2014 on, as hundreds of thousands of refugees and migrants crossed the Mediterranean from both the Middle East and North Africa, European politicians became increasingly desperate to suppress their own far-right parties, which were gaining popularity by riding on a wave of anti-immigration sentiment. That response was often framed in terms of combatting smuggling and trafficking. "Let me explicitly assure you that no refugees or migrants intercepted at sea will be sent back against their will. Their rights under [the] Geneva Conventions will be fully honored,"[36] EU foreign policy chief Federica Mogherini told the UN Security Council in May 2015, as the EU sought approval from the UN Security Council to carry out military sea operations. "The European Union is finally ready to take its own responsibilities: saving lives, welcoming refugees, addressing the root causes of the phenomenon, dismantling criminal organizations . . . It is our firm intention to always respect international law, international humanitarian law, and human rights," she continued, explaining that she was in contact with UN Secretary General António Guterres and wanted to support UNHCR's work in Libya, too.[37]

That year, the EU trebled funding for its own Mediterranean missions.[38] Then, in November 2015, the Valletta Europe-Africa Summit took place and the EU Trust Fund for Africa was created. This was a highly significant multibillion euro pot to be distributed across much of Africa, aimed at stopping the movement of refugees and migrants.[39] "Border management" was the second largest thematic area of spending, in a continent where borders— carved out by colonialists—had nonetheless remained quite fluid, with people crossing back and forwards every day, without undergoing formal checks.[40] Spending would include the training of police and border officials, donations of surveillance equipment, helicopters, patrol ships, and vehicles, and a significant chunk of funding for the UN, including money for programs to return migrants back to the countries they originally came from. Between 2016 and 2021, more than 4.8 billion euro was committed through it, funding more than five hundred projects in twenty-six African countries.[41] By mid-2021, the EU would pledge 455 million euro specifically towards Libya through the Trust Fund, and another 245 million euro through other funding instruments, all labeled "EU support on migration in Libya."[42]

The full Trust Fund was classified as "emergency" funding, meaning it was not subject to the same oversight as most EU spending and did not have to follow the same public procurement procedures. Effectively, half of the countries on the African continent were considered to be in "crisis."[43] Most money would be distributed through UN agencies or those run by European governments, especially France, Italy, and Germany.

Particular projects were especially egregious. In Eritrea, for example, the EU spent tens of millions on materials to build a road, even though the work was carried out by forced conscripts.[44] In a 2020 report, anti-poverty charity Oxfam decried the Trust Fund, calling it an example of development aid being used as leverage to pressure African countries into cooperating with European demands to combat migration.[45] "European governments seem determined to prevent migration at any cost," said Oxfam's EU migration policy advisor Raphael Shilhav. "They are putting short-term wins over strategies that work in the long run, at the expense of those most in need. The EU needs to stop undermining its own values and make sure that all of its engagements in Africa promote stability, democracy, and resilience—not the opposite."[46] The charity called for more transparency.[47]

In many cases, Trust Fund money strengthened abusive systems rather than improving life for civilians, so people kept crossing the water. Between 2014 and 2016, more than half a million people arrived in Italy by sea, while at least 12,480 died trying.[48]

––––––

It was back to the drawing board for the EU, and the next option was to stop the boats. The international law principle of non-refoulement prohibits sending a person back to a country where their life is in danger and they could be tortured or persecuted. In 2012, the European Court of Human Rights ruled that refugees could not be returned to Libya by European boats because of the huge risk to their lives there.[49] The EU found a way around that by equipping, training, and supporting the Libyan coastguard to do interceptions themselves.

As an entity, the Libyan coastguard was much looser than it sounded, even once it recruited more people who could sail. Different militias were involved at various points along the coast. Smuggling was a lucrative business, and in the years following the revolution, many of the coastguard's members had been actively involved in it themselves. A number still were. "Those Libyan coastguards are wicked, they're violating the rights of migrants and refugees," a South Sudanese man who spent sixteen months in a government-associated detention center complained. "The EU know[s] that Libya is the largest human market in the world, and they're still paying the Libyan coastguard to bring back migrants."

> *"The Libyan coastguard just work for money. Let's say the EU stops funding the coastguards, then the coastguards would work for the smugglers . . . There are some boats that make it to Italy. Do you think the coastguards don't see the boats? The smugglers and the Libyan coastguard were co-workers before. Sometimes the smugglers give them a higher percentage of money, then they let them pass through. This is business, Sally. Money. The coastguards are working with Italy now because they are giving more and more money."*

The policy developed quickly, despite apprehension. In early 2017, Fabrice Leggeri, the director of EU border agency Frontex, said he was looking at Libya with concern. "There is no stable state there. We currently have practically no contact person at the operational level to promote effective border security. We are now helping to train sixty officers for a possible future Libyan coastguard. But that is at best a beginning," he told a German newspaper.[50]

"Europe has proven it is able to close down irregular routes of migration," European Council president Donald Tusk said around the same time, referring to a multibillion euro deal between the EU and Turkey to prevent new arrivals to Greece. "Now it is time to close down the route from Libya to

Italy . . . It is within our reach. What we need is the full determination to do that." He was speaking ahead of an EU leaders' meeting in Malta where 200 million euro more would be pledged towards this goal.[51]

Budget documents show the EU was already aware that roughly seven thousand refugees and migrants were being held across twenty-four detention centers associated with the Tripoli-based government, along with countless other unofficial ones.[52] "Migrants and refugees do not undergo any kind of formal registration and don't have access to legal process before and while being in detention," one read. "Conditions in detention are generally inhumane: severely overcrowded, without adequate access to toilets or washing facilities, food, or clean water. In several detention centers, migrants are held in large numbers in a single room without sufficient space to lie down."

Yet Italy and Libya signed a memorandum of understanding on February 2, 2017 confirming support for the Libyan coastguard, while focusing on a newly popular term: "migration management."[53] The Italian Interior Minister who presided over this was Marco Minniti. In a fawning profile, *The New York Times* described him as "an old spymaster," a former communist who worked from an office "surrounded by bookcases filled with tomes about espionage and religious fanaticism." He loved philosophy, airplanes, free diving, and the poet Catullus, the piece said.[54] (When I googled Catullus, the first excerpt I found of his poetry was: "All this is great, but the greatest of all is the owner, no ordinary man, but in fact a mighty menacing cock.") Part of Minniti's plan was a willingness to pay anyone in Libya who could help achieve his aims. By August 2017, refugee and migrant arrivals were down 87 percent on the previous year.[55]

With the encouragement of the EU, Libya also requested control of an area of the sea off its coast from the International Maritime Organization, meaning foreign rescue ships could not enter it anymore without requesting permission, and Europeans could no longer be held responsible for drownings there.[56] Elections were looming in Italy, and politicians were scrambling to hold onto power (they would lose to the anti-establishment Five Star League and Matteo Salvini's right-wing League, leading to Salvini, who was even more staunchly anti-immigration, becoming interior minister).

————

The EU initially pledged 46.3 million euro to go towards training, vessels, and equipment for the Libyan coastguard, in what they called the "first phase" of the project, and 45 million euro for the second phase (this was revised down to 15 million euro in 2020, with an updated document, which included a section called "risks and assumptions," warning, "if the treatment of migrants during [search-and-rescue] interventions will not be improved, then it will further damage the narrative and reputation of the EU."[57])

As Europe removed its own ships from the Mediterranean, it also flew planes, helicopters, and later drones to locate boats full of refugees and direct the Libyan coastguard to them, ensuring their interception.[58] Frontex, the EU border agency, might fly as many as three planes a day, spokesperson Ewa Moncure told me during a phone interview in November 2020. While she emphasized that they wanted to save lives, when I asked Moncure how Frontex measured success, she laughed before saying: "We are there to survey the border. So our measure of success is detection."

Analysis by investigative journalism network Lighthouse Reports found that Frontex regularly failed to inform nearby merchant vessels or charity-run rescue ships when they spotted a boat in distress, instead sending WhatsApp messages with the coordinates of refugee boats to members of the Libyan coastguard. Sometimes, these delays cost lives immediately, while others would die later, unnoticed, back on Libyan territory. So was this violating international law? Many experts said the level of engagement and direction by Frontex meant it was.[59] The interceptions could be aggressive, with Libyan coastguard members ramming migrant boats or shooting at rescue ships.[60] In certain cases, they led to chaos, with people jumping in the water and drowning, or families being separated in the commotion. In 2018, a 10-year-old Sierra Leonean boy ended up being apprehended by the coastguard while his father made it to Italy.[61]

Once refugees were returned to Libya, or even brought within twenty-four miles of the coast, Frontex played no monitoring role at all, Moncure said, while acknowledging she had heard allegations of human rights abuses. "The situation in Libya, what it is, that's outside our mandate . . . It's not important what I feel. We have a very clear mandate of what we are to do." I posited that Frontex had a duty to do more, given they were supporting the Libyan coastguard, but Moncure said there's a difference between giving training and "monitor[ing] the operation of a sovereign country, however messy it is."

The UN also worked with the Libyan coastguard. As part of a 2017 54-million-dollar appeal, UNHCR said it was going to provide "light communications and IT equipment (e.g. generators, desktops, radios) to one hundred Libyan coastguards involved in night rescue operations" and "support Libyan officials with IT and biometrics equipment."[62] IOM, the UN's International Organization for Migration, which was also involved in coastguard training, even gave them "crisis communications" advice, according to one former staff member, in an effort to improve the Libyan coastguard's image. (I asked an IOM spokesperson about this but did not receive a reply.)

More regularly, in the years to come, UN staff would be at the positions where migrants and refugees intercepted at sea were brought onto land again. They handed out water, food, and clothes or provided a minimal level of medical care. Afterwards, they would watch the scared, sad, bedraggled captives be taken away to detention.

———

What happened to refugees forced back to Libya was not a secret. In January 2017, days before Libya and Italy signed their memorandum of understanding, German Chancellor Angela Merkel received a diplomatic cable from

Germany's embassy in Niger that described Libyan detention facilities as a place where "[e]xecutions . . . torture, rapes, blackmail, and abandonment in the desert are the order of the day," there were "the most serious, systematic human rights violations," and "concentration-camp-like [conditions]."[63]

According to the UN, by December 2017, less than a year after EU support for the Libyan coastguard began, there were more than seventeen thousand people in detention.[64] Large numbers were then sent back to the countries they came from through the EU-funded, IOM-run return scheme, dropping the number down to around five thousand, but new people kept arriving. More than two thousand detainees at that time were Eritreans, followed by Sudanese and Somalis. As many as 70 percent were from countries known as "refugee-producing"—which meant they were experiencing war or dictatorships, or people were widely persecuted there. By late 2018, at least twenty-six government-associated detention centers were operational.[65]

Africans heading for Europe had been detained under Gaddafi, too. Libya's Department for Combatting Illegal Migration (DCIM) was created the year after the revolution, under the Tripoli-based Interior Ministry. Even though many detention centers were run by militias, if they came to an understanding with DCIM they could make sure some of their men received government salaries. In practice, the Geneva-headquartered Global Initiative Against Transnational Organized Crime said it was "impossible" for detention centers to operate without the involvement of armed groups, and that DCIM's control was "nominal."[66]

The migrant detention business was profitable. "The human smuggling industry has gone from monetization of movement to monetization of captivity," explained Mark Micallef, who worked with the initiative.[67] Guards and management demanded money for releases, sold goods and services inside the centers, or procured catering contracts to provide detainees with their meager daily food. Refugees could be rented out as hired labor, returning to detention at night. Aid workers told me that any humanitarian efforts had to include a benefit for the Libyans running each center. "If you do a scabies campaign, you bring new mattresses and give the guards ones [too]," said one aid official. "If you bring vitamins and oranges, you give the guards some."

Notably, Libya was not a party to the 1951 Refugee Convention, which gives people fleeing persecution international rights. Refugees were not able to claim asylum in Libya, so they were always at risk of being imprisoned. A review of the EU Trust Fund, commissioned by the EU itself, would later describe Libya as a place with "total state collapse."[68]

Drownings continued. In 2018, the year Kaleb made his own attempts, an average of six people a day died trying to cross the Mediterranean Sea, making it the world's deadliest sea crossing.[69] In Libya, as in Europe, bodies washed up along the shore. "We can't eat the fish anymore," one Libyan man complained to me. Others were more sympathetic.

———

Through FOI requests by the charity Privacy International, I obtained a copy of a timetable for a three-week Libyan coastguard training run by Frontex. Much of it was redacted—thick black lines blocking out details. What I could see included an hour of stress management and two days of first aid classes. The first two Fridays were to be spent on "law enforcement: special tactics and techniques." Another of the skills they would learn was "basic self-defense techniques that can be used during the apprehension of suspects on board," the timetable said, "including the use of force and its limitations."

For the first two weeks, coastguard members would attend five hours of teaching per day, with two hours for lunch, and a half day each Friday. The final week was more practical, with a full day on forged documents and three hours on crime scene investigations. At the end, there was an hour-and-a-half-long closing ceremony.

What must it have meant to these men—and I believe they were all men—to be taken to Europe, sat down in a classroom, and told about "fundamental rights and protection," which the first day focused on. Did they

nod and smile, or did they speedily lose interest? Would they consider alter-
ing their working methods, or did they feel like it was a waste of time, despite any money they thought might come their way as a result of it? At least
one Libyan is known to have absconded in Italy following this type of
training.[70]

Libya's coastguard describes itself as humanitarian. At three in the
morning, on one of the last days of Ramadan in 2021, I interviewed Colonel
Reda Essa, a coastguard commander who has been involved in sea opera-
tions since Gaddafi times. He spoke, through a video call, from Libyan city
Misrata, sitting hunched in a white plastic chair, wearing a wine-colored
V-neck sweater and khaki trousers, another phone clasped in his hands.
Along with "illegal immigrants," Essa said they patrolled for drug, fuel, and
weapons smuggling.

He had traveled to Italy to meet with Frontex and other European agencies, but laughed when I asked if the EU is giving the Libyan coastguard
orders, saying the EU gives them barely anything. At the time, he said they
had close to three thousand coastguard members but only five boats, two of
which were about to become unusable. They were supposed to cover a stretch
of 300 kilometers of Western Libyan coast, from Misrata to Zuwara. "We
don't have the right equipment. We can't get into the rough seas sometimes
and save lives . . . We, as the Europeans know, are capable of doing the good
work . . . If we receive new equipment, up-to-date, not old equipment, then
we can stay in the sea, not hours, we can stay for longer, days, and that way
we can stop the illegal immigrants."

He said he could not account for where all the EU money was being
spent, but he was not seeing it. "There's a lot of things that work under the
table," he said, adding, perhaps as encouragement, with thought to future
income: "The stability of Libya is the stability of Europe."

Essa said the coastguard worked well with the UN, whose staff were
usually present at the disembarkation points back in Libya. His biggest problem was the independent charity rescue ships, which he described as "crimi-

nals" and a "mafia," "watching us like hawks." These ships sailed missions on the Mediterranean Sea, attempting to rescue refugees and bring them to Europe, but also documenting the coastguard's failure to respond to distress calls and how it treated people whom it did apprehend. "You notice that when there's the NGOs that there's big numbers of illegal immigrants in the sea," he charged. "If they are really trying to save the lives of those illegal immigrants in the sea, instead of wasting all the money on boats and things like that, why don't they come to the desert and try to help them from there?" (Migration experts have said the numbers dying in the Sahara Desert en route to Libya could be double the number that die at sea, though there is no way of verifying these numbers.[71]) Essa then steered the conversation back into European far-right scare tactics, suggesting that there could be terrorists among the migrants, meaning it made sense to block their entry.

Like Frontex, he emphasized his mandate and its limitations. Once the refugees and migrants were offloaded back in Libya, Essa said his responsibility ended, and he was not concerned with what happened to them next. "My job is to get them from the sea to the land and hand them over to those illegal immigrant centers. From that point, it is not my job," he said.

———

Though European officials clearly already knew what was happening, I started getting contacted by consultants the EU had hired to do research who were writing internal reports or conducting audits and wanted to know what was going on inside the detention centers. I was also receiving requests from human rights organizations, other journalists, UN organizations, and an array of researchers. Almost always, those people would ask me for refugees' phone numbers. I usually passed on information, but not direct contacts, because of concerns over my sources' safety and their fears about talking to new people. I was surprised that few of these organizations seemed to have their own contacts inside the centers. Why was no one talking to the refugees already?

Then there were the Libyan aid workers on the ground, who were often being directed by foreign colleagues in neighboring Tunisia. Some began to contact me, too, explaining that while they saw refugees being mistreated all the time, they were in danger, their families could be hurt, and they had no power but to let guards do whatever they wanted. They would describe being inside detention centers, having to ignore what was happening if they wanted to protect themselves. They were particularly vulnerable if they did not have family members in the government or in powerful militias. In Libya, *wasta* could determine your future. *Wasta* translates as clout—who you know and how influential you are. Some Libyan aid workers did have *wasta*—clear connections to militias and less of a conscience than others, they would say.

"We do put ourselves at risk every time we go," one frustrated aid worker told me, as she worried my reporting was portraying all Libyans badly. "Unlike the detainees, I am a national . . . You never know when they might target you. I've received Facebook messages telling me not to show up anymore and not to come. [They] threatened me [saying] where I live and how many brothers and sisters I have."

Libyans had suffered massively. Years of turmoil meant that even inside the detention centers, it was not just refugees who were traumatized. Some detainees expressed sympathy for their Libyan guards. "You see Gaddafi created bad things for his people," one Eritrean in Abu Salim told me. "Most people aren't educated, there are no good Libyan doctors [for example], they're mostly from other countries. A lot of people here speak bad language. [Gaddafi] made them think about taking drugs. Gaddafi was a bad president. Many people died, their homes fell down . . . They are very much victims, they have a lot of trauma, but they don't want to evaluate it."

There were certainly questions to be asked about whether the EU was empowering militias and making Libya a hell for its own citizens through its focus on stopping migration above all else.

Speaking in November 2020, former UN Special Envoy for Libya

Ghassan Salamé said he was not even sure if the EU wanted Libya to become a functioning state that it could not interfere with. "Have they resigned themselves to Libya as a space where they try to limit the damage, to contain the risk?" he asked, sitting in front of an array of books during a Zoom conference call. Salamé had resigned from his UN position eight months before, saying the job was too stressful.[72] He sounded frustrated and exhausted. "There is no legitimate institution in the country . . . The whole political class is so corrupt and so attached to their positions that they don't want an election . . . They are there to make money."[73]

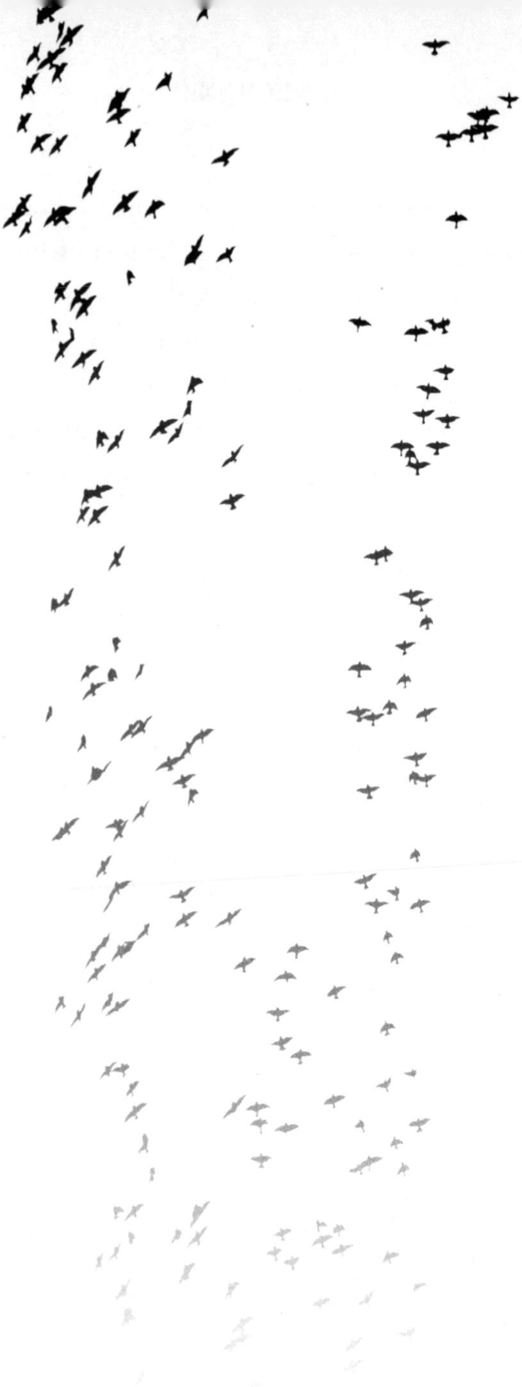

CHAPTER 6

TRIQ AL SIKKA: BURNED ALIVE

"He who has a why to live can bear almost any how."
—FRIEDRICH NIETZSCHE

From a cell in Triq al Sikka, a detention center in central Tripoli, Samuel, an Eritrean in his late twenties, messaged me through Facebook. "Hiiiii me Samuel," he wrote. "How are you?" I responded.

I was excited to hear from him because of the significance of where he was. Triq al Sikka was not just a standard detention center, but effectively the headquarters for the Libyan Department for Combatting Illegal Migration (DCIM), the body that ostensibly managed all migrant detention centers—at least in the part of Libya controlled by the UN-backed government. That meant the stakes were raised for everyone locked up there. It was the center of power, where any wrong move could be costly. Militia leaders, as well as UN staff and diplomats, came and went from this area all the time.

Despite their prime location, refugees were dying. Anywhere between seven and twenty detainees perished before the 2018 outbreak of conflict, this number shifting up and down depending on who I spoke to (there are no records to confirm this, just testimonies from refugees). "When they die, [the guards] just take the body and that's it," said one, adding if friends did not hold their own remembrances or attempt to inform families, "no one would do anything."

Hundreds of men and boys aged fifteen or sixteen were held together in a dark hall, secured by mesh. The oldest was in his mid-forties. "A crowded mob huddled in a cage," is how one described it. Mattresses were infested with insects. The toilets were clogged. At night, with stomachs too empty to sleep, they would lie still, wondering how their lives had come to this. Some were sick or disabled. There was barely space to walk around anyway. During the summer, detainees sweated profusely. Every day, they ate plain macaroni.

They spent hours, weeks, discussing their chances of being selected for evacuation to a safe country. It felt like a real-life hunger games, a competition where their suffering, and the horrors they had lived through, were evaluated and weighed up against each other, and yet there was a randomness to it. This was the most important lottery of their lives. Since 2017, when the evacuation program began, they knew around two thousand people a year could be taken by UNHCR to neighboring Niger to wait before finding out to which European or North American country they would be transferred. A lucky few even went straight to Italy.

Some captives repeated proverbs to themselves in an effort to build internal strength. "If it is a long night, sun must come in the morning," went one. How many months could a human live without sun?

In 2018, nearly 4,500 migrants and refugees were transferred into Triq al Sikka.[1] There were Eritreans and Somalis, sometimes joined by Ethiopians, Sudanese, Yemenis, Syrians, and South Sudanese who had been caught on the sea or apprehended at city checkpoints. West Africans came, too, but they were more likely to only stay a few weeks before they were sent back to the countries they were born in.

There were also the *capos*, Eritreans and Somalis who worked directly with the guards, giving the Libyans information about what was going on inside the cells, dishing out food to the prisoners, and even leaving the detention center to go on errands. They, too, were hoping for evacuation from the center and had little incentive to escape.

"It's just like hell. An abomination."

"Day and night is the same for us."

Samuel told me how Triq al Sikka was used as a show center for touring European diplomats, such as the Italian and German ambassadors to Libya.[2] The refugees would know visitors were coming as the electricity would suddenly be turned on. The sickest detainees, or those with injuries from thrashings or torture, would be hidden at the back of the hall, locked up in a dark room accessed through the guards' toilets, or even made to lie under out-of-service buses in the parking lot. Visitors, including UN staff, called ahead before they arrived, and guards would warn detainees not to speak out. One of the most high-profile people Samuel saw there was UNHCR high commissioner Filippo Grandi, who visited Triq al Sikka multiple times.[3] His June 2018 trip was timed to coincide with the evacuation of 121 refugees from the center, including 38 children and 74 women. "We were confronted . . . with the pain, sometimes the despair, of those that are not leaving. And conditions in this detention center, especially on the men's side, are truly appalling," Grandi said.[4]

By this stage, Samuel was well aware of the dangers that came with talking, but he saw Grandi's visit as a chance that could not be wasted. He pushed past others to come face to face with the Italian UN boss, words tumbling from him. It was a list of indignities that had been building up, a string of sentences he had practiced and extended since his ordeal began. He was flushed, his heart pounding. Maybe it sounded basic and his long-mulled-over thoughts seemed obvious. "I know all the problems," he remembered Grandi replying.

"I wish they would get locked inside with us. Then they would see . . .
People want to die in the sea rather than in the detention centers. At this
time, human rights are sleeping. Life is very cheap."

Samuel was punished afterwards. In the meantime, nothing changed. This made him realize the abuse was not a secret. A foreign journalist who visited Triq al Sikka around that time told me refugees were hit in front of him. "Libyan guards do not care about these people at all. That was clear to me across every place I visited. They really did seem to consider these people like animals," the journalist said.

A UN employee told me participating in diplomatic visits to detention centers used to make her cry. The detainees were lined up like "animals in a zoo." During one visit, when her delegation arrived late, she remembered asking a refugee how long they had been sitting in the scorching sun. He answered that they had been there for hours, before a guard snapped at him to be quiet.

———

Among Triq al Sikka's detainees were around thirty married couples. They were separated upon arrival: women and children had a bit more freedom and were kept outside, in an open area. Once a week, the couples could see each other for around ten minutes. It happened in a yard under the watchful eyes of armed guards, usually on Fridays, the Islamic holy day. The women tactfully built cordial relationships with the Libyans. In their area, they were even allowed to buy goods, including phones they could use to contact their families. Soon, women began to take advantage of the weekly supervised meetings to sneak phones to their husbands. "Baby Nokias" or "J1 phones" were the most favored kind because of their small size. The women took the handsets apart and hid the pieces in soda bottles, shampoo containers, or boxes of rice. An empty juice carton could fit three phones, packed with paper so there was no rattle. The bottom was glued together again, before the carton was placed in a box under another carton of real juice. They would brazenly give them to their men as gifts while under surveillance. Sometimes a phone and charger, snug in a sock under an arm, was pulled out when armed guards were looking away. Detainees later used those phones to contact me.

Physical contact was prohibited, even between married couples. "At that moment, the guards stand about one meter from you," one man told me later. "You get afraid to touch each other because they don't love like us. The police don't like it." Instead, they communicated through their eyes, speaking in pleasantries and avoiding anything meaningful.

Back in the men's cell, there would be jostling when darkness fell and it came time to charge the newly acquired phones. While the guards were sleeping, thin electrical wires—a live and a neutral—were connected to a power supply feeding a light in the toilet. The plastic at the other ends of the wires was peeled off and they were wrapped around the metal part of the charger pins, which were covered in clothes with a sponge mattress placed above them and a "keeper man"—a refugee volunteer—sitting on top of that. Sometimes the wires they used had been discovered around the detention center, such as a long black one that once connected to a disused television, while others were smuggled in. Getting electricity this way was dangerous. If the two wires touched each other they could spark, while if someone touched the live wire they could be electrocuted.

"In a bad situation humans discover many ways to solve their problems."

This operation meant every man was exposed and at risk—if a guard caught one person with a phone he would be pounded until he snitched on others. Sometimes, the culprit would even be given his own phone back, on the condition that he became an informer. The punishment increased if there were any photos stored on the phone, or even if it had a camera—the guards did not want the poor conditions they were keeping people in to be exposed.

Guards particularly liked searching for phones at night, when they could get away with keeping confiscated items for themselves rather than handing them over to their commanders. Many times, a detainee would log onto a friend's Facebook or WhatsApp account to tell me not to message their own account anymore, in case the guards—who had just seized their phone—saw the message pop up on the locked screen.

Refugees used hidden phones to speak to their families and friends in other detention centers with whom they had traveled before. They felt like they were saying endless goodbyes, their words loaded with the guilt, anger, and sorrow they could not articulate. "No one thinks he will leave from those centers, I'm sorry to say that, dear," one man told me.

———

With nothing to do, Samuel would think about his grandmother. She lived until she was ninety-six. Having an old person in your home is the same as having a vast library or a thick history book, he thought to himself. Eritreans dying young across North Africa, and in the sea, meant the destruction of that kind of deep knowledge. Looking around at the squalor, he found it easy to believe that European countries did not want African people to develop and be smart or educated. That must be why they were locked up for trying to make a success of their lives. "They are killing our time, killing our brains," Samuel mused.

He was constantly bothered by the Libyan guards, who would "insult Jesus Christ," spotting the rough crosses some Eritreans carved from wood to wear around their necks. "Are you Muslim or Christian?" he was asked sporadically.

"If you answer Muslim, the Libyan person will be happy."

Around him were detainees weak from kidney problems or hepatitis C. Fevers flared. Disease spread quickly in that humid hall, where refugees breathed the same air for months at a time, but in October 2018, the situation escalated. Detainees knew the Arabic words to describe what was happening: *kuha* (cough) and *marad alsul* (tuberculosis). But words were not necessary. In audio files I was sent, the sound of coughing became a constant backdrop.

Infectious disease was a problem everywhere. In October 2018, MSF reported a fourfold increase in the number of tuberculosis cases they were treating in other Tripoli detention centers—but at least those people were being cared for. Triq al Sikka was the center of power, a place where Libyan authorities could not distance themselves from responsibility, but no one tried to prevent tuberculosis from taking over. Soon, detainees worried they all had it. One watched a man spewing blood beside him. When it seemed like a victim was close to death, friends would cling to the mesh of their cage and call out that it was an emergency. Sometimes, they had to become aggressive to get a sick person seen.

Samuel paid guards thirty dinars to buy him a pink bottle of Amydramine Expectorant cough syrup, which he shared with four others, despite knowing it would have little impact.

"We are living by the power of God."

"It's been a month, I am coughing every night. Headache. I feel dizziness when I sit and wake up . . . Every one here is coughing every night, Sally. Starting from myself, we all think we have TB already . . . Everyone here is faint, shortness of breathing, headache, pain in their stomach, stress and so on."

Right when they were most needed, the UN partner organization supposed to be providing medical care, the International Rescue Committee

(IRC), made the decision to stop treating infected detainees after two of its own staff members tested positive for tuberculosis.

> *"They stopped everything. They even stopped TB medication to the infected persons, and we are living all together. Even the police they don't come near to us. People here are kind of demoralized."*

The IRC was founded during the Second World War, partly on the suggestion of Albert Einstein.[5] By 2018, it was led by David Miliband, a former UK Labour Party Foreign Secretary who earned almost $1 million dollars a year in his position at the charity's helm.[6] The organization had only recently begun working in Triq al Sikka. On the phone from Tunis, Thomas Garofalo, the IRC's Libya country director, told me his staff were "overwhelmed." "The conditions in the center are just not adequate, that's the problem," he said. Logistically, their access to detainees was limited. Guards insisted on deciding who got medical treatment, and visitors never had a full oversight. "Let's face it, this population is very vulnerable, they have been rescued at sea," Garofalo told me. "If you put them in an enclosed space like that it's a very big public health danger, and a danger for them . . . Ultimately we need to get these people out of detention."

> *"Here the doctor and the police have the same behavior. They are laughing, it means happy. They don't have mind. Libyan is Libyan."*

Beginning and then interrupting treatment can cause strains of tuberculosis to become drug resistant. "The cost of a dose of tuberculosis drugs is less than a beer in the pub," said Aaron Oxley, the executive director of Results UK, a British anti-poverty charity that campaigns to end the disease, when I told him about the situation. Without proper treatment, "of course it won't stay in the detention center," he said. "Anyone who breathes the air that's anywhere near there will transport it around."

"The place is like a cave, there is no airway out and in."

Tuberculosis is a disease of the disenfranchised, so it does not garner much international attention, but in 2018, the same year as Triq al Sikka's outbreak, 1.5 million people died from it globally.[7] It affects the poor and the incarcerated, those who live in damp or cramped conditions, and could impact someone for life, flaring whenever their immune system becomes compromised.[8]

A UN official told me efforts to encourage a response to the tuberculosis outbreak in Triq al Sikka by the Tripoli-based government went nowhere. The man recalled asking what could be done for migrants and refugees who were infected and not being treated: "They said send them to their countries." I asked him why the Libyans seemed unconcerned about the disease, given its damage would not differentiate between nationalities. "That was my question," came the frustrated response. "But they are ignorant. I hope they will understand one day."

While writing an article about the outbreak for a newspaper in the UK, I asked the British Foreign Office spokesperson whether they felt responsible or could react, given that they were partially funding the UN's work in Libya and the Libyan coastguard's forced returns.[9] The response came quickly. The UK government was "deeply concerned over conditions in these centers in Libya," but they were the responsibility of the Libyan authorities. "We continue to pressure the authorities to pursue alternatives to detention, to improve conditions for migrants in [the] country and to respect human rights."

———

Abdulaziz, a slim, 28-year-old Somali, was one of a small number of captives allowed to leave the men's cell. Doing chores for the guards meant a chance to stretch his legs. On his last day alive, he went outside to clean the yard as usual.

He must have noticed the containers of fuel, used to power the genera-

tor, many times before. Some refugees say he had even been asked to fuel it
himself. When no one was looking, Abdulaziz doused his body with petrol,
then set it alight.

> *"Please help, today one person self dead by petrol because hopeless*
> *from UNHCR. Burning. Name Abdulaziz 28. Somalia. Waiting*
> *nine months."*

In 2016, Abdulaziz fled al-Shabaab, the Islamic militant insurgent
group with ties to Al Qaeda that controls large swathes of Somalia and
carries out deadly terrorist attacks. In areas the group presides over, music
and movies are banned, and punishment can include stoning and amputations.[10] Abdulaziz survived a kidnapping. He traveled with his wife, whose
father was murdered by al-Shabaab. After a failed attempt to cross the sea
from Libya, both of them ended up in Triq al Sikka.[11] They were locked up,
separately, for most of the year.

> *"UNHCR said to him you go back to your country, your case is failed.*
> *After that, he killed himself. He was hopeless. He spent a long time here.*
> *He put petrol on his body and then he lit it. First he did it secretly, but*
> *then he was shouting, people were running over."*

I began receiving panicked messages describing what had happened, so
I asked the UN for confirmation. In response, IOM spokesperson Joel
Millman said the Somali had been carrying out an "act of protest."[12] But
that was not the impression inside the detention center. Those who knew
Abdulaziz described a hopeless man, frustrated and frayed, with nothing
left to give.

His end echoed another death: that of Mohamed Bouazizi, a Tunisian
street vendor who set himself on fire nearly eight years earlier. Bouazizi
dreamed of a university education. He was embarrassed and ashamed when

a local official took away his vegetables, claiming he did not have a license to sell them. He could have paid a bribe but he sent himself up in flames, sparking the Arab Spring, setting off protests and revolution across the Arab world and reshaping the Middle East for all time. The ripples of what he did inspired uprisings and toppled dictators, including Gaddafi in Libya.

If Abdulaziz was thinking of revolution as he poured the petrol and lit the fatal match, his death would not have the same effect. In the days after Abdulaziz set himself on fire, I saw no journalists reporting on it apart from me. Would it have ever been documented except for the bravery of the detainees who sounded the alarm? Would I have even believed them if they had not contacted me on the very day it happened?

"All refugees have [a] very bad feeling. Today [we're] not eating at all because so many people have died."

Even the reason for Abdulaziz's death was glossed over, the story shifting as UN agencies moved to defend themselves. Friends claimed Abdulaziz had asked visiting UNHCR staff whether he had a chance at being evacuated from the country and was told no. At the time, UN employees were heavily involved in what they called "managing expectations," something staff from all aid organizations I spoke to told me was an important part of their jobs. For UNHCR, this involved going around Libya's detention centers to tell people how low their chances of evacuation were. Later on, the agency denied staff had ever spoken to Abdulaziz in Triq al Sikka, saying they only talked to Eritreans there.[13] They also misstated the day that Abdulaziz died. "We cannot comment on a death when we are not there to verify it or understand what happened," said a spokesperson.[14] Actually, they claimed, Abdulaziz and his wife were going to be evacuated to Niger the very next month, they had just not been informed yet.

"In Libya, so many people are dead. It's nothing."

Libyan officials would chime in too, though they blamed the UN. During an interview with journalists the following year, Naser Hazam, the manager of Triq al Sikka, said Abdulaziz could not handle it when he was told he would not be evacuated, though he also got specifics wrong. "Some Ethiopian and Somali people in this center remained for two years here," he said. "[Then] UNHCR informs [them] that you are refused and not allowed to be resettled." He said Abdulaziz had been waiting for years and killed himself because of "depression" after he was rejected.[15]

In the days after the death of Abdulaziz, refugees collected small amounts of money to pay for coffee, biscuits, and candles, so they could celebrate his life. Yet their thoughts quickly turned to who might be next. By November, medics had not visited them, or distributed tuberculosis medication, in a month. Another detainee tried to hang himself in the toilet but was interrupted.

"If I spend time more here it means I am waiting to die, because the situation is very bad."

In some detainees' minds, as they tried to pass time by staying motionless, bickering, or sleeping, was an image of Abdulaziz going up in flames. Whether or not they had seen it themselves, it was seared deep within them, as persistent as the sound of his wife crying over the three months afterwards, until she was finally evacuated. Other journalists later tracked her down, living in a tent in Niger, still waiting to be taken to Europe or North America.[16]

Abdulaziz set fire to himself on Wednesday, October 24, 2018. He probably did not know that it was "United Nations Day"—the same date the UN Charter came into force seventy-three years before.[17] The UN recommends that member states declare October 24 as a public holiday, saying it is a chance to celebrate the UN's achievements.[18] Across the world, its staff were marking the day with meetings and speeches as Abdulaziz died.

CHAPTER 7

DISUNITED NATIONS

"They call us romantics, weak, stupid, sentimental idealists,
perhaps because we have some faith in the good which exists even in our
opponents and because we believe that kindness achieves more
than cruelty. It may be that we are simple-minded, but I do not think that we
are dangerous. Those, however, who stagnate behind their political
programs, offering nothing else to suffering mankind, to starving, dying
millions—they are the scourge of Europe . . . Everyone must join in
this work. We must take up the fiery cross and light the beacons so that they
shine from every mountain. We must raise our banner in every
country and forge the links of brotherhood around the world.
The governments too must stand shoulder to shoulder, not in a battle line,
but in a sincere effort to achieve the new era."[1]

**—FRIDTJOF NANSEN, THE FIRST HIGH COMMISSIONER
FOR REFUGEES, APPOINTED BY THE LEAGUE OF NATIONS, SPEAKS
AFTER WINNING THE NOBEL PEACE PRIZE IN 1922**

"Sometimes our minds would never comprehend the low level of ethics
and lack of professionalism and integrity that can come from people who are
supposed to be the ones pushing the humanitarian agenda."

—A FORMER UNHCR STAFF MEMBER IN LIBYA

Like many people throughout the planet, I always had a vague awareness of
the United Nations as a force for good. In secondary school, I participated
in model UN, drafting and voting on made-up resolutions in front of teams
of students from other parts of my city. Years later, I taught a similar class as
part of a program for academically gifted children in north Dublin (my
clearest memory of it is the boy who represented North Korea throwing
balls of paper at other students while saying he was "nuking" them).

In particular, I admired the UN Refugee Agency. I knew it operated in the most troubled countries, assisting millions of people in need. In 2014, I interviewed UNHCR's then-chief spokesperson, Melissa Fleming, and was starstruck at the chance to speak to someone so inspirational (when I left my staff journalism job two years later, she told me to send her a CV in case they had any opportunities for me there).[2]

As I began to report across Africa more, it became harder to ignore the extreme differences between UN staff—who were usually incredibly well paid and secure inside massive white 4x4s or guarded compounds—and the people they were supposed to be helping. This included the value placed on life, which unsettled me in security briefings. In one I attended with the UN Children's Fund (UNICEF), staff were told not to stop driving if their car hit a child because they'd run the risk of angry locals attacking them.

Another time, I was among a group of European journalists invited to see UN work combatting female genital mutilation in one of the world's poorest countries. Prior to arrival, I was asked if I would rather stay in a hotel with a golf course or a swimming pool and was offered a daily allowance of $216, which was supposed to cover expenses, but was equal to more than three months of the average income of a local citizen.[3]

In social settings, too, I would be reminded of how much money international, or so-called "expat," UN staff earned. I remember one UNHCR employee, a friend of a friend, telling me she had amassed enough to start building a holiday resort. Staff in other organizations constantly joked about the inflated salaries of UN workers while wondering aloud when they would capitulate and join them, too.

Aside from all this, it was going to Sudan, in 2017, that really made me question which stories we hear about refugees, and how murky the truth can become when the biggest organization filtering them is also constantly angling for donations from states. As a journalist, my job is to elevate voices that may be overlooked while making efforts to hold powerful individuals, organizations, and governments accountable. The power imbalance between UNHCR's staff, who have the ability to grant refugee status and the accompanying documentation and even transfer people to another state, and refugees, who have fled their countries and often lack legal rights, property, belongings, their family and communities, is one of the largest I can imagine, and therefore ripe for exploitation.

In Khartoum, I arranged interviews with refugees from Eritrea and Ethiopia. Instead of the tales of escaping oppression and surviving smuggling routes that I expected, they all wanted to talk about UNHCR and how corrupt they said the organization was. They told me staff were taking bribes of tens of thousands of dollars from refugees who wanted to be resettled to a safer country. Resettlement may be an unknown term to anyone who has grown up with peace and relative freedom, but for refugees it is a golden ticket to a better life. Priority is supposed to be given to vulnerable people who claim asylum in developing countries with no chance of building a secure life there. But the process relies on wealthy states offering spaces, and the number available has always been woefully inadequate. In 2017, just over 102,000 refugees were resettled globally, out of the 1.2 million UNHCR said needed it.[4] Around 2,000 of them came from Sudan, which was hosting more than 200,000 refugees at the time.[5]

When something is scarce, a corrupted gatekeeper can take advantage. Refugees in Khartoum said the going rate to speed up a resettlement process for unregistered asylum seekers was about $15,000. Resettling a whole family boosted the price as high as $40,000—money usually raised by relatives in Europe or elsewhere. Bribes were paid to a network that included middlemen and UNHCR protection staff. This racket had been going on for years, refugees told me, but nothing was being done and no one would listen. When they tried to protest at UNHCR's offices, they were beaten by police. One protester I met, her leg still in a cast, showed me X-rays of her broken bone, while a man told me he was deaf in one ear after being boxed in the head. (UNHCR at first denied police were present at all, until I showed them videos with police clearly visible; they then denied force was used.[6])

What happens when your supposed protector is the one exploiting you? You may be out of the frying pan, yet find yourself thrown into the fire. Money was the deciding factor: if legal resettlement through the UN was too expensive because of the bribes required, many felt they had no choice but to travel to Libya and attempt the illegal route to Europe. I embarked on an investigation.

UNHCR was set up in 1950, in the aftermath of World War Two, initially to help Europeans displaced during the conflict. Over the following decades, the agency ballooned into a worldwide organization, receiving the second-most funding for humanitarian aid from international governments behind fellow UN agency the World Food Program.[7] By 2017, it had an annual budget of nearly eight billion dollars, while employing around 18,000 people in more than 125 countries[8]; by 2021, its budget had risen to 9.15 billion dollars.[9] UNHCR has a legal mandate to protect refugees, with the goal of finding them long-term solutions, such as resettlement to a new country, the chance to integrate in the society they fled to, or voluntary repatriation to the place they left, if it becomes safe again.[10] In conversations with governments and other international bodies, it is often UNHCR, and almost never refugees themselves, representing refugee voices.

In Libya, many refugees simply called it "the organization." They were well-versed in the 1951 Refugee Convention and knew they should have an international right to protection. For people who had left home and were now without citizenship, UNHCR could be their only hope, if an overwhelmed and unreliable one.

But the UN made Faustian bargains with states all the time, with vulnerable people the ones who suffered. After the 2017 Rohingya crisis, for example, when hundreds of thousands of Rohingya Muslims fled to Bangladesh to escape ethnic cleansing in Myanmar, UNHCR shared refugees' personal and biometric data with Myanmar's government. Human Rights

Watch, the organization that exposed this, said it was done without informed consent.[11] Refugees they interviewed ended up going into hiding for fear of being forcibly returned. "Are we instrumentalized by states?" asked UNHCR Special Envoy for the Central Mediterranean Vincent Cochetel while speaking about Libya, at an activist-organized event in Germany, in early 2020. "Yes, we are instrumentalized by states in that we are an intergovernmental organization. That's what states have created us for. But they also created us to monitor their obligations."[12]

It took me ten months to complete my investigation about UNHCR staff in Sudan taking bribes for resettlement. All that time, I was in touch with refugees in Khartoum, who grew increasingly frustrated, convinced that no one cared. I managed to interview a former UNHCR Sudan employee, who told me his employment was terminated after he complained about corruption. More evidence followed, and more UNHCR whistleblowers came forward—highly ethical people who loved their jobs and wanted to do good, but were upset at misconduct they had seen and the failure of the organization to tackle it. I traveled to France to meet Frank Montil,[13] a gruff, leather jacket-wearing Australian intelligence officer turned senior UN investigator who had uncovered a similar multimillion-dollar bribe-taking scheme by UNHCR staff in Kenya in the early 2000s. One afternoon, in his home city of Dijon, France, we went through my notes. It was like corrupt UNHCR staff in Sudan had read his 2001 Kenya report and used it as a "how to" guide, he quipped.[14]

On May 15, 2018, my report was finally published.[15] Two days later, to my great surprise, UNHCR issued a press release saying that refugee resettlement had been completely suspended from Sudan pending the results of internal probes into possible fraud.[16] This was not the reaction my sources wanted; they felt it punished the neediest once again by removing their only means of escape. As time wore on, witnesses were threatened. They worried they could lose their refugee status and be arrested or deported. Those already scheduled for resettlement were left in limbo. It took UNHCR a year to find just one staff member guilty of soliciting bribes and abusing power (the employee was dismissed in February 2020).[17] Resettlement started up again, but spaces remained limited, and refugees complained there had been no real reform.

This experience changed my thinking. While this was far from the only international organization or UN agency dealing with corruption allegations, UNHCR was mandated to look out for a uniquely vulnerable group— people who had lost their homes, but also the protection that comes with citizenship. I realized it was not only persecution, violence, and war pushing refugees to take dangerous journeys, but the belief that legal routes to safety were closed or unfairly administered, and that the organization supposed to be looking out for them was not on their side.

More would come from my reporting in Sudan—not least, it was how the detained refugees in Libya eventually came across my name. For better or worse, my involvement was not about to end.

———

One of the common complaints I heard from current and former UNHCR staff was that the agency was becoming increasingly corporate, with an extreme focus on public relations. It even had a 57-page brand book instructing employees that all of their "messaging and content" needed to "convey the three attributes that will make people support" them. These were: "1) Gets things done. 2) Makes a difference in people's lives. 3) Can be trusted." The book offered advice on "applying the UNHCR brand to everyday work." It spoke about photography that should "show our work in action, capture images of staff wearing or working with branded items or interacting with people forced to flee. An example would be a photo of staff wearing UNHCR-branded items offloading an airlift onto a truck with a large UNHCR logo on the side. A UNHCR convoy loaded with supplies moving across rough terrain also works well. UNHCR's logo should be clear."[18]

The agency recruited celebrity ambassadors, like actors Angelina Jolie, Ben Stiller, and Kristin Davis. They went on trips to refugee camps, promoting the organization on social media and using its hashtag, #WithRefugees.[19] "A growing area of our work is based around the activities and advocacy of UNHCR's Goodwill Ambassadors, high-level supporters and social media and digital influencers," a 2021 UNHCR social media manager job advert read. The new hire would be placed within a communications service that "works to lead the narrative on forced displacement, generate empathy, and mobilise action."[20]

Social media was a key place for UNHCR to get attention. The agency invested large amounts of time and money and had millions of followers. Its Twitter handle was @Refugees,[21] and for a long time its high commissioner went by @RefugeesChief. But the agency's communications were targeted at donors rather than refugees themselves. "Whenever they do a publicity, the photographer and the commissioner come and take a picture of the[ir] logo, and then they write expressive words," said a Darfuri refugee who was visited in detention by UNHCR staff, upset that nothing subsequently changed.

"The amount of time and money that they spend on visibility and public relations is more than they are spending on the actual work," complained another person who worked with the UN in Libya.

As the internet became more easily accessible, those traditional dynamics were challenged. Increasingly, UN staff began to be confronted by refugees online, with uncomfortable results. Refugees complained about being blocked by UNHCR officials on Twitter—which meant the refugee could no longer tweet opinions or pleas for assistance at them, but also could no longer access any information they shared. A Sudanese man, who had fled from Libya to Niger and ended up stuck in a refugee camp in the desert, told me he was blocked by the UNHCR Niger country representative, Alessandra Morelli, for tweeting at her twice. One of the tweets, which I saw, included a picture of a poster that read "We suffer in Sudan and in Libya and even in Niger," and accused UNHCR staff of lies and corruption. The other, sent less than two weeks prior, was more of a plea. He asked Morelli to "save them from (a) slow death."

When I spoke to Morelli on the phone in mid-2020, her voice was fast and high pitched, like a frustrated schoolteacher. "Allora," she said. "I blocked them actually because it's the same Twitter they're sending. I had seven, eight of those Twitters going, du du du, du du du, nonstop. Nonstop. Nonstop." She said she would rather enter into dialogue that is "equal and correct."

Morelli's Twitter bio read: "Safeguarding dignity, leaving nobody behind. Standing #WithRefugees because we are part of one shared humanity."[22] She had recently been lauded by the actress Cate Blanchett—one of UNHCR's celebrity ambassadors—who called her "absolutely inspiring."[23] When I spoke to Morelli, she quickly began comparing protesting Sudanese refugees living in a largely destroyed and deserted camp to children having a tantrum.

"We are all psychologists, we understand the trauma," Morelli said, her exasperated voice slowing down as if I were having trouble following her words. "We understand that like children, when they don't like what their parents are doing, they are going to 'na na na.' I take it, we [UNHCR] are mature, we're here to continue saving lives, but the message I'm giving them is you can't force your entry into Europe, you cannot force it through us, this is not how it works."[24]

CHAPTER 8

TUNIS: THE LAST DAYS OF ROME

"Are all humans human? Or are some more human than others?"
**—ROMEO DALLAIRE, COMMANDER OF UN PEACEKEEPING
FORCE DURING THE RWANDAN GENOCIDE**

"One day, I hope, everyone will look back with incredulity
on the EU's complicity with human rights abuses in Libya and the UN's
failure to speak out on this matter."
**—JEFF CRISP, FORMER HEAD OF POLICY DEVELOPMENT
AND EVALUATION AT UNHCR**

By the time I started reporting on the situation for refugees in Libya, there was a huge amount of disquiet among people involved in the humanitarian response and how it related to the tens of thousands of refugees and migrants who were being funneled into detention centers. A lot of this had to do with the role of the UN.

Though there are dozens of UN agencies, the two specifically focused on migration issues are UNHCR and the International Organization for Migration (IOM). While UNHCR's mandate is to protect refugees, IOM has a less defined task, but it largely deals with migrants who might not legally qualify for international protection.

Both agencies were regularly mentioned by EU spokespeople when they were questioned about the atrocities resulting from Libyan coastguard interceptions. "We, together with the IOM and UNHCR, are providing life-saving assistance to vulnerable people held in detention centers while urging the Libyan authorities to close detention centers and replace them with reception centers that meet international humanitarian standards," an EU spokesperson told me in 2019. EU documents, detailing the funding for the Libyan coastguard, named both agencies as the "main . . . international stakeholders" with whom "close cooperation and permanent operational links [would] be established."[1]

Former Italian interior minister Marco Minniti, who presided over the signing of the 2017 Italy-Libya deal, also mentioned the UN when justifying his anti-migration policies.[2] "Have we sorted the issue of detention centers in Libya? Obviously not. We still have a lot to do," he told the BBC. "But the fact that the UN are in Libya and can visit the centers is a step ahead."[3]

IOM only became a UN agency in 2016.[4] That same year, an external audit carried out by a UN oversight body found UNHCR's work in Libya to be "unsatisfactory," with failures including that the agency had only registered six of a planned eight thousand refugees in a year and that none of them had received identity documents.[5] Still, in 2017, as the EU started funding the Libyan coastguard to intercept boats, UNHCR's donations grew, and its expenditure in Libya almost quadrupled (from $12 million to $44 million). Over the next four years, UNHCR spent just under $190 million on its operation there.[6] In 2018, an EU Commission spokesperson said they had allocated 185 million euro towards UNHCR and IOM, 38 million of which was directly in support of resettlement and evacuation through UNHCR.[7] In 2020, the charity Oxfam documented IOM and UNHCR receiving 29 million euro specifically as part of a project that would include rehabilitation works and infrastructure maintenance inside detention centers.[8]

After I started getting contacted by refugees in Libya, I noticed that UN-HCR and IOM regularly thanked the EU through their social media accounts, without mentioning the role Europe was playing in sending refugees and migrants to detention centers in the first place. One UNHCR tweet, posted on July 30, 2019, read: "Friendship means no one is left behind. UN-HCR is grateful for the support provided by the EU #AfricaTrustFund for the humanitarian evacuations of refugees from Libya . . . #FriendshipDay."[9] That type of selective messaging seemed to clash harshly with the organization's most regularly used hashtag, #WithRefugees.

———

"Before I came to Libya . . . I was ready for many problems and I knew I may die. The surprise is UNHCR. I didn't think about this first because we were happy when we were registered by UNHCR, but after we saw everything we were sad. UNHCR is cruel. I can't see any kind thing in UNHCR."

———

Staff from both IOM and UNHCR, as well as people involved in the wider aid response, began to contact me, asking to talk anonymously. They described a working environment where maintaining a good image for their organizations was seen as more important than the lived experience of refugees and migrants.

In extensive interviews, more than thirty aid officials working in Libya also accused UNHCR and IOM of allowing themselves to be used by the EU to sanitize the devastating impact of migration policies aimed at keeping refugees and migrants away from Europe, effectively whitewashing a brutal system of violence and torture. All of those officials wished to stay anonymous for fear of professional repercussions. They said that while UN-HCR and IOM were doing some important work, they were also focused on safeguarding their own funding. One researcher, who interviewed both donors and UN staff working on the Libya response, said there was an unspoken rule "to not bite the hand that feeds them," meaning they would not speak out about what the EU was doing.

"They are constantly watering down the problems that are happening in the detention centers," an aid official told me more bluntly. "They are encouraging the situation to continue . . . They are paid by the EU to do [the EU's] fucking job."

Some of this came down to language choices. On their social media accounts, in 2018, UNHCR was still calling the Libyan coastguard interceptions "rescues"[10] (later, they would replace this wording with "intercepted/rescued," while IOM used the word "returned"). In Arabic-language reports, UNHCR referred to detention centers as "shelters."[11] ("This is not a matter of language. This is a matter of camouflaging what's happening in Libya," a former UNHCR staff member complained). In 2021, during a press conference with European Home Affairs Commissioner Ylva Johansson, UNHCR head Filippo Grandi called the funding of the Libyan coastguard "legitimate," saying there is "nothing wrong" with strengthening its forces so it could do a job that was "both efficient and principled," though other Libyan institutions should also be built up to make sure returnees would not be abused.[12] This statement ignored the fact that tens of thousands of people had already grossly suffered because of this policy, and countless deaths—in detention centers, while resisting interception, or during subsequent sea crossing attempts—were a direct result.

> "The UN can't do anything. I have lost hope from the UN and from anyone. I am here since 2016, I have passed [through] the worst situations . . . I decided I don't need anyone except God. If it's written that I will reach Europe I will with God's help. If it's not my destiny I will accept it."

It was clear the UN was operating in difficult conditions. UNHCR did not have an official agreement with the Libyan government, meaning it lacked legal status inside the country. The agency was only allowed to register refugees and asylum seekers from nine nationalities.[13]

Another problem was that wealthy countries were not offering an acceptable number of resettlement places—most years, less than 5 percent of the refugees UNHCR determined to need resettlement globally actually traveled.[14] Only around two thousand refugees were legally evacuated from Libya each year, before the COVID-19 pandemic put these departures completely on hold.[15]

Still, aid workers said they were frustrated that UN agencies were unwilling to admit the limitations of what they could do. "In almost every country where there is an emergency there are always complaints, there are always issues and critics, but what we see in Libya is a complete mess," said one aid official. "Here what we are missing is willingness to talk about it. People are scared."

"If UNHCR cannot protect people in Libya, they have to say it," said another. "Libya will always be a black mark on UNHCR," said a third.

"UNHCR just got fucked," a fourth official said. "They set out with good intentions, but the good intentions were corrupted with the realities they were faced with."

Many aid workers I spoke to accused UN spokespeople of misrepresenting the extent of their access to detention centers. They alleged that tasks that UNHCR and IOM claimed to be carrying out either were not happening or were not effective. "They're lying, they're using fake numbers, they're using medical teams that are not even there," one official told me. Two audits of UNHCR's work, by an external UN body, pointed out that "inaccurate reporting of achievements was a recurring weakness."[16] Another aid worker said it was clear the UN agencies were "totally overwhelmed," yet their management was always "on the defensive."

When I asked about this in 2019, IOM head of communications Leonard Doyle said the agency was "present across the east, west, and south of Libya. Our teams conduct regular visits to detention centers, delivering emergency medical assistance and core relief items and coordinating voluntary humanitarian return assistance to those wishing to go home. Suggesting that the organization is falsifying reports is utterly preposterous."

UNHCR spokesperson Cécile Pouilly also responded to a list of the aid workers' concerns. "Your questions seem to indicate an incomplete understanding of the humanitarian and security situation and the severe constraints UNHCR faces on a daily basis in Libya," she wrote. "Our efforts to help vulnerable refugees and asylum seekers in Libya is based on a humanitarian imperative—saving lives—which is forcing us to deal with complex realities and sometimes jeopardizes our own staff security. We take this opportunity to reiterate that we only have restricted access to detention facilities and that we limit ourselves to providing humanitarian assistance to those in need."

———

Libyan visas took time to be approved, if they were at all. Any individual who made too much noise could be declared persona non grata and become unable to travel there. In 2018, the vast majority of UNHCR Libya's roughly forty international staff lived in neighboring Tunisia, and not Libya, though some would fly in and out, receiving significant financial bonuses each time they made the journey.[17] There were less than one hundred Libyan staff members, fifteen of whom also lived outside the country. That same year, IOM had 253 Libyan staff and 9 international staff, saying they could not have more because of the security situation.[18]

Tunis, a seventy-five-minute flight away, was far from a hardship posting. One humanitarian organization head described it as the best city in the world in which to live, while another aid response worker said the atmosphere among UN and NGO staff there was like "the last days of Rome." "People are signing up because they want to live in a lovely city like Tunis," he said. "[They get] massive salaries. It's a gravy train . . . People always talk about the crisis of accountability in the conflict, but there's just as big a crisis of accountability in the humanitarian response."

"The senior management of almost all NGOs working in Libya are permanently based in Tunis," said a senior aid official in an organization which took EU funding. "This is great for the NGO expat parents who want their kids in private French schools and the single NGO expats who want to enjoy shitty Tunisian beer on the beach while prowling for hook-ups on Tinder. However, having a permanently remote management team means that snap decisions in Libya are often taken by 20-something Libyan colleagues without much experience outside of petroleum engineering and binging American sitcoms [on] Netflix to perfect their English. It also means that the people making strategic decisions about how to use EU funding are in a different country, time zone, and culture than Libya, since the EU delegation and all UN agencies are mostly in Tunis with only short forays to Tripoli."

UN employees got up to forty days holiday a year, and they usually did not pay taxes on their income.[19] A senior UNHCR communications officer or external relations officer in Tunis, with seven years' work experience, could make between $110,000 and $140,000 per year. In Libya, they could get between $159,000 and $195,000. On top of that, there were bonuses that could add up to tens of thousands of dollars, like allowances for children or dependent spouses, moving costs, education grants, and the so-called daily subsistence allowance if they traveled for work.[20] In Tripoli, the daily allowance went as high as $335 a day, and in Tunis, where the monthly minimum wage was $121 in 2021, they got $281 a day.[21] "We have competitive salaries, we have prestigious status . . . expat life, all these privileges. So many people are doing their jobs not actually driven by the principles and values rather than the material values," said a former UNHCR Libya staff member. It was not necessary to have a "bleeding heart," the former staff member said, "as long as you are delivering on your job . . . But this is not even that."

"Ninety percent of UN staff were not in Libya," said another humanitarian worker, who traveled between Tunisia and Tripoli. "That's a huge problem with remote [aid] responses, and we see it time and time again."

———

In 2018, some international UNHCR staff stayed in a holiday resort during their visits to Tripoli. On its website, Palm City was advertised as "property for the lifestyle you deserve"—a luxurious spot on the coast with indoor and outdoor pools.[22] At the head of the agency, between 2017 and 2019, was Roberto Mignone, an Italian whom colleagues remember working on his laptop while swinging in a hammock at the beach there. A journalist who visited the complex in 2019 wrote that it was home to oil executives and frequented by militia bosses.[23] Members of the EU delegation also stayed in Palm City. When the security situation got tough, UNHCR's staff were likely to be evacuated again.

Even in Tunisia, in most UN and aid agencies, there seemed to be a large rotation of staff, meaning institutional knowledge could be lost when people left their jobs. A posting there could be a sort of "semi-retirement" taken by senior officials who were ready to slow down, I was told by some aid workers. But others cycled in and out, staying for a year or less before moving on to the next assignment. It meant I was constantly talking to people who had never heard of a major incident that happened several months ago. "That was before my time," they would say.

———

*"When we talk about UNHCR, UNHCR is just a business . . .
UNHCR is a legal organization, but they are letting people die in
fucking detention."*

———

Around the same stage that my contact with refugees in Libya began, there was something of a quiet revolution within the humanitarian response.

UNHCR and IOM, together, ran regular lengthy EU-funded meetings in Tunis under what was called the Mixed Migration Working Group. Attendees complained that little of use was discussed when it came to improving the situation inside Libya, and they were aware that Frontex representatives and European law enforcement agents were either present or being updated on what was said.[24] "It was very clear the Mixed Migration Working Group was not a humanitarian forum" and not "conducive to a humanitarian principled response," said one person with knowledge of what transpired. "A lot of blah blah blah. Things that are not important . . . They collected a lot of money and prevented others from doing what they needed to do," said another, while a third called the meetings a "money grab."

The group was responsible for allocating seventy percent of the 266 million euro allotted to Libya under the EU Trust Fund.[25] A large proportion of that funding was targeted towards detention centers, though conditions inside them remained abysmal. (A 2021 review of the EU Trust Fund would say that the magnitude of EU money available led to increased competition between organizations jostling for the cash, preventing proper coordination and leading to "too many large" contracts "that may not have been the best fit for purpose.")[26]

The Mixed Migration Working Group was eventually dissolved after aid agencies working in Libya began boycotting meetings, but this led to a sense of "futility," one aid official said, as "the system struggled to respond to what coordination should look like," and UN staff were hesitant to suggest an alternative after having been "stung." Another person who attended UN and donor meetings in Tunis in later years called them a "shit show," saying European embassies were "willing to tolerate literally anything," while UN leadership was weak and "there's not a lot of urgency."

"There's just a sense of Groundhog Day," he said. "Nothing is ever achieved in this humanitarian response . . . There's tremendous lethargy and a sense they've given up or something."

———

There were more irregularities in spending within UNHCR. An audit, published in March 2019, found UNHCR was not doing assessments to verify the needs of the people it was meant to be helping.[27] This led to unnecessary purchases, like two thousand bags of cement, which expired in six months after being used for nothing. A complaint box, for refugees that could access it, was opened only six times in eighteen months. Between January 1, 2017, and May 31, 2018, nearly $200,000 was spent on flights booked with two travel agents without a competitive bidding process. Nearly $750,000 was spent on hiring out an office, with another $200,000 going towards office security. Eight laptops were bought at a cost of $5,883 each.

"UNHCR are smugglers really, but the only difference is the source of money for them is not from us but from the EU. They keep us here to die to get that money."

"The UNHCR listens to the soldiers and not us."

"UNHCR does not work for us—it is a criminal organization."

"UNHCR are playing us."

A dysfunctional banking system and problems obtaining hard cash inside Libya meant the black market currency exchange rate, from dollars to dinars, was hugely different to the official rate that UN agencies had to follow. While they paid for goods and services in dollars, Libyans they did business with could convert the money on the black market rate, leading to a potentially huge profit. This meant there was far less aid than there should have been, humanitarian workers said.

"It would have been much better for us to fly to Tunis with a suitcase full of dollars and buy on the black market. We would have quintupled or quadrupled our effectiveness, but obviously we can't do that . . . You have to use the legal banking system, which was broken," said Alan Bobbett, the former head of the International Medical Corps in Libya, a UN partner agency that worked in roughly a dozen Libyan migrant detention centers over several years.

"Your suppliers could be making an absolute killing," said another senior humanitarian official, who asked not to be named. "By doing everything in accordance with the law and good ways of doing business, you were likely to be exploited." He said it was also evident that everyone doing business in Libya was dealing with militias in one way or another, whether it be by paying protection money, providing benefits in order to operate in certain neighborhoods, or engaging with companies or individuals that did. "Just by participating in the economy, [the militias] already stand to benefit," he said.

———

On top of this, UN staff complained about being fired or not having expiring contracts renewed if they spoke out about failures in the UN operation in Libya. Two people working for two different UN agencies told me they felt they had been flagged as troublemakers and were encouraged or forced to leave their positions. "That's not only in Libya, that's everywhere. In the UN you don't open your mouth without your boss telling you to open your mouth," said one person who sat in on Libya-related meetings with high-level UN staff.

People employed by so-called UN partner organizations were careful about what they said as well because they knew they could lose access to detention centers if they were too outspoken. "We had to keep our heads down," said Bobbett. "It was the tightrope you walked all the time. If you got vocal about what you saw there, you would be denied access. If I open my mouth, people are not going to get medical treatment. So the detention centers themselves kind of mandated that." Aid agencies working inside detention centers found it easier to get funding, he said. "The EU was throwing money, Italy was throwing money, lots of different programs across Europe were throwing money at detention centers. So that was where people gravitated towards, it was low-hanging fruit, it was easy."

Another senior aid worker said this meant there was basically "a race to the bottom" among aid agencies to secure access to detention centers. They would almost compete to be the easiest for militias to work with, because a lot of the decisions about which organization provided services in each center were made on the basis of personal relationships. "For some, it was just a case of a tick box exercise in terms of delivering on project objectives, rather than ensuring that humanitarian assistance was provided in the best way for the population," he said. Then the organizations would do "glowing" assessments of their own work back in Tunis, when the realities on the ground were very different. These discrepancies could be blatant, as simple as the difference between UN social media posts showing distributions of blankets and photos taken by detainees later that day in which guards could be seen removing the stacks of blankets again, putting them on the back of vehicles and driving away.

———

Whether to speak out or maintain access in the hope of doing some small good is an age-old problem for aid organizations. It was only in 1996 that the International Committee of the Red Cross, which has a policy of neutrality, admitted it knew about the Holocaust and the persecution of Jewish people during World War Two. The organization argued that if it had made that information public, it would have lost its limited access to prisoner of war camps.[28] Historians accuse the Red Cross of making the problem even worse by doing a superficial 1944 visit to a concentration camp and settlement in German-occupied Czechoslovakia, Theresienstadt, and speaking well of it. "This helped perpetuate the German charade by discrediting the accurate reports trickling in about concentration camp horrors," one historian wrote to *The New York Times* in the 1980s.[29] The US Holocaust Museum describes the camp being "beautified" in advance.[30] "Gardens were planted, houses painted, and barracks renovated. The Nazis staged social and cultural events for the visiting dignitaries."

Marwa Mohamed, the head of advocacy for the organization Lawyers for Justice in Libya, argued it would have been better if UNHCR left the country completely so as not to fall into a similar trap. "I think their presence is a lot more counterproductive [than it is helpful]," she told me during a WhatsApp call from London. "Because when you look at it, yes, they can provide medical [care], but so can MSF, and MSF does it a million times better. They've set up community centers that [are] difficult to access. They have hotlines that they say work, but in reality they don't . . . Their resettlement is a drop in comparison to what is actually needed."

Mohamed, who previously worked for UNHCR in North Africa, said she is a big believer in the 1951 Refugee Convention and the values the agency should stand for, but called their actions in Libya "shameful." "They are sending the message that this is manageable, and it's not . . . What is their purpose there, other than [as] a cover for whatever policies? The stronger method would be [to say they] are not going to be involved in any of this anymore . . . If UNHCR pulls out with a very, very strong statement as to why they have pulled out, it becomes very difficult [for the EU and member states] to continue to engage," she charged.

When it came to refugees in Libya, often the only big organization willing to speak out in a meaningful way was MSF. From 2016, MSF refused to take any EU funding, including from individual European countries, in protest over the 2016 EU-Turkey migration deal, which saw the EU pledge six billion euro to Turkey in return for stopping the departures of largely Syrian refugees who were crossing the Aegean Sea to Greece. The number of crossings dropped from 856,000 in 2015 to 10,000 in 2020[31]; by then, more than 3.6 million Syrian refugees were living in Turkey, where many faced harassment, exploitation, and the constant risk of deportation.[32]

"This is jeopardizing the very concept of the refugee," Jerome Oberreit, MSF's international secretary general, told Reuters news agency. "It's really important to see the real people instead of the political football that they have become. We're talking about Europe's refugee shame." Before taking that stance, MSF received more than fifty million euro in a year—around eight percent of its budget—from the EU and its member states.[33]

As part of their work in Libya's detention centers, MSF staff laid down conditions, including that they should be able to access all detainees inside a facility; that they could observe living conditions and report them to other organizations or the government; and that all MSF employees would be allowed to enter, including international staff. Despite pushback from militias running the centers, MSF employees who visited detention centers tried to stick to these rules, suspending operations at points where they were not met.[34]

————

When I started communicating with refugees in Libya, I sent regular updates to UNHCR staff with information from detention centers. Sometimes they were responsive or said they would pass it on to teams on the ground. Other times there was no answer. There was pushback, too. Various staff members told me I was putting refugees at risk by publishing details of the conditions. One UNHCR employee even said they heard two senior officials in the Tunis office call me the agency's "enemy."

Throughout my engagement with the agency's staff, I noticed that there seemed to be an institutional unwillingness to trust what refugees said. For example, when I emailed a senior UNHCR official in October 2018, asking about the number of deaths taking place in detention, he said it was not possible to obtain that data. But he added that I should not be so quick to believe refugees, despite the fact that I was triangulating information using multiple sources and he did not seem able to highlight any factual inaccuracies in what I had reported.

Saying he had noted my "recent renewed criticisms of what my colleagues are doing/not doing in Libya," he wrote: "We can all make mistakes and I would be the first to recognize them, but you should not either take at face value what you hear/we hear from individuals in Libya, even [if] they are in a dire situation." I was shocked. This was a person who represented refugees at the highest levels and had regular interactions with politicians crafting anti-migration policies. I wondered how often he repeated his comments in meetings where refugees had no seat at the table and he was their only advocate.

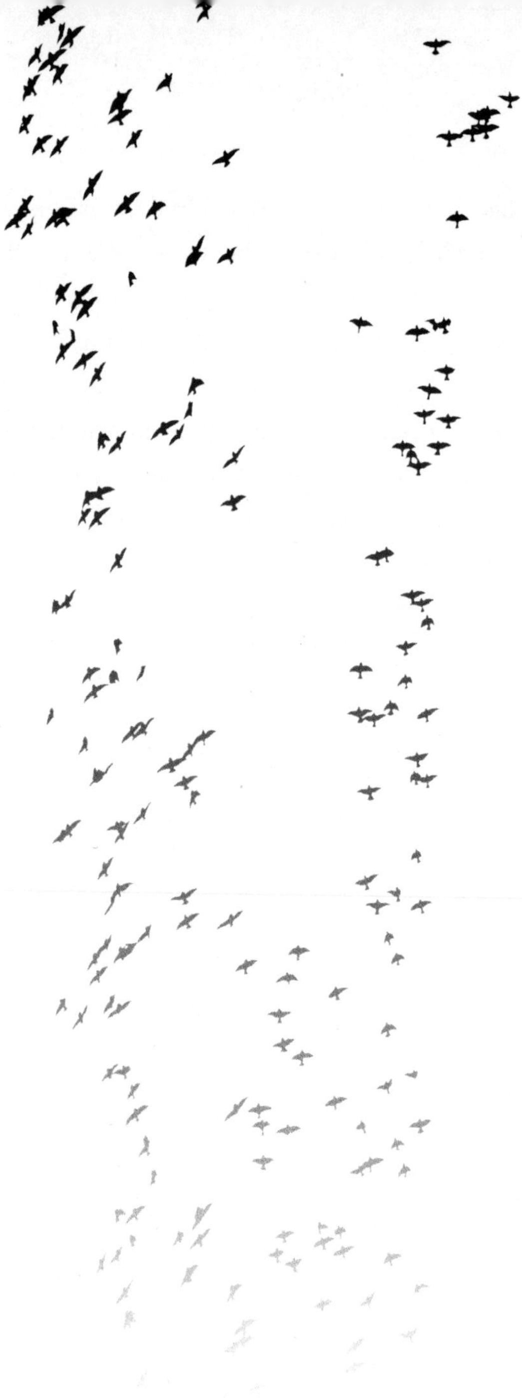

ABU SALIM: LOVE FINDS A WAY

"I loved you as if I had never seen anyone else in the universe."
–FACEBOOK STATUS BY A SUDANESE REFUGEE IN LIBYA

"The worst thing about distance is you don't know
whether they'll miss you or forget you."
–FACEBOOK STATUS BY AN ERITREAN REFUGEE IN LIBYA

The first war had subsided, but the Libyan guards who disappeared as fighting raged across Tripoli had not since returned full-time to Abu Salim detention center. Technically, Kaleb and the other refugees could have walked out of the compound completely, but they had nowhere to go. After two years or more under smugglers and in detention centers, they were fearful of enslavement and drained of money. The only strength they had was in numbers, and they wanted to stay together. Tripoli was unpredictable, and there were dollar signs on their heads. Abu Salim was now their sanctuary.

Food and water were the most obvious requirements. Men began to cautiously venture out of the center at dawn, lining up with other African migrants living in the area to look for work.[1] There were estimated to be more than 660,000 foreigners in Libya at the time—including Arabs, who found it easier to integrate because of similarities in language and culture, and Sub-Saharan Africans, who were likely to be exploited and paid little for labor.[2] Abu Salim's detainees found they could earn around 15 dinars a day (about $4) in construction, a restaurant, or even in a militia's barracks.[3] All options were risky, as they had no identification papers. There were armed groups and smugglers, and checkpoints dotted across the city where they could be caught. Some refugees who left for work disappeared for weeks before reemerging, either with cash or after being conned and toiling without reward. They had stories of pistols waved by employers with "dangerous eyes" or police who pressured male laborers to have sex with them.

> *"If they try to arrest you on the street, and you run, Libyans will shoot you and throw the body in the sea or in Tripoli's streets."*

For women, there was also the risk of sexual violence. Libyan men would invite refugee women to work in their homes as domestic help; once there, the men might rape them. Victims would stay silent, knowing that if anyone found out it would be passed around the detention centers, bringing shame upon them. "People will say she must have wanted it or she shouldn't have gone," said Kaleb.

Better off detainees received money from relatives. Libyans living locally started a taxi service. They would drive Abu Salim's refugees to shops to collect funds sent through the informal hawala money transfer system. Arabic-speaking refugees, like the Sudanese, could negotiate Tripoli's streets more easily. They even set up a market inside the detention center, hawking foodstuffs they bought outside at inflated prices.

Most days, one of the former guards called by the center. He collected payment—what he called "rent"—from the Sudanese men who ran the market while having a cursory look around to check everything was in order. When detainees asked him to call the UN or medics to request assistance for

them, he would. The man was profiting and thus had no incentive to inter-
rupt the status quo by informing other Libyans about the lack of management there, though the refugees suspected it was only a matter of time
before some other militia or authority figure realized what was going on and
tried to retake control. They decided to form a committee and govern the
center themselves. Twenty people were elected. The eldest was in his forties,
chosen for his wisdom; others were picked because of their religious leadership, or simply their confidence. Most detainees were Eritrean men, and the
committee reflected that, but there was also a Somali, an Ethiopian, and
one woman. Kaleb was the youngest member. His role was talking to me,
usually through Facebook.

The committee divided up the cleaning and nominated other refugees to
act as guards: five at a time on twelve-hour shifts. Appointees stayed by the
gate, observing whoever approached through a slit in the wall.[4] Those with
the best Arabic were selected so they could defuse a situation when outsiders
arrived. The refugee guards also enforced rules, with the aim of making sure
no Libyans who came there were angered. Any vexation felt by a Libyan
visitor would increase their risk of being confined again.

"They wanted a small mistake to lock us back in."

Sometimes, the refugee guards would hit people with sticks to enforce
regulations. Inside the detention center building, men and women were allowed to speak to each other, but not outside, in the compound, where they
might be seen. Women were ordered to cover their hair and wear long skirts
and t-shirts, or the refugee guards would shout at them or beat them into
conforming. They said this was so Libyans who might visit unexpectedly
would not be angered by the refugees' inability to conform to Islamic rules.

*"There were refugees who had no respect so it was good to beat them. I
don't like refugees when they do bad things."*

"Instead of talking we believe [in] sometimes [using] a stick . . . They do it for your own benefit."

The committee was also in charge of redistributing food, making sure everyone had something. They collected money and purchased coffee, sugar, and flour—though they refused to buy communal cigarettes, to the consternation of a few. On holidays, there was popcorn.

Ahead of an all-detention center assembly, committee members would shout "*akaba*," the Tigrinya word for "meeting." The gathering meant everyone could be updated on new rules or challenges. Kaleb took to the floor. He shared anything I had said about their chances at evacuation or the general situation in Libya, unless it was very bad news, when he kept it to himself so as not to dampen their morale (I knew nothing about this until much later). He would sometimes take photos, or gather other information I had asked for. As time stretched on, though, Kaleb found it hard to summon the energy needed for these assemblies and occasionally slept right through them.

———

In the months after the Libyan guards abandoned them, Abu Salim's detainees broke into an empty room in their compound and spent four days fashioning a Christian church. A refugee artist painted religious drawings. People compiled holy books they had carried with them to Libya. There was a priest among the detainees. Every evening, and between 6:00 a.m. and 10:00 a.m. on Saturday and Sunday, the Orthodox Christians gathered to chant and bow in prayer. In detention centers across Tripoli, at the same times, there were Ethiopian and Eritrean Christians bent over in worship and supplication, devotedly practicing their religion even in a country where there was total hostility to it.

Later on Sundays, refugees would gather around to sing and drink coffee—or *bun*—that they had pooled together money for. They would perform songs in Arabic, Tigrinya, Amharic, or English. Eritrean musician Yemane Barya's songs were a particularly popular choice. When listeners appreciated a rendition, they would throw cigarettes or a carton of juice at the singer, as a gift.

Another way to pass time was by playing a game similar to two truths and a lie. One person made a statement about their life, and the others had to guess if it was true or not. They even created alcohol, putting yeast, rice, sugar, and macaroni or dry bread in a container and closing it for three days if the weather was cold, or one if it was hot (any longer and it would explode). This was a drink Eritreans learned to make in military camps. They called it *dumu dumu* (cat cat).

A few refugees procured blades and set up a barber, despite knives being previously banned by the Libyan management. The men wanted their hair short and tight to their head to avoid lice.

At the time, there was little external outcry about this detention center being abandoned by its management, and few organizations spoke publicly about it—it seemed like a best-case scenario for detainees who had been through so much trauma already.

————

UNHCR made rare visits to Abu Salim, and in late October 2018, the day came when Kaleb and many other refugees were registered. They lined up in front of UN employees with laptops, reciting their names, date of birth, country of origin, and the reasons why they left. Each person was given a case number written on a yellow piece of paper that they quickly memorized, aware that any documentation could be stolen from them. It was an exciting occasion, a rare moment when they felt like something promising might be on the horizon.[5] Finally, the agency knew they existed and there was a chance—however tiny—that they would be chosen for evacuation.

MSF kept visiting, too, providing Plumpy'nut nutritional bars and milk for the babies. Sometimes, their staff arrived with readymade meals, even chicken, to boost the immunity of the refugees. They brought scabies medication, footballs or dolls for the children, and the occasional book, too, which Kaleb was always excited by.

"Our whole life was dependent on MSF."

Their staff occasionally spoke to refugees about their mental health, though many were reluctant to divulge how they were feeling—they were so used to keeping their lips sealed to protect themselves. Instead, the medics taught them breathing techniques to stay calm and sleep easier at night.

It was during darkness that the impact of what they were going through felt most raw. While others slept fitfully, an individual might get up and start whistling or dancing "just to disturb the memories," as Kaleb explained. No one would stop them.

————

In total, the Libyan guards were absent for nearly three months. One of the unexpected consequences of this newfound freedom was how many refugees began to fall in love. The Libyans had maintained that mixing between the sexes was *haram*—forbidden. Now, those rules were gone, and they mingled freely.

"Love doesn't choose a place, every place there's love. You start to meet a girl without the police. Everyone was sleeping in every corner."

There were couples who had met in the smugglers' warehouses or in the Sahara Desert. There was love that had grown over time, throughout the endless, spirit-crushing challenges, and love that had sprung in an instant. There was love that had grown out of dependency, and there was love that arrived with the growing realization that no one else would ever understand what their minds, bodies, and souls had gone through.

"You see amazing love. One woman waited one year [with smugglers]
until the man's family could pay [the ransom for him]. They met in the
Sahara and she waited one year."

The new romances lightened the general mood across the center, but
also made it harder for refugees pining sweethearts they had left behind.
Some were not able to contact home at all, and they wondered if their partners were alive or dead, or had simply moved on, unwilling to wait for a
lover in limbo. Mustafa, a good-looking guy with a bright smile and a fond-
ness for selfies, told me his personal tragedy: the beautiful woman he was
deeply in love with; the relationship he had unknowingly sacrificed to make
this journey to nowhere. In photos he sent me, she smiled shyly into a camera. He had mapped out their life together, fantasized about their wedding.
If he reached Europe she could come and join him there, he imagined, but
he got stuck along the route.

Mustafa was from the border of Sudan and Eritrea. His girlfriend was
Eritrean, and marriage was the only way she could avoid indefinite conscription. She told him she was unwilling to leave her country because all her
siblings had already gone, and her parents were old and needed to be cared
for. That meant the end of their future together. "Her mom said to my dad
we can't wait a long time because maybe the policemen will take her to the
military camp," Mustafa told me. As he counted seconds, days, years incarcerated in Libya, Mustafa's father agreed the woman should wed someone
else. "My story with her [is] finished," Mustafa brooded. "Another man will
marry her."

To distract himself, Mustafa worked out in Abu Salim's yard each day,
fashioning weights with metal bars he found lying around. At each end, he
placed a plastic bottle filled with cement. He set himself challenges, but
they did not stop Mustafa from thinking about his lost love constantly. He
compared her fate to Eritrea itself—caught up in the whims of a dictatorship exercising brutal control over its population.

*"Dear Eritrea is like a sweet girl. A selfish person came and killed her love
and made her like darkness!"*

———

In Abu Salim, there was serious pressure on relationships. It came from the understanding that women were given priority for evacuation, and, if they were married, their husbands would accompany them. Refugees usually flee without documents, or lose any they bring with them, so proof was not necessary. It was not long before recently formed couples would have a conversation, reaching an understanding that they would register as married if the opportunity arose.

There were loveless relationships, too, the women taking pity on the men. "It starts like a game, and then they have a baby," Kaleb would tell me about some of these. "If the woman is good [the man will] stay with her. It's too hard to find a woman in Europe . . . You have to marry someone from your own country."

This was not unique to Abu Salim. In Tajoura, a detention center in eastern Libya, marriages were organized by letter. A man would write, giving his carefully worded script to a detainee who worked with the guards— the *capos*—before it was passed on to a woman in a separate cell. He may have never seen the woman in person, but, if she accepted, for the sake of their evacuation bids they were together and in love.

*"We are in different hangars but they write letters and give it to
the migrants who are working together with the guards who give letters
to the females, so this is how they marry. As she is from your country,
she will accept marrying because she knows that UNHCR is [only]
dealing with those who are married. UNHCR doesn't transfer single
[men], so people are marrying here in Tripoli so that UNHCR
will evacuate them."*

In the days before an evacuation, the guards in Tajoura would allow refugee couples to meet for the first time, for around thirty minutes. It was a chance to say hello and exchange bashful smiles, or to be met with steely eyes, hardened in pursuit of an escape route. These were Libya's marriages of convenience.

In several cases, the women did not consent. One refugee, who acted as a translator in Abu Salim when international organizations visited, told UNHCR he was married to a woman in the same center without her understanding what he was saying. They were registered, and he convinced her not to correct the mistake. Eventually, they were evacuated to Italy together, but she told friends she hated him.

Other times, men would pull out of the arrangements last minute. One young Somali man told me he came to an agreement with a woman in Tajoura to whom guards allowed him speak to for five minutes, face to face, after a day of forced labor. He later panicked, worried about the pressure of being responsible for a wife, and decided he could survive more easily alone. The woman was later evacuated with another man.

As UNHCR began to register more detainees inside detention centers, a select number of refugees living in the city outside—including those who had bribed their way out before—began paying money to the guards to let them enter, out of desperation to have their asylum claims heard and their details taken by UNHCR.[6] Married couples were particularly likely to come in, hopeful that they would be selected.

It was especially hard for those who were already married and had left spouses behind them with whom they wanted to be reunited one day. They could not allow a fake marriage to be listed on their documents and rule out the possibly of applying for family reunification down the line. "For someone like me, I'm married. My wife and son are suffering somewhere [but] UNHCR can't believe that I am married unless they see my wife and my son. That's unfair treatment," one South Sudanese man in Tajoura complained to me.

There were also people in detention with spouses already in Europe. One young Eritrean, Hamid, arrived in Germany in 2014 without a hard copy of his marriage certificate, which he lost while escaping. Even with it, the German authorities said the union would not have been recognized, as it was carried out in a church and not certified by the Eritrean government. Though he had gone ahead to save his wife, Kedija, the perils of the journey, she ended up having to make the same trip, too, without his protection. Kedija was caught by the Libyan coastguard. After months in Ain Zara and Abu Salim, she called him saying she wanted to die.

I became aware of their case when a German pastor, who was looking out for Hamid in Germany, contacted me asking if there was anything I could do (I referred him to the UN). In late 2018, I interviewed Hamid, asking whether he felt his relationship could recover from this lengthy separation and all they endured apart. "Although the trauma we both have, I believe that we could live a normal life again," he said. "We still love each other like five years ago. Love makes you strong, and there is always hope." He told me he was doing well: he found a job as a systems engineer, had an apartment, and was ready for her arrival, whenever it might happen. All he had achieved to date was for his wife.

Kedija was evacuated to Niger, en route to Europe, after being chosen by UNHCR for resettlement. It came too late. In November 2019, she revealed that she was pregnant with a baby from another man. She severed the relationship with Hamid and was resettled to another country instead of Germany. Later, she would lose her baby and attempt to reconnect with her husband, but he was unwilling to speak to her. He became depressed, unable to concentrate to the extent that he risked losing his job. The future he had projected for them, the goal that had kept him going for so long, had crumbled into pieces. Theirs was just another tragedy in the broad tapestry of destinies irrevocably altered by this inequitable, treacherous system.

———

Word got around Tripoli that Abu Salim was now an open detention center—a place with some measure of freedom. By late 2018, victims abandoned by smugglers started turning up on the doorstep en masse. They had paid ransoms but were not sent to sea; smugglers told them the European funding of the Libyan coastguard meant the route was "closed."

Over roughly a month, around 260 new people arrived. They had a litany of torture scars. One woman cried constantly from electrocution marks on her breasts inflicted when she resisted a rape attempt by a smuggler; men lamented similar scars on their buttocks. Some had tuberculosis or were severely malnourished and found it difficult to walk, they were so weak. At least five people died shortly after they got there.[7]

"A lot are mindless."

A series of women and girls arrived pregnant, saying they had all been raped by the same smuggler. Some tested positive for HIV—another lifelong burden to bear. About half of the pregnant women in detention centers had conceived through rape, a Somali woman who was held across three centers told me. They had problems accessing healthcare, toiletries, and enough food. Abortion was illegal throughout Libya.[8]

"Many women lose their babies. The people facing the most problems are women and children."

———

Freedom could not last forever. The novelty of their situation had worn off, as had jubilation from being registered by the UN, and the Abu Salim refugees began bickering. They were no longer united, Kaleb said. When committee members came up with ideas about how they could advocate for themselves or improve their living conditions further, others would ignore them or say it was more effective to do nothing. People slept long hours and became angry over tiny things. Kaleb knew this weakness meant the Libyans could easily reassert control over the center. "We are not strong enough to fight them like before," he said.

Then one day, late that year, it happened: the Libyan guards returned full-time. Detainees were presented with a choice by the detention center's manager: "freedom or food."

> *"One day, the boss came and gave us an option: either to be locked up without facing the sunshine, or to be free without food. We had spent two years without facing the sun in the smugglers' store, and our choice was fresh air without food."*

Choosing "freedom" meant they could at least walk around the compound but would have to continue paying exorbitant prices for anything they ate instead of the (admittedly meager) meals being provided without charge. When they could get away with it, the more enterprising would eat from the guards' trash: a mix of couscous, macaroni, and—when they were in luck—chicken.

Once again, management started a divide-and-conquer strategy. This even extended to mothers with newborn babies, who fought when the Libyan manager only brought milk for the women he liked. In December 2018, a guard shot a gun inside the women and children's area to scare them.[9]

> *"After the guards came back things got bad."*

Soon, even the refugee committee stopped trusting each other. If they planned a protest, the manager would find out about it in advance. Anything they said to each other in confidence could be leaked, and there would be a resulting punishment.

Under the darkness of night, one of the refugee leaders, Hassan, made an exit. He had discovered it was suddenly possible to pay $600 to be smuggled to Tunisia, driving long, risky distances in a vehicle and then walking by land across the border. He told no one of his plan, apart for one friend in the center and me. Hassan felt guilty, believing his departure would be demoralizing for everyone he left behind. He messaged right before he left and again after arrival, when he sent me photos. They showed skinny Eritrean men crowded around a fire they lit to stay warm during the journey and a selfie of his face in front of a tall white UNHCR reception center in Medenine, a town in southeast Tunisia close to the Libyan border. "I see the Freedom after one year and six months, sis. I hope my friends get to see this," Hassan wrote, capitalizing freedom in a display of how much value that word had for him.

In the weeks after Hassan left, the cost of being smuggled to Tunisia went up to $800, then increased again. As the glow of "freedom" wore off, he questioned whether he had made the right choice. The influx of refugees from Libya, when the route opened up, meant services in Tunisia became overwhelmed, and the early arrivals were ordered to leave their free accommodation. Within the next year, hundreds of refugees who made the same journey would start paying smugglers to take them back to Libya again after realizing there was no functioning asylum system in Tunisia, it was illegal to work, and racism was rampant.[10]

In Abu Salim, more questions were being raised about how information was becoming public. I noticed that people there were messaging me less, including Kaleb, but it was only later on that I found out why. The management began making threats against those who revealed the conditions inside the center. In return for fruit, cigarettes, or other benefits, refugees were snitching on my sources. Detainees began to form their own select groups of people they trusted, making a pledge to support each other and limit conversations with anyone else, but they could not relax; one eye was always scoping out who might be listening.

"[There were] too many tricks happening in that house, especially as time went on."

Kaleb was called in for questioning. Ali, the manager, ordered him to the detention center's administrative office, before commanding him to open the photo gallery in his phone so they could see if he had been taking photos to send to me. "They checked my mobile but did not find anything. If they did, they could take me to prison and torture me," he recalled, months afterwards. Kaleb was worried about the small isolation room on site, the *shella*, where refugees could be locked up.

"There are snitches around us, from our own people."

During one of their sporadic visits, Kaleb says a UNHCR staff member even warned him that if he continued to talk to me he would get in trouble. "He said if I do this I will be harmed, but I didn't admit it," Kaleb said. "He told me we can't change anything by doing such things."

Despite this, other refugees wanted information to be broadcast. I kept sharing their messages on Twitter and publishing articles in international media. Even when Kaleb became worried for his own safety, people would approach him, asking him to send news to me. He had the best English and had been given the phone for this purpose. "In the middle of the night I [would] text you, I [would] write you," he told me later. "Something happens, they had someone at least to tell in the outside world. Before there was no one. If something happens, someone should know. In one day, many things happen inside the compound. Many fights. [The manager] makes a deal with you, a new deal. They want it [all] to be reported, they say tell her."

UNHCR rotated staff. On one occasion, a white man visited and spoke to the hundreds of detainees together, telling them he had only been in Libya two weeks so was still trying to get to grips with how things worked. "I wanted to come and see for myself," he said, gazing at them hunched on the ground.[11] But they were tired of being gawked at, and exhausted by the leap of anticipation and the subsequent plummet into despair that accompanied each of the UN's visits, which always seemed to lead to nothing.

"He makes us lose our hope. UNHCR told us that they are not responsible for our life."

They waited, and were presented with ways to disengage even further. Libyan guards would give detainees their first try of black hashish for free. Some quickly got hooked, finding that it shut off their memories. The second time, of course, cost money. And the third, fourth, and fifth. Those who stayed away from hashish smoked cigarettes.

"Even a 35-year-old woman with two kids started smoking in Libya. Everyone starts smoking in Libya. People start beating down doors for smokes. You can do without food but not without addiction."

The children in Abu Salim were losing their innocence. A ten-year-old picked up cigarette butts from the ground and put them to his mouth. A three-year-old, who had been in Libya since he was just six months, uttered the words "*barra neek*" ("go fuck yourself"). Sometimes, children reenacted behavior they had seen while with the smugglers or by the Libyan guards, hitting each other and shouting "pay dollar, you son of a bitch." The Arabic they were learning was the language of control, abuse, and exploitation. *Hawel massari* ("transfer some money"), *weld el gahba* ("son of a whore"), and *khush dakhl* ("get inside").

"The words, the actions they use are just like the smugglers. Children are just like a white sheet of paper, we are the ones who should write good things on them."

Later, I would hear that there were discussions among the humanitarian response back in Tunis about providing schooling or building playgrounds in detention centers, but there were concerns about the "optics" of creating anything permanent that might be perceived as legitimizing the situation. "Children didn't even have books to read," recalled Alan Bobbett, the former International Medical Corps Libya director, who worried that this had been the wrong decision.

"A child who grows up in a gutter camp will not be a good person, there is no one to guide them."

———

After the Berlin Wall was built in 1961, German psychiatrists began noticing a new phenomenon. Symptoms included depression, suicide attempts, fear of confined spaces, and delusions of persecution. They called it *"Mauerkrankheit,"* or "wall sickness," as it particularly affected people with homes close to the wall, who lived with the daily feeling of being blocked or fenced in. The term was coined by a doctor working in an East Berlin mental hospital, Dietfried Mueller-Hegemann, who eventually fled to Western Germany.[12]

Imagine those mental health effects compounded. People trapped with no idea how long they might stay there. The lack of a future. Not being able to plan a single day in advance.

"Depression if you are a fighter it makes you cool, if you are cool it makes you a fighter. Some people were like an angel when they came to Libya and after some time you become a devil."

Indefinite detention took a toll on everyone. In Abu Salim, apathy sunk in and community spirit disappeared. It was each man or woman for themselves. "There are four people who have gone mad, they're just sitting down, they don't talk, even they start peeing on their trousers like a baby," one Eritrean messaged me. "There are some people who cannot tolerate [this]." He said the most serious psychological problems emerged after people were caught by the Libyan coastguard, because this was something no one was mentally prepared for. "Most people started [behaving] like that after they came back and tried the sea." Refugees quickly learned about the dangers in the Sahara Desert—the thirst, torture, starvation, and opportunistic smugglers—but they did not know the whole odyssey could end in a rescue that was not really a rescue, and indefinite confinement in a prison that was not officially a jail.

Even that Eritrean, a committee member in his late twenties, felt like he was going crazy. "We are losing hope, even from God," he messaged another time. The next day he apologized again for not answering my questions. "Sorry I am late. My mind is not working like before. Everything is becoming darkness."

Across Libya's detention centers, people started making up wild stories to explain how they came to be there. One man said he was a filmmaker who wanted to document the migrant crisis but was kidnapped after his investigation began. Maybe this was true, but his peers were skeptical. "The real story is too sad," explained Kaleb. Detainees crafted fiction for themselves, repositioning their existence in a way that made things bearable. "You are the actor, the smuggler is the director and you are the star," Kaleb told me.

Words stopped flowing. They felt paralyzed, disconnected, useless. They felt their deaths had already come to pass.

"Every day still now we are listening to bad news. I don't know what we can do. I see the people, when they stay together, everyone with his hope and wishes finished. We have had a long time with our families worrying, they don't want us to tell them bad news. Also, we are not

reaching our little dreams. We can't go on or return. Please, we need to leave here. After a short time we will be mindless."

Winter was fast approaching, and the cold weather made their bodies hurt, particularly because so many were badly malnourished. At night, the temperature dropped to around 46 degrees Fahrenheit. They felt pain in their backs, feet, and heads. They would lie without moving, unable to sleep, wishing time to pass. UN-distributed blankets were not enough to keep them warm.

A LETTER WRITTEN BY A POET IN KHOMS
SOUQ AL KHAMIS DETENTION CENTER

Irate (Angry) Letter to a Friend

Dear Friend,

All of my attention is focused on standing and saluting you, my dear friend, it's been a long time.

This world is a sorry place but it has been graced with your presence. Sleep well, old friend. You are not in my heart, you are in my soul. Now you are nothing, but you meant everything and you are me.

Best friend, we are one, not just two, because we had a lot of fantasies together. We wanted to achieve things others only knew from a screen.

You taught me a lot from what you experienced: how to survive in a hell.

Many people thought we were not going to survive but we responded "YES, WE CAN." But now I am starting to feel guilt. And I am so down, I'm feeling it and living in it emotionally, dear friend.

Why did you choose to fall and disappear? Why don't you come back? I'm waiting alone counting the stars.

When we separated I tried to tell you how dangerous the path you were choosing was. I didn't believe you might fall, but I was stressed you would not return, and I was afraid of losing you. And I lost you, it's real, it happened and it hurts badly. You taught me that if I felt seven I have to try to wake up at eight, but you stopped waking up. You left me alone with my tears. Are you happy with that?

But you are my backbone.

Fragile bottles, they get broken, they don't have the courage or capacity to hold my tears. Tears may seem as small as candle drops but every drop has its own strong memories of what we went through.

Each drop of my tears has its own unique, unforgettable, beautiful, sad, successful, and powerful experience. Even if we failed together we wanted to wake up together again and start to move forward.

Try to understand the dead body smells that disturb my nostrils. Yet I am smiling when I say you are me. The rest of me is drying while my tears continue to fall. My eyes feel thirsty.

You chose to rest. I don't care why you chose it but you left me in a hell, you condemned me to live while mourning. I say loudly and angrily: "I AM HURTING, YOU GOT ME TO HURT."

You resemble love for me. Not just love but life.

I never thought that you might leave me with my loneliness and now I suffer from being alone without you.

How could you do that, my old friend?

May Heaven calm you, you lived hard and struggled a lot in this earth full of fakes.

But me, I will always accuse you of leaving me behind in this world of evil.

May your soul rest peacefully, long live my most beloved dear friend of mine.

You are nothing but you are me.

Because I was nothing but I am you.

—In the memory of all Eritreans who lost their lives in the Mediterranean Sea. The world, even your own people, don't care about you, but we do.

MJ Waliku Arsema

CHAPTER 10

KHOMS SOUQ AL KHAMIS: A MARKET OF HUMAN BEINGS

"I wish I could be a bird to fly away where I wanted."

—AN ERITREAN REFUGEE LOCKED UP IN KHOMS SOUQ AL KHAMIS

"A refugee is someone who survived and who can create the future . . .
The world will not be destroyed by those who do evil, but by
those who watch them without doing anything . . . We can say that there is
killing, threats, raping, hunger, but it's already known by the world."

—DETAINEE IN KHOMS SOUQ AL KHAMIS[1]

On the walls of Souq al Khamis migrant detention center in Khoms, a port city in Libya's northwest, Tigrinya-language warnings for new arrivals were marked on a gray wall.

"Who comes to this house, may God help you," one said. "Libya is a market of human beings."

"Where is UNHCR?" read another. "Three people were sold here."[2]

They had been written with a toothbrush, using a mix of toothpaste and carbon.

*"Once we came in Khoms, we got warning messages written on the walls,
[saying] don't let anyone go outside or work with soldiers outside the
prison, otherwise they will sell you."*

Khoms Souq al Khamis was one of the so-called disembarkation centers: a place of nightmares, a worst-case scenario for those who tried to reach Europe. Thousands of refugees and migrants who were intercepted on the Mediterranean Sea by the Libyan coastguard passed through this center. Some were covered in painful burns caused by fuel mixing with seawater in the bottom of the boats. Everyone was hungry and dehydrated. Now was the time of reckoning.

A few had held SIM cards in their mouths during the long sea journeys. First, they wrapped the cards in tissue and then surrounded them with plastic, burning the edges together with a lighter. These small packages stayed in cheeks or under tongues as they were caught at sea, and while Libyan guards searched them upon arrival at the detention center. Inside the locked rooms of Khoms Souq al Khamis, they would quietly ask who had a phone that they could insert their SIM card into so they could send a message to their families to let them know the bad news.

"A lot of people's families died of stress, their father and mother, while they were in Libya."

Kaleb had also been in this detention center once, nearly a year before, right after he came off the water. Many of my sources were inside Khoms Souq al Khamis at some stage. From the cells and halls detainees were held in, they could see the sea, around fifty meters away, and hear its lapping and crashing waves. The buildings were old—this used to be a military training base.

During one particularly horrific week, nearly a month after a shipwreck that had killed as many as one hundred and fifty people, detainees watched corpses wash up on the sand and lie there for days.[3] Twelve survivors from the same shipwreck were incarcerated there when this began. Detainees asked the guards if they could bury the bodies, but said they were threatened with being shot if they tried. During a toilet break, a number of the longer-term detainees walked down to the shore and attempted to scoop sand onto them. But there was such a short period of time before they had to return, it was impossible to restore dignity to the dead.

Sometimes, new arrivals in Khoms were moved on quickly to other detention centers in Tripoli or elsewhere. They even paid for the privilege, thinking that relocating to the capital city meant UNHCR would be more likely to evacuate them. Others stayed in Khoms for years. Then there was a third group: those sold directly back to smugglers by the guards watching over them, whether they consented or not.

There was ongoing communication between the guards in Khoms Souq al Khamis and human smugglers; the guards would even facilitate escapes for detainees who had money to try and cross the sea again, in return for a payoff. But they also arranged the transfer of unwilling captives. I had heard about a group of eighteen detainees who were sold directly from Khoms Souq al Khamis to Bani Walid traffickers in late 2017. The refugees were lured out of the center by guards who claimed they were being taken to find work. The guards were reportedly paid by the smugglers. "It's beyond my word to explain the inhumanity that happened," a man, held in the center at the time, told me. "We heard some of [the detainees who were sold] lost their lives by tremendous, brutal beatings. They were electrocuted with so many volts. I know them, they were little guys. Their only hope was to step in to Europe, nothing more."

Several of them later ended up back in government-associated detention centers. One man was evacuated to Niger, and another agreed to return to Eritrea through the IOM repatriation program. Eight of that group were killed, friends of the survivors said, after their families could not afford to pay sums as high as $20,000.

"They don't talk . . . They don't remember . . . They had nightmares every night."

This was why detainees in Khoms began to write warnings on the wall. A year later, the same behavior was still going on, and EU-funded returns to the center were continuing, too. I started getting live updates on the fate of new arrivals to Khoms in early December 2018 when several detainees were removed from the center by force and their friends first contacted me about it, panicking and begging for action.[4] Among those taken were two Somalis, aged 15 and 21, and a 16-year-old Eritrean. After that, refugees began demonstrating. They sent me a video showing detainees gathered outside in the compound walking en masse towards a guard, who shot the ground by their feet with live ammunition to force them to withdraw.[5] Another video showed guards in blue khaki uniforms smoking by a wall, a gun slung across the back of one, as detainees crouched on the ground, some of their wrists crossed in front of them in the protest symbol that means "freedom."

> *"I'm not going to lie to you, I don't know even if this center is being run by the government or not; I couldn't differentiate it. Yes, they wear police officers' clothes but they work like smugglers. They torture, they kidnap, they steal, how can we differentiate?"*

That same month, on December 29, 2018, nearly three hundred more refugees and migrants were intercepted at sea and taken to Khoms Souq al Khamis.[6] They brought scabies with them and little else. Photos showed the group huddled together, dejected, under gray, standard-issue blankets. None were registered with the UN, so there was no list of their names anywhere. I tweeted about their plight in real time as the guards began to beat them with guns and metal rods, telling them they should go straight back to smugglers.[7]

> *"The new migrants are really in danger. The leaders are trying to push them to get out every day. They're beating them. They make them stressed.*

It's a way to make them get out. They want to sell them to the smugglers
and the smugglers will send them to sea."

It took just a week from their disembarkation by the EU-backed Libyan coastguard for dozens of those new detainees to exit the official system again. They were told they were being moved to a new center by the guards, as Khoms Souq al Khamis was full. Instead, they were sent back to the smuggler who held them before—a man called Abdusalem, who transferred them to Bani Walid and demanded another ransom of between $1,000 and $5,000 per person.[8] When UN staff visited Khoms in mid-January, they confirmed there were "a number of people . . . unaccounted for."[9]

"They stole our friends," one detainee told me. "I'm afraid for my friends." He said there were ten women left in the center and fewer than ninety men. Everyone was worried about being next. "Policemen in Libya and smugglers are just like hand in glove," he said, adding that this was a clear sign the EU should not be condoning returns to Libya or working with Libyan authorities.

Dying would be less painful than his relatives being asked to pay money again, said another Eritrean, who spent two years with smugglers, during which his family raised more than $9,000 in ransom payments by selling their home. The guards in Khoms were "boasting, saying they will kill us, or take us to a place [where] nobody can find us," he said.

"Sally, are you here?"

He did not need to go far to be reminded of the dangers of smugglers, and sent me photos showing the torture marks on the inmates detained with him. An arm and chest missing patches of skin; a lengthy scar skirting a belly button; a crescent-shaped slice across a palm all compounded their fear.

"If you want to say it publicly do now. Anything that you think can help
us, please do. Even if you can tell the president of the United States,

Donald Trump, tell him. Tell the world about our life."

Around twenty people tried to kill themselves in the months before Christmas 2018 and New Year's, according to one of my sources in Khoms. "The world can't find us, we're especially isolated," he said. "Some are getting mental desperation. We are living in a dark hell." The man was registered with UNHCR, but he would stay incarcerated in Khoms Souq al Khamis for almost two years. The saddest times came during the night, when the guards took women out to rape them, he told me. Detainees could hear the sound from the men's blocks.

The detention center eventually became a labor camp, with select refugees going out during the day to work and returning back in the evening with money to buy food. The guards encouraged this, knowing refugees would not escape—even though they remained frightened of the guards, they were more anxious about losing any chance of being selected for evacuation. On the evenings when they got paid, and not threatened or tricked out of their earnings, detainees cooked, with one person preparing a meal for four or five others. They crowded around together, taking fistfuls of macaroni from a shared bowl.

In October 2020, the detention center was finally closed and its inmates moved to Tripoli by UNHCR, where they were left to fend for themselves.[10]

CHAPTER 11

SIERRA LEONE: THE TEMPLE RUN AND THE LEFT-BEHIND WOMEN

"Amazing Grace, how sweet the sound, that saved a wretch like me. I once was lost but now am found. Was blind, but now I see."

—JOHN NEWTON, A FORMER SLAVE TRADER WHO WORKED IN SIERRA LEONE[1]

"Wae bod wan fly you shake di tik."
(If a bird wants to fly, you shake the tree.)

—KRIO PROVERB

The mobile phone game is called Temple Run. "Use amazing powers to cheat death," reads an advertisement on the app store. "Collect coins to buy powers." You must dodge dangers, including gaps in the stone path, electrical currents, and large rocks, which you jump over or slide under. Evil demon monkeys chase you. There is no way to stop running without dying. The longest I lasted was seventy-two seconds.

In Sierra Leone, a West African coastal country of roughly eight million people, that's also what the route to Europe is called. Thousands have done the real-life Temple Run. They travel by land through Guinea, Mali, Niger, or Algeria and on to Libya, entrusting their lives to unscrupulous smugglers.

Since the hardening of EU migration policy on the Mediterranean, there is another game this odyssey could be compared to: Snakes and Ladders. In Libya, West Africans are generally not considered to be refugees, so they have no chance at legal evacuation. If they do not drown or die in the desert or make it across the sea, there is a large chance they will be repatriated to their birth countries through a vast EU-funded return scheme. Back at square one, they will have to decide whether to give up on their dreams or attempt the journey all over again.

———

Joseph K. Conteh was born in 1991, the same year Sierra Leone's civil war began. His family was from Bumba, a village in the northern Makeni province, where his father worked as a palm wine—or "poyo"—tapper. As a small child, Joseph said he could carry gallons of poyo on his back. Joseph was the eldest boy and the second oldest of seven siblings, two of whom died young. He grew up in the capital city Freetown, 200 kilometers from his family's village, where he was cared for by his grandparents.

His grandfather was a pastor in Wellington, a neighborhood in Freetown's east end. In 1999, eight years into the civil war, the city was stormed by rebels, who mutilated victims as they moved. Joseph says the rebels came to his grandparents' church and asked for the "leader of the house." When his grandfather ventured out, the rebel fighters said they would "dress him," asking if the pastor wanted "long sleeves or short sleeves." The old man said "short," and the fighters chopped off his arms above the elbow. Joseph recalls hiding in the church with his grandmother while his grandfather bled to death outside. His mother would later confirm Joseph's grandfather's death, though not how it happened. She had just given birth at the time and was reluctant to speak about the war, except to say that she stayed indoors as much as possible, and the worst thing she witnessed was a man whose lips had been padlocked shut by rebels.

"It affects you."

Joseph spent the next decade selling his grandmother's vegetables in the morning before school began. When he was around twenty-one, Joseph met Blessing, who was a year younger and still studying. Her uncle lived in his neighborhood, so they kept running into each other. They started a relationship.

Blessing attended lessons in the morning and then sold goods in a market, like her mother had always done. Many of Sierra Leone's traders worked hand to mouth, trying to earn enough to eat dinner each day, but Blessing had a plan. Despite being in a state where as many as 75 percent of women, and 59 percent of men, are illiterate,[2] she was academically driven. She wanted to be accepted into university and become a nurse.

In colonial times, Freetown had been known as the "Athens of Africa" because of the quality of education available, but by the twenty-first century universities were expensive and teaching standards were poor.[3] Job hires were often chosen through corruption and favors, tribalism, or patronage. The odds were stacked against most citizens, yet still they tried.

In 2012, Joseph finished his final exams and realized he could not afford to go to college. At most, he could have lasted one semester before running out of cash for fees and other expenses. He got a job riding a rented okada motorbike instead—carrying passengers, dodging traffic police who pestered him for bribes—and tried to ignore updates about former classmates who were building up qualifications, heading towards well-respected jobs.

"For me, now, nothing."

Blessing realized she was pregnant. The couple still did not live together, but Joseph knew his responsibilities were about to grow exponentially—and there was another challenge coming, too.

In 2014, an Ebola outbreak began. Many Sierra Leoneans had never heard of this deadly disease that made victims bleed from their noses, mouths, and other orifices and condemned the majority of those who contracted it to a painful death through organ failure or dehydration. Nationwide, there were only around one hundred and forty doctors—one for every fifty thousand people in the population.[4] Isolation centers were set up across the country, with makeshift mass graves nearby. Within months, bodies were being left to decompose in the streets.[5] Nearly four thousand victims would die by November 2015—part of a more than eleven thousand West African death toll.[6] Blessing's uncle was among them.

Sierra Leone's borders were shut to curb Ebola's spread, but there were unofficial ways to leave, and Joseph wanted out. As an eldest son, he was expected to earn enough to support his extended family. Joseph's mother was a farmer, but he did not want that kind of life for himself. He started talking about "greener pastures" and "taking life to the next level." He wanted to make money "fast" and told Blessing he could reach Europe, get a lucrative job, and send funds back to her. Blessing agreed that it was a good idea, even though they never discussed her going to join him; she had no notion of when they might meet again.

Across Earth, humans plot and plan. They take a myriad of actions in the hopes it will make their lives better. Joseph was no different. Poverty presents as a lack of opportunity, and Joseph seized on the biggest opportunity he could think of.

Joseph is bad with dates, but he described his departure as being after the Ebola outbreak, which Sierra Leone declared over in late 2015, and before the mudslide, which happened on August 14, 2017, on Freetown's Sugarloaf Mountain. Unusually heavy rains created a torrent of mud, burying poor families in homes they built on a steep slope out of necessity. No one knows the true death toll, though the World Bank identified at least 1,141 as dead or missing—the worst natural disaster in the country's history.[7] A year later, many bodies still had not been found.

Joseph and a friend raised $750 between them—a huge amount in a state where 2016 World Bank figures listed the average annual income as just $490.[8] They traveled overland to Gao in Mali, a human trafficking and smuggling hub nicknamed "The Ghetto." African migrants from across the region gather there, taking chances on which truck is the best bet to bring them across the Sahara Desert—a five- or six-day trip.[9] Human cargo travels north towards Algeria, and fridges and electrical appliances, or even noodles and pasta, come back in the other direction.[10] Any poor soul who dies on route, or falls out of the vehicle, is left in the sand. The UN says at least 690 people perished in the desert in 2017 alone, though the number is likely much higher.[11] Of the thirty people Joseph traveled with, six died.

"They sold me twice."

In Algeria, Joseph tried to find work, but he was worried about being caught without a permit and abandoned in the desert by security forces. He called his mother twice for money, and she took out a loan from a local women's cooperative to send it to him. Joseph says he went to Morocco, where he begged for food and unsuccessfully tried to storm the border fence into Spain. Then he went east, to Libya, where he attempted to cross the sea but was caught by the coastguard and locked up. He says one of his friends drowned. That's when Joseph contacted Blessing again.

––––––––

Across West Africa's hills and coasts, in its markets, churches, and mosques, are the widows of Libya. They are the women left behind, the ones who often do not know whether their husbands and boyfriends are alive anymore. While some women and girls go to Libya from West Africa, too, it is noticeably rarer. They are more likely to fly to Lebanon, Kuwait, the United Arab Emirates, or Oman as domestic workers, in trips organized through dodgy recruitment companies. Blessing considered making her own journey to the

Middle East but decided it was not worth the risk. Those women are regularly raped and even tortured, their passports confiscated while they toil for years with no respite until they are abandoned or deported without the pay they were promised in the first place. They return to stigma and accusations that they worked as prostitutes. Instead, Blessing resolved to hold down the fort at home, caring for her child, Joseph's relatives, and their aging parents while Joseph gambled for a better life for them all.

Blessing prayed and fasted for Joseph's safety, and eventually dropped out of school to focus on earning money. When she finally heard from her boyfriend again, he said the police had caught them. He was stuck in detention; everything was too difficult; he had no money left over for another boat journey and was ready to give up.

He sent her a number for the UN's International Organization for Migration, the UN agency that repatriates migrants from Libya to their home countries, but the person who answered was aggressive and shouting, she says. Then he gave her my number, which he received from a fellow detainee. Blessing told me her son was starving, that she needed Joseph back home. I forwarded her questions, and her boyfriend's documents, to a contact in IOM.

> "Please help me to talk with IOM so that my husband will be with me next week, please. I am not in a good condition now. Help me for the sake of Allah. I'm going down on my knees. I have no way to communicate with my husband because the police took his phone . . . I don't [know] what is wrong, my heart is stressed now as I'm talking to you. I am talking with tears in my eyes. I don't even have anything in my hands to pay the rent, there is no food with me at home, my child's school fees, there is nothing."

Joseph kept his phone in his boxer shorts, taking it to the toilet to record his pleas on WhatsApp. His voice was low. "Ma," he would say to me. "I want to go home." In detention, the guards held their noses as they looked at him, calling him smelly and saying detainees were "slaves." At night, he listened to the cries of women.

On October 24, 2018, Joseph signed his "voluntary return declaration form" with a fingerprint, a requirement of the system. "I understand that I may be interviewed and/or questioned by authorities upon arrival," the form read. "I further understand that IOM will not be in a position to interfere with rules and procedures established by airport or immigration authorities in transit or upon arrival. I acknowledge, for myself and for any person for whom I have the right to do so as well as for relevant heirs and estate, that IOM will not be held responsible for any damage caused, directly or indirectly, to me or any such person in connection with IOM assistance that derives from circumstances outside the control of IOM."

Under a question about his status, the "other" box was ticked, indicating that Joseph had no recognized rights to asylum. "Do you have concern that you/your dependents will be targeted for violence or abuse, including arrest or detention, in your country of origin?" Neither yes or no was ticked. He gave consent for his data to be used for research purposes, and his photo, too, though where that would go was not clear.

Joseph waited. His name was left off the next list of Sierra Leonean passengers who flew back. "We are not doing fine," he messaged on December 17, worrying he had been overlooked. I contacted IOM again. He was given a flight date: December 26. "I will never forget you in my life, may God bless you," Joseph messaged. That Christmas Eve, he wished me "compliments of the season," and asked me how I slept.

On New Year's Eve, I was delighted to get a message off Blessing's phone from Joseph himself. "Hello ma, is me Joseph K. Conteh. How are you? How the work, ma? Am now with my family, am so happy."

"May God bless you, may God take you to another level," messaged Blessing.

———

In Senegal, the journey towards Europe is called *la recherche*—"the search"; in Gambia, the "Back Way"; in Guinea, *"tounkan,"* or "the adventure." On a daily basis, West Africans face extreme poverty, endemic corruption, discrimination on the basis of tribalism, problems accessing education, and a lack of decent medical care. In many countries, government institutions do not function effectively and there is no social security net for citizens.

The absence of services that Europeans might take for granted was brought into sharp focus for me in 2018, when I happened across a human body on a beach during a reporting trip to Liberia, which neighbors Sierra Leone. It had been there for days, locals in this Monrovia neighborhood said. When I asked the health ministry about the dead man, authorities told me they had no funding for transport costs so regularly left abandoned corpses—people who died through violence or disease—lying in public areas for days before collection and burial could be arranged.

This is just one example, and an extreme one, but it underlines the societal struggles many people in this region are facing and the value they see placed on life by the authorities in charge. Tens of millions of West Africans live hand to mouth: whatever they earn that day determines how much they can eat. Studying is expensive, scholarships are rare, and jobs go to the well-connected. A journey to Europe can be perceived as the only option: a coming of age, a communal sacrifice, and a way to secure your family's future.[12]

When the EU began funding the Libyan coastguard to carry out interceptions on the Mediterranean Sea, West Africans were also caught in the vicious cycle between smugglers and detention centers in Libya. Given that they were not listed in the nine nationalities UNHCR could register for possible evacuation, a key part of European migration policy focused on so-called "voluntary humanitarian returns"—sending people back to their country of origin through the UN agency IOM. Between 2015 and 2020, EU Trust Fund money enabled IOM to return more than fifty thousand people from Libya to forty-four different countries.[13] Detainees were not officially charged or given court hearings, so these returns were their only legal way out of Libya's migrant detention centers, making them effectively a deportation.[14] From Libya, people have been sent back to countries including Nigeria, Sierra Leone, Guinea-Conakry, Ghana, the Gambia, and Mali.

"They say voluntary repatriation, but this is not voluntary, this is our way or the highway," said an aid worker who sat in on meetings with IOM about Libya. Libyan authorities were generally happy to get rid of West Africans who were stuck there, he added, because they did not have big diasporas or access to a lot of money, making them harder to for smugglers and militias to profit from. "[West Africans] are poor, they cannot extort them for anything. They will call their families who will sell the generator, the chicken, and can still not afford to pay the ransom. [Libyan authorities] don't waste their time on those. Those they deport through IOM and they keep holding the cash crop [of East Africans]."

Some IOM returnees even came from so-called "refugee-producing" countries. By mid-2019, more than fifty Eritreans had been returned from Libya through IOM, according to Eritrea's minister of information, meaning they were flown straight back to a dictatorship where human rights abuses are rife.[15]

In Triq al Sikka at the height of the 2018 tuberculosis outbreak, detainees recalled Eritrean embassy officials arriving to the detention center, with IOM, to encourage them to go home. "Why are you dying like this? Go to your country, you can live together with your family. Libya and UNHCR are using you as a business, why are you spending your time here?" one Eritrean recalled an official asking them. Despairing, and convincing themselves they would die of disease if they stayed, four men agreed. One had been having nightmares, remembering being tortured by smugglers. Everyone could tell he was floundering.

"They said here they are facing death and in our country it's the same. It's better that we die in our motherland. They definitely have stress and don't have a normal mind."

An IOM source told me the Eritreans arrived back in capital city Asmara, where they were put on buses to the regions they came from, though IOM staff did not accompany them. After that, it was unclear what would happen, but friends worried that they could be sent to the military or prison.

————

Online, IOM regularly posts videos celebrating its program repatriating Africans. There are filmed interviews with men and women disembarking from charter flights or working in bakeries and poultry farms back in their birth countries, cut to upbeat music.[16] One, from early 2017, showed Nigerians clapping and singing the P. Diddy song "Coming Home" on board a plane from Libya.[17] The intern who edited that video, Tenley Garrett, would later write a blog saying she became detached from the images she saw working for IOM, "because admitting that what I was witnessing was in reality absolutely horrific, or that local and international systems had failed to protect the rights and lives of hundreds of thousands of innocent people, kind of implicates me in the crime."[18]

From the IOM headquarters in Geneva, she described a "quick realization" that "the burden of covering rent . . . supporting a family (if you made time to have one), and affording basic amenities and the (extraordinarily high) cost of living in one of the world's wealthiest cities seemed to swallow up the sincere good-heartedness and eagerness-to-fix-the-world attitude that most newcomers feel upon first joining the ranks of the UN.

"[I would] sit back and feel utterly hopeless as I watched conniving people dirty the hallways of what looked to the outside world like an esteemed, distinguished, and benevolent organization seeking only the best for the oppressed," she wrote. "I started to question if these people (myself included) were really the good guys, if we even gave a damn, like we claimed to, about victims of abuse or children held in detainment camps or mothers given false identity papers and forced to work like slaves in countries far way. If we truly cared about the human faces of these stories, why did we modestly celebrate over shocking new developments overseas or the anomalous media recognition?"

Over the years in which I reported on migration and refugee issues, I, too, had been asked to take part in IOM-sponsored events. This included an invitation to speak at a training in Sierra Leone where returnees from Libya and local journalists were given lessons on how to produce stories about migration that might dissuade others from setting off for Europe (I declined). Similar sessions have taken place in other African countries, with one journalist attendee in Nigeria describing her surprise at finding out she was now being targeted by the type of EU-funded project she should be investigating. "We soon realized that no journalist in this room was going to learn to critically examine European Union (EU) migration policy," she later wrote. "This was a language course: a lesson in Migration-speak, as spoken in the EU."[19]

As IOM's work returning migrants increased, its budget did, too. By 2019, the agency was spending more than $2 billion a year, up from one eighth that in the late 1990s.[20] Nearly half came from the EU and its member states.[21]

The money did not always trickle down to returnees. People in countries including Sierra Leone, Ethiopia, and the Gambia told me that IOM staff promised them reintegration support if they agreed to leave Libya, such as money towards setting up businesses, but it did not materialize or was less than expected (IOM did not respond to my request for comment about this). Less than one in three returnees to Sudan received economic support, according to a Euronews investigation published in 2020, and similar figures seemed to be echoed elsewhere. Instead, those who took up the offer were faced with shame, debt, and unemployment.[22] A Harvard University study on Nigerian returnees found that the majority had no work after they got back.[23]

Loren B. Landau, a migration professor at Oxford University, called IOM an "agent of the EU." He said it cannot be called a voluntary choice to leave when the alternative is staying in a detention center and barely being fed, adding that IOM is not subject to much scrutiny. "The only people they essentially report to are the people who are paying them to do this work. If they report to the EU on what they've done the EU is going to be happy," Landau said, when we spoke on the phone. "The EU I don't think cares, as long as the program remains effective."

During a face-to-face interview in early 2020, Federico Soda, who became head of IOM in Libya the year before, told me that only a quarter of the people who left Libya through the EU-funded voluntary return program were coming directly from detention centers. The other 75 percent were not incarcerated at the time of departure, something which gave him "some comfort" in that it was more "acceptable," he said. They were generally living independently in Tripoli and other cities, though many had also been caught up in the cycle of smugglers and detention centers at various points.

"Do you have concerns that people are being forced to go back to places when it's not really a choice?" I asked.

"I don't have those concerns," Soda responded. "I think you're right, we have to be realistic about what the options these people have are. And I think if they had better options it might not be what they choose, but I don't think that means that it's not . . . voluntary. It's not forced, but it is a lifeline out of a very bad situation. But I still . . . the trauma of the experience for a lot of these young men and women is very serious. I think that the repatriation is probably for a lot of them just about as badly as things could end. Obviously, they didn't leave thinking of coming back in that way without much of a success story. So I think that's also probably quite hard on them."

———

Joseph's flight back to Sierra Leone was his first time on a plane. He watched in wonder as it "entered the cloud." The turbulence that came later felt like a galloping horse. His fear of flying made eating impossible. He transited in Tunisia and again in Morocco. Later, I would make the same final approach towards Freetown's airport, Lungi, the plane looping in to the coast over deep green forest and an expanse of sea.

Lungi is separated from the capital by a large estuary. Wealthier arrivals can get a water taxi for forty dollars that jets across ten miles of choppy waves after seated passengers pull bright orange lifejackets over their heads. Those who cannot afford this luxury take an overcrowded ferry or buses, which drive for as long as four hours across bumpy dirt roads.

In Aberdeen, on the northern tip of the city, cargo ships hulk across the horizon, passing casinos lit up with neon lights and fancy hotels with rows of identical white balconies. They are heavy against the big, cat-like speed of multideck motorboats or the long wooden canoes the local fishers use, one man standing shirtless at the helm while the others crouch behind him.

When I first arrived, I stayed in a mostly empty hotel a bit out of town. It vertically jutted out of flat ground between a mountain and a long, empty beach, which I walked through rice fields to get to. Dotted across the land-scape around us were a mix of ruined homes and half-built houses: an odd clash of new hope and faded dreams. At night, the orange sun dissolved into the glistening water.

During the week, Freetown's outer beaches had the feel of an abandoned holiday town. In the 1980s, Sierra Leone had a booming tourism industry, but the civil war, and then the Ebola outbreak, put things on hold. More recently, the coronavirus pandemic had shut down foreign travel again. There were a smattering of white people in bikinis or swimming trunks lounging outside colorful restaurants and bars—mostly diplomats, charity or UN workers. Like many beach towns in Europe, there was an undercurrent of unhappiness, a sense that while the foreigners found time to relax, locals were trapped there.

Life was sharply divided between wealthy Westerners and most Sierra Leoneans. One night, I went to a pool party in a huge gated compound, high above the city's shining lights, where staff of a certain embassy live with their families. Each "expat" was designated a multibedroom bungalow. They were not allowed to use public transport, meaning people without cars barely left—but they hardly needed to. They danced and drank, or cooled down in the pool, drinks floating beside them in inflatable flamingo and pineapple-shaped cup holders.

I did not want to talk about the reporting I was doing, but an embassy employee pushed me on it before telling me it was pointless questioning the status quo, that nothing would change. "The people in Europe, who are the 'haves,' are not going to be willing to equalize with the 'have nots,'" he said. "No European government would agree to the free movement of people, even if there are moral and historical reasons for it."

As in most African countries, foreign charity workers in Sierra Leone lived a nice life, too, getting driven around in shiny white land cruisers, going to beach resorts on the weekend, and being waved through police checkpoints where Sierra Leoneans would be forced to pay undeserved bribes. The daily subsistence allowance for visiting UN workers, on top of their usual salaries, was $254 a day.[24] It made me think again about who foreign aid, this multibillion-dollar industry, was serving in the long term. Surely allowing migration to richer countries was a necessary kind of aid, too, letting Africans earn money from the systems that had abused them for so long, send it to their families, and eventually fly back themselves if they wanted to. In 2017, while Joseph was in Libya, remittance flows to Sub-Saharan Africa were expected to be worth $34 billion—significantly higher even than the EU Trust Fund spending.[25]

Being desperately poor is not a reason to be granted asylum. If Joseph had reached Europe, he was unlikely to be given the legal right to stay.[26] Yet Sierra Leone was becoming even more impoverished, while Europe became richer. Between 2017 and 2018, while Joseph was in Libya, a new global billionaire was created every two days.[27] In 2019, Oxfam said the world's twenty-six richest people owned as much as the poorest half of our planet.[28]

———

I began to imagine a link between Joseph's return and something that took place a long time before, when another group arrived in Sierra Leone after being abused by Europe and North America.

For more than one hundred and forty years, from the seventeenth century, as many as fifty thousand people were sent across the sea as slaves from Sierra Leone's Bunce Island, one of around forty major slave forts on the West African coast.[29] Relics of Sierra Leone's slave-trading past have made their way into our lives today. I had not known, for example, that the hymn "Amazing Grace" was written by an English former slave ship captain, John Newton, who regularly sailed out of Sierra Leone with human cargo. Later in life, he turned to religion, becoming an Anglican minister and abolitionist, and penned the song now estimated to be performed around ten million times a year—sung publicly by everyone from Aretha Franklin, to Johnny Cash, to Barack Obama.[30]

In 1787, Freetown was founded as a home for rescued and repatriated slaves. The initial group of four hundred came from London.[31] A few years later, more than one thousand more arrived from Nova Scotia in Canada, and in 1820 a group arrived from New York, following the abolishment of the transatlantic slave trade in the US.[32]

Some of the people brought to Freetown were known as "recaptives": they had been intercepted at sea by the British navy (Britain colonized Sierra Leone in 1808).[33] Life was not easy for them. They were born in different African countries but had to build a new life together, even as their continent continued to be looted by the West. The still-spoken national language, Krio, is a form of pidgin English that formulated among these disparate Africans. "How de body?" means "how are you?"

"De body fine," comes the reply.

Across Sierra Leone, the stamps of colonizers remain in the names they left behind: Aberdeen, Waterloo, Kent, York. To the north of Freetown is

White Man's Bay. The US would later pay half a million dollars to refurbish Bunce Island and ready it for tourists.[34]

After slavery ended, there was one early, initially promising example of migration from Sierra Leone to Europe. In 1873, Christian Cole, a Sierra Leonean, was said to be the first black student to study at Oxford University.[35] Cole read classics and spoke at the Oxford Union. He would later become the first black African to practice law in an English court, an environment where he must have felt desperately alone. The odds were still stacked against him. He is said to have moved back to Africa after he could not get enough work as a barrister and died of smallpox in Zanzibar at the age of just thirty-three.

———

Sierra Leone got independence in 1961, but that did not stop its plunder by the West.[36] "It should be the Saudi Arabia of Africa, but it's not," wrote Greg Campbell in *Blood Diamonds*, the nonfiction exposé that inspired the multi-Oscar-nominated movie starring Leonardo DiCaprio. Its people remain some of the poorest in the world.[37]

History books say that diamonds were first discovered in Sierra Leone in the 1930s by a British geologist, J. D. Pollett. Between 1930 and 1970, the diamond reserve he found produced more than 50 million carats.[38] The lure of this treasure would eventually spark a war over profit and territory, which lasted from 1991 to 2002. The Revolutionary United Front (RUF) rebel group originally promised to equitably share diamond revenues, but instead became known for their incredible cruelty towards civilians. Its fighters gave their missions names like "Operation No Living Thing" and had a regiment christened the Bastard Brigade, so called because it was formed of orphans and led by a commander called Man Friday.[39] Like Joseph described happening to his grandfather, Sierra Leonean rebels would chop off body parts—hands, lips, breasts, tongues, ears, or legs—along with raping, looting, and executing. At least fifty thousand people were killed during the conflict, many by indoctrinated child soldiers.[40]

As this violence continued, the UN ranked Sierra Leone as the least developed country on earth.[41] The UN's peacekeeping mission there became the world's largest and most expensive, deploying more than seventeen and a half thousand soldiers from thirty-one countries and spending $612 million in 2001 alone.[42] One study found that 99 percent of people interviewed in Freetown suffered some degree of starvation; 90 percent saw people being wounded or killed; and at least half lost someone close to them. One in three people were held hostage, while more than half of the interviewees witnessed torture.[43]

Even today in Sierra Leone, the diamond trade continues. In the Radisson Blu Mammy Yoko, one of Freetown's most upmarket hotels, diamond exporter Age International has an in-house office. When I asked a local journalist whether Sierra Leoneans had finally started to benefit from this business, he shrugged: "Not really."

That the West has profited from Sierra Leone is undeniable, and some academics and activists argue that allowing migration from Africa to Europe is an essential form of reparations, given all that has been stolen from the continent. In 2019, E. Tendayi Achiume, the UN Special Rapporteur on contemporary forms of racism, racial discrimination, xenophobia, and related intolerance, wrote in Stanford Law Review that "economic migrants of a certain kind have compelling claims to national admission and inclusion in countries that today unethically insist on a right to exclude [them]," arguing this would simply be a matter of "corrective, distributive justice," given that the "European colonial project involved the out-migration of at least 62 million Europeans to colonies across the world between the nineteenth and the first half of the twentieth century alone."[44]

On top of arguments around corrective justice and reparations, there are questions around what constitutes a threat to life that go beyond the recognized legal definitions. At the time that Joseph left his country, life expectancy was just fifty-one for men and fifty-two for women (up from just thirty-eight the year Joseph was born).[45] By their mid-twenties, men and women had realistically finished half their lives, while the average European was not even a third through theirs.[46] Western European men lived an extra twenty-nine years on average, and women thirty-two.

In 2016, UNICEF said Sierra Leone had the worst maternal mortality rate on the planet, with one in seventeen mothers likely to die giving birth.[47] Of every ten children born, one would die before their fifth birthday.[48] A nurse in a Freetown children's hospital told me staff applauded on the rare days they did not lose a child from malnutrition, malaria, or other preventable illnesses; usually the death toll was around 20 percent of admissions. When the coronavirus pandemic hit, there were no ventilators available in public hospitals, and patients died because their families could not afford to buy $75 canisters of oxygen.[49] Considering these factors, the differentiation made between so-called "economic migrants" and "refugees" did not seem so clear cut.

———

This is not a love story, but it is a human story. When Blessing saw Joseph for the first time after his return, she thought he looked physically and mentally fit, though he carried barely any belongings, not even a phone. He had no money, either, a travesty after all he had put her through, she thought.

There were months of silence, and then, in May 2019, Blessing messaged me to ask how everything was going. I inquired after Joseph. "That man, as soon as he came home, he disappointed me for another woman. Joseph didn't want to know about me and my son," she replied. "But I left everything to God, God will fight for me. God will take control." The man "scattered," she explained in Krio. "He didn't play me well."

I would later meet Blessing and Joseph in person, separately, numerous times. She cooked me chicken and fried plantain with lavish dollops of

Hellmann's mayonnaise, then listed her worries in the dark room she rented alone, sitting on a mattress covered with a Barcelona Football Club sheet. Foodstuffs were piled in boxes on the floor, her clothes hanging on a peg on the wall. A plastic covering on the ground was decorated with flowers and square patterns. Her son was back in her family's village—she had not seen him in more than a year. She said she was too embarrassed to go there empty-handed, certain people would talk badly about her. "Men neglect responsibilities, women take it all on," she complained.

There are many things that a relationship cannot survive. Their accounts of what happened over those difficult years would align and diverge, as Blessing was subsumed with bitterness, or Joseph wondered if what he told me could create "problems." It made me question who I was to be asking this former couple intimate questions about their personal life.

Joseph said he caught Blessing with another man, and, as she was already a financial burden, he cut her off. She said he cheated. Either way, the love was gone. When you live life on the edge, everything is immediate; you do not have time for olive branches or slow reconciliations.

One Sunday afternoon, I got on the back of an okada motorbike heading towards Joseph's neighborhood, Blackhall Road, in eastern Freetown. We sped down dusty roads, past boys playing football, their goalposts marked out with stones. To my left were roofs of turquoise, baby blue and dusky pink, under a cloudy sky. On the right were rolling green hills. A strolling man wore a T-shirt that read BONJOUR BITCHES. Some hustlers held a rope across the road and demanded money to let us pass. The motorbike driver asked which continent I came from and laughed when I said Europe. Graffiti at an intersection read: "When there is corruption, individuals gain but the country loses."

Joseph literally lived on a precipice. He greeted me, and we climbed steep steps carved from rock to reach the home he shared with his new fiancée, Khadija; his friend, Yusuf, who also unsuccessfully tried to reach Europe; and more than ten other family members. Yusuf began smoking marijuana heavily when he got back to Sierra Leone, robbing Joseph to feed his addiction and later threatening him, too. When I saw Yusuf, he was red-eyed, his body lax, as he ranted about the hardships he had been through. In contrast, Joseph was sharp and warm.

The Atlantic Ocean was visible from the concrete ledge where we sat on multiple evenings, watching the sun set and lights start to shimmer. We were on the slope of a mountain, every layer filled with construction and human life. A cloud of dust rose from the football pitch below, where two local teams—one in a white uniform and one in blue—faced off against each other. It coated our faces, adding another light brown layer to the corrugated metal roofs of shops and homes. Joseph could spot friends on the road beneath us, which was lined with small stores, some painted with UK or US flags. They called up to him.

Houses were packed together in the surrounding area. Joseph gave me a tour. We stepped over muddy streams of water, passing children pulling toy cars fashioned from yellow jerrycans. Joseph introduced me as the journalist who helped him return from Libya. "She's come to see how I'm doing," he excitedly told an older woman, who smiled and said she knew what a hard time he had been through. Close to the football pitch, Joseph greeted another fellow IOM returnee, who had come from Algeria.

For a year after his return, Joseph says he slept in the local "cinema," a room created from corrugated iron with three TVs where people pay an entry fee to watch football matches. At night, it becomes a shelter for boys and men who have nowhere else to go. When I visited, an unconscious man was sprawled out on the floor.

High up another hill, we could see Joseph's mother's house. She waved at us once, a dot in the distance, and he smiled widely. Another day, we climbed to her, hiking thirty minutes up uneven, impossibly steep stone steps and dirt slopes so treacherous—even in dry season—that Joseph held my hand to stop me from falling. Joseph's relatives would make the same climb with jerrycans after fetching water; there was none running in the house. We sat in a sparse, cement room as his mother told me she had been suffering from chest pain for years, which made it impossible for her to work as a palm wine trader, like before. She could not afford the cost of getting tests at a hospital and did not have the energy to descend the hill anyway, so she bought pills and drips supplied by a "quack doctor"—an unlicensed and unqualified drug salesperson who walked from house to house flogging his wares. Suddenly animated, she explained that she had been preparing to go to the market the day Joseph unexpectedly came back to Sierra Leone and broke a bucket in her rush to run to him when she heard his voice outside.

———

Freetown is a hub of activity. Boys and girls do somersaults on the beach, play volleyball, sell crafts, and sometimes breathe fire for money. There are parties, packed markets, and fervent preaching. This liveliness can distract from the lack of protection for the vulnerable. Joseph was struggling, and he was not alone.

In a third-floor office near Freetown's ferry terminal, I visited the Advocacy Network Against Irregular Migration, an association founded by returnees from Libya. IOM had paid their $1,500 annual rent, but the organization's leaders told me they were volunteers with little other funding. They attended government meetings to discuss new migration-related legislation, while requesting assistance for their members, and spoke on local media encouraging other Sierra Leoneans not to make the same journey they had attempted. Along with a local colleague, I was the first journalist to visit in two years. In something like desperation, founder Sheku Bangura invited more than one hundred returnees to gather and meet me. There were men who had returned from Libya and women who traveled for domestic work in the Middle East, where they were raped and abused before being deported.

Bangura recalled being dumped at Sierra Leone's national stadium, with around two hundred others, when they came back from Libya with

IOM in 2017. "There was no place for us," he said mournfully, explaining why he set up the organization. He wore a short-sleeved mauve shirt and tie and sat behind a desk with UK and US flags propped upright at the front (he said the flags had no relation to his work, he just liked them). Somewhat ironically, given that his new position involved advocating for people to give up their dreams of Europe, he told me he had managed to marry a UK resident the previous year and was hoping he could get a visa to travel there at last, though he was concerned the organization would fall apart without his leadership. Even with a marriage, the process to get a visa was arduous, humiliating, and expensive. "The real problem is the way the [Western] embassies treat the people," he complained. "Some [Sierra Leoneans] have been rejected five or six times for visas because they're Africans."

He said it was normal for relationships to break up after one half of a couple came home from North Africa or the Middle East. "Husbands reject the women when they come back, saying they were doing prostitution . . . Women have high expectations. When [men] come back with nothing, the women will reject them."

Returnees often start taking drugs, he said. They feel shame and can be easily offended, which leads to fights. Their thoughts keep cycling through what they have experienced. When I asked the organization's media manager, Sisqo Alimamy Kargbo—a tall, well-dressed man in a wine-colored suit—whether there was an image that haunted him from his own journey, he described Libyan guards lining bread rolls up on the ground, peeing on them, and smirking as detainees still scrabbled to eat them afterwards.

In Sierra Leone, traffickers and smugglers continued to advertise on Facebook. Legal repercussions were a new and rare thing; the country's first human trafficking convictions only happened in 2020, according to IOM.[50] Returnees were even tempted to try their luck a second time.

When I asked Joseph why he was not involved with the returnees' association, he told me they demanded a fee before he could be recognized as a member. He was in debt, and it rankled him to be asked for cash again, so soon after returning home. (I questioned Bangura about this; he said they used to ask returnees for one or two dollars as a registration fee, after they first set up the organization, but they made everything free in 2019.)

————

Joseph still had lingering mental and physical pains from his time in Libya. He felt a constant "cold" inside his body and had problems in his lungs. One finger broke when he tried to escape a detention center, and it never properly healed. He received some assistance from IOM, but not as much as he said he was promised.

He applied to join Sierra Leone's military in 2019, but said he was told he would need to pay a large bribe to be accepted. ("I want to defend this country," he explained.) In early 2021, Joseph tried to join the police force, but said he was told the same. If he was a police officer, he would never ask poor civilians for money, he declared emphatically. (Later, Joseph asked me to bribe a recruiting police officer with three million leones ($300), so he could secure a position. I declined.)

The police or military would have been a means to an end. He wanted to study to become an accountant but the fees were too hefty, and with a security job he would have a chance at being supported while receiving a qualification. He worked instead as a keke taxi driver in a rented tuktuk-style vehicle. It earned him roughly 100,000 leones a day ($10), but came with its own struggles. While I was in Freetown, Joseph spent a day in a police station after he was accused of parking badly. Weeks later, as Sierra Leone marked its sixtieth independence anniversary, thousands of motorbike drivers would take to the streets to protest police exploitation and corruption, saying constant arrests and overregulation had turned into a profit-making racket, of which they were the victims. Security forces fired off tear gas in retaliation. At least one driver died in the ensuing chaos, with an eyewitness saying they saw his brains splashed over the street. "This is the main reason so many people want to leave this country, this is why they do the Temple

Run," a motorbike rider, who had just been released from a police cell after paying a bribe, complained to me in the aftermath. The man who rented Joseph the keke taxi took it back shortly afterwards to loan it to someone else; once more, Joseph's income was gone.

Three families were now reliant on Joseph: his fiancée's, his mother's, and his sister's. Joseph began to think about traveling again, despite knowing there was no way he could legally get a passport. He told me, quietly, that he was contemplating returning to Libya to make another attempt at reaching Europe. Even then, after all he had been through, he was considering another Temple Run.

CHAPTER 12

BRUSSELS: MIGRATION CRISIS "OVER"

"NO, I don't care. Show me pictures of coffins, show me bodies floating in water, play violins and show me skinny people looking sad . . . There is no stopping them . . . What we need are gunships sending these boats back to their own country . . . Make no mistake, these migrants are like cockroaches. They might look a bit 'Bob Geldof's Ethiopia circa 1984,' but they are built to survive a nuclear bomb. They are survivors. Once gunships have driven them back to their shores, boats need to be confiscated and burned on a huge bonfire. Drilling a few holes in the bottom of anything suspiciously resembling a boat would be a good idea, too."

–BRITISH COLUMNIST KATIE HOPKINS WRITING IN THE SUN, THE UK'S THEN-BIGGEST SELLING NEWSPAPER, APRIL 2015[1]

"Enough of Sicily being the refugee camp of Europe.
I will not stand by and do nothing."

–MATTEO SALVINI, FORMER INTERIOR MINISTER OF ITALY, JUNE 2018[2]

"The reduced migrant flow in the Central Mediterranean Sea proves today that the model described above has been successful."

–OPERATION SOPHIA BIANNUAL REPORT, JULY 2019, WHICH REFERS TO TRAINING AND EQUIPPING THE LIBYAN COASTGUARD[3]

On October 3, 2013, a boat carrying more than five hundred people caught fire and sank within sight of Lampedusa, the windswept island that marks the southernmost part of Italy. After hours grasping for life in the water, just 155 people were rescued, including a mere five of the eighty women who had been on board.[4] A massive retrieval operation led to the recovery of 339 bodies, including a young mother who had just given birth, her baby still attached by an umbilical cord.[5]

Italy's president Giorgio Napolitano called the tragedy a "slaughter of innocents." José Manuel Barroso, the president of the European Commission, traveled to Lampedusa and said he would never forget seeing "hundreds of coffins lined up" there.[6]

The shipwreck jolted the Italian government into action. It launched a major search-and-rescue mission, Operation Mare Nostrum, within three weeks. Mare Nostrum translates from Latin as "our sea," but the Romans used that term to refer to the Mediterranean Sea itself. Over the next year, the Italian mission rescued roughly 150,000 migrants and refugees, at a cost of nine million euro every month.[7]

When I interviewed him in February 2020, Enrico Letta, who was prime minister of Italy between early 2013 and 2014, would say he was still "very proud" of their response to the Lampedusa tragedy, but he wished Mare Nostrum had been supported by the rest of Europe. By then, the slim, bespectacled academic had become the dean at the School of International Affairs in France's Sciences Po university. He told me the Lampedusa tragedy was completely unexpected. It shocked the public, provoking an outpouring of empathy that has not been seen since. "In the very beginning, what happened after Lampedusa was something completely different, it was horror and sadness."

In the seven years before the shipwreck, the EU had allocated nearly two billion euro towards solidifying its external borders.[8] This was despite all European countries being signatories to the 1951 Refugee Convention, meaning refugees could not be penalized if they entered a country illegally looking for asylum; could not be sent back to a place where they would be in danger; and their appeals for protection must be heard. Mare Nostrum was an attempt to do good, but Italian politicians complained that other European countries should be contributing. In November 2014, it was ended and replaced with an EU operation called Triton, which only patrolled up to thirty miles off the Italian coast and had a significantly smaller budget. The number of drownings increased tenfold.[9]

To Letta, it makes sense that Africans try to reach Europe. "It's not their fault. We live in a world of inequalities," he told me. "Geographical inequalities, social inequalities. You can't make these people guilty." It was the reaction to these journeys that was "mismanaged," he said. The biggest initial mistake was acting like search-and-rescue was a negotiable part of policy, when saving lives should always be an imperative. "Search-and-rescue is something that is not related to migration policy. It is something that is related to our constitutions, to our values," Letta said, adding that European countries were more responsible than European institutions for how everything developed. "The European institutions did what the member states wanted them to do, or allowed them to do."

We were sitting in the foyer of his university. In a room nearby, academics and lawyers debated who was culpable for the tens of thousands of Mediterranean deaths before breaking for a lunch of salads, sandwiches, and canapés. The conference was partially sponsored by the EU itself.[10]

"A huge number of people have died," I said. "Do you think there's ever going to be any reckoning, or that there should be?"

"What does it mean, reckoning?" Letta asked.

"Where you face up to what happened and analyze it," I answered.

"I hope so," he said. "But the big problem is the shift in public opinion. Public opinion has completely shifted in the last five years."

"So potentially it's the European public that are guilty, really?" I said.

He almost laughed, before catching himself. "It's a mix, it's a mix."

"Can something else happen to shock the public opinion?" I asked him.

"Unfortunately, I don't think so . . . Today there is a sort of business as usual, [refugees and migrants] die because they want to come."

"Do you have any guilt about not doing enough?" I asked Letta.

"I tried. It's not my responsibility to judge myself."

"Is there anything that makes you feel hopeful?"

"No, I'm very pessimistic," he replied.

———

In April 2015, two more devastating shipwrecks, in which roughly 1,100 people are thought to have perished, occurred just six days apart. The dead came from around twenty countries, as far apart as Bangladesh and Mauritania. Around one hundred children were thought to be among them.[11] I covered what became known as the "Black April" incidents as a staff journalist for VICE News.[12]

A month later, a new EU military effort called Operation Sophia was launched, with the aim of disrupting the "business model of human smuggling" in the Central Mediterranean by European forces boarding and seizing vessels.[13] Given that the operation had little focus on lifesaving, it felt cynical that it was named after a baby born to a rescued Somali woman on a German navy ship. Speaking in Rome in September 2015, then-EU foreign policy chief Federica Mogherini said the moniker was given "to honor the lives of the people we are saving, the lives of people we want to protect, and to pass the message to the world that fighting the smugglers and the criminal networks is a way of protecting human life."[14] The subsequent destruction of the boats used by refugees and migrants actually resulted in the journeys becoming more dangerous, as smugglers began to send out cheaper dinghies instead of the sturdier, costlier wooden vessels.

The arrival of hundreds of thousands of refugees in Europe between 2015 and 2016 sparked a surge in anti-immigrant, xenophobic, and racist sentiment across the continent. This alarmed some political leaders and was capitalized on by others. While the UK dramatically voted to leave the EU completely on June 23, 2016, after pro-Brexit campaigns focused on anti-immigration scaremongering, other countries also experienced political upheavals.

Poland, Bulgaria, and Denmark were among a raft of countries with growing far-right movements in the years following the so-called "European migrant crisis."[15] French liberals were shaken when Front National leader Marine Le Pen won 21.3 percent of the vote in the first round of France's 2017 presidential election, compared to 24.01 percent for Emmanuel Macron, the eventual winner. The lawyer and certified cat breeder, who shoots as a hobby, took over her political party from her Holocaust-denying father. She has compared Muslims praying in the streets to a Nazi occupation, and called immigration "the engine of insecurity in our country."[16]

Months later, in September 2017, Alternativ für Deutschland (AfD) became the first far-right group to enter Germany's Bundestag since World War Two, taking 94 of its 709 seats.[17] In Hungary, where Prime Minister Viktor Orbán decried "migrant armies" and "Muslim invaders" while building a razor wire fence at his southern border, human rights groups worried the country was descending into full-scale authoritarianism.[18]

European politicians with more moderate or leftwing views struggled to know how to respond. In his final state of the union speech in 2018, after four years as EU Commission president, Jean-Claude Juncker warned against the rise of "exaggerated nationalism . . . riddled with both poison and deceit."[19]

———

One of most notable and consequential rises of the far-right happened in Italy. Between June 2018 and September 2019, League party leader Matteo Salvini was Italy's interior minister. During his time in office, the man nicknamed "Il Capitano" was labeled "the most feared man in Europe" by *TIME* magazine.[20] He compared African migrants to slaves, saying he would rather Europeans procreated instead of inviting in "new slaves to replace the children we're not having"[21] and claimed that "immigrants" committed "seven hundred crimes" a day.[22]

In March 2019, the EU ceased sea patrols in the Central Mediterranean completely, after Salvini and Italy's populist government threatened to have Operation Sophia shut down.[23] A report that year said Europe had already trained 355 members of the Libyan coastguard and navy. The average distance migrant boats were covering before interception was 135 nautical miles, while the Libyan coastguard—which it said had thirty ships operating—responded to more than 50 percent of cases, stopping a majority of attempts.[24]

In a factsheet, the European Commission declared the so-called migration crisis "over." It was two months before the May 2019 European elections, and many incumbent politicians feared losing their seats to far-right candidates (the subsequent results did lead to greater representation for populist and far-right parties than ever before, though it was not quite as significant as anticipated).[25] Incoming European Commission president, German physician Ursula von der Leyen, created a new post called the "vice president for protecting our European way of life," which would be responsible for migration policy, in what was seen as an adoption of far-right rhetoric.[26]

"African governments [are] under the control of the first world. Me, I am always in pain about my people."

All this time, drownings continued. Between 2014 and 2020, more than twenty thousand men, women, and children would die on the Mediterranean Sea.[27] Yet independent search-and-rescue efforts were slowly but effectively being criminalized, as were efforts to help refugees on land. From 2014 through 2019, more than two hundred and fifty Europeans were arrested, charged, investigated, or threatened with fines or imprisonment for supporting refugees and migrants, according to data gathered by news website Open Democracy. They listed cases involving rural farmers, pensioners, a university professor, local politicians, firefighters, and priests, most of whom provided transport, shelter, or food in countries including France, the UK, Germany, and Spain. Renting accommodation to migrants could attract criminal charges, as could driving them in a car. Reporters suggested this was just a snapshot: the real number of arrests could be much higher.[28]

———

The EU, which is both a political and economic union, was set up following the Second World War with the aim of ensuring lasting peace across the continent. Around 446 million people live within its roughly four million square kilometers, surrounded by more than 12,000 kilometers of land borders and 45,000 kilometers of sea borders and dotted with six hundred international airports.[29] Its founding values are listed as human dignity, freedom, democracy, equality, the rule of law, and human rights.[30] One of the EU's key objectives is the free movement of people, goods, and services. But this is not a right for everyone.

In 2018, a study found that almost 1,000 kilometers of border walls had been erected by EU member states and states in the European Schengen travel area since the fall of the Berlin Wall nineteen years before. Seven new border walls were built in 2015 alone.[31]

In tandem, Frontex, the EU border and coastguard agency, grew steadily—its budget soaring from a little over six million euro in 2005 to 460 million in 2020. Frontex was established in 2004 and headquartered in Warsaw, Poland. In 2019, it began a recruitment drive to hire its own uniformed border guards, with a plan to have ten thousand in place by 2027. By that point, European taxpayers will have spent 5.6 billion euro on the agency.[32]

Yet it is increasingly mired in scandals, including accusations it coordinated the illegal pushback of refugees in the Aegean Sea off Greece, with its officials later lying to cover this up.[33] In 2021, former deputy head of Frontex Gil Arias Fernández told *The Guardian* newspaper that he was worried abuses against migrants and refugees are ignored by the agency. "Frontex pains me," he said. "I do not believe that the agency has proactively violated the rights of migrants, but there are reasons to believe that it has turned a blind eye."

Arias claimed he lost out on the top job in Frontex after he failed to link refugees with the Paris terrorism attack in November 2015, when 130 people were killed and 350 wounded (Frontex spokespeople did not reply to my request for comment on this). He left his position that year, but said increasing numbers of people with extreme far-right views may have joined the EU border agency in the meantime because there was "no filter" in the recruitment system. "You cannot prevent people with extremist ideas from entering, unless they clearly express their position in favor of hate crimes, xenophobia, and racism," he said.[34]

———

A few months after I started getting contacted by refugees in Libya's detention centers, I was invited to the European Parliament to speak to politicians about my reporting. I took a Eurostar through the Channel Tunnel and across France, arriving in Brussels on a gray November day, and made my way to the labyrinthine EU buildings, which had begun to symbolize, for me, the way the EU operated.

Through glass corridors crossing the outside concourse, I could see posters promoting the EU's 2018 Sakharov Prize For Freedom of Thought winner, Ukrainian film director Oleg Sentsov. "The NGOs protecting human rights and saving migrant lives across the Mediterranean Sea" had been listed as a finalist.

In another window nearby, there was a photo of a grinning brown-haired white boy with his arms around his mother. They sat on a nice couch with framed family pictures lined up behind. "Because we need to work together to secure our borders," was written beside them, along with the image of a coastguard vessel at sea.

The most high-profile person I met in Brussels was Claude Moraes, a British Labour Party politician and the chair of the European Parliament's Civil Liberties, Justice, and Home Affairs Committee. Moraes had been listed as the most influential UK Members in the European Parliament by think tank Vote Watch Europe.[35] I told him about the hundreds of children in detention, about the role of Europe, about the thousands of people desperate to be saved, and about the Somali man Abdulaziz burning himself to

death. Moraes responded that it was already all over the news. I was surprised, given I felt there was still very little coverage considering the scale of
what was happening, and only I had reported on Abdulaziz's death by then.[36]
Maybe he was reading my articles, I said. Maybe, he conceded.

I explained I was a journalist, that it was not my role to propose exact
solutions, but I wanted to make sure European politicians were aware of the
consequences of what they were doing. Surely someone should be held responsible? Moraes said it was difficult to implement change when public
opinion and political will had shifted so far away from empathizing.

In a meeting of the Council for Civil Liberties later that morning, time
was allocated to speak about the Central Mediterranean and what was happening to refugees returned to Libya.[37] We sat in a big room named after
József Antall, the first democratically elected prime minister of Hungary.
His father, a government commissioner for refugees, is said to have saved
the lives of thousands of Polish Jews during the Second World War by issuing them with documents.[38]

"This matter has been on the agenda a number of times," Moraes said,
opening the session. "Colleagues will have seen all the various press reports
and so on. I've had some discussions with a journalist who has very ably
produced some of those."[39] He would go on to call some of the EU propos-
als regarding how to deal with refugees in the Mediterranean Sea
"Kafka-[esque]."[40]

The invited speakers, including representatives from the European
Commission, the European External Action Service, and the IOM—all
white men in suits—sat in a raised section at the front, faced by a collection
of parliamentarians, their assistants, and translators.[41] They each spoke
briefly to the attendees, speaking broadly and reiterating their stances in a
way that made it easy to forget there were thousands of real humans caught
up in this nightmare right at that moment. The European Commission
representative—Michele Avino—was asked if they would consider suspending support to the Libyan coastguard and whether they were making

efforts to get more refugees to safety. He did not answer directly, instead saying the number of arrivals in Europe that year was 80 percent lower than the same period the previous year.[42] Libyan coastguard members chosen for trainings were vetted, he added, and human rights segments were always included.

Dutch politician Sophie in 't Veld interrupted. "We've been listening now to lots of technocratic babble, we didn't get an answer to the question. The questions are very simple. What are you doing to evacuate people, and what are you doing to make sure that they are not put in a place where their lives are in danger? How difficult can it be?" she asked.

Moraes said he was worried attendees would get "wound up" and leave the room if they could not ask questions, but then allowed the other men to focus on what they identified as their "key points."

Vincent Piket, the spokesperson for the European External Action Service, said the EU had been "strengthening border management" and improving conditions in the detention centers, including by "refurbishing" them, while putting pressure on Libyan authorities to close them down.[43] He said 34,000 people had already been sent back to their home countries from Libya and therefore "rescued."

"Detention centers, we visit them every time we can through our ambassador, through our other staff members of the EU delegation, of course we work together closely with the UN organizations," Piket added later. "Why do we go there? Just to make it clear to the Libyan authorities that we don't accept the situation as it is. Secondly, we go there in order to see that the assistance we're providing to these centers to refurbish them to some sort of adequacy, to try and ensure food supply, that that works. But as I said earlier, our policy is to have these centers closed."[44] This was a long-term goal, he said.

German politician Cornelia Ernst interjected. "Is there any degree of moral shame alongside all the nonsense that they're telling us here? I find this outrageous. This is shameful for the EU. It's shameful for each individual that's sitting here."[45]

In the end, the session ran out of time. There had been a lot of talking, but nothing was agreed and many of the posited questions were not even adequately answered. Everyone in that room would now move onto other issues. No change was possible from here, I felt.

"At this time, human rights is sleeping. Life [is] very cheap."

As the speakers gathered their belongings and said their goodbyes, I approached Piket. I asked him who was counting the number of refugees dying in detention centers—a question that had been put to him from the floor to which he failed to respond. He told me he did not know, but gave me his business card. I emailed him later the same day.

"I've been told by UNICEF, as well as detainees, that at least five people died in the two months from mid-September in an 'official' detention center in Zintan, Libya," I wrote. "I've also been told by detainees that many have died this year in Triq al Sikka, possibly more than twenty according to one detainee (that doesn't include the man who burnt himself to death in October). I'm trying to get an answer as to how many people have died, and who is tracking those deaths. Earlier, you said you don't know, and maybe UN-HCR [would know]. I was wondering if you can add anything to that?"

There was no response.

———

Reporting on the EU side of this story was hard. Officials working directly on migration were rarely allowed speak on the record to journalists, and media requests were funneled through the EU Commission instead, where spokespeople would give a few lines of often slightly irrelevant text. I requested interviews with a range of EU figures, including home affairs commissioner Ylva Johansson, who was in charge of migration policy beginning in 2019, and Dimitris Avramopoulos, who served as EU migration commissioner for the five years before—but their teams did not respond. The whole system was opaque—something even European parliamentarians complained to me about, saying they struggled to understand who was making certain big decisions and how to raise concerns.

Many aid workers told me that the EU ambassador to Libya between 2016 and 2018, Bettina Muscheidt, did care about improving conditions for refugees and migrants (Muscheidt declined to speak to me for this book, instead referring me to the EU Commission and her successors at the EU delegation in Libya[46]). But I was told she sometimes asked for minutes not to be taken when she discussed Libya's detention centers, making it hard to find documentation detailing her real thoughts. "Nobody would want to publish this dirty laundry," said one person who sat in on meetings with her.

In April 2019, then-EU commissioner responsible for migration, Dimitris Avramopoulos, called conditions in Libya's detention centers "dire" and "a disgrace for the whole world" during an interview with Channel 4 News. He even agreed with reporter Paraic O'Brien that it was "a contradiction" to oppose the centers while the EU funded the Libyan coastguard to transport people there. "It is an irony, also in my eyes," Avramopoulos said.[47]

The month before, Andrew Gilmour, the UN Assistant Secretary General for Human Rights, told the UN Human Rights Council about interviews he carried out with former detainees. "Every one of them—men, women, boys, and girls—had been raped, many repeatedly, and tortured by electrocution. All testified about the widespread extortion technique whereby the torturers force the victims to call their families, who are then subjected to the screams of their loved ones, which, they are told, will continue until they pay a ransom. I can honestly tell the members of this council that in thirty years in this line of work, these were the most harrowing accounts I have ever heard."[48]

Yet, in October 2019, the European Parliament rejected a motion, with 290 votes to 288, that would have called on the EU to end cooperation with the Libyan coastguard if it carried out serious fundamental rights violations, for rescues to be stepped up in the Mediterranean, and for more to be done to evacuate people from Libyan detention centers and move them to safe countries.[49] There was no sense of urgency.

———

"I decided to enter the sea. Please, I've told you but I didn't tell my family and friends. I don't know when we will leave. Promise me you won't say or write anything until I enter Europe or die or I'm caught . . . I have to tell you because you are the only one who I complain to about everything that happens to me."

———

One of the first things you learn reporting on different sides of a war is the power of language. Opponents can use completely distinct vocabularies to refer to the same things. For example, in Syria, supporters of Bashar al-Assad say they are ruled by a president and a government fighting terrorists; for opponents, he is a dictator heading a regime who brutally suppressed a revolution. A few simple words make it clear where anyone's allegiances lie.

In the same way, the EU has created its own vocabulary for the forced interceptions and return of refugees to Libya. It says it is engaging in "migration management" or "breaking the business model of smugglers." We hear of "irregular migration" and "illegal immigrants."[50] The EU has funded trainings for journalists in Africa where these terminologies are taught, and refugees I spoke to even adopted the phrasing. Personally, I had to continuously remind myself to question the language I heard and how it related to real people—the ones experiencing these policies firsthand.

In June 2019, popular American congress member Alexandria Ocasio-Cortez referred to US detention facilities on her country's southern border as "concentration camps," spurring a heated discussion about the meaning of the term and when it is acceptable to use it. "Even this back-and-

forth over naming the camps has been a recurrent feature in the mass detention of civilians ever since its inception, a history that long predates the
Holocaust," wrote journalist Andrea Pitzer in *The New York Review of Books*.
"At the heart of such policy is a question: What does a country owe desperate
people whom it does not consider to be its citizens?"[51]

Alan Bobbett, who was Libya director for the International Medical
Corps between July 2017 and January 2019, told me German donors ob-
jected when he referred to Libya's detention centers as "concentration camps"
in meetings. "But I said, listen, people have no freedom of movement, they're
being sold. They're being traded," he recalled during a 2021 phone interview.
"Someone's got to do something about these things, they're God-awful
places, and in this day and age that we have even children locked up in detention centers is ridiculous . . . I will say the Europeans built a wall, they
just built it over in Libya. That's really all I can say about it. I mean, their
policies are directly contributing to the imprisonment and death of thousands of people trying to cross the ocean. Migration is nothing new. It's always happened. And I understand that countries like Italy are overwhelmed
with [arrivals] and don't have the resources. I get that part. But there has to
be a better solution . . . it's unconscionable."

"I was there when the Italian prime minister came through and toured
those detention centers," he continued. "To say they didn't know would be
ridiculous. They knew exactly what their policies were funding. They were
there, physically present . . . The long-term implications are going to be
staggering. The EU needs a reckoning on this. They really do. I hope you
bash the hell out of them."

CHAPTER 13

TRIQ AL SIKKA: GOING UNDERGROUND

"The revolution is not an apple that falls when it is ripe.
You have to make it fall."[1]
–CHE GUEVARA

"The tongue hasn't got a bone, but it can break a bone."
–ERITREAN PROVERB

Samuel, the Eritrean medic who first contacted me from Triq al Sikka, decided that I was losing energy and needed to be motivated.

"All Eritreans should know about the famous, smart, and kind journalist, Sally Hayden," he wrote on Facebook, along with two photos of me he
found through Google searches: one with my hood up, surrounded by bottles of alcohol in an liquor store in rural Kenya, and another from an awk-
ward-looking photoshoot with Ireland's foreign affairs minister after I
won a student journalism grant many years before. "Sally Hayden is one of
the biggest journalists. She is helping the refugees in Libya, especially
Eritrean refugees in different detentions suffering with different kinds of
disease in Libya, and for evacuating to safety countries and not taking

refugees back from crossing Mediterranean Sea," he wrote. "She is working day and night with the biggest mass media and also directly contacting with EU and UNHCR in Libya, struggling to change the European policy and stimulating the human rights. So all my brothers and sisters, Eritrean people, Sally Hayden deserves more and more applauses for her astounding jobs. We have to SHARE and LIKE for the motivation and keep her going . . . THANKS!!!"

It got more than one thousand likes and more than 520 shares. I laughed and cried and grappled with the idea that a person in such a wretched situation could feel like they needed to lift my spirits, or maybe just encourage me to stay interested.

This also made me think again about the gross power imbalance in our situations. Already, I had been questioning how unfair it was that the voices of refugees in Libya were constantly filtered through privileged journalists like me. I started helping detainees write their own op-eds, compiling messages they sent me to hit the correct word count and sending them back for final approval. The testimonies were published in British newspapers and magazines like *The Guardian*, *The New Statesman*, and *The Independent*.[2] Samuel's, sent through a series of furtive social media messages during the Triq al Sikka tuberculosis outbreak and published under a pseudonym, went on to be long-listed for a prestigious Amnesty International Media Award.

This was far from his consciousness by the time it happened, though, when life at Triq al Sikka had been altered forever by a protest.

"Sally, we are planning to do a big aggressive protest here in Triq al Sikka. No one can tolerate the life inside this detention center. Everyone is ready for the bad things that are going to happen. We are doing this because there is not enough food, not enough place to sleep, no doctors, no sanitation, people are sleeping in the toilet, every one is feeling weak, disease is spreading, everyone is coughing. There is no one to ask about our

conditions, no one is responsible for us. Sally, we are not criminals, we are refugees seeking a better life, that's it. But these people injected evil in us. Why? Why are we facing such horrific suffering? Why?"

"Here we die."

———

At that time, in early 2019, there was relative peace in much of Tripoli. Perhaps predictably, I noticed that oppression in detention centers often increased when the management and guards were not distracted by conflicts outside. Still, the number of refugees reaching out to me through hidden phones continued to grow.

I had a new contact in the men's cell in Triq al Sikka. Ben used to call me "Dr Sally." "I miss outside so much, Dr," he wrote. "This condition is very, very hard for human beings, Dr Sally . . . Please, Dr Sally, help us please." He was thirty-three, but worried his face and body looked forty. When we spoke about the difference in our ages, he said years were not the same for me anyway because I could manage my own time. "My age is increasing and time is going meaningless. I am very angry for my life," he said.

Ben had a bad injury from a gunshot wound he said was caused by a Libyan guard for which he never got medical treatment. A picture he sent showed what looked like a chunk of flesh missing from his body. There were other people inside Triq al Sikka with similar wounds. "We were broken by police, those who work in the detention prison," he told me.

His initial messages, typed late at night, were an appeal. "We've spent a long time here, over thirteen months with many miracles. But we can't get a solution from any humanitarian organization like UNHCR. We're refugee asylum seekers, but here we are prisoners without anything, like criminals, for a long time. We're human beings, but here we are animals." Ben told me his girlfriend had died crossing the Sahara Desert, and their child was still in Eritrea with his mother. He never left the caged hall and had not seen women in a year. "Now I am alone, except GOD. Under GOD you. Thanks GOD, bless you. Goodnight," he signed off.

Ben spent the first half of 2017 with smugglers before being intercepted at sea in June. Upon return to Libya, he fell into the hands of another group of smugglers, who demanded $5,500, yet never delivered on an offer to let him try to cross the Mediterranean again. He was locked up with no provisions and left to die, but managed to break down the door and get away. When he asked for help in the streets, he was taken to a detention center.

"Because of the shortage of food, clean water, no medication, and not enough sleeping space, it is very dirty, a bad smell. We've stayed a long time without fresh air, enough sunlight, with no communication with family and others."

Ben worried he did not have long left to live. "Follow me, please, like a journalist," he wrote. "Thanks more to meet you. Have a nice dream about us. God bless you." Over the coming months, he elaborated on the financial cost of being incarcerated ("Life is very expensive") and the mental state of those around him ("Some people have crazy here").

"You know prison is very sensitive for the mind. When you stay a long time in prison, without anything, you have to go crazy or die. We're even very sad. In Libya, life is meaningless, Dr Sally."

At least five people had begun talking to themselves. "They sleep in the toilet and they're angry," he said. "They play with the same dirty things. At the same time they don't eat food, this stupid macaroni." He would apologize for messaging late and keeping me awake. "Me, I've adapted to not sleeping in Libya. Day and night is the same for us."

Then, on February 18, 2019, he asked for my direct phone line (we had been messaging through social media). I did not realize how significant this would be, and what the detainees there must have already been planning. "God bless you forever," he wrote. "I will never forget you in the whole of my life. Even if I die, maybe if God takes me to heaven, I will never forget you."

"I know you are not sleeping day and night for us. You are very smart, but here the situation is not changed. Especially in Triq al Sikka prison: UN-HCR is not evacuating from here. Me now, I think I've made my decision. I want to go back to my country because I want to die on my land. Finish life. Prison is painful for me. If I die in my country maybe my family will get my dead body. In case, send me your number, dear Sally, because we don't have another choice. From any place or by any number I will call you quickly, pick up for me. Thanks for every thing, you did good things for us. I WISH ALL THE BEST FOR EVER YOU."

That was the last time we would message for months.

———

I started working with Channel 4 News in the UK. We pieced together photos, videos, and audio clips that I had received over the preceding months. Before this, I had trouble getting media outlets to publish this kind of imagery: they all said it was too graphic, and even I was shocked when I saw it all come together. But how would anything improve if the public was never shown the shameful and horrifying reality of what was happening?

On the evening of February 25, 2019, our report finally broadcast, leading the nightly news bulletin in British homes.[3] "Is this the Abu Ghraib of the migrant crisis?" the tagline asked.[4] There were images of torture and abuse: a man with a gun to his head and vomit by his face; another dangling upside down; a woman in chains. Videos from Khoms Souq al Khamis were in there, showing detainees protesting after recently disembarked refugees were sold to traffickers by the center's guards. Another video, taken with the aim of extracting a ransom, captured a man writhing on the floor as molten plastic was dripping on his back. I was interviewed, too, in the kitchen of the London apartment in which I was subletting a room at the time, looking slightly uncomfortable and unused to being on camera.

The report was shared thousands of times on social media by the direc-

tors of major charities, human rights organizations, and a host of other notable people. Maybe videos and photos could achieve what text could not, I
thought as I scrolled through the reactions, standing in the Channel 4
newsroom. During a debrief after the news program finished, other journalists congratulated me and producer Darius Bazargan. The report was later
written up in *The Times of London*[5] and sparked at least two written questions from Members of Parliament to the British government, including one
on the number of deaths occurring in Libyan migrant detention centers
("The British Government does not hold information on the number of migrant deaths in detention centers in Libya," came the answer). Still, I should
have known better than to expect change.[6]

————

The next morning, on February 26, 2019, around one hundred and fifty
detainees broke out of the men's cell at Triq al Sikka. This coincided with a
visit by a delegation from the Dutch embassy.[7]

"Holland embassy came, we talked to them a lot. [The diplomat] told us
the Europeans have a problem with resettling refugees and I told him we
don't need Europe at this moment. We need shelter, good food, fresh air, a
place to walk, and a place we feel freedom. He told us he cannot help us, and
I asked him why he came to us."

They demanded a visit from UNHCR. The diplomat left.

"We break the door and we are outside, all the police are around us. I am
writing you secretly. The leader of all detentions are here . . . They said we
are not responsible for you, we are calling the responsible person. They said
if you don't agree with the UNHCR boss we will let you go free. We carried
all our stuff with us: clothes, blankets, everything is with us."

The management called for reinforcements. As many as one hundred
guards surrounded the group, holding wooden sticks, strips of plastic, and
metal piping that looked like it came from building sites. In advance, they

carried out a search and confiscated phones from the women, who were being held nearby, so they could not film what came next or call for help.

"First they make sure that there is no one around. They are smart, Sally. That's why they waited until the embassy left the detention."

Women started to scream as the guards beat the men and boys. Four people passed out after being hit in the head. The International Rescue Committee later confirmed to me that two were taken to a hospital. An EU spokesperson said they were aware of the reports of a protest.

"The only thing you can do is to inform, Sally."

Dozens of detainees were rounded up afterwards and taken to other detention centers, but not before their spare clothes and documents were seized from them. Around seventy phones were confiscated.

"Now they will sell all the phones and use the money for drugs. That's their life, Sally. The Libyans live a poor life, money makes them crazy."

Those suspected of being ringleaders—people who were caught filming the protest with phones or leading chants—were brought to a room underground in Triq al Sikka itself, accessible through a black door close to the entrance to the men's cell. Several of them were underage. "That place is so bad. There's no place to walk, it's dark, it's so small," worried a refugee whose friend had been held there before.

The following night, I got a call. Ben managed to get hold of a phone—he told me the source, but even now it would be too risky to share that publicly. This is an abbreviated version of our conversation, which I recorded.

Ben: "We are underground, we are underground."

Sally: "You're in an underground detention center?"

Ben: "We are not in detention, yesterday they take us to . . . Prison in underground . . . Yesterday they beat us, people are suffering . . . We are in underground prison, they take us to underground."

Sally: "Do you know where the prison is? Do you have any idea where the prison is, which location?"

Ben: "In Triq al Sikka. In the same place, in the same place but it is underground . . . don't tell anybody about this phone."

Sally: "I won't tell anyone, don't worry. Do you want me to tell the UN?"

Ben: "Yeah. Yeah please tell them." [Then he said people were being taken out one by one for beatings.]

Sally: "You mean they're torturing people?"

Ben: "Yeah . . . So even . . . they take him outside, they beat him."

Sally: "You're waiting to be beaten."

Ben: "Yeah, yeah, yeah, they, they, they . . ."

He asked me to take note of each of their names. We spent long minutes stumbling over sounds and spellings as I wrote them down, counting the list when I had sixteen, and then twenty-one, until I finally had all twenty-two and could read them back to him.

Sally: "Okay. And should I, should I phone you back at some stage or is that dangerous?"

Ben: "Yeah."

Sally: "And, and what happened, what happened yesterday? They beat everybody? Did they beat everyone or was it just a few people, or what happened?"

Ben: "Everyone. They beat everyone, everyone . . . they, they put in underground the other, they sent to another prison we don't know we don't have any . . . about them, nobody . . ."

Sally: "Okay . . . Do you know how many people were taken to a different prison?"

Ben: "We don't know, we don't know we have . . . they take them . . . they take them we . . ."

Sally: "Okay okay, I'll do what I, I'll do what I can and call you back at some stage if that's, if that's safe and the phone will be hidden."

Ben: "Don't call, don't call."

Sally: "Okay, I won't call then, don't worry."

Ben: "Yeah. I call you me myself, I call you."

Sally: "I'm praying for all of you, let's hope we get you out soon."

Ben: "Yeah, we are, we are in the underground . . ."

Sally: "Okay. See you, good luck, good luck."

Ben: "Yeah, pray, pray, pray for us, pray for us."

———

A week after the protest, on Saturday, March 2, I published a report on Al Jazeera with the title: "Refugees in Libya 'tortured' for breaking out of detention center."[8] The next Tuesday, the Dutch Minister for Migration was due to visit Triq al Sikka, but his aides were informed the visit had been moved to another migrant detention center, Tajoura, for "security reasons." That same day, an EU spokesperson emailed me saying they were "following the situation [in Triq al Sikka] very closely through our EU Delegation and [are] in close contact with the UN agencies and humanitarian operators . . . We hope a solution can be found swiftly, in line with international law."

The spokesperson reiterated the usual spiel that the detention centers should be closed, and said, "The EU's priority in our work in Libya when it comes to migration has always been and will continue to be saving lives, protecting people, fighting trafficking and smuggling, supporting vulnerable migrants to voluntarily return and reintegrate in their countries of origin, and creating legal pathways to Europe for those in need of international protection."

"I am in the hell, Triq al Sikka. I don't know how to I say to you. I don't
know what is happening. Before seven days was the worst day in my life.
My friends all in the dark room. Underground. Yes, is terrible."

UNHCR's spokespeople emailed me calling the protest a "riot" and said
they were following through on prior plans to visit the center. Two days later,
they released a statement saying they did not have access to Triq al Sikka,
but were "troubled by reports of the use of force" and heard around fifty
detainees had been injured.[9] IOM released a stronger statement: "According
to reports, migrants detained—many for months—launched a protest . . .
and were punished severely," it read. "We condemn the use of violence in
detention, and ask for urgent access to individuals who have been removed
from that detention center . . . No matter the circumstances that led to this
particular incident, violence against migrants cannot be justified."[10]

Triq al Sikka's guards announced they were carrying out an "investigation" into the protest and its origins. Before long, Samuel, one of the few
refugees left in the upstairs male cell, was also taken to the underground
rooms and interrogated. He was threatened, too, with guards asking whether
he was in contact with a "British" journalist, presumably me. They took out
a photo of a deep pit and told Samuel he would be put down there and never
come out again if he was found guilty of communicating with anyone
outside.

The guards were angry. During the protest, a participant had thrown
something at Naser Hazam, the manager of the center, a usually unruffled
man never seen without a cigarette.[11] "Police saw him as a God," one detainee told me. *"Kus umak,"* the guards began shouting at the refugees in
response. "Fuck you."

"The ones responsible for us are UNHCR, and we don't think they will
come for us, because they are in a fight with this detention center."

I heard nothing further from Ben or the other twenty-one people who remained underground. I emailed UN and aid agency contacts, giving details of where the group was, including a photo of the black door that led to the underground prison and a description of exactly where it was located. Later, some aid officials would accuse IOM and UNHCR officials of failing to properly advocate for the victims.[12] (When I asked them about this, an IOM spokesperson said IOM repeatedly called for the group to be released and for its staff to be granted access to them.) Hazam, the manager, eventually invited UNHCR to register and interview the remaining Eritreans in the upstairs cell, but said the group underground would never be evacuated as punishment. When UNHCR called some of their names for interviews, Hazam refused to produce them.

Sources inside the UN later told me their staff were not willing to take a strong stand on the protest, and subsequent torture in Triq al Sikka, because of the broader political situation in Libya. "At the time, they were trying to avert a war," one well-placed person told me. "So this wasn't the biggest priority." Representatives from the UN Support Mission in Libya (UNSMIL)—which was operationally separate from UNHCR and IOM, though still part of the UN—had spent the last eighteen months meeting thousands of Libyans and collecting tens of thousands of online comments and suggestions ahead of a planned national conference. It was scheduled to take place in mid-April, with the aim of bringing together different parties and leaders from across the country and setting Libya on the path to democratic elections.[13] That conference was doomed to fail, and the twenty-two men and boys subjected to torture in Triq al Sikka would stay underground for months.

A storm was certainly brewing. Bosses from different militia groups kept turning up at Triq al Sikka to strut around and hold meetings. Samuel watched them from his cell with trepidation. Weapons, even bombs, were stored in a room beside the remaining detainees, who now shared space with new migrants caught at checkpoints around the city.

Months passed, and then at 1:38 a.m., on the morning of April 4, 2019, Ben "waved" at me on Facebook—an animation of a little yellow hand popping up on my screen.

"Hii dear Sally. Thanks GOD. Today we are outside. From the under. Now we are in detention."

That very day, a new war would begin.

TRIPOLI: WAR ERUPTS AGAIN

"Libya is on the verge of descending into a civil war, which could
lead to the permanent division of the country. The damage already done will
take years to mend, and that's only if the war is ended now."

**—UN SPECIAL ENVOY TO LIBYA, GHASSAN SALAMÉ,
SPEAKS TO THE UN SECURITY COUNCIL, 2019**

The war started on April 4, 2019, while I was at the annual International Journalism Festival in the city of Perugia in central Italy. Just hours before, I had spoken about my reporting in a small room on a panel with other journalists who covered migration. Members of the audience asked what they could do to change the situation in Libya and the Mediterranean. I said I am not an activist, it is not my role to direct them, but I strongly believe that everyone should be aware of the consequences of EU migration policy and the human rights crises that are being compounded by it.

I was grateful for the interest. One of the things I had noticed, in the seven months since I started sharing testimonies from Libya online, was that more activists, lawyers, and journalists in Europe and the US seemed to have begun communicating directly with detained refugees. They would share their stories publicly, too, or appeal to politicians and international organizations on their behalf. The more individuals involved, the greater the chance that something positive might happen. But there was always another setback.

After the talk, I was invited to a dinner arranged by an organization that supports independent journalists. Roughly a dozen of us sat at a long table in a room lit by golden light. Beside me was a Pulitzer Prize winner whose work I greatly admired, but I could barely speak to him. Instead, I stared at the phone on my lap as messages, and an accompanying sense of dread, began flooding in. The familiar sounds of warfare were rumbling far away. Tripoli was under attack.

One of the dinner attendees was Libyan, and we talked quietly afterwards, in the warmly lit restaurant entrance, as heavy rain poured down on the cobblestones of Perugia's Piazza IV Novembre. She was sad for her country and worried for her family, who would have to live through fighting all over again. Would it turn into civil war this time, she wondered. It was always civilians who endured the most.

Renegade eastern general Khalifa Haftar, a mustachioed man with a drooping, dour face, had ordered his troops to advance on Tripoli and take control of the city, right as UN Secretary General António Guterres was there. Guterres's trip was aimed at drumming up support for the UN-organized national conference, set to take place in less than a fortnight.[1] That morning, Guterres had met al-Serraj, the prime minister of the UN-backed government, before visiting Ain Zara detention center, which was once again filled with refugees caught on the sea. The Secretary General said he was "very moved and shocked" by the level of suffering and despair he saw there. "This is, of course, not only a responsibility for Libya, it's a responsibility for the whole of the international community," he said.[2]

Haftar had long condemned the Tripoli-based government and its associated militias and fighters, labeling them Islamists and terrorists.[3] Born in

1943 and now seventy-five years old, he had helped Gaddafi—who once described him as a "son"—seize power.[4] When they fell out in the 1980s, Haftar moved to northern Virginia, in the US. He sometimes worked with the CIA, which is headquartered there, while trying to oust his former boss from afar.[5] After the 2011 revolution, Haftar made his way back home. In 2014, he launched "Operation Dignity" against Islamist militants in Libya's second largest city, Benghazi, flattening neighborhoods in his bid to rule. His fighters were self-styled as the Libyan National Army, he managed to attract some international backing, and his effort was rewarded. Within a few years, he controlled more territory than the UN-backed Government of National Accord, though Libya's capital city, Tripoli, remained the ultimate prize.[6]

———

I was supposed to go directly to Tunisia after the journalism festival, flying to the Libyan border to meet refugees who had escaped in the months before. They paid their way out of detention centers and had firsthand stories and evidence of torture, rape, and other abuses. I carried out a risk assessment with a security team, secured government permission to work, and booked flights and a place to stay. Apart from the stories I hoped to report, I was excited to meet my contacts in person after such a lengthy time communicating at a distance.

The day after the war began, the trip was canceled. A contact had received warnings—first from the UK's MI6, and then from the CIA in the US—saying my safety appeared to be at risk. I was given little further information but would return to London instead.

Had someone betrayed me? I wondered. Who in Tunisia knew I was coming? Only a few refugees, a Tunisian driver, the government press department that granted my accreditation, and some aid agency staff I organized interviews with. The most devastating part was disappointing the refugees I had arranged to see. I did not want them confined to messages anymore, text on a screen. I did not want me to be that, either—or worse, a foreign journalist exploiting them for career advancement, making demands from afar without any real investment. I could not even tell them why I was no longer coming, as I was instructed to keep everything quiet. And now I was back in London, in a Stoke Newington sublet, confused and frightened.

Weeks later, I would learn that there is a US policy called intelligence community directive 191, which says the CIA has a "duty to warn" a potential victim if they receive "credible and specific information indicating an impending threat of intentional killing, serious bodily injury, or kidnapping,"[7] which are defined as follows:

> "Intentional Killing means the deliberate killing of a specific individual or group of individuals.
> Serious Bodily Injury means an injury which creates a substantial risk of death or which causes serious, permanent disfigurement or impairment.
> Kidnapping means the intentional taking of an individual or group through force or threat of force."

My fear was nothing compared to the waves of terror flowing through Libya's detention centers. The conflict escalated quickly, and by mid-April around 2,700 refugees and migrants were being held in areas close to Tripoli's front lines.[8] Around eight hundred were with Kaleb in Abu Salim detention center, where detainees did not sleep for two days, alarmed by the sounds of rockets flying over them. Despite the constant threat of attack, the first refugee death I heard of during that war would not be from a bomb or a bullet.

When Meri, the Asmara teenager Kaleb had met in the smuggling transit point in Kufra, close to the Libyan border, had showed up at Abu Salim months before, Kaleb had not seen him for almost two years. Meri was among a group of refugees dumped directly at the detention center's gate by smugglers—malnourished and physically damaged. He never even made it into a boat.

Kaleb was shocked by how much Meri had changed. "The first time I met him, he was [a] normal person," recalled Kaleb. "I knew him before he became stressed."

Meri still smiled, but he had lost the ability to speak. No one seemed to know exactly what the teenager had been through, and he could not tell them. There were rumors that he had been sold between smuggling gangs who tortured him by electrocution, as had happened to many others. He had probably been starved and beaten, with his family listening on the phone. That might be consistent with his mental state afterwards, detainees suggested: certain humans cannot survive such horrors. "His mind was gone," said Kaleb. "He had mind depression, he was acting like a crazy. He was not the old Meri I knew. He didn't talk, he didn't eat, when I met him he couldn't walk."

Despite this, Meri had energy. He was only seventeen—"still young, just like a fire . . . a joker," Kaleb said.

"Even after he had made a mind depression he was still happy. When he was stressed, if we played music for him he danced."

The war would prove too much for him. One week after Haftar declared the beginning of Libya's latest war, Meri killed himself by jumping into a septic tank in the detention center compound.[9] It took other refugees more than thirty minutes to get his body out. Women sped over without shoes, headscarves, or the other coverings they normally wore outside, where Libyan guards might object to the sight of them. They looped a rope around a burly man, Papa, who used a length of iron to measure the depth of the septic tank before lowering himself down, taking a deep breath and going under.

Meri's body was laid on the ground. It was not clear if he was alive. At one point, on the phone to me, Kaleb began to cry from happiness, saying it was a gift from God that Meri had survived—a message to us all about resilience. Later, it emerged that several of the detention center's ruling committee, the refugees who had taken charge when Abu Salim's Libyan guards ran away, had lied to calm detainees down, saying Meri was recovering.[10]

"He liked to play with everybody, so everybody misses him. Today I hated living in this shameful world. I lost my friend, brother, my everything . . . Meri was a good boy."

They held a mourning period after Meri's death. That meant three days without food; women walking bent at the waist, tapping their thighs, and singing, calling to God for help. Muslims and Christians came together. When the public grieving ended, refugee leaders called a meeting to say Meri's death had been God's will and they all needed to move on from it now. "There is a war," one announced. "If we keep crying, we will be targeted."

"We will die one by one, either by war, by suicide, by starvation."

One month later, Meri's body was still being held in what the Abu Salim refugees called "a fridge." Authorities were distracted, or maybe they had no idea what to do with him.

Around Abu Salim, the fighting became worse, its noises constant. Rockets and shells landed close by. The sound of gunfire was a violent rhythm, a relentless tapping. The few Libyan guards now stationed there confusingly switched uniforms, making refugees wonder if they had swapped allegiances and were now on Haftar's side. As expected by then, the guards eventually got into their cars and drove away.

*"People are very angry and afraid. And the sound of the weapons are
coming to us. We hear [them] from near. The children are scared and cry
all the day and night. The pregnants and all the ladies are very scared.
Every thing is not good now. All people [are] stressed."*

Sky News' Alex Crawford, the courageous British journalist whose image was broadcast around the world when she rode into Tripoli's Green Square with rebels during the 2011 revolution, was back on the front lines.[11] "Many of the revolution fighters have picked up arms again, and some are clearly a bit rusty," she said in a voiceover to a report on April 15 with footage showing men in jeans and hoodies trying to fire guns.[12] "There's little binding them together, just a desire to keep out the forces outside, led by a former Gaddafi general. But it's messy and very disorganized."

Prime Minister al-Serraj appeared in her report, appealing for help from the international community. Around two hundred thousand people would be displaced in the first six months of this war, with Libyans suffering badly themselves.[13] Yet, even then, al-Serraj turned the conversation back to migration, making the exact same threat Gaddafi made when he tried to rally support during the revolution. "What's going to happen with this security breakdown is that 800,000 illegal migrants temporarily on Libyan ground will have to leave Libya and will cross the sea towards Europe," al-Serraj told Crawford, sitting hunched in a cream-colored chair with a Libyan flag behind him. "And among those 800,000 there are terrorists and criminals. This will be disastrous."[14]

———

As the war accelerated, Libya's propaganda wars stepped up a notch, too. Sky News Arabia got in touch with me to ask if they could broadcast audio I had gathered—testimonies from refugees who were forcibly recruited by the Tripoli-based Government of National Accord-aligned militias. The producer wanted me to be interviewed live on air. After asking for advice from a Libyan friend, I declined. She said the Arabic version of Sky News was perceived as supporting Haftar, and being associated with a partisan outlet could stop my other reporting from being seen as credible.[15]

Soon after this, I received another email, from a US- and UK-based public relations company, Mercury Public Affairs.

> "Dear Sally,
> I am writing on behalf of the internationally recognized Government of National Accord in Libya.
> Given recent events, including the attack on Tripoli by forces connected to Khalifa Haftar, as well as shifts in support for the UN-sponsored political agreement, it would be great to organize a quick meeting to introduce myself and the work we are doing to support the GNA.
> Let me know if you are available this week in London.
> In the meantime, please find attached a statement from the GNA following the most recent air strikes on the city.
> Please let me know if you have any questions."[16]

According to different media reports, the GNA had signed a $2 million deal with Mercury.[17] The agreement was confirmed shortly after then-US President Donald Trump appeared to switch his allegiance away from the GNA by phoning Haftar and saying he supported the eastern general's "significant role in fighting terrorism."[18] International involvement would play a large role in exacerbating the conflict and empowering each side. Backing the Tripoli-based GNA were Turkey, Italy, and Qatar.[19] France supported Haftar, as did Russia, Egypt, and the UAE.[20] But both sides knew US support could sway the course of the war significantly.

Haftar had also hired his own public relations firm, Linden Government Solutions, which had a base in Washington, DC.[21] "It's actually very fascinating that the GNA are working with western public relations firms—it reminds me of Gaddafi days," a Libyan friend said when I told her about the email.

My meeting with Mercury was scheduled. I was on edge, wondering why they had contacted me. The potential threats on my life were still on my mind. Could it be a trap or a test? A journalist friend suggested I try to secretly record everything. He set me up with a contact in north London who carried out undercover investigations and owned a car keyring with a camera in it. I charged the keyring and then practiced surreptitiously aiming the camera, but I could not even figure out when it was turned on or not.

Waiting on the pavement outside Mercury's office in Mayfair near London's Bond Street, I tried again. Almost no one had a car in London—no one I knew, anyway. For me, a disheveled 29-year-old, to turn up with a car keyring would be suspicious. Undercover filming, without evidence of wrongdoing by the people you were targeting, was illegal too.[22] I left the camera in my laptop case and resolved to brave this alone.

Sitting on a leather chair in a wood-paneled, expensive-looking reception area, I contemplated how this chic public relations firm fit into the wider Libyan story of militias, horrific detention centers, and hardship on an incomparable scale. On its website, Mercury says it is a "high-stakes public strategy firm" that offers strategic media relations, crisis management, and political consulting.[23] It counted union-busting for an automaker in the US as one of its successes, as well as helping Republican politicians win elections in traditionally Democratic states. It claimed to have executed successful election and public affairs campaigns on five continents, with "a particularly strong capability in Africa, the Middle East, and the Islamic world."[24] Regarding media relations, it specialized in "crafting the right narrative for our clients."

Mercury had represented Turkey and Qatar—autocratic states with dire human rights records—as well as Haitian President Jovenel Moïse when he was facing calls to step down amid protests he was installing a dictatorship.[25] Two years later, Mercury would sign a $120,000 per month deal with Israeli surveillance giant NSO Group, the creator of Pegasus, a program which governments used to spy on journalists, activists, and opposition politicians around the world.[26]

The man and woman who met me that day were slim and good looking. They asked what they could do to help my reporting, and I said I was having problems getting responses from Libyan officials. While I had been calling, texting, and emailing the Libyan authorities in the hope of including their responses and perspectives, replies were not forthcoming—especially after I explained I was a journalist. It could take time, the two said, joking about how bad the GNA were at emailing, but it was definitely possible.

I asked more questions, but they could not offer explanations for behavior by the Tripoli-based government, or explain the conditions in detention centers and the treatment of refugees. I felt more confused than ever: here was another organization making money off this crisis, another spin clouding the harsh reality. We said goodbye, with the man telling me he was going to Kiev, Ukraine, the next day on a work assignment. For the first time, shortly afterwards, a Libyan official responded through Mercury when I contacted them looking for a comment on a report.

In early May, as a result of a podcast I recorded, Ibrahim Sahad, a Libyan Interior Ministry Supreme Security Committee member, gave another statement through Mercury.[27] "The Libyan government takes any allegations of abuses, even isolated occurrences, extremely seriously," he said. "We are working with the international community to build capacity within relevant agencies and ensure that migrants are afforded the rights and dignities that all human beings deserve. The scale of the challenges facing Libya is enormous, and the issue of large-scale migration is an international problem that cannot be left for any one country to solve on its own. The UN-recognized Government of National Accord (GNA) has worked long and hard to create peace and stability in Libya, gains which are now being put at grave risk. Violence and chaos will make it difficult to ensure that vulnerable groups, including migrants, are supported and that systems are operating with appropriate standards and accountability."

Shortly afterwards, Libya's interior minister, Fathi Bashagha, spoke to

Euronews, saying that putting Libya in charge of managing Europe-seeking migrants was like "a sick doctor being asked to treat patients."

"Libya has internal problems," he told Anelise Borges, Euronews' Paris correspondent. "Since the state fell apart, Libya has not been able to provide adequate services even for Libyans. The EU demands Libya secures the coast, fights human traffickers, cares and pays for illegal migrants in accordance with international standards . . . [But] Libya has many other problems, service problems, security problems, terrorism problems, economic problems . . ."[28]

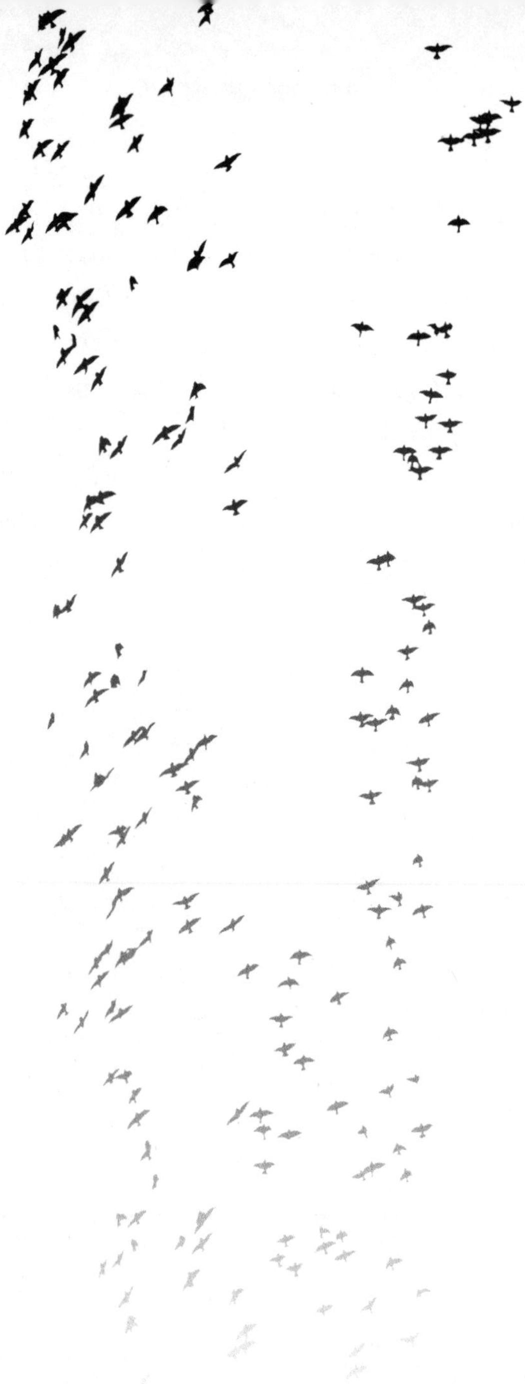

CHAPTER 15

QASR BIN GHASHIR AND ZAWIYA: SHOTS FIRED

"War does not determine who is right—only who is left."
—BERTRAND RUSSELL

Binyam loved reading. If he had books, it would be tolerable to spend months in Qasr bin Ghashir, a detention center around twenty-five kilometers south of Tripoli, the 23-year-old told me. In Ethiopia, where he previously lived as a refugee, he had been a "star" at reading. "What society needs is books," he messaged through Facebook. "Especially psychology books."

He listed off his favorites. *Thinking Fast and Slow*, by psychologist and Nobel Prize-winner Daniel Kahneman; *The Power of the Habit: Why We Do What We Do in Life and Business*, a 2012 bestseller by Charles Duhigg; and his all-time top choice, *Mistakes Were Made (But Not by Me): Why We Justify Foolish Beliefs, Bad Decisions, and Hurtful Acts*, by Carol Tavris and Elliot Aronson ("This is the best book that I love").

Binyam missed reading in the library the same way he missed fresh air, spending time outside, his family, and seeing children learn in classrooms. "Even there is no Bible dear," he told me from detention. "Nothing except disease and stress." Instead of books, he was now being educated in insults. "We are learning the stupid words of the Libya police. To say *zeb* it means dick. *Haywan*, it means animal," he said. "There's not any education here. If they had an education they wouldn't treat us like animals." Like everyone else, he waited. He had been caught after seven hours at sea in June 2018, and described the evacuations as slow, "like a tortoise," but he was hopeful his time would come.

Qasr bin Ghashir's detainees had faced much the same problems as everyone else, except they very quickly ended up on the front lines of Tripoli's new war. In April 2019, when Haftar ordered his troops to advance, Qasr bin Ghashir was one of the first areas he took. Within days, electricity supplies were cut, meaning water pumps stopped working and taps ran dry. Detainees sat in total darkness all night. The toilets were blocked.

> *"The problem we face with women and children is serious. Mothers can't breastfeed their infants because their breast doesn't have enough milk. The reason is a lack of drinking water and food. The children have become so slow. Sometimes when they are hungry they try to cry but they do not have the strength."*

By then, the center contained more than seven hundred people, including almost fifty children and more than one hundred women, some of them pregnant. Roughly half had been intercepted on the Mediterranean—the others were arrested in the city or surrounding areas, or arrived there straight from smugglers. Now they were squarely in the middle of warring factions: a Tripoli government-aligned militia also had a base nearby. As had happened in other centers, most of their guards disappeared when the conflict began, leaving them without food. Two Eritreans who ventured out of the center in search of water returned with serious injuries after being beaten up by Haftar's soldiers.

"The jet is coming, they are bombing a lot of things, a lot of houses of the people," Binyam told me on Monday, April 8.[1] He started phoning me regularly, his voice high-pitched and frantic, the words coming out at double speed like he knew his time was limited. On occasion, he even imitated a news wire, with "breaking news dear" prefacing many updates. He sent voice memos that were long and repetitive, important information repeated over and over again. In the background were the cries of young children.[2] "Even the Libyan people are running. All the way—backwards, forwards— there's a lot of military. We don't have any person who can take responsibility (for us). We are in a bad condition, dear. Report for us to the world."

"Hi dear, the war is continuing like yesterday. Today, also, it is very hard to imagine . . . Four days now, starting from Thursday night until now we don't have any food. Actually, there's no water, there's no light until now. We are in bad condition, dear. But who can we report to? Only we are reporting to God.[3] Our messages continue, praying only, there is not any solution . . . There's big weapons, even the jet is coming, dropping a lots of things in our detention center. But everything is very bad, everything is very bad, only pray for us, dear. This is the news for today."

An air strike hit nearby. It left a craterous hole in the dirt ground behind where the women and children were sleeping. Mothers began recording voice messages for me to share with the media, their young, quivering voices underpinning the urgency of their situation. They were broadcast by BBC World Service, who also interviewed me. "Please if you can help, help us, everybody," beseeched one woman. "Tell to them, everybody, the world . . .

Please, please, I can't say more than this because it's too much war and too much bad life."[4] They sent photos and videos showing their heads bowed, many headscarves—yellow, red, turquoise, blue—in resigned supplication.

The center's former manager disappeared and then came back to tell detainees they would be moved to Zintan, another detention center, located 180 kilometers southwest of Tripoli. It was known as Libya's "Guantanamo" because of the large number of people who had died there from medical neglect. For Binyam, Zintan was the "home of grave or hell." Others agreed that they would rather be killed by bullets or bombs than risk losing access to international organizations with bases in Tripoli. Either way, death was a strong possibility, they speculated.

On April 11, 2019, a UNHCR staff member called me, sounding panicked. She said that day would be the UN's only chance to move the Qasr bin Ghashir detainees. Negotiating access had been hugely difficult. Was she asking me to help? As a journalist, I told her, I am not allowed to advise sources on what choices to make, it is their decision. She said she knew that, but wanted me to be aware that UNHCR had tried to do something. This might mean life or death, she said, and UNHCR could not be held responsible for anything that came next if this offer was rejected. She asked me for phone numbers for female refugees in the detention center, saying she wanted to convince them to take the offer. I passed one on.

Buses arrived. The first was gray, with "Leptis Magna" emblazoned on its side. Detainees gathered for a group meeting and a show of strength. They stood, or sat on the ground, and took turns to speak. The eventual decision was seemingly unanimous. They would not leave.

Binyam said UNHCR did not understand the situation. How could they, he asked—they evacuated their staff to Tunisia when things got tough. They had no qualms about putting their lives first and leaving refugees behind, he said. "A lot of our brothers and sisters are suffering more than anything in [Zintan]," he said. "This is not the solution . . . All Libya is a war zone."

"This message is from Qasr bin Ghashir detention center. We need
emergency evacuation from Libya. Please, UNHCR Libya and IOM
Libya, help us. We don't want evacuation from detention to detention
center . . . Take us from Libya, please. WHERE IS HUMANITY
AND WHERE IS HUMAN RIGHTS? WHERE IS [THE] UN
AND WHERE IS THE WORLD? PLEASE, WE ARE IN HELL.
LIBYA DETENTION CENTER ONE FULL YEAR. WE ARE
PEOPLE OF PEACE, WE LEFT OUR COUNTRY BECAUSE
OF LOST HUMAN RIGHTS AND LACK OF DEMOCRACY.
PLEASE, WE NEED EMERGENCY HELP."

After four hours, the buses left. Not one refugee was on board.[5]

———

In a statement on April 12, UNHCR said its efforts to move refugees were being "frustrated by access and security challenges," calling the attempted move "a last resort and a life-saving measure."[6]

"Although the Zintan center is far from suitable, it is in a safer location and is accessible from Qasr Bin Ghashir. UNHCR's medical partner, IMC, also has an on-site clinic to rapidly assist refugees and migrants. However, refugees and migrants refused the transfer, asking instead to be evacuated out of Libya. Currently, evacuation possibilities from Libya are extremely limited."

Qasr bin Ghashir's manager began to threaten the detainees with violence.

"We refused to go to Zintan, so he told us 'I will kill you all.'"

"The manager told us we are the target of the air strike and the main
target of smugglers. Our sisters are shocked, they are afraid of rape and
every bad thing."

Then the final Libyan guard left Qasr bin Ghashir, and they were alone again.[7]

"We find ourselves in a fire."

"There are no words to describe the fear of the women and children. We are afraid of [the] noise . . . fired from the air and the weapons. I feel that we are abandoned to our fate."

"They didn't leave us anything to defend ourselves with."

On April 13, a Libyan organization called Migrace managed to reach the center. From a truck, its staff offloaded food, juice boxes, and a liter of water for every three people. With their bellies full for once, there was a sense of celebration. "All refugees are very happy and feeling good. Even the war is not like before," Binyam said, thanking God again and calling Migrace's staff "humanitarians for the people."

Over the next few days, Migrace came back.[8] On April 14, as they delivered supplies, a jet was downed close by, leaving a trail of black smoke through the blue sky.[9] On April 18, UNHCR again contacted detainees to ask whether they would go to Zintan, but they refused. That same day, one person attempted suicide. Then the food stopped arriving.

"Some people get diarrhea, especially all small babies [are] sick."

On April 21, Binyam messaged: "People are very weak and losing power, especially babies, mothers, and pregnant women. The problem is humanity is lost from the world, I don't know the reason."

———

Christians were praying inside Qasr bin Ghashir when the shots began. It was the afternoon of Tuesday, April 23, 2019. Refugees had not heard the approaching militia, who wore uniforms showing they were aligned with Haftar's Libyan National Army. "When they saw the cross of the people praying, they said 'Stop praying,' but people didn't hear . . . After a few minutes [they] started shooting," one witness told me later. "They came without any reason. They came to get inside."

"Right now they are attacking the center, shooting more people . . . They are shooting us directly. We need medical treatment right now because the people with us, their injuries are really a lot."

A detainee from Darfur, Sudan, said he thought the fighters were still in a vehicle when they began to shoot. He remembers people falling like dominos, women fainting, men downed by bullets. "Then they entered the hangar and began to stab people with a knife. They want phones. On a phone call [one of the men] said the orders came from [the center's manager], 'kill them all.'" In response, some refugees began to drop and break apart blocks of cement that had been lying inside the hall they stayed in so they could throw the pieces at the armed men.

"People are bleeding a lot; now, I need emergency assistance. Please share for us to the world. Please, please, please, dear, we are in danger."

My contacts were quick thinking. They knew they needed evidence to be believed, so they pulled out phones they usually kept hidden and took videos. In one, what sounds like gunfire could be heard outside the center, as refugees and migrants called out. In another, pools, splatters, streaks of blood were visible on the concrete floor as detainees dressed the wounds of those shot. Gaunt men lay on thin mattresses, beside blue UNHCR-branded mats.[10] One man had a bloody wound on his neck; another on his chin.[11] A tourniquet, to stop catastrophic bleeding from a leg injury, was fashioned out of a scarf; an orange sling strung together from clothing. All that time, through WhatsApp and Facebook messages, they begged to be rescued.

"They are beating and shooting people. We are in a bad situation, Haftar's soldiers attacked us . . . The network is very poor. Now all people are stressed, do something, dear."[12] .

Some people had died, they said, and around twenty were injured. Then we lost contact.

———

When we regained a connection the following day, refugees in Qasr bin Ghashir told me an ambulance had already taken away some of the dead bodies; they had no idea who sent it.

Meanwhile, UNHCR spread disinformation—incomprehensibly issuing a statement saying guns were only fired in the air, and there were "no bullet wounds," though "twelve refugees endured physical attacks that required hospital treatment."[13] They said they were aware of no deaths.

Everyone I spoke to who had witnessed the attack said UNHCR's statement was painfully untrue. "That is false news," said one man. "All are shot by bullets."

"Two people dead immediately," said an Eritrean refugee. A humanitarian worker who had contact with UNHCR at the time called their statement a "huge error" and "key fuck-up," saying they were likely passing on information they received from "someone who had an interest in saying that no one was shot."

On the ground, there was an active cover-up. Along with dead bodies, around sixteen of the most injured people were taken to a military base by armed men in what others said was an attempt to hide evidence of the crimes. They managed a phone call out, sounding the alarm. Back in the detention center itself, survivors who had to spend another night there screamed in their sleep.

"There are injured people until now. The ambulance did not return back.
All of them have a dangerous injury on their leg."

MSF, whose staff treated some of the injured, confirmed there were bullet wounds, too. "It is the clearest example yet of why all refugees and migrants in Tripoli detention centers must be urgently evacuated out of Libya," said their project coordinator for Tripoli, Craig Kenzie, in a statement.[14] The day after the attack, Amnesty International called for it to be investigated as a war crime.[15] Human Rights Watch concurred when I told them about the evidence I had. "Deliberately firing on detained civilians, including migrants and refugees, would be a war crime," said Gerry Simpson, Human Rights Watch's associate director for the conflict and crisis division. "[Even] indiscriminately firing on a detention center known to contain fighters and civilians breaches the laws of war."[16]

I asked the EU for a statement. "Alleged violations of human rights and violence against civilians, including refugees and migrants, are completely unacceptable and must be denounced in the strongest terms," an EU spokesperson emailed back. "We are working in close cooperation with the UN to protect the refugees and migrants affected by the clashes."[17]

In Tunis, humanitarian workers said the bloodiness and brutality of the Qasr bin Ghashir attack marked a "turning point" among UN agency staff and aid workers. One aid official told me that, before this, issues regarding refugees were not considered at the "same level of seriousness" as they should have been. It compelled a lot of officials to reflect honestly on how they had acted or failed to act.

"That Libyan context was full of [questioning] did I do enough? Did I do everything that was in my power at the time?" he said. In the wake of the attack, he remembered many conversations about what had gone wrong, with officials asking themselves, "did I pull all the right levers . . . to convince people that [in this case, moving to another detention center] was the best option? Because what happened later was so much worse."

————

I was working hard to get the story out, but the Qasr bin Ghashir attack also marked one of my first experiences of direct censorship as a journalist. Days before, I had been approached by an editor at the United Arab Emirates-based *National* newspaper to write an update on how detained refugees were managing during the conflict. *The National* had recently hired a series of well-respected international journalists whose work I admired, and when one had previously asked me to write about the testimonies I was gathering from refugees in Libya I submitted two articles, which were published without any problems.[18]

This time, I led my report with what was clearly the most shocking recent development: the shooting at Qasr bin Ghashir. I said the attackers appeared to be aligned with Haftar and his LNA. In response, a senior editor wrote to me saying it was "a really good read," but they could not publish the article. "I'm actually really embarrassed about this but we can't actually run it. Seems there's a party line we can't cross at the moment and I said I wouldn't ask you to change the story/omit something to make it palatable for those with thin skins here. It seems that the line about LNA forces opening fire on migrants was too much for us, which in my opinion—for what it's worth—is insane." The UAE was actively involved in Libya's war, funneling in weapons and fighters to support Haftar, which explained their decision.[19] I never worked for that newspaper again.

————

Why exactly had the attack taken place? Rumors swirled that the militia running Qasr bin Ghashir supported Haftar and had been longing to use it as a military base, but the refugees were getting in the way. If it was an inside job, it worked. The survivors agreed to leave. More than three hundred were moved to another detention center. In a statement, UNHCR again said the group had been "evacuated . . . to safety"[20]—their statement accompanied by a photo of smiling children. But quickly, those driven away came to the stunning realization that they were right back in the center of human smuggling.

AL NASR DETENTION CENTER, ZAWIYA

As soon as the first busloads of refugees arrived at Al Nasr detention center in Zawiya, an hour's drive away on the northwest coast, all hopes they had of a warm welcome evaporated. The hundreds of survivors were greeted by guards with growling dogs who told them they would be locked inside with no sunlight, indefinitely, if they did not agree to pay money quickly in order to go to sea.

"He said pay for me 4,000 dinars, I will put you in the sea. Or if you not want to pay 4,000 dinars I will send you back to your country."

From that day on, refugees knew they needed to raise between $500 and $1,500, depending on their nationality, to be put in a rubber boat. The Nigerians among them called these sea journeys "pushing."

"It's the daily movement of this detention center. Daily, people go to the sea, it's a big market of smuggling. Smugglers in this detention center and this city are famous."

Osama, the manager of Al Nasr detention center, was a short, tempestuous man; detainees were amazed to see his willingness even to beat Libyans. They thought he was drunk a lot, or maybe on drugs. He would speak openly about his smuggling business. "If you talk to [him] about the Mediterranean [he] will answer: 'Yes, we have good boats,'" recalled a Sudanese detainee.

> "*The boats leave in the middle of the night. I think they leave when the number of people is enough to fill the boat and the situation of the sea is ok.*"

Shortly after they were transported there, detainees overheard him boasting that one of his vessels had made it to Europe. "The joy was clear in Osama's face," said the Sudanese man, "because if he managed to get his boat to Europe, he would attract many immigrants now."

Osama seemed to be referring to a group rescued by German charity-run ship the *Sea-Watch 3*. On Friday, May 17, 2019, the same day Osama was gloating about his success, eighteen families rescued by its crew were permitted to disembark in Italy. Two days later, the remaining forty-seven people on board arrived on Italian soil after further negotiations with authorities there.[21] The following month, the *Sea-Watch 3* would pick up another one hundred and sixty-five people off Zawiya's coast. This rescue would become infamous after three of the men on board—a Guinean man and two Egyptians—were arrested and accused of carrying out torture against other migrants in Al Nasr detention center. Refugees said they were *capos*—detainees who began to collaborate with their guards. The Guinean man, who was just twenty-two, was sentenced to twelve years in prison, down from twenty after an appeal.[22] Osama was mentioned seventy times in the prosecutor's report.[23]

That May, 1,224 people were caught at sea and returned to Libya—more than all of the rest of that year so far combined.[24] A large number went straight to Zawiya. The newcomers were locked up in separate buildings, close to the Qasr bin Ghashir survivors. They were not registered with UNHCR, and they were treated even worse than the others.

"People are still tortured, beaten, made into slaves, and sold like a goat. It's clear how many prisoners are dead from secret torture and poor medication, even a lack of nutrients, food. We hear in the middle of the night noisy screaming sometimes in the locked hanger."

The halls became suffocating, and detainees had no choice but to sleep in the toilets if they wanted to lie down. A Sudanese man, calling for help, sent me a photo of two men curled up in a toilet, which I posted on Twitter after obscuring their faces. Somehow, Osama discovered that the photo had been published and embarked on a hunt for my source. Refugees said he called them all outside, put his hand on his penis and told detainees he would put it in their mouths one by one, then hit his own head against a door while saying he was prepared to kill them. Eventually, they were allowed to go back indoors.

"When the guards want to sell [detainees] no one can stop them, even UNHCR. UNHCR and IOM must take responsibility for these sold people because they were brought here from the sea. We are facing a big problem in front of us. We do not feel safe. We are living in a very dangerous place."

On the night of June 3, I received audio with the sound of gunshots, several paced out, almost leisurely, and others fired in quick succession: guards firing at detainees who tried to escape.[25] New captives kept arriving. The lack of space meant some detainees now stayed outside, though if they tried to construct shelters for shade Osama would randomly order them to be dismantled again. There was a growing psychological crisis. In August, a man was killed in his sleep by another detainee, according to multiple witnesses. "He was beaten by a girl with mental problems. The girl was hurting mentally," said an Eritrean who was present. "She beat him [while he was] sleeping in the night, with stones. He was a good guy."

One of the people now in Al Nasr was Violet, a 23-year-old Nigerian who said she came to Libya after being promised a job as a "sales girl" in Europe. She was the eldest of four children raised by a single mother; their father died when she was young. There was never enough money, and Violet dropped out of school to sell drinking water so they could eat.

A woman she met while working convinced her that getting a job in Europe would enable Violet to support her family and further her own education. "I agreed because I had no hope," Violet recalled. Three days driving through Niger's desert, to reach Libya, culminated in an accident. Others who fell from the truck broke their legs and arms; Violet fell on her forehead and never received medical treatment. Once they crossed the border, she was passed between smugglers before she was instructed to work as a housemaid in Tripoli for three months. Around this time Violet said she and another Nigerian girl were told to have sex with a man in exchange for food.

She tried to cross the sea twice. The first time the boat capsized, and those on board were rescued and brought back. The second time, they stayed on the Mediterranean for two days. When the situation became critical, they called the Italian coastguard to rescue them, but the Italians contacted the Libyan coastguard. In detention, a UN employee asked if she would return home, "but I refused because of my future and that of my younger siblings," Violet told me.

She began to video call me from the female section of Al Nasr detention center, where controls on phones were lax, likely because of how often people were ordered to appeal to their relatives for money. "I really need your help, ma, I can't go home empty-handed. I wish you all the best and amen to all secret prayers," she told me. She was terrified of her own family, picturing their disappointment.

In the end, though, she did go back to Nigeria, and another detainee commandeered her SIM card. I never heard from Violet again.

———

In 2019, a report by the UN Panel of Experts of the International Sanctions Committee on Libya would describe the Al Nasr detention center as "a known hub for human trafficking, where migrants are subject to various forms of human rights abuses."[26] The report, which was presented to the UN Security Council, identified Osama al-Kuni Ibrahim as the man in charge. "Either he or the individuals under his control facilitated the exploitation, abuse and extortion of migrants," it read. "Sexual exploitation and violence, beatings, starvation, and other degrading treatment, including to minors, frequently occur." A 2021 report by the same body would echo that information, saying Osama "had committed several violations of international humanitarian law and international human rights law" and that his "victims recounted acts of kidnapping for ransom, torture, sexual and gender-based violence, forced labor and killing."[27] The same year, he was sanctioned by both the United States and the UN, with US Secretary of State Antony Blinken urging the Libyan government to hold him accountable.[28]

The center was under scrutiny before the UN reports. In 2017, its then-manager admitted to *Washington Post* journalists that smugglers came inside and removed detainees.[29] In June 2018, Mohamed Kashlaf—commander of the Al Nasr Brigade, the militia controlling the center—was put under UN sanctions for human smuggling and trafficking, including allegations that female detainees were being sold as "sex slaves."[30] Kashlaf was a close associate of Osama's, as documented by the Panel of Experts report. Members of his militia ordered Qasr bin Ghashir survivors to clean their weapons, refugees told me, sending photos of their friends crouched over guns.

The head of Zawiya's section of the Libyan coastguard, Abd al-Rahman Milad—known as "Bija"—was also associated with the detention center. In May 2017, Bija had traveled to Italy for meetings with intelligence agencies, during which he appealed for more European money to stop migrant flows.[31] Photos show him sitting at a desk in a gray suit jacket, a lanyard around his neck and a handout of papers in front of him. In 2018, he was sanctioned by the Security Council due to accusations he collaborated with smugglers, including Kashlaf. He was also accused of sinking migrant boats using firearms.[32] Later on, Bija was even arrested by the UN-backed Tripoli government and accused of trafficking, but he was set free less than four months later.[33] Qasr bin Ghashir survivors told me Bija visited the center while they were there.

All of this raised further questions about Europe's relationship with Libyan authorities, why UNHCR had moved hundreds of traumatized refugees to a center associated with sanctioned smugglers, and why the EU was funding the interceptions of ever more victims, who ended up there, too. When I asked an EU spokesperson, he answered, unconvincingly, "The EU has always taken very seriously any allegations of criminal activities. Our engagement in Libya aims precisely at limiting any risks of unlawful activities." The Libyan coastguard funding was "crucial to save lives at sea and fight trafficking and smuggling," he said.[34]

CHAPTER 16

ZINTAN: LIBYA'S "GUANTANAMO"

"We have made an engagement with death, so pray
for us before the wedding comes."

–FROM A SONG WRITTEN BY DETAINEES IN ZINTAN DETENTION CENTER[1]

"Does the world have eyes? Tell the world we are humans, not animals."

–AN ERITREAN REFUGEE IN ZINTAN DETENTION CENTER

Over three days in October, 2018, Fatima Ausman Darboe watched her young son, Abdou Aziz, die from appendicitis. His stomach swelled, and he writhed in pain. She held him as his condition deteriorated. Most other mothers could have brought their child to a hospital, but Fatima was incarcerated. She only had her voice.

"Come and look at my boy, his stomach is swelled up, I don't know why his stomach is swelled up like that," she would cry. "What is this, what is this?" She clutched his small body in her arms, holding him aloft so the guards outside could see his protruding stomach. The uniformed men repeatedly told her there was nothing they could do as their manager was not in the vicinity, though she was convinced they were lying. The International

Medical Corps (IMC), the organization supposed to be providing life-saving care in the detention center, and the UN agencies, which should have been monitoring conditions inside the center, were nowhere to be found. Fatima's appeals were ignored.

"They didn't worry about it, I don't know why. He was just a boy, just six years old, why they are doing that? When a child is sick he's not supposed to stay in detention, they're supposed to take him to hospital," she said later.

The detention center's manager finally turned up and took pity on the pair. He could not get medics to come to the center, so he drove Fatima and the child towards a hospital himself. It was too late. Fatima's son died in the car.

Long negotiations ensued regarding the burial, and the boy was not laid to rest for a month. Fatima and her husband were being detained in different rooms, but they traveled together to see their child's body one final time. Fatima's husband then accompanied the boy to a burial place, which Fatima would later see as her husband's final undoing.

"Why [are] you crying, get up, you have another child," a Somali woman with her own three-year-old remembered guards in Zintan telling Fatima in the aftermath. "They didn't have any mercy for her. They think we are animals, cows, they don't think we are humans."

Fatima was born in the West African nation of the Gambia, a small sliver of a country surrounded by Senegal. For more than two decades, from the mid 1990s, it was ruled by an erratic dictator, Yahya Jammeh, who headed death squads, promoted fake cures for AIDS and infertility, and ordered literal witch hunts, during which elderly people in rural villages were rounded up and forced to drink hallucinogenic liquids as a means of control.[2] Fatima traveled to Libya at the height of Jammeh's lunacy, in 2009, where she met the man who would become her husband, another Gambian. He had been there for a decade already, and they quickly fell in love.

They managed to survive in Libya and had three children together. It was only when Fatima's husband developed a heart problem that they tried to cross the Mediterranean Sea to reach Europe in the hope of finding affordable medical care. "It was due to my husband's health condition, that's why we wanted to find a greener pasture," Fatima explained. They were arrested off the coast of Zuwara, a city around 100 kilometers to the west of Tripoli, and driven the 180 kilometers to Zintan detention center two days later. Fatima, who was pregnant again, gave birth to her youngest child inside the detention center.

Her eldest son's death was not the final tragedy. Weeks after the boy was buried, her husband died, too, seemingly from a stroke triggered by shock. Fatima was still locked in a separate women's hall, and she never got to say goodbye. "If he fell down or if he was sick the guards should have come and told me [to] go and see him," she recalled later. "Maybe he wanted to tell me something. Or maybe I wanted to tell him something. They didn't know." She only found out about the death when a guard asked her to confirm her husband's full name. Her heart stopped; she felt cold, like she had been put "in the fridge."

> "They did not take me until the next day, in the morning. He was already dead. They took me, they said you're going to see your husband. The policeman told me your husband passed away. I could not talk, I could not do anything, just my body, all my body was just shaking. I was just looking but I did not see anything . . . I didn't cry. I don't remember, oh my God. They told me that maybe it's up to one or two hours I didn't talk, I didn't do anything, I was just looking in the same place."

The guards allowed her one phone call, and she dialed her brother-in-law in the Gambia. "Your brother is dead," Fatima told him, and the line was immediately cut. Had he hung up in shock, or had he even heard her? Fatima felt so alone.

Her husband's body was not buried for three months. She regretted asking to see him a final time; she no longer recognized his face. Other detainees would remember Fatima leaving the detention center suddenly, soon after this, with no explanation. I knew where she had gone: back to the Gambia with her remaining children, on a flight organized by IOM. She traveled through the so-called voluntary return program. She had been out of the country so long she hardly knew what she was going back to, but felt there was no other option.

Over the following years, Fatima would message me every so often.

"Hi. Miss you."

"Things are very bad. No work, no money."

"I am just managing."

Sometimes she called me in the middle of the night. She was lonely and easily became upset, recounting what she had gone through, remembering how bleak Zintan was, reliving the moments she discovered her son and husband had died. "RIP my dear husband" became her name on WhatsApp. Her profile photo was of him too: a serious-looking man in a navy sports jumper gazing at the camera, with pink and blue hearts (Fatima's addition) superimposed on his chest. She sent me pictures of her eldest boy, taken when he was alive. I looked at the images of this cheerful-looking child—in red shorts and a blue t-shirt, posing on one leg, his hands intertwined under his chin; in a baggy white shirt, lips pursed with bright eyes looking straight at the camera—and wondered what his life could have been like if he had lived.

———

Through the desert and deep into Libya's Nafusa Mountains, 180 kilometers southwest of Tripoli, was Zintan, Dhar-el-Jebel, the detention center refugees nicknamed "Guantanamo."[3] During the fighting that broke out in Tripoli in September 2018, hundreds of refugees and migrants were bused to Zintan from Tariq al Matar, a center in the capital city that closed after it was shelled and one detainee injured.[4] Italian news agency ANSA reported that the move was coordinated by UNHCR and the Libyan authorities.[5] It was the beginning of an ordeal that would last years, from which dozens would never escape.

In his book *The Burning Shores*, Frederic Wehrey described the Nafusa Mountains as "a natural haven for dissidents" where "remote villages sit atop its bluffs, each one accessible only by narrow roads that snake through ravines." He said the mountains were divided between militias: "alliances and checkpoints shifted; you had to tread the landscape carefully." When there was no visual clue, like a flag, to tell you which fighters controlled the territory you were in, "you were flying blind, hoping that your guide knew the right turnoff, was friends with so-and-so's cousin, spoke the right dialect, or had the right last name."[6]

According to a report in US weekly magazine *The Nation*, Dhar-el-Jebel center in Zintan used to be a training center for children who studied Gaddafi's *Green Book*, before the dictator was ousted and killed in 2011.[7] The biggest danger to refugees locked up in Zintan was not abuse or torture, it was being forgotten. This was an outpost, removed from international organizations, diplomats, and any real oversight.

"It's too far. No one can help you. They can do anything they want."

Shortly after they were moved there, detainees began to perish.

———

In the biggest hangar, there were three toilets for hundreds of men and boys (more than 130 of whom were under the age of eighteen[8]). Refugees had to pee in buckets, and a large pile of rubbish, buzzing with flies and crawling with maggots, took up one section of the hall.[9] Insects scurried across mattresses as they slept. No one from outside would enter this hall for a full eight months, and food was delivered through a hatch. Detainees ate once or twice a day—a small bread roll or around 200 grams of plain macaroni or couscous, garnished with a dollop of tomato paste if they were lucky. Everywhere, people were coughing. Some lost up to 30 kilograms of body weight.

> *"The UNHCR wouldn't enter when they came because they don't want to smell us, they don't want to see you. If they're a humanitarian organization why won't they see us? If they care about refugees, why won't they enter and see how we live?"*

A section of the hangar was reserved for the mentally ill. Four people who tried to electrocute themselves by grabbing hold of electrical wires were deposited in this zone, their feet bound and hands tied behind their backs so they could not attempt it again.[10]

> *"At this time all people are in a big stress, because in every two weeks one person is dead . . . If they're sick no one thinks he is going to be ok, he just thinks death is my destiny."*

Over the next nine months there would be at least twenty-two deaths, a 16-year-old Somali girl and an Eritrean dentist among them.[11] Haftom, the dentist, used to tell a joke that went like this: "God was watching the globe and saw Eritrea was green. 'How did this country become so green,' he wondered, and went to investigate. But when he got there, he saw the green was overcrowded militias."

Of course, this was black humor. Like tens of thousands of others, Haftom fled Eritrea. The 32-year-old wanted to get away from brutal leaders who controlled every aspect of his life, from his profession and salary to where he could live and what topics he could speak about. Friends described him as a "quiet, smart" man, who had eventually despaired of any chance that things would get better. By February 2018, Haftom had survived smugglers in the Sahara and police in Sudan. Twelve hours in a rubber boat ended with a Libyan coastguard interception. He died days before Christmas that same year.[12]

Though friends believed Haftom developed a heart problem in Zintan, it was not clear what the final cause of his death was. "So many people [are] getting ill," messaged another detainee. "They take them and [put] them in one house and they don't give them any medication." Haftom had been moved into the building where tuberculosis patients were held. Those who saw him around this time say he knew he had reached the end. "Everyone in here [thinks that] if he gets sick. No one is thinking that they are going to be OK. They are thinking only it's our turn," said a fellow detainee.

Underlying every illness was starvation. "People were dying of hunger," a detainee later recalled. Ten pieces of bread could be bought for one dinar (around $0.20 on the black market rate), he complained, but they got nowhere near that. He wondered where all the funding meant for refugees had gone. "Those people wouldn't have died from disease if they were being fed," he said.

"Where is humanity? People die there more than the smugglers. The smugglers say we are better than UNHCR because they see the outcome. Under UNHCR, even with our money, we cannot get food."

———

When refugees died, there was no formal process to let their families know. There had never been an official list of their names anyway. Sometimes, other detainees posted photos of those who had passed away online, and these would be shared over and over again on Facebook by sympathetic social media users with crying emojis and written prayers to whatever God the person supposed was listening. *"Mengsti semayat ywarsoo,"* meant "rest in peace" in Tigrinya. I sometimes shared the news of these deaths, too.

Later, critics would tell me it was inconsiderate to put information about the deaths online, for fear of upsetting families who had not been informed. But surely the death itself was the most upsetting part, and some of them would want to know?

Abel, an Eritrean who had made it to Germany, found out his younger brother, Teddy, had died through Facebook. In a crackly call, he told me they had gone without contact for two months when he saw Teddy's picture online with "RIP" written beside it. Abel contacted the poster. "I said how do you have that information?"

The man who made the Facebook post was in Switzerland, but his brother was in Libya, too, and had apparently been with Teddy during his final days. After that conversation in late 2018, Abel said I was the first person to contact him about this, seven months later.

Teddy left Eritrea in 2013 and crossed the border into Ethiopia, where he worked illegally. He made his way to Egypt, and then to Libya. "Five years in this harsh life," said Abel, with regret.

From Libya, Teddy occasionally got a chance to call. "He said we are in a bad situation, we don't have medicine, we don't have food." Teddy tried to reach Italy, but he was caught on the sea. He ended up in Zintan and died at the age of just twenty-six. "I didn't hear he was sick, but most of the people who are in danger in Libya don't have the chance to talk a lot. Once a month or once every two months they will contact you. It was such a shock," Abel told me. "There is lot of bad history [like this] in each and every family in Eritrea."

In early 2020, I met Abel in person. He suggested a bar in Berlin's trendy Kreuzberg area. He was thin, in a blue spotted shirt. I bought him a beer, then he bought me one. The room was smoky; stylish young people squashed into armchairs of various shapes or perched on wooden seats, cigarette in hand.

Abel was one of six children. Another sister was in Italy, and a brother was in France. There was Teddy, who died, and a 19-year-old, who had just escaped Eritrea for an Ethiopian refugee camp. The teenager had spent the previous two years in the military, crying constantly throughout the few times she was given leave. "You should know that girls and women are raped there," Abel told me.

He had been in Germany for three years but still shared a room in a refugee reception center. One week, three people there killed themselves, he told me. He worried about his mother, back in Eritrea, who was prematurely old (he suspected through heartbreak) and physically ailing. Occasionally, Abel phoned her, but he could usually afford just five minutes before the line was cut off.

In the bar, by coincidence, we met another Eritrean man. He told us he worked seven days a week in multiple jobs, including as a cashier in a Berlin airport souvenir shop. Eventually, he aimed to set up his own bar, with spaces upstairs where Eritreans, down on their luck or newly arrived, could sleep when they were stuck. He smiled at Abel, conveying a common understanding of what their people were going through.

Abel also traveled through Libya on his way to Germany. That country was "the mother of chance . . . always bad and worse, like the devil," he said. "All of us Eritreans, we came the same way . . . Eritreans, they are all over the world. Like a farmer spreads seeds on the land, Eritreans are like seeds all over the world."

When the conversation turned to Teddy, Abel became like a bird reluctant to perch, unable to find a branch sturdy enough. He did not want to think any longer about tragedy, but life was nothing without family, he said. "Life means to be with your father, your brother, your mother, your family. It wasn't my dream to come here. I just couldn't stay in my country."

———

By early 2019, so many people had died in Zintan that it became a logistical problem. The refrigerated area where the bodies were stored was full, and the local community of Muslims would not allow Christians to be buried in their cemetery. "Administrative reasons," an aid worker explained to me. "Having dead people is a burden."

"Dead bodies. Until now they did not bury. We ask so many times about this."

So there was a selection among the living. The decision was made to move the sickest people to another remote center, 110 kilometers northwest, with a better capacity for disposing of corpses. Detainees said they believed those chosen were going to Tripoli for medical treatment: they were told this by Zintan's management, they recalled, and that was why they gave consent.[13] In early 2019, around fifty people were transferred to Gharyan.[14] By May, at least eight of that group were dead, detainees said.[15]

"When we arrived, we were immediately locked in a container," one person told an aid worker who visited Gharyan later on. Gharyan was notorious already because roughly 150 detainees there had been sold to traffickers and ransomed for $20,000, while five left behind were shot. Aware of this history, one of the new arrivals tried to hang herself.[16]

———

Back in Zintan, detainees began to construct a church. The four-and-a-half-foot-high structure was crafted from food cartons and mattress sponge, colored red with bits of towels, green from cut-up sheets, and white from the Colgate toothpaste handed out in aid packages. A blue UNHCR mat lay in front of crosses fashioned from candle wax.[17] Every day, at 11:00 a.m., hundreds of detainees would gather to pray for the dead. This continued for the best part of a year as the death toll rose. They attempted protests, too, using tomato paste mixed with pepper to inscribe pleas on sponge mattresses, holding them up to a phone's camera. "We need emergency," "we are innocent refugees," "we are being starved to death," they wrote. They built up contacts among activists and journalists. Receiving messages from supporters outside was "like a candle in the night," one man, who contracted tuberculosis and lost 25 kilograms in Zintan, later told me.

"We are victim by UNHCR in Libya. We are abused by human rights organizations."

"Give up suffering from TB; improve our drugs; UNHCR should care."

"We are urging them to hold a funeral for those stored in the refrigerator in Zintan al Jabal DC."

———

I started asking questions about IMC, which was supposed to be providing medical care in Zintan. The Los Angeles-headquartered organization was established in 1984 and had staff working in around thirty countries, including Afghanistan and Somalia. Its website, which featured pictures of IMC "global ambassadors" Sienna Miller, Jude Law, and *Vogue* editor Anna Wintour, among others, stated that IMC had "changed the very definition of relief work."[18]

But in Libya I repeatedly heard that detainees' health rapidly declined in centers that IMC was working in. A reporting document compiled by IMC in 2018, which was sent to UNHCR and someone leaked to me, said the organization ran through their annual budget quickly and stopped referring detainees to private clinics as early as May that year.[19] Public health clinics often refused to treat refugees and migrants, leaving them no other way to get urgent medical care. The same document even described a day, in December 2018, when the management of Zintan refused to let IMC's staff leave the center without referring some of the sickest detainees for medical treatment; the staff seemingly agreed but then transferred two to another detention center instead.[20]

Zintan seemed to be the worst center IMC was presiding over in terms of the medical situation: "a major scandal," as one aid worker described it. When they did visit, IMC staff would look at detainees in the big hangar through a grate in the door, or simply rely on the detention center's guards to select patients for them. People who needed treatment for tuberculosis, chest infections, anemia, kidney problems, diarrhea, scabies, and malnutrition said they were offered paracetamol and ibuprofen. "Do you think by these methods they'll cure us?" asked an Eritrean man skeptically.

"IMC are very stupid doctors, no sense about life. They take salaries. People are dying."

I began emailing both UNHCR and IOM about the mounting number of deaths in Zintan in October 2018. A month after detainees were moved there, four people had already died, and it was clear something was terribly wrong.

IMC was receiving funds from the UNHCR, the EU Trust Fund, the UK, and Germany for their work in Libya. They had a staff of more than seventy people, almost all of whom were Libyans, and an annual budget of $11 million,[21] more than $10 million of which came from UNHCR between 2018 and early 2020.[22] IMC boasted of being "one of the few" international organizations supporting conflict-affected populations in Libya, and one of three that relocated expatriate staff back after fighting escalated in 2014.[23] Yet it would not admit there was a problem in Zintan.

I first tried to contact them in October 2018; the following month, a spokesperson in Washington, DC, responded, saying they were "not in a position to help."[24] In February 2019, IMC's Director of Global Communications, Todd Bernhardt, told me they would not speak to me "due to security concerns and the sensitive nature of our work in Libya."[25]

In March, more emails where I documented detainees' calls for help went unanswered. When I tweeted saying IMC were refusing to talk to me, Bernhardt emailed complaining that I was misrepresenting the organization. "I'd hoped that at some point we'd be able to talk to you about the situation in Libya, but you clearly are not operating according to journalistic guidelines,"[26] he wrote. All this while people were dying an average of one every fortnight.

When I showed the message from IMC to Isaac, one of the Eritreans in Zintan, he responded. "OMG, why would they say it like that. This is inhuman beyond belief. They don't have time for us. No organization will take any responsibility."

He was not the only one frustrated about the behavior of IMC. "If they had said they cannot cope, some people would have been saved," said an aid worker with knowledge of the situation. In an email as late as May 2019, sent to other aid agencies after concerns were raised, the IMC claimed both its staff and IOM employees visited the center every day and said the only reason Zintan was being discussed was because detainees who wanted resettlement and evacuation had "rioted."[27] (Ironically, the IMC program director who wrote this email, Anil Kangal, has written and spoken extensively about her own love of recreational travel across the world, which gives her "unlimited freedom" and "defined the person who I am today."[28])

Instead of admitting their own shortcomings in Zintan, another aid official, who attended high-level meetings, said they had seen UNHCR and IOM representatives defending Zintan's management. The aid official also said an IOM representative dismissed the reports of deaths in Zintan as "fake news," and both IOM and UNHCR staff emphasized that refugees and migrants are prone to exaggeration. These agencies are actively "blocking" the truth from coming out, the aid official said. In an emailed response to me later, after the UN finally admitted the scale of the deaths, IOM chief spokesperson Leonard Doyle said his agency had "always been vocal about the grim conditions in detention centers" and had "jointly, with UNHCR, publicly called upon the European Union and African Union to adopt a new approach to the situation in Libya . . . The suffering of migrants in Libya is intolerable and is of great concern to the organization. Any statements attributed to IOM and IOM staff suggesting otherwise are inconsistent with the organization's core principles."[29]

I tried to get a reply from the Libyan authorities, but nothing came back.

In the week of May 13, 2019, Haben Dirar, a 21-year-old from Eritrea, was the twentieth death since mid-September.[30] "He was a student before he fled. Young, quiet, excellent," said Isaac, who was the same age. "He had a bright passion, he told his friends he wanted to continue his education when he arrived in a safe place." That same month, 1,224 people were intercepted on the Mediterranean Sea and returned to Libya by the Libyan coastguard—more than the rest of the year combined.[31]

MSF began pushing for access to Zintan, and its staff eventually got in. An official who arrived mentioned my Twitter account, Isaac told me—saying he had seen the refugees' pleas for rescue online. He walked around the hall they were locked in, staying around forty-five minutes—the first time an outsider had entered in about seven months. "I must say that I never saw people abandoned as much as in Zintan and Gharyan. The level of despair of the detainees is beyond words," the official would write later, in an email to IOM, IMC, and the World Health Organization.[32] That day, MSF staff distributed milk and water to children and referred five people to hospitals, including one who went directly into intensive care. Detainees felt better after this visit, but the next day everything got worse. On Friday, May 17, management shut off the electricity and water. There was no food. "Nothing has changed, we are crying in the locked hall," Isaac messaged.

"Still, we are alive."

A video sent to me the following Wednesday showed what happened when guards turned on the water taps for just ten minutes. Five buckets were filled up, but hundreds of people were desperately thirsty. A detainee filled a cup and handed it to each man who stepped forward in turn to gulp down quickly. The others stood back and stared, but soon they began jostling, realizing the buckets were nearly empty, and those at the back would not drink anything at all. It was their first water in days, and perhaps their last. (An email from an IMC staff member, sent that month, described the detention center manager "utiliz[ing] access to water as a mechanism for punishment."[33])

The same day, Isaac said the windows of the hall they were locked in had been covered in electrical wire to stop them escaping. Around eighteen people managed to get away before that, traveling the dangerous road to Tripoli by taxi. Two more were caught, and Isaac said they were taken to an isolation room. "They beat them and scare them," he said, "so all people are losing their hope, desperately so . . . Please, we are thirsty, we are hungry, for how long can we stay like this?"

"Is it true the EU rescued or saved our life? They are just sentencing us to death. This is an awful life. It's better to die rather than to stay here.

We lose our hope. A lot of us have developed mental disorders because we have been detained for one year and six months in this terrible condition.

We are around 620 Eritreans refugees detained in one hall. A lot of people are suffering from TB, hungry and dying every two or three weeks . . .

Death is nothing, just that is our fate.

There is some hidden issue about Zintan. We are the victims, we need a safe life. We need our rights . . . Dear Sally Hayden, we want you to know our pain . . . We need your help and support. Whatever you do, just do it. Please stand on behalf of us. Denounce it or write an article, whatever."

———

How many were dying in detention centers? Hundreds? Thousands? I asked Federico Soda, the head of IOM in Libya, why the UN tracks the numbers of people drowning at sea but not the numbers dying in detention. He told me there was no real reason, and hearing me say it was lacking made him consider it again. "I would like to see if we [can] contribute in a more systematic way to [getting] this kind of information . . . It's extremely important. But we don't have that information," he said. "Ideally, it should be the authorities that are responsible for the center[s]."

IOM compiled estimates of deaths on the Mediterranean by triangulating evidence and testimonies from survivors, international organizations, the Libyan coastguard, and other sources, though the real numbers were widely believed to be higher than listed. ("I hate it. It's just so depressing," Soda said.)

When it came to informing families, Soda confirmed there was no real process. With sea deaths, the bodies would be decomposed and hard to identify; DNA testing was very expensive; and families rarely came forward. In Libyan detention centers, Soda said, "these people are just like everybody else. They have friends. They have acquaintances that they've traveled with. So I suspect that somehow that information of what's happened to the person gets back home."

I knew that was not always true. Abel was not aware of Teddy's death until he saw that Facebook post. Others, whose friends died in detention, told me they had no idea how to contact bereaved family members to inform them. As the casualties in Zintan mounted, detainees there sent me a list of the names, photos, and nationalities of most of Zintan's dead, through WhatsApp.

———

Luckily, the MSF visit made a difference. An urgent meeting was convened on May 27, 2019, with UN agencies deciding they should travel to the center one week later. After their visit, ninety-six of the detainees—mainly

women and Somali men—were taken to the UNHCR Gathering and Departure Facility for potential evacuation.

According to the report the UN agencies produced afterwards, which I
obtained a copy of, their delegation met Nasser En-Nakou'a, the head of the
center.[34] He stated that 750 people, including eight children, fifty-seven
females, and 685 males, were being held in Zintan. Inside the biggest hangar were 432 male Eritreans, including 132 minors.

En-Nakou'a confirmed that twenty-two people had died by then: eighteen men, three women, and one child. An IMC staff member told the
visiting delegation that they suspected 80 percent of detainees still alive in
the center had tuberculosis, though most were not being treated or tested.[35]

The report was written with an almost ghoulish practicality. "Mr. Nasser
En-Nakou'a reported on the difficulties in handling the deceased, including
[the] burial of corpses as Zintan and Yafren hospitals do no longer have the
capacity to deal with these. Also, the local community has refused to bury
the bodies of non-Muslims in the cemetery of Muslim people. The most
prevalent cause of death was tuberculosis. Sick migrants are transferred to
Gharyan detention center, where most of them die." When the manager
appealed for help feeding detained refugees and migrants, UNHCR and
IOM staff told them food is the responsibility of the Libyan authorities.

After this visit, the hundreds of men and boys who had been rammed
into one hangar were moved and separated by guards into smaller rooms,
which were still very cramped. They began to sleep outside instead, fashioning their own shelters from sheets.

The UN finally spoke publicly after that visit. "Conditions in Zintan are
dire," read a UNHCR statement, though they seemingly found a way to
criticize the refugees' behavior again. "Tensions amongst the detainees are
rising as they become increasingly agitated and desperate."[36] Of course, little
would improve anyway, and many of those who had survived their first year
in Zintan would go on to suffer through a second.

"Europe is responsible for the deaths of our sisters and brothers."

After that shocking number of deaths, there was never any inquiry or internal investigation, no reckoning about what had gone wrong. "It's criminal . . . it's absolutely sickening," one person who attended meetings between humanitarian agencies in Tunis told me, more than a year after that interagency visit. "No one's been [held] accountable . . . It's mad that up to now they've completely gotten away with it."

"What about UNHCR, do they take responsibility for the ones who have died in the jails who were registered?"

In early 2020, UNHCR stopped visiting Zintan again, saying they had lost access.[37] ("It's total bullshit," said the person who sat in on humanitarian coordination meetings.) More detainees died: a 24-year-old with tuberculosis, unable to run away when an electrical fire broke out; a father of three who experienced heatstroke.[38] Friends told me that the father, Tewelde Andom—a quick-to-smile, mustachioed 39-year-old whose body broke out in a lumpy rash in the days before he died—used to joke that they must have been sinners to have been condemned to this life. To reach Europe, "your heart must be so clean," he quipped.

That July, nearly two years after he was first transferred to Zintan, Isaac escaped. He fled to the coast and boarded a boat with ninety-four others, including a newborn baby. Each of them paid more than two thousand dollars for the trip. They were left drifting in the Maltese search-and-rescue zone for thirty-five hours after they issued a distress call for help, until, at long last, they arrived in Europe.

CHAPTER 17

UNHCR GATHERING AND DEPARTURE FACILITY: THE HOTEL

"If you tie a chicken with a long string, it will think that it's free."

—ERITREAN PROVERB

Refugees called it "the Hotel" because it was the nicest place any of them had seen in years. It was a guarded compound in central Tripoli, across the road from Triq al Sikka detention center and a short drive from the Libyan prime minister's office. This was the UNHCR-run Gathering and Departure Facility, known among aid workers as the "GDF."

"Water, food, and everything is available, dear. It's not a hotel but people, because they find it suitable for living, call it a hotel.
Dear, when you leave detention center you might call it paradise, 'hotel' is not enough."

UNHCR touted the GDF as an "alternative to detention" with "the potential to save lives," "the first center of its kind in Libya."[1] As early as 2017, the same year that the EU entered into its deadly deal with the Libyan coastguard, the agency began to promote this still-unopened compound as "an initiative that offers viable alternatives to [refugees'] dangerous journeys along the Central Mediterranean route."[2] The idea was that people could be assembled there from detention centers around the country, as well as Tripoli's streets, before they were evacuated to Europe or moved to another country in Africa, where they could go through more medical tests and interviews and have their asylum cases assessed. International donors contributed around $6 million towards the GDF's running,[3] 2.1 million euro of which came directly from the EU.[4]

"We hope that thousands of the most vulnerable refugees currently in Libya will benefit from this forward-looking initiative," said Roberto Mignone, then-UNHCR Libya head.[5] "We now need EU member states and others to step up with offers of resettlement places and other solutions, including family reunification slots. Together, these will be an important platform for securing solutions for these vulnerable people, based on shared responsibility."

Among staff at other international organizations, the GDF was known as a waste of time, money, and energy—at best, a bandage set up in this precarious militia-run area; at worst, a diversionary tactic that helped the agency cover its total failure to protect refugees. "If you squeezed UNHCR [about other problems], they said they are waiting for this to open," said one person who worked on the aid response. "It took them years to open it."

The GDF began to be mentioned regularly in UNHCR and EU statements, which struck an optimistic tone, suggesting change was about to come. It would not actually begin to be used until December 2018, when UNHCR announced it had a capacity for up to one thousand vulnerable refugees.[6] It was fated to stay open for just one year.

Kaleb was one of the lucky ones: he made it inside. Amid rockets, shelling, and sleepless nights in April 2019, as the war echoed throughout Tripoli, UNHCR staff came to Abu Salim to carry out a long-awaited relocation. Over two days, they moved around 350 people, including Kaleb[7]; another 475 men and boys were left behind. The fighting got so bad that month, Amnesty International would later call for a war crimes investigation because of the "indiscriminate attacks" on the Abu Salim neighborhood.[8]

Kaleb messaged me as he boarded a bus to leave the detention center, but then he lost contact. The next time I saw his face was on Twitter that same day, where UNHCR posted his picture, along with his full name, saying they had helped him "find safety." I was surprised. After years when Kaleb had kept his identity a secret for fear of potential repercussions, I questioned if he had agreed to this. Later, he told me he had not. He believed he was being interviewed for internal UNHCR purposes until he saw it played on Libyan TV. He had not even been inside the GDF when he was filmed. All he wanted to speak about was his fears for the people they had left behind, but the camera people told him to say something positive.

"I didn't know they were recording."

He described his surroundings to me. The GDF was a compound within a compound, the outer area still controlled by militias, but the inside was supposed to be a safe space. There were more than one hundred rooms, he guessed, with beds for six refugees in each. Outside was a small playground for children and benches where their parents could sit and watch them. There was grass broken up by concrete walkways. Couples shared rooms with other families, marking the first time in years they could stay together after forced separation in detention. It was a bit of a shock having everything they needed after so long without it, and some people had some difficulties adjusting. Families even got in trouble for washing clothes in the sinks; one refugee complained others were ruining the furnishings. But everyone was delighted to eat regularly and have access to staff from UNHCR, "the organization" that had long felt so distant. Some even built up rapports with individual employees.

———

"Today is a unique day for me and friends because we have got freedom from the militias of Tajoura detention center. Forty-one people have been called by UNHCR. We are now at the gathering Hotel. You are suffering with us and you have to be happy with us."

———

Ramadan, the Islamic holy month, started in early May. During the day, the Libyan staff running the GDF fasted alongside Muslim refugees, but Christians said they were not fed during daylight hours, either. At night, they claimed there was discrimination, and Muslims were provided with better food for the *iftar* meal to break their fasts. Before daylight, only the Muslims ate again. Children, in particular, began suffering. Their parents mixed water with sugar so the children could drink it and trick their stomachs into feeling full.

"They give only to the Muslims. We eat yesterday dinner only. So sister, please, we want [you] to ask UNHCR now because we are very hungry. This GDF is managed by UNHCR but look how they think and do . . . We stay for 24 hours without food, sis. We have kids and pregnants and sick people, and if we want to buy food with our money they won't give us permission, so what we do?"

A 21-year-old pregnant woman began vomiting blood. A medic on site from the Libyan government agency LibAid gave her an injection, but the pregnant woman said it did not help. Refugees claimed the healthcare clinic was badly stocked and its employees were not doing hospital referrals. Later, an Associated Press investigation would allege that nearly half of the LibAid staff supposed to be based in the GDF were effectively "ghost employees" who were paid but never turned up.[9]

After the first few weeks that Kaleb spent in the Hotel, a meeting was called. There would be new rules, said the GDF's manager. That night, fresh, aggressive guards arrived, wearing blue uniforms. "They kick people, they do whatever they want," Kaleb complained. "This place is the same as a detention center."

> *"They entered to the couple's rooms, they disturbed them at night. We are exposed to danger. Children are crying because of hunger, some of them didn't eat food up to now. Still the food crisis isn't solved. Even there's no shop to buy bread. We don't know what we can do. May Jesus solve the problems. Libya is the place of the devil."*

On Friday, May 17, 2019, one of the new guards hit a teenager and broke his tooth. The guards were accused of stealing two phones and money as well, including from a pregnant mother of two, who sobbed when she discovered her belongings missing.

Some refugees recognized the new guards from Triq al Sikka, the detention center across the road. I confirmed with separate sources that they were associated with Libya's Department for Combatting Illegal Migration, which had maintained jurisdiction over the GDF despite the UN's involvement. Though the guards were supposed to stay on the perimeter, Libya's Interior Ministry had seemingly decided there had been breaches of regulations. It seemed like an excuse to get inside. Quickly, the new guards set up a business selling food to hungry refugees, who secretly cooked smuggled-in pasta in metal kettles. The same men might even confiscate the remaining food later, after pulling a profit.

"They can't even give us enough food. Sometimes they give us it once per day, and the food on the plate is very small. It's not enough. We have pregnant women and children, that's why we need more food and can pay with our own money."

"Two days ago they collected the food from us that we bought with our money, and yesterday the soldiers came and said get inside, no going outside. The soldiers are still here in the compound and they shoot in the sky to scare us."

Emanuel, another Eritrean, said the new guards made him want to escape the UNHCR center. "We really are starving. And we have fear." One day, a guard called him over and began insulting him for no reason. "I freaked out and yelled at him," Emanuel said. "They didn't expect that kind of answer from me. I told them I only fear God. From that day they started spying on me."

They would hassle him as he walked by, or call him over and order him to show them his room. "They searched everything. They were trying to find drugs. Black hashish and tramadol, they think I use that. They are just waiting for one chance to find me doing something wrong." He said everything was "screwed up" now. "I can't stay for nothing in this place."

Emanuel and others were getting hungrier. If anyone snitched, they could have more food, meaning the temptation to reveal or fabricate another's misdeed increased whenever meals were denied.

"Still, they are hitting us. We are at risk now because they use force over us. They hit us without reason and they take our stuff from the gate and today at the kitchen they said 'only three minutes for feeding,' after that they took the plates and throw them into the garbage."

The refugees were waiting for interviews with UNHCR staff. When the time finally came, a few included small or big lies: Ethiopians pretended to be Eritrean; older teenagers said they were under eighteen—all desperate to improve their chances. The way decisions were made was very opaque. "[It's] if they like your face, I swear to God," said Kaleb about how people were chosen for evacuation.

"Just I am waiting for the future. May God help me with the coming fingerprints. I don't know which order they are using, I don't think they have a procedure. You just wait to hear your name."

————

Kaleb began reading the Bible earnestly, looking for a sign or resolve.

"Anyone who does not love does not know God, because God is love," he read and pondered. "Whoever fears has not been perfected in love. We love because he first loved us. If anyone says, 'I love God,' and hates his brother, he is a liar; for he who does not love his brother whom he has seen cannot love [a] God whom he has not seen. And this commandment we have from him: whoever loves God must also love his brother."[10]

Back in 2015, I met a lot of Syrian refugees who said they had lost their faith in Allah on the journey to Europe. One told me it became impossible to believe there was any higher body looking out for him. He fled from a country of sieges, where his countryfolk were starved and barrel bombed, while his brother was arrested and crippled through torture. He traversed Turkey, where he labored for free; the Aegean Sea, where drowning was a very real possibility; and arrived in Europe, where people were thoroughly oblivious about the suffering he had seen. Using Google Maps, he crossed continents alone, no holy power by his side. The world is unfair, he realized. The world is unjust.

For Kaleb, the opposite happened. Governments—both African and European—had repeatedly let him down, as had so-called humanitarian organizations. The only thing left to believe in was God, he concluded, because he had no free will anymore. Decisions that changed the course of his life would always be made out of his own sight. Whether he ate or starved, got medicine or a flight to a new beginning, even lived or died was decided by local officials in offices, aid workers in protected compounds, or diplomats in faraway capitals. Even then, there was no reason why the opportunistic vultures who circled in Libya, like traffickers and militias, would not swoop to reclaim him first.

Kaleb called his mother, asking her to pray for him. Along with Kaleb's younger brother, Yuel—a slim boy the spitting image of Kaleb—she set out for the holiest place she knew: Tsadkane Maryam church. It meant a 200 kilometers' journey northeast from her home in Addis Ababa that began at 6:00 a.m. in a bus of pilgrims. The area around the driver's seat was decorated with a picture of a lion and Jesus, plastic green leaves bordered with red, pink, and yellow roses strung up overhead. Hanging beside them were blue and white tassels and miniature decorative pots, fashioned like those *Habeshas*—Ethiopians and Eritreans—used to make cheese.

She leaned against the window, Yuel's head on her shoulder and their arms linked, listening to a priest in a red frock with a bejeweled cross, preaching, encouraging them to clap along as he sang. Markets, churches, and farms rushed by outside. There were donkeys, cows, green fields, and small hills coated in stones.

Kaleb's mother wore a white *netela* scarf covering her dark hair and a crucifix around her neck. When the bus stopped after four hours of driving, the gentle figures of mother and child trekked across rolling hills, the lowest areas layered with mud that liquified so deep during rainy season they had to use a stick to test the ground in front of them before taking a step.

She took off her shoes and queued up with other women who had cancer, poor eyesight, or were having trouble getting pregnant. Each took a turn standing under a pipe that poured holy water straight from a well. All morning, they had gone without food and avoided drinking liquids to be pure for this. A number of women who made the journey believed they were possessed by the devil, and when the sharp cold water hit them they would shriek and cry.

Afterwards, Kaleb's mother dried herself off, gathered up her belongings, and hiked another steep stone path with Yuel, pausing at intervals to breathe deeply. Along the track, beggars—the blind, the old, the sick—extended cupped hands for alms. At the top was a monastery, positioned inside caves set in a stone cliff. The air was still, but heavy with wishes. No talking was allowed; no shoes, no phones. Incense wafted past walls covered with pictures of Jesus. The floor was thick with woven mats, and that is where Kaleb's mother bent down, her face touching the ground, and prayed for his deliverance. She asked God to take her eldest son out of Libya. She silently begged for him to make it to safety, and she promised to give the monastery a donation if he did.

Then she put an arm around Yuel, and they retraced their steps down the hill before climbing into the bus, their bodies close, comforting each other. They were ready for injera flatbread, their first food that day, and the drive back to Addis Ababa. By their feet were plastic bottles filled with holy water. For the next few days, it would be the first thing that touched their bodies each morning. Maybe that would augment their prayers.

Much later, during a visit to Ethiopia, I retraced the same pilgrimage with Kaleb's mother and brother. I would witness firsthand the love they carried for him, the depth of his mother's faith and the sacrifices she had been ready to make. Close to the monasteries, we spent a night sleeping on floor mats in the back of a local farmer's home beside a brightly lit shrine to Jesus and Mary. A church dominated the small, poor town, where wandering residents sometimes shouted unintelligibly at pilgrims who bought small wooden crucifixes and religious books from street stalls. A donkey with a bloody, injured leg limped in circles as the sun set. The following morning, we woke at 5:00 a.m. to hike down to a valley containing a holy waterfall beside yet another monastery. One by one, we stepped under its frigid water, a rainbow shining in front of us that was said to be a sign of the goodness of God. When it was her turn, Kaleb's mother beamed and ululated.

This time, her praise was triumphant. Kaleb had been evacuated to Italy.

————

In mid-2019, more than two years after he arrived in Libya, Kaleb finally left. He called me from Rome, saying everything was "cool."

"Can I ask you one question? Is life good in Italy? I mean when you compare it to other European countries," he messaged me later. "What about the economy? Many people have said it's not a good country. Some people are advising me some stupid things."

Most of the small number of refugees evacuated from Libya to Italy would not stay there. They knew that Italy was hosting a lot of refugees and migrants—it was obvious from the number of African, Middle Eastern, and Asian people they saw sleeping on the streets. They heard stories about the increasingly harsh treatment of foreigners, including tens of thousands of black people who were effectively being used as slave labor in fruit farms, often under the control of the Italian mafia, in the country's south.[11] This convinced them that Italy was not the right place for them. Instead, they escaped, moving on towards countries like Germany, Belgium, or France, with the hope of trying to reach the UK. The lucky ones got away before they were properly registered and fingerprinted—those who did not risked being sent back to Italy when they tried to claim asylum elsewhere under a law called the Dublin Regulation, which said that refugees must stay in the first EU country they entered. Now, Kaleb had to decide whether he also wanted to take the same risk, embarking on another illegal journey, this time across Europe, to improve his future prospects once again.

CHAPTER 18

TAJOURA: WAR CRIMES AND WAR SLAVES

"I used to be afraid of smugglers in Libya, and now I'm afraid of organizations that claim humanity."

–TAJOURA BOMBING SURVIVOR, OCTOBER 2019

A UN source once told me that while Zintan detention center may have been known as "Guantanamo" among Libya's refugees, Tajoura was the real Guantanamo. The migrant detention center in eastern Tripoli was located within a huge military complex that also served as the headquarters of the Daman militia.[1] It was "a Gaddafi kind of fort," as one aid worker called it. Unlike in Zintan, its detainees were regularly put on display for visitors.

Take, for example, December 18, 2018, and the UN-designated International Migrants' Day. An audience of Libyan officials; diplomats from Sudan, the Ivory Coast, Mali, Niger, and Bangladesh; and Libyan aid workers arrived to watch detainees who had been ordered to reenact the experience of drowning at sea.[2] Men and women hunkered down on ledges of wood, fashioned in the shape of a boat. They rowed in time. When a voice called out a command, they fell to the ground in unison. Behind them, a Libyan Red Crescent ambulance drew up. Medics, wearing outfits with their symbolic red cross, ran over, feigning concern. They begin to treat the people who were splayed out on the cement floor. These theatrical treatments brought them back to life. As the detainees feigned drowning, it was impossible to see the baby, who sat alone, gurgling, in the middle of the faux wooden boat, before being revealed by the acting medics. They continued to play the part of saviors, with one lifting the infant in the air. Watching on were fellow detainees—women and children who had been forced to sing and dance earlier in the performance. (Others, who stayed locked up in halls that day, said the audience was chosen for their lack of Arabic, so they could not communicate with the visiting delegations. At least one person was beaten for refusing to perform.[3])

"After twenty hours of sailing, they returned us to Tripoli and imprisoned us in Tajoura center."

The whole spectacle was recorded for Libyan TV. This was not the only place incarcerated refugees were coerced to look happy on camera that day—I received panicked messages from Abu Salim detention center, where a film crew arrived with biscuits, tea, and big speakers to play music.

"They want us to enjoy ourselves but all people refuse. We say no . . . They took a camera, they want to record us . . . People are in a big stress now. How can we dance and enjoy when UNHCR are playing with us? We want evacuation."[4]

But Tajoura put on the biggest show. At the time, roughly one thousand refugees and migrants were locked up there. They knew they could literally be tortured to death if they attracted the ire of the guards.

"Tajoura is the most dangerous part of Tripoli, where you can find soldiers mixed with terrorists. They don't fear God at all."

"The guards pee and spit on food so that no one approaches and eats it. I asked my friend 'why do they put food there if they do not want anyone to eat?' They said to me it is in order for the UN to see that food is being provided to the prisoners . . . You have to focus on the prison of Tajoura, there are undeclared deaths."

As the festivities dragged on, detainees were conscious that a fellow refugee was spending the day in a torture chamber as a punishment for speaking to a visiting international delegation. It was nearly two months since they had seen him. The same could easily happen to any one of them.

"The police asked me 'who allowed you to talk the delegation?' They beat me on my back, legs, and my chest. They asked me 'are you a Christian?' I said yes. Then they treated me worse than before. They poured cold water on my body and left me without a blanket to cover me during the cold weather."

———

In March 2019, I got a message saying three Sudanese men were being punished in Tajoura, this time for an attempted escape. They were in a room in the administration block—my source even gave me a map. One note, a call for help, was written in blue ink on lined paper, folded up and wedged inside a loaf of bread, and smuggled out. It was not addressed to me, but another detainee took a photo and sent it on.

"My dear,
How are you? I hope you are good. I told you before that I want to escape from Tajoura.

I escaped, but they caught me and my three friends, and they killed one of us. They broke my hand and the legs of my three friends, also they put us in a private room far away from the others.

Every day they punish us: no water, no eating, we are about to die. You have to do your best, my lady, in order to take us out of this place. They ignore us. Nobody knows we are here.

The room they put us in is underground. You have to help us!

And tell my brother about what has happened to me.

Please don't share this on your Facebook page. Do your best."

I gave the information to other sources, who verified that it was true. That building was known as a torture chamber. A refugee who worked there, helping guards, even claimed he had been forced to carry the bodies of detainees who had been murdered inside. Later, I would hear that at least one of the three men who got out the note was eventually released, and made it to Europe, but I never found out what happened to the others.

> "If you're dead they throw the bodies in the sea, and they say in the news another boat drowned. Over time, they torture someone until death . . . They put you in a place [where] no one knows to hide their crimes. People die here for no reason and their families don't know if they're alive or dead or how they die, and they don't see the bodies."

The administration block was not the only place of torment. A visiting official described a network of underground cells connected by tunnels in Tajoura, where there were "people in bad shape."[5] A Tajoura detainee who was punished underground told me some prisoners had been down there for years, including a Libyan from Benghazi with uncut hair, a long beard, and fingernails like claws.

———

When Haftar's assault on Tripoli began, detained refugees across the city were ordered to help militias fighting on the side of the UN-based government. In at least five detention centers, refugees told me they were forced to move weapons, clean, and cook in military bases, or were even instructed to fight themselves.[6]

In Tajoura, refugees had long been made to man weapons stores. Even before the conflict, one young Somali used to send me videos showing himself surrounded by bombs. His favorite film was *Mission Impossible*, and he thought back to Tom Cruise's adventures as he considered his fate. In audio messages, his voice rose up a few pitches when his anxiety peaked.

> *"Once I reach Europe I will show the world the truth about Libya by acting [in a] movie. The true story about the innocent refugees in Libya."*

> *"Do you see these weapons? If you post this video on the news they will kill me. They will kill me and I will die."*

In wartime, fighters patrolled the migrant halls each morning, selecting the strongest-looking men. There were slim pickings, since everyone was weak because of the lack of food. The daily payment for those chosen might be five dinars ($1), or vegetables and a packet of cigarettes, or nothing at all. It was a devil's bargain. They would be treated as a combatant, despite being a slave.

> *"The soldiers give us military uniforms. I told them to return me back to the detention center, but they refused. And while I was complaining one of the soldiers pointed a gun at my head. I washed a military ambulance which was full of soldiers' blood, who were killed on the warfront."[7]*

My contacts started sending me photos of themselves in camouflage uniforms in Tajoura's military base, a short distance from the migrant halls. They cleaned tanks, or loaded bombs or guns into vehicles. "The first time they told them they wanted people for a little work and would give them food and cigarettes," said a Darfuri. "They took them to the store to carry guns. After they finished they told them it's not allowed for them to go back to the cell. You see it a lot."

> "The soldiers forced me together with the other refugees to load weapons and unloaded them in the front line. They forced me and because I feared for my life, I did it. I don't want to be forced to work or load weapons. I don't want to live in fear. I don't know what I can do in the future because I can see that my future is closed."

> "Tajoura is a militia area, they are fighting for two months now with the military. We have had many brothers taken, more than twenty disappeared in this period of time. They took them and they come all the time and ask for more. I'm so scared right now, I can't sleep at night."

Some of them did become fighters. A Sudanese man told me he was taken out of the compound and given an AK-47.[8] "They gave us three AK-47s and then two of us, they gave them RPGs. So we're in the line, the front line, where we fought," he told me by phone. "They don't even ask you. We are not soldiers at all." He eventually managed to escape.

> "I have a friend now, he is out serving in the war by force. They came asking for mechanics. My friend and four other refugees thought the work was here in the center. They took him to the war zone. He called two days

ago and said two of them were shot. One in the shoulder and the other in
the leg. Now he's trying to escape, but they threatened him, saying
'anyone who tries to escape can count himself a dead man.'"

A 14-year-old was among those chosen from Tajoura, others told me. He went to work as a cook. I sent UNICEF the boy's photo and name, his age apparent from his chubby cheeks, asking them to do something about it, but it seemed to go nowhere.

"You are going to hear one day that the refugees in Libya, all of them are
going to die or they will join the militias or other groups in Libya."

In the first month of the new war, around four hundred people were killed and fifty thousand displaced.[9] Haftar was undeterred. "Officers and soldiers in our armed forces and the auxiliary forces, I salute you in these glorious days and urge you with your strength and determination to teach the enemy a greater and bigger lesson than the previous ones," he said in an audio message in May 2019, pledging to "uproot [the enemy] from our beloved land."

Schools became shelters for displaced civilians. The LNA were pushing hard. Amru Salahuddien, a photojournalist who lived on the front line, counted thirty-one air raids in just one day in Salah Al-Din in southern Tripoli. He called it an undisciplined war, saying the young Libyan fighters almost believed this was a video game in which, if they got shot, they could jump back up and begin a second life. Rivals were close, even two houses away from each other. Fighting was door to door and window to window. Many of the people Salahuddien photographed were killed within months.[10]

Prime Minister al-Serraj traveled through Europe meeting state leaders and appealing for support.[11] A UN call for a week-long ceasefire in Tripoli, to enable humanitarian aid to reach those who needed it, quickly failed.[12]

———

One day that May, an air strike hit one of Tajoura's weapons stores. Shrapnel from the blast burst through the roof of the women's hall, barely missing a sleeping baby.[13] An Egyptian man was burned.

> *"Tonight they attacked . . . They bombed places so near, and the electricity is gone, we don't know what will happen and the door is closed. [It's] really very frightening. Everyone is so worried."*

As I spoke to witnesses, I came to a stunning realization. There could be a sickening explanation for why most of the migrant detention centers now doubled as military bases, a reason that went beyond it being the militias that ran them. It seemed clear to me now that the refugees were being used as human shields—which, if true, was another war crime.[14] A Libyan contact I spoke to agreed, describing the situation as a "win-win" for government-aligned forces. If Haftar did not bomb the bases to avoid targeting refugees, the weapons would be safe. If Haftar did bomb, refugees would die, and Haftar would be internationally condemned—a bad result for a military leader currying international favor.

> *"My situation is very scary. We are here, more than 400 people in one room. The bombs fly north . . . We are among the most dangerous firefighters because we are in the middle of weapons stores."*

I felt a sense of dread so strong that day, as understanding dawned on me, that when the worst happened, two months later, it would seem we had known it was coming all along.

It was the night of July 2, 2019, when the first bomb hit the nearby weapons store. An Eritrean called Kit phoned me in terror. Detainees in Tajoura's smaller hall ran for the doors but found them locked. They dashed to the windows, trying to shatter the glass, but the guards outside started shouting and then shooting, telling them to get back. One man who pushed forward was hit in the chest by a bullet, witnesses would later remember.

"Terrible moment is happened before three minutes. Air strike bombing. Oh my God, we are in terrible," Kit told me. His English failed him. He asked me to pray before his connection failed, too. Another man began to film. In the video, you see the dust and hear hollering, almost celebratory, like a lot of weak people have suddenly remembered that they are alive, adrenaline coursing, blood pumping. Twenty-five seconds later comes a second huge crash, then more dust and darkness—a direct hit. Not capable of being captured on camera was the smell of burning flesh.[15]

More than one hundred newcomers were crowded into a smaller hall. They were a mix of nationalities: Nigerians, Nigeriens, Egyptians, Moroccans, Bangladeshis, Sudanese, Gambians, Malians, Ghanaians. Some, like Kosofo, had been arrested just a week before, caught on Tripoli's streets by Libyan security forces and ordered to pay money to be released. The Darfuri still had not managed to raise enough to get out when the bombing began.

Others in that hall had been there six weeks after coming from the sea. They were left without food and water for days at a time and had not been registered with UNHCR. On the Summer Solstice, less than a fortnight before, two people were killed trying to escape and more were taken away to an unknown location. Unexpectedly, this may have saved their lives.

"We stay here for a year and a half waiting for the UN, suffering from serious problems. No one wants to help us. When you choose to escape they kill us. We aren't criminals, we are someone's sons. We go across the world illegally because we haven't any papers."

On the gray walls, graffiti read, "One day I will be free," "Fuck life," and "Follow your dream." Now, the people who wrote those messages had breathed for the last time. The second air strike landed on the smaller hall. It had been packed full of human life, immediately extinguished. "The other cell already destructed, the people are lost," messaged Kit. With others, he finally ran outside, in among the trees and bushes to cower.

Kosofo was hiding in the bathroom of the hall that was hit. "Everything was silent. The shouting of people, the crying of people, it was silent totally," he recalled later. "So we stayed in the bathroom about five minutes. After that, we went outside, and we found dead bodies lying on the ground and the legs and heads of men . . ." he trailed off. "It was so confusing. We found the policemen, they were sitting on their chairs. They didn't move and they didn't say anything. They were sitting and chatting."

"I saw the hell with my eyes. I saw things that I had seen during the Darfur war," Kosofo continued.[16] "Then they contacted the ambulance, and the ambulance came and took all the injured people, all the sick people. They took us to the hospital."

In one of the photos of the destruction, taken later by AFP photographer Mahmud Turkia, a dead man is curled up like he is sleeping. His body is gray, his arm reaching in front of him. He appears to be missing a leg. Another journalist who visited later found a playing card lying on the ground: an eight of hearts. The bombing left a deep crater.

"We all feel sorry for those young people," mourned another Sudanese detainee. "We picked up parts of their bodies." One of the dead was his friend, a Gambian called Jabrill. He had no contact for Jabrill's family, no way to tell them his fate. "He was a good man. I'm so sad about his lost five years in Libya trying to cross the sea. Every time they got him, this was his last chance. [Jabrill] always told me, 'Believe in your dreams.' We want a better future for our kids. That's why we need to go to Europe, to build families and life and happiness. We escaped from our countries looking for peace. Now, I know he rests in peace."

———

Over the following days, fresh statements were issued. UN Secretary General António Guterres called for an independent investigation "to ensure that the perpetrators are brought to justice, noting that the United Nations had provided exact coordinates of the detention center to the parties."[17] He "condemn[ed] this horrendous incident in the strongest terms" and "express[ed] his deepest condolences to the families of the victims and wish[ed] a quick recovery to those injured."

"Such an attack deserves more than condemnation," said a joint statement from UNHCR and IOM.[18] "This attack clearly could constitute a war crime, as it killed by surprise innocent people whose dire conditions forced them to be in that shelter," said Ghassan Salamé, head of the UN Support Mission in Libya.[19] The UN put the death toll to "at least forty-four."

Survivors thought that figure suggested a cover-up. I got dozens of messages saying there should be anywhere from 120 to 200 people dead, judging by how many were inside the hall that was hit. One Somali, who worked as a translator, would even say later that the Libyan guards ordered him to tell journalists fewer than fifty people died, though there were 185 people in the hangar and more than one hundred were murdered, from what he witnessed. Bodies were dispersed to different morgues and eventually buried in unmarked graves.[20] Attempts to identify the dead went nowhere, and their families were never contacted through official channels.

On Friday, July 5, the UN's stated number rose to fifty-three, including six children.[21] As it climbed, the UN Security Council met for several hours, behind closed doors, to discuss the attack. Afterwards, they held back on issuing a statement—reportedly because the US opposed the proposed wording.[22]

"We're still sleeping beside the dead bodies."

The GNA's interior minister, Fathi Bachagha, said the Libyan authorities were "currently reviewing the closure of shelters and the release of illegal migrants to ensure their safety and security," adding that the Tripoli government did not have the capacity to protect migrants from air raids.[23] The GNA also denounced refugees' claims that guards had shot at those trying to escape as "rumors and false information."[24]

While diplomats and aid officials debated semantics, the most seriously wounded survivors took up an entire wing of a hospital in Tripoli. Some underwent amputations. In a meeting with various UN agencies on Thursday, July 4, the GNA's undersecretary for migration, Mohammed al-Shibani, said morgues had run out of space.[25] Though they would bury those already dead, he said the UN had to take responsibility for injured people who might die in the coming months.

UNHCR Libya chief, Jean-Paul Cavalieri, went to the site of the Tajoura bombing to film a video condemning the air strikes, but he seemingly spent no time meeting survivors who were camped out there. A spokesperson later suggested Cavalieri was not allowed "access" to them.[26] But hundreds remained in Tajoura. They lay under the blazing sun during the day and slept in the grass at night, or pulled the remaining mattresses outside. Libyan guards tried to force them back into a locked hall, and they refused, withstanding threats. The hall that guards wanted to put them in was edged by weapons stores, survivors said. The only time they would go in was to use the bathroom. "The place is so big, there's a wide empty area we can stay in, but they force us to stay close to the buildings," worried a Sudanese survivor. "There are three buildings around us full of weapons."

When I asked others about this, an aid worker said the guards were trying to avoid detainees being bitten by snakes and scorpions. "[Snakes are] better than air bombs," Kit responded, dismissively. "Nobody needs to enter that cell, because it's a target. We are dying here in Tajoura."

For once, they were getting attention. Three hundred detainees queued to get food, a sandwich and 1.5 liters of water, as guards waved guns to make the lines orderly. "The UN came and saw the situation, they left us to go and do paperwork, there is no humanity in the world," said the Sudanese man. Drones flew overhead.

Medics arrived to offer psychological help. Detainees were grateful but skeptical, knowing their fears were justified and would not go away until they were out of this place. With fighting sounding in the distance, they were depressed.

"Now all the world looks nasty and dirty, trying to show us they feel our pain. I hate this life, really, I hope I die soon. We are too tired to live in this world. You can't know this feeling. If you see people here, just the shape of their face tells you a long story."

Okot, from Sudan, was just twenty-four. Most of his direct family died when he was a child, apart from an older sister, who had three daughters and a son. Seeing her struggle in their birth country made him determined to reach somewhere he could envisage a future, he told me. As Okot typed out his feelings, he watched people sift through the rubble for bodies.

"I try to find my way in this life and build a family in a place where my kids would never lose their parents for no reason. It seems impossible for me. All my life, I'm trying to do the things my mamma taught me. Never hurt someone, never take something that doesn't belong to me. I remember her voice. It's like she's always with me, saving me from bad things. I'm trying to make her proud, all my life, but it's too hard."

Spokespeople for Haftar's LNA initially denied carrying out the bombing, but then said Tajoura detention center was a legitimate target.[27] Detainees were only ninety-five yards away from weapons stores, it emerged.[28] An investigation presented to the UN Security Council later revealed that the air strike had most likely been carried out by a fighter plane from a foreign country supporting Haftar, with sources telling journalists it was the UAE.[29]

As survivors waited, refugee women arrived at Tajoura's gates. They paid their way in, taking a gamble that the UNHCR would carry out evacuations after the air strike and knowing that women were usually first in line. This led to consternation among survivors, including a significant number who had been locked up in Tajoura for almost two years. There were always leeches ready to take advantage of any situation, they lamented.

———

On Saturday, July 6, four days after the bombing, Tajoura's survivors went on hunger strike.[30] They refused unusually good offers of food from visiting aid organizations keen for a photo opportunity, saying they did not need sustenance, just safety. As the self-deprivation started, UNHCR staff arrived, holding an hour-and-a-half-long meeting with the detention center's management.

"We are still waiting in the sun's heat," messaged Okot, from outside those shut doors. "Our brothers are dead, why is no one answering?"

On Sunday, July 7, UNHCR made an offer to move up to seventy people to the "Hotel"—their Gathering and Departure Facility. A staff member said certain detainees had already been selected—though detainees feared the group would include the frauds who had paid their way into the center after the bombing.

In a rare display of power, survivors en masse rejected the deal, refusing even to listen to the names of the people who had been chosen. As UNHCR staff applied pressure, they were flustered but did not falter. "Humanity is in books only, it's not in humans at all," said one man after witnessing these discussions.

"UNHCR HERE IS A FAKE UNHCR, BECAUSE STILL NOW
THEY DID NOT TAKE ANY ACTION FOR OUR SITUATION."

Early in the morning of Tuesday, July 9, 2019—a week after the bombing—three air strikes hit around 500 meters from Tajoura detention center in quick succession. Then UNHCR staff called refugee leaders and again tried, unsuccessfully, to broker a deal. In the end, five different refugees told me a UNHCR official said she could not do anything more for them and they should just leave the detention center. It was almost inconceivable, something they would not have dared to attempt without her presence. The center's management looked angry but resigned.

Several refugees hesitated, too frightened to venture out of a complex they had lived in for as long as two years: worried about fighters, smugglers, or militias who could murder or brutalize them. A number went a short distance and turned back, hoping that the UN would return and realize how vulnerable they were. But these were the minority.

Something historic was happening. Hundreds of people were walking out of the detention center where they had been starved, beaten, and bombed, striding forward on a proud march through a war zone—a journey that would last hours.[31] They were frail and weak after three days of hunger striking and months with only one meal a day. They carried a white flag as protection, thin arms grasping meager belongings—a spare t-shirt, a blanket, a Bible, or an ID card. The marchers were filled with dread and excitement. They were taking their lives in their own hands. They decided the destination: the UNHCR "Hotel."

On their phones, other refugees who had left Tajoura in the previous months tracked the group's progress from afar. "It is wonderful after two years to leave Tajoura detention center. They were living in darkness," said David, a former detainee who had been evacuated to a camp in Niger. His heart was soaring. "When I was leaving Tajoura I didn't believe it, just that I was created again. That was my feeling. It isn't easy to feel sunlight after two years."

What David said was true: the marchers' eyes hurt from the sun. "Our fatigue on the road is severe," a Sudanese man messaged me as they moved along towards central Tripoli. "My mind did not believe we would get out of there. We expected to die."

In a tweet posted almost straight away, UNHCR said it "thank[ed] the Libyan Ministry of Interior for releasing refugees and migrants from Tajoura detention center . . . 350 persons were still at risk in Tajoura and [are] now free."[32]

"Free" was not exactly the right word, and it was certainly too early for celebration. But they were walking with determination, risking their lives, knowing they had as much as 40 kilometers to walk to reach the UNHCR center and no guarantee they would be allowed in. They regarded each vehicle with suspicion; every person on the road was a potential foe who could murder one of them with impunity. Then the Libyan police did an unexpected thing.

They were different from the guards in Tajoura, whose sadism was familiar. These police took charge of the road, making way for the marchers, even taking a few of the weakest refugees into their cars. "At the end, they were even proud of us," Kit said. "Because they didn't expect that kind of walking by foot. Imagine, we're all refugees arrested and imprisoned between one year and two years."

When the hundreds of survivors finally arrived at the UNHCR center, another miraculous thing happened: they were allowed inside. A hastily issued UN statement insisted they could not stay long. "Today, a group of some 260 refugees and migrants managed to leave Tajoura detention center and have reached the Gathering and Departure Facility. The GDF has a limited capacity, however, they were allowed to stay to spend the night and provided with emergency assistance, food and water."[33] The statement asked the Libyan authorities to identify another "open shelter" for the survivors "in order to maintain the transit nature of the center, which is a facility for the most vulnerable refugees for whom a solution outside Libya has already been identified." Nothing like that existed, though, and they knew it.

The survivors spread out flimsy mattresses on the floor. They smiled at each other, suddenly shy, anticipating their first proper sleep in more than a week.

"We hope that the organization will not lag in the evacuation work until we get clouded again and lose other people. We must speed up the process. Libya is not safe."

In the following days, they were both criticized and had their experiences rewritten. UNHCR spokesperson Charlie Yaxley claimed all Tajoura survivors had been "evacuated . . . to safety" by the agency.[34] On Thursday, July 11, in response to international broadcaster Voice of America's coverage of the great march, UNHCR Special Envoy for the Mediterranean Vincent Cochetel tweeted criticizing the refugees for not being "patient" and going to Libya in the first place. "No one can pretend that they did not [know] it's not safe to go to Libya, yet they keep going there. There is no right to resettlement and no priority for those putting themselves at risk in Libya," he said.[35]

Cochetel's tweets would provoke refugees and activists again not long after. "I am very concerned by the radicalization of the migratory dreams and demands of some migrants and refugees in Libya, and neighboring countries," he wrote on August 18, 2019.[36] This was sparked by a development on the Open Arms rescue ship, which had been stranded in the Mediterranean. Its crew refused to travel the long distance to Spain, saying the rescued migrants and refugees on board should be disembarked in nearby Italy because they needed emergency help. "Radicalization of migratory dreams? Just wow," responded Alessandro Siclari, a communications adviser for MSF.[37]

On August 22, after a news outlet noted this tweet had sparked "controversy," Cochetel doubled down. "There is no controversy, it is just abnormal that some refugees refuse to attend language and vocational training classes, job placement in some countries, because they claim that they only want to go to EU and that UNHCR has an obligation to resettle them!"[38] But he had originally been referring to Libya. Where were the language and vocational training classes? Where were the job placements?

———

The EU began to utilize the Tajoura detention center bombing as an excuse to not release information and documents about their workings in Libya. When I filed freedom of information requests, looking for details from their discussions about Libyan detention centers, I got responses saying that information was too sensitive, and Tajoura showed "the risks described" in the country "are not hypothetical."[39] The killings of dozens of refugees and migrants—including people who were returned to their deaths because of EU policy—were now being twisted into an excuse for the EU to avoid scrutiny.

For Tajoura's survivors, memories of the bombing remained in their minds and in photographs on their phones that they kept as evidence for the day someone cared. A hand, its fingers curled, on a stone step. A black plastic trash bag with body parts inside. A torso with arms attached, raised above it as if in supplication to a higher power, its mouth crushed by a cement block that fell from the sky. A mass of flesh that used to be a person with dreams. A dead man in blue boxer shorts, his face turned to face the ground. Another corpse with chin tilted upwards, distracting from the missing skull, its skin white from debris, whiter than if this person was born with a skin color that might have been deemed by Europeans as worth saving. Underneath the stretcher he was loaded on, the blood-covered legs of two more bodies protruded.

Later, one survivor told me that when he finally reached the UK, he refused to sleep in a bed at night in honor of his friends from Tajoura, who never got that chance.

CHAPTER 19

RWANDA: A NEW ROUTE TO SAFETY

"The EU and the UN are natural partners!"

–NICOLA BELLOMO, EU AMBASSADOR TO RWANDA, DURING A VISIT BY UNHCR HEAD FILIPPO GRANDI TO RWANDA, APRIL 2021[1]

Fly over Niger, a landlocked nation on the Libyan border, and you will be struck by its brown, dry landscape. More than two thirds of its territory is desert.

Western countries were rarely willing to take refugees directly from Libya, partly because of the limitations of the assessments that UNHCR and their embassies could carry out inside detention centers, so there needed to be a transit site. From late December, 2017, Niger was where the lucky few refugees selected for evacuation were flown to have their resettlement cases assessed and processed, their histories interrogated and their suffering evaluated.[2] They would live there for months, or even years: in the capital, Niamey, or in dry, barren, and remote desert camps, where temperatures reached as high as 104 degrees Fahrenheit.

"When we got the plane to Niger the airplane host [a Libyan man] told us we smelled badly. He sprayed us."

Problems soon arose. Not enough of those evacuees were found to meet Western countries' criteria (for example, that they were single women or families, or that they had never served in the military, despite that not being a choice in Eritrea). Some got stuck in Niger indefinitely. There was a bottleneck. New spots became scarce. Protests escalated, and refugees living in camps contracted malaria or other potentially deadly diseases. As of May 2019, 2,782 people had been evacuated from Libya to Niger, but only 1,378 were resettled onwards.[3]

It became necessary for the UN to find another state that could step up and help with evacuations. Thousands of kilometers southeast, Rwanda—a small country of roughly 12 million people, infamous for the bloody 1994 genocide in which 800,000 Tutsis and moderate Hutus were killed in just one hundred days—stepped forward.[4]

In November 2017, following international outcry over slave markets in Libya due to CNN's undercover report, Rwanda's government had suggested they could host up to 30,000 refugees.[5] In a statement, its foreign ministry said it was "horrified" that "African men women and children who were on the road to exile have been held and turned into slaves . . . We may not be able to welcome everyone but our door is wide open."[6]

"The desperate situation in Libya is disturbing, and we are prepared to provide support and sanctuary for our African brothers who are stuck in the immigration debacle in Libya, and who are willing to move to Rwanda," President Paul Kagame reiterated the following year.[7] On September 10, 2019, Rwanda's government signed an agreement with UNHCR and the African Union, confirming it would take an initial group of five hundred people.[8] The EU agreed to provide 10.3 million euro in funding.[9]

Refugees in Libya were apprehensive. A number even refused to travel, despite being offered a space on the plane out. They thought they had better prospects trying the sea again. "People want to go. We want to go," said one detainee, with slight desperation, before asking me if Rwanda was a good place to live. "Please, if you know about Rwanda, tell me."

"We heard about the evacuation plan to Rwanda, but we have a lot of questions," said another detainee, in Zintan. "Maybe they can forget us there," he worried.

Rwanda had previously been accused of involvement in a scheme to remove refugees from a rich country. In 2017, a year-long investigation by *Foreign Policy* magazine found that Eritreans who had taken dangerous migration routes to Israel and were locked up in government-associated detention centers after arrival were sent to Rwanda.[10] Officials made promises of legality, visas, and work permits, but instead those who agreed to go were tricked into illegally crossing into neighboring Uganda, where they had no chance to make an asylum claim.

There were other examples of developing countries taking responsibility for asylum seekers or stateless people in return for money from wealthier states. Starting from 2008, Kuwait and the UAE made deals with the Comoros, an impoverished Indian Ocean archipelago off the African coast, to give passports to their bidoon populations—stateless, often nomadic groups who lived in the Gulf states but whom the leadership did not consider to be citizens. The Comoros, which had an average annual income of $1,402 per person in 2021,[11] is said to have made upwards of 200 million euro from the schemes.[12] In 2014, Australia struck a $40 million deal with Cambodia to send refugees there (only ten people took up the offer).[13]

Officials working on the new Libya-Rwanda deal told me it was being negotiated with good intentions, and they were trying to make sure refugees moved there were not abandoned. The program would cost $10 million for the first four months alone, including accommodation, basic aid, and services for the evacuees.[14]

"We are afraid, especially in terms of time. Because we stayed in Libya more than two years, and have been registered by UNHCR for almost

two years. Will we take similar time in Rwanda? It is difficult for
asylum seekers."

Rwanda was already sheltering around 150,000 other refugees, mostly
from neighboring Burundi and the Democratic Republic of the Congo.[15]
For Kagame, the Libya evacuation initiative was a chance to show the world
his country's progress. During a speech to the UN General Assembly in
New York, he said Rwanda was ready to "receive and protect" the refugees,
and called the agreement "a clear sign we can cooperate to address complex
problems."

"Africa itself is also a source of solutions," Kagame—a thin, austere
man, whose steely eyes conveyed his past as a rebel commander—told assembled delegates.[16]

In late September 2019, the first group of sixty-six new arrivals stepped
off a plane, their smiling, anxious faces captured by a UN photographer.[17]
Among them was a two-month-old baby born in detention and twenty-five
other children, many of whom were unaccompanied. Everyone was Sudanese, Eritrean, or Somali.

"I think they are happy."

"They accepted going to Rwanda because everyone needs to escape from
Libya to any country to save their life. At this time, life in Libya is
becoming worse."

The next month, another group of 123 people made the same trip.[18] On
board were many of my contacts, including Samuel from Triq al Sikka, the
detainee who had sent me updates about the tuberculosis outbreak, taken
part in the protest, and been threatened with disappearance. We messaged
as he made the journey, and I decided I had to meet them in person as soon
as I could.

———

It was not my first time going to this small African Great Lakes country. In 2014, soon after I started working as a journalist, I covered the twentieth anniversary of the genocide—a month-long period of events commemorating some of the most severe crimes against humanity and war crimes the world has seen.

Rwanda has changed dramatically in the decades since that terrible period. The streets are clean, plastic bags are banned nationwide, and there is a booming technology industry.[19] It has become a darling of international donors, and capital city Kigali is heavily promoted as a destination for international conferences.

During that first trip, I spent time in close proximity to President Kagame, the former leader of the Rwandan Patriotic Front (RPF) rebel group, which fought for control of the country and eventually brought a halt to the bloodshed. In Village Urugwiro, Kagame's headquarters, I photographed UN Secretary General Ban Ki-moon and the president shaking hands following a private meeting. Upon entry, my phone had been confiscated—it was for safety reasons that no phones were allowed near Kagame, I was told.

The main event of the genocide commemorations was held at a thirty-thousand-person capacity stadium.[20] In the VIP seats, Kagame was flanked by former British Prime Minister Tony Blair and former UN High Commissioner for Human Rights Mary Robinson, along with the UN Secretary General. Yoweri Museveni, the long-serving dictator from neighboring Uganda, made a speech about the dangers of trusting the West and the legacy of colonialism. In front of us, actors reenacted UN peacekeepers abandoning Tutsis to their fate and the ensuing violence and bloodshed, when friends and neighbors methodically killed each other with machetes and hoes, before more actors, dressed as RPF soldiers, ran onto the grass and brought victims back to life. Around the stadium, survivors collapsed and wailed, overcome with memories. I thought about trauma, how the powerful determine the way history is presented and atrocities memorialized, and how hard that might be for survivors to bear.

I knew that Rwanda had a bad reputation for press freedom: it was ranked in the eighteen worst countries in the world in the Reporters Without Borders press freedom index.[21] That night, a leading journalist, Cassien Ntamuhanga, disappeared on his way home from the stadium, with security services only admitting he was in custody a week later.[22] Also arrested was Kizito Mihigo, a gospel singer and Tutsi genocide survivor who recorded a song widely perceived to be accusing Kagame's forces of revenge killings (years later, after a cat-and-mouse game with authorities, during which he was pardoned, released, and captured again, Mihigo died in a Rwandan police station cell, in disputed circumstances).[23]

Though the country was undoubtedly peaceful, these arrests were a small sign of the ongoing problems its citizens face. Kagame had clearly emerged as an authoritarian dictator, accused of physically beating his own subordinates, crushing opposition, and ordering the assassinations of his opponents abroad.[24] He employed Western public relations firms to bolster the image of both him and the country he reshaped to his will.[25] Rwanda was calm, but also a police state—certainly not a place where you could speak freely.

———

While traveling to Rwanda was easy, getting permission to actually visit Gashora camp, where the Libya evacuees were staying, was impossible. First, I went to the Media High Council in Kigali to collect my journalist accreditation, which had already been approved online.

Next, I requested the necessary permission at the Ministry of Emergency Management. It was a Friday, and the administrative staff in a downstairs reception told me to come back the following Monday. On Monday morning, I was told to come on Tuesday afternoon. On Tuesday, they said Wednesday morning. I waited for four hours in a corridor on Wednesday before giving up.

On Thursday, I was at last told that I would not be allowed to go to Gashora.

A man called Claude Twishime, who was in charge of communications, said I should never have expected to be allowed to visit there alone anyway.

Twishime said he had been on annual leave until that day, even though all week I had been told the person who needed to grant the permission was in a meeting. "They gave you accreditation because we believe you will write good stories about us," he said after looking at my media card. "We deny some people accreditation, I think you know that."

Twishime said I should leave Rwanda for now but could join a group of at least twelve journalists who would go together the following month, accompanied by UNHCR and government officials. Was it all an elaborate stalling technique? "They are killing time," one of the Eritreans said when I told him about it.

Was Twishime's invitation also a ploy to prevent me from publishing unflattering material in the interim? I had seen these tactics before on other reporting trips—officials delaying rejections so you could not come up with a second plan when permission was denied, or offering the promise of greater access as you were leaving (implicit was the understanding that anything you wrote in the meantime would need to be flattering).

Despite this, of course I met many refugees outside the camp. We had been messaging and speaking on the phone since long before they left Libya, and they suggested I just come there—no one could stop them walking out to me. It took two buses and two motorbike drives to reach Gashora from Kigali, and it was worth it. In a restaurant newly set up by a Rwanda-based Eritrean entrepreneur who saw an opportunity to sell traditional food, I was surrounded by former detainees of Zintan, Ain Zara, Abu Salim, and Triq al Sikka centers. It was overwhelming, putting so many names to faces at once while remembering what each person had gone through. We took selfies, the women pouting, the men smiling widely. We ate a meal of injera and meat, and drank beer. We talked about everything and nothing. I felt so grateful that they were finally out of Libya.

———

It is generally understood that there are government informers throughout Rwanda.[26] For privacy reasons, and to converse freely, I arranged meetings farther afield with a few of my closer contacts. In Nyamata, a town about a thirty minutes' drive away, I sat at a secluded wooden table beside a dusty road in the center of town. With me were Samuel and Eyob, who had been held at Triq al Sikka, and Milion, who had been in both Khoms Souq al Khamis and another detention center called Sabaa, where management launched missiles on the peripheries and deliberately starved detainees as punishment.[27] After more than a year of secret phone contact with each of them separately, I could not believe we were sitting there together, that they were alive and okay. There was so much to say.

First, we ordered tea and talked about Rwanda. They marveled at locals eating bananas (plantain, matoke) with dinner or lunch as a savory food. They thought the Rwandans were polite, "civilized," welcoming and "humble." But they were worried that they had been lured there, tricked into moving much farther from Europe with no guarantee of future opportunities.

They had reason to be uncertain, too. That week, the UNHCR Special Envoy for the Central Mediterranean, Vincent Cochetel, tweeted suggesting that they should be grateful. "African refugees in Rwanda do not want to stay," he wrote, "[but] the expectations of some of these refugees are wrong, we have no obligation to resettle all refugees in/from Libya. This is one solution among others for those evacuated out of Libya."[28] This ran counter to assurances refugees received before traveling, with UN officials telling them Rwanda would be a place of transit. Official UNHCR communications had left things a bit broader, saying that while chosen evacuees may benefit from resettlement to wealthy countries, they also might stay in Rwanda long term; return to places where they had previously been granted asylum; or be sent back to their home countries, if safe.

More than 430 people had been intercepted by the Libyan coastguard in the previous week, but a few of Eyob's friends had made it onto Mediterranean rescue ships heading towards Europe—he knew by their joyful posts on Instagram. The news made him question his situation again. Why was he in Rwanda, he wondered, when he might have been among them? He started repeating that he had "a choice" not to come there; he, too, could have gone again to sea.

"We stayed in detention centers for more than two years because we wanted to go through a legal way," he said. "I came to Rwanda because they told me they'd take me through the legal way [to Europe]. Still no one really feels or understands what we've been through . . . We resist all the suffering and torture only to get what we want. We resist everything only to get our goals."

For Eyob, this was not just about getting to Europe; it was about having the freedom and security of a European citizen. "Africa is Africa," he said, pensively. "Today is OK, but after some time it's not going to be OK."

Like the others, he was in massive debt. He owed $16,000 to six relatives, including around $10,000 to his oldest sister. "Our families sold gold, their house, they sold everything they had for us," he told me. "This is always with us."

In Tripoli, he was treated like a war slave. "I was one of them, they used to involve me in the military. We used to load weapons," he said. "I didn't kill or anything, but... they took us to the war to work. They took us by force . . . It made me know that there isn't real humanity in this world." He held out one hand, showing me where his fingernail had cracked while lifting heavy weapons under the control of Triq al Sikka's guards.

"When we were in Libya we were a tool in a political game," Eyob continued. "So we suffered."

"Coming to Rwanda does not mean that we left our dreams. What about our long-term goals? . . . Our brothers are in Europe, they keep telling us

Europe [has] the most safe countries, government, they give you human rights. But we don't know about Rwanda, we have no insurance. They say to us if we want to stay here they will make it like Europe, they will give us everything like we'd get in Europe. But if you see the reality, those governments, they didn't even prepare for their people like that . . . We saw the people in the village, how they live, so I can't expect that they will give us anything like Europe. This government, they just like diplomacy, they are just making themselves look like the good ones."

Eyob wanted to finish his degree in electrical engineering. Milion wanted to be a teacher, and Samuel a nurse. They were angry at being trapped in a system where everyone else seemed to be profiting from them: hosting countries, UN agencies, NGOs. "When we get to a country Europe makes a deal with the government, they give them money and the government keeps something from that," said Eyob. "We're like property . . . We feel like in every country we get to, the government [gets] a benefit from us . . . All the UNHCR, all the organizations, they are involved in the political schemes. That is why we are suffering too much . . . European countries are responsible, especially the European Union."

All three Eritreans wore crosses around their necks, under their t-shirts. Milion carved his in detention out of a piece of sand-colored wood. Samuel's came from Eritrea; he had kept it with him for four long years.

"I want my own house, my privacy," Eyob said. In detention, in smugglers' warehouses, there was never any privacy. "I will be a free man . . . We can start a new life, it's like we will be born again. All the suffering and all the torture, this only makes us stronger."

When I asked how they felt about the possibility of going to different resettlement destinations to each other, despite their friendship, Milion said that is the curse of being Eritrean. He had seen high school reunions in movies, where adults meet up with their graduating classes years later, and he knew that would never happen for him. His school friends were scattered around the world, their lives stunted in sprawling refugee camps with no opportunity, or their bodies damaged for having the gumption to try and make it far away from the heartbreak that scarred them. There was no tally showing how many were already dead.

"We can't trust anyone."

We stayed at that Nyamata table for hours, drinking tea and talking. They spoke about how Albert Einstein was a refugee, how politicians in the West should understand that, like Einstein, they could make meaningful contributions to society if their time was not wasted and temperaments destroyed. Milion pictured his brain filling with "serenity" once he was in Europe. "Most of our minds are completely spoiled," he said. "We're afraid of motorbikes. Of helicopters. Your mind becomes creative when you're safe."

"Our destiny was to get serenity. In our country there's no serenity . . .
our brothers and sisters tell us in Europe there is safety and human rights.
If you have safety and human rights, you will get serenity. This is my
thought. Still now we don't know how to get peace . . . It's a different
type of colonization."

We talked about time passing, years they saw as wasted and how to recover from them. Eyob spent roughly a year in Triq al Sikka, including twice being sent out to work with munitions or in construction for militias. Inside the detention center, he managed to watch *The Time Traveler's Wife*, a film about a relationship between a man who involuntarily time travels and the woman who lovingly waits for him. At night, under a blanket, Eyob squinted at the downloaded video flickering on the phone he shared with others.

Milion brought up the equation $E = mc^2$ and the theory that you could be moving at the speed of light, hurtling through space, and your body would stay the same age while the earth advanced. You could never go back to the place you left, he noted.

I told them one of the stories we grow up with in Ireland: that of Tír na nÓg. How a warrior, Oisín, met a beautiful, unearthly woman, Niamh, and rode away with her to a land of eternal youth. It was when he began to pine for his birthplace that he got in trouble. Oisín went back to Ireland, only to realize that everyone he knew and loved had been dead for hundreds of years. When he stooped down to touch the ground, disembarking from his magical white horse, he rapidly aged, too, undone by his longing to reconnect with his country.

For refugees, such questions of time and home and family are ones they will grapple with for the rest of their lives.

———

I never said it to the Eritreans, but as well as being the most convenient town to meet in between Gashora and Kigali, Nyamata was home to one of the most gruesome genocide memorials Rwanda has. Around fifty thousand victims were buried there.

One day, after a meeting with another source, I visited it alone.

I stepped into what was once a Catholic church, where a massacre had taken place—grenades thrown in ahead of killers who finished survivors off with machetes. Inside were plastic boxes filled with the musty clothes of the dead. A little girl's frilly white dress was laid out, as if her mother had left it ready for the next day of school. A tiny boy's sweater reading "skate actor," a cartoon character embossed on it, was on another bench. There were lovingly knitted blankets. The colors—baby pink, lime green, deep blue, bright orange—were faded by rot and covered in brown dust.

At the front, on the altar, were leg braces that had belonged to people with disabilities, along with a pile of rosary beads. Pipes, bracelets, handkerchiefs were all watched over by a statue of the Virgin Mary, her hands held together in prayer.

A Rwandan guide, Rachel, waited outside, then led me to the mass graves around the back, where the remains of some of the tens of thousands of victims are still visible. The first time she came there, she told me, she could not sleep for the whole night afterwards, but she believed it was important to keep this kind of memorial open and accessible. "It's a kind of healing," she explained. As history shows us, it is important to remember the atrocities that have taken place and can so easily happen again.

————

Back in Gashora, unaccompanied minors who had been evacuated were acting out. They started sleeping with Rwandan prostitutes who seemed to have moved to the area expecting business. Samuel was worried they could contract HIV or other STDs. These were highly traumatized young boys who had gone years without education, and it was hard for anyone to reason with them. "Those underage, they have stress," he said.

The camp became more difficult to live in. Refugees would remind each other that they had a duty to be well-behaved, so more evacuees, still suffering in Libya, would get the option to come to Rwanda after them. It felt increasingly difficult. There was depression and a feeling of inertia when everyone realized they would be waiting indefinitely again. They also believed their rights were being infringed upon. The refugees had organized "congregations" in Libyan detention centers—everyone coming together to make communal decisions and hear out anyone who wanted to opine—but in Rwanda, these gatherings were banned.

When the coronavirus pandemic spread to Rwanda in March 2020, a curfew was introduced. Shortly afterwards, a minor who returned to the camp after the designated time accused a senior police officer of trying to rape him. The officer was never removed from the site, even during what authorities said was an investigation. Online, the Rwandan police force called the boy a liar, and UNHCR told media that a subsequent protest by refugees was against pandemic-related restrictions, rather than distress over the lack of any response to the attempted rape allegation.[29] When I subsequently reported on the claims for a British newspaper, the Rwandan government-associated *New Times* accused me of writing "refugee porn."[30] "[There is] no fucking justice in this society," said someone who saw the minor on the night of the alleged assault. "They want to suppress our voice totally. They will fade this incident, and we can't do anything about it because we are refugees."

———

Nearly two years would pass before Samuel was transferred to Canada. Eyob had reached Norway by then, and Milion Sweden, where he began to write his own book about his long struggle to escape a dictatorship, survive Libyan detention centers, and find serenity. They were lucky; many of their friends still had no assigned country. The stay in Rwanda became another limbo, another purgatory.

CHAPTER 20

TRIPOLI: CLOSING THE GATHERING AND DEPARTURE FACILITY

"In this messy world, there are only a few having humanity."
—AN ERITREAN FATHER WHO WAS EVACUATED TO SWEDEN AFTER YEARS IN LIBYA

Now that the UN Refugee Agency's Gathering and Departure Facility—"the Hotel"—had hundreds of Tajoura bombing survivors in it, UN-HCR staff were confused about what to do with them. Outside, Tripoli's war was continuing. Grad rockets, mortars, and artillery were being fired during indiscriminate attacks by both sides, hitting field hospitals, a school, and civilians in their homes.[1] Despite this, UNHCR staff began to discuss ways they could get the traumatized group to leave, saying their facility was over capacity. A UN employee, present during a meeting with the EU and other aid workers and diplomats in July, 2019, later recalled UNHCR staff claiming refugees and migrants who had been held in Tajoura for up to two years could "easily mingle" with communities outside in Tripoli. "I was not convinced," the concerned UN worker said. "The main question is what would be next? Where will they go? Where will they sleep? Who will feed them? It is a premature decision that is being taken before proper planning, and it will lead to another mess. They will end up in the hands of smugglers and then get detained again."

By September 2019, Tajoura survivors say they were offered two options: either accept money and go live in so-called "urban" areas of Tripoli, where they would need to find work and take care of themselves, or be sent back to a different detention center by the Libyan authorities and associated militias.[2] Either way, they would not be considered for evacuation or resettlement as long as they stayed inside the UNHCR center.

"They will leave us to an unknown fate amid the ongoing war in Tripoli. We don't know where we are. We were detained for two years now."[3]

"I'm afraid to go outside."

UNHCR spokespeople told me they did not threaten to use force, but a video taken by one of the refugees shows their then-deputy chief of mission, Lucie Gagné, telling Tajoura bombing survivors that if they did not agree to leave, "they're going to come here, take you back to detention." She looked exasperated and made the gesture indicating *halas*, that she was washing her hands of something.[4]

In reality, many refugees who had left their countries to seek asylum would have preferred staying in detention centers, terrible as they were, than being on the streets. They were frightened about being kidnapped or enslaved—particularly those who were not Muslim and did not speak Arabic. They did not know how to take care of themselves after being so long incarcerated. They could not afford rent, and they were worried they would lose access to the UN.

"I am sure there is no preparedness from UN side. They are saying that they will establish community service centers and migrants can go there to access services, but I am not sure if that is feasible," said an aid worker who attended planning meetings at the time. There was already a community day center run by UNHCR in an area called Gurji, but refugees living in Tripoli described endless, fruitless waits to get inside and little help from its staff.

That same month, Germany announced it was giving an extra two million euro to UNHCR to help refugees in Libya.[5] "Who benefits from this, it is already known," a detainee complained in a Facebook group. "Seventy-five percent of it is going to be corrupted, twenty-five percent may be offered to the victims. Because there is no proper management . . . So offering this much money is not the solution. The refugees require, especially now, urgent evacuation."

Even refugees who had been moved directly to the GDF by the UN, expecting imminent evacuation, were soon put under pressure to get out.

———

On October 17, Libya was elected to the UN Human Rights Council, winning 87 percent of a secret ballot.[6] That same day, refugee women in the GDF were given bad news: they had been rejected for evacuation.

Among them was Hibaq, a 20-year-old Somali woman who had been in Libya two years and already tried to cross the sea twice. Shortly before the Tajoura bombing, after nine grueling months of pregnancy without the nutrients or toiletries she needed, Hibaq was operated on in a hospital. Her baby was not breathing—the result of poor medical care in the detention center, she told me. After this stillbirth, she went right back to Tajoura. The scar from her cesarean section was oozing when the air strike happened, and during the long walk to the GDF. Her husband, a fellow Somali she married while in the smugglers' warehouses, partially to avoid being raped, was with her. "We had nowhere to go," she recalled. "We were in a trap."

"Go to your own country or stay in Libya," another Somali woman with a three-year-old son said she was told by UNHCR staff. She had been moved to the GDF from Zintan, the detention center where so many died of neglect. She claimed she was offered $500 to return to Somalia. "How can they reject women and children? I'm two years in prisons . . . All that time my baby grows up day by day," she told me. "In Libya, it's like Somalia, they are fighting each other. If you go outside there is a lot of violence. They will cut you, they will ask you for money. When we are taken from Zintan we got food, our life was changed, we thought everything will be ok, but now we are rejected. Broken hearts, sister, you can't imagine how we are feeling."

"They make hope because they register, then three, four years later they say we're rejected."

UNHCR staff said the rejected people were not seen as a "priority."[7] "For the majority of those who have not been prioritized, it is because of credibility concerns—for example, issues with their identity, their country or place of origin, with events in their country of origin or linked to their flight, etcetera," said spokesperson Charlie Yaxley. "We understand the frustrations of those who have not been identified as a priority for resettlement . . . However, the reality of the situation is that there are simply not enough evacuation and resettlement places available."[8]

This group of Somalis decided they would not even wait for the small amount of money the UN offered them to leave the GDF, as it would not all be distributed at once and was too little to go through the hassle of the process. Instead, they agreed to exit with one solution on their mind: trying the sea again. They knew this meant possibly drowning, but staying in Tripoli could also result in death. They paid a smuggler 2,000 dinars each (around $500) for another place in a boat. In late 2019, this group was rescued by a charity rescue ship and taken to Europe.[9] A crew member on board messaged me, saying she had met them and they mentioned me. There were "more obstacles" in Libya than the war they fled in Somalia, they told her.

Others were informed they would not be registered with UNHCR at all unless they left the GDF. They were offered 450 dinars each to get out (roughly $115 on the black market exchange rate),[10] as well as food, medical referrals, and basic healthcare—though many were doubtful those promises would be delivered on.

––––––––––

By this stage, the GDF could easily have become a target in the ongoing war. Its perimeter was being used as a weapons store and a military training center. Detainees in Triq al Sikka, the detention center across the road where protesters had been tortured, were brought to work in the GDF under the deputy DCIM head Mohammed al-Khoja.[11] The refugees later recalled offloading weapons, including RPGs, rifles, and F1 bombs—some of which were stored in an ambulance—as well as constructing a stable for Khoja's seven horses. They slept on the site for almost four months. It seemed horribly ironic that the long-anticipated "alternative to detention," trumpeted by the UN, had become a site for refugee slave labor. When I asked UNHCR about this, they did not respond. On the accounts of weapons being kept in the GDF, a UNHCR spokesperson said they were not aware of it. "The GDF remains under the jurisdiction of the Ministry of Interior, [which is] responsible for security," he said.

"Sally, inside the GDF, so many weapons they have. Underground and overground."

Al-Khoja was an interesting character: both an EU accomplice and a known militia leader. He had attended at least one UN-sponsored migration meeting in Rome.[12] A former Triq al Sikka detainee recalled seeing Italian officials visiting al-Khoja's office in Tripoli. An aid worker who knew al-Khoja described him, and Naser Hazam, the Triq al Sikka detention center manager, as a "gang," despite them having official government titles. According to the Associated Press, a catering company linked to al-Khoja named "Ard al-Watan," or "The Land of the Nation," was receiving millions of dollars in food and aid contracts related to the operation of the GDF.[13]

"Every day [al-Khoja] came to the hall to see the horses. I think he loves horses. And he told us what kind of food and services we should do for the horses . . . When he saw us stop working and chat to each other he used to say bad words to us: 'I will fuck your mother.' Every single Libyan was frightened when they saw him. He is dangerous, Sally."

I perused his Facebook.[14] "Enemies everywhere my friend," al-Khoja posted one day. On another, he joked about the lack of public services in Libya: "When [Thomas] Edison, the electric inventor, died in 1931, all the world's electricity was turned off in honor of him, and the Libyan cities are still honoring the man to this day." (When I sent al-Khoja a message requesting an interview, he did not reply.)

———

Things were about to get more crowded in the GDF. The hundreds of men and boys who had been left behind in Abu Salim detention center, after Kaleb left for evacuation, would stay there six more months, much of that time without running water and electricity. More than a year had passed since official food distributions had stopped.[15] At least three others died from poor health, including a 20-year-old and a 17-year-old. The number of tuberculosis cases increased by almost forty.[16] Libyan guards pulled guns on some detainees, demanding they go "to work," though refugees suspected they would be compelled to assist on the warfront.[17] An increasing number bribed their way out and returned to smugglers on the coast.

"Today all night and still now we [are] hearing sounds of heavy weapons closer to us than before. It continues still now and they are launching from the area around us."[18]

"Hiiii Sally, yesterday and today there is no water and electricity all day except a few hours at night. So it is difficult to stay all day without water because at this time the temperature reaches above 36 degrees celsius [96.8 degrees Fahrenheit]. There is more suffocation in the hangar which is crowded by many people, especially for the sick people it is so dangerous."

"1) We are locked in detention centers more than two years, since 2017, in inhumane living conditions, in overcrowded hangars, with different transmitting conditions like TB, which it is easy to transmit in this overcrowded situation, and we have lost many brothers by these transmitting diseases. 2) Libya is not a safe country for refugees. Now we are trapped and close to the clashes area, to the front line, with no one taking responsibility to bring foods and basics needs for us. 3) We need urgent evacuation out of Libya to safe places."[19]

On October 29, 2019, hundreds of Abu Salim detainees walked out of the center for a final time following a dispute with the management, who never managed to lock them all back in halls.[20] I emailed UNHCR a photo showing the crowd of skinny young men, rucksacks on their backs, and said the group was on its way to the GDF. They asked for protection upon arrival, but the gates remained locked in front of them. UNHCR tweeted saying the situation was "tense."[21] That night, everyone slept on the street outside. The next day, four representatives were invited to meet UNHCR staff, but these four said they were simply advised to return back to detention.

"We tell them to allow us into the GDF and to support us. Otherwise we will stay here."

They were finally allowed into the outer, militia-controlled perimeter of the GDF on Halloween in 2019. Photos from the night showed the group crouched en masse in the dark. One man near the edge carried a weighty, much loved picture of Jesus, turned on its side.

There were now 1,200 people in the GDF, which UNHCR claimed was double its capacity, despite saying it could hold 1,000 people when it opened.[22] Separated from everyone else, a period of starvation began for the former Abu Salim detainees, who got water from a pipe, a few biscuits from IOM and UNICEF, and little else.

"Hiiii Sally. Please tell UNHCR, IOM, MSF to bring food. For six days we have not got any food."

"Still no food. Bad feeling, I can't explain it."

"More people getting weak."

On November 4, 2019, and again on November 11, I emailed UNHCR to ask when the former Abu Salim group would be fed. "I'm wondering if this is a deliberate policy on UNHCR's part? They seem to be starving,"[23] I wrote, but no reply came.

IOM carried out an assessment. It was written in broken English but circulated around many aid agencies. It called the situation for the Abu Salim group "distressful" and said that one quarter of the four hundred people were minors. "They are currently starving except for some casual food assistance that they get stealthily from their friends in the GDF," it read, adding that those present had coughs, colds, and skin infections, and no access to health facilities. "The lack of food in the locations is hindering the sick people to get improved and jeopardiz[ing] the health of others to sickness and malnourishment, in winter times the body requirements of calories increased and when there is no sources of enough daily calories to take in food, body will lose weight faster and malnutrition with cold will be a perfect match for diseases to spread among migrants . . . Water in the location cannot be guaranteed from being contaminated, it is obtained by water trucking and stored in a big plastic reservoir, no cases of diarrhoea are recorded at the time being, but the risk of contamination is there if people run out of the chlorine tablets which they get from UNICEF."

———

It was of course predictable that Libya's refugees, desperate for security, would risk everything to gather at a heavily promoted UN-associated center, but UNHCR management apparently had not considered this. "The GDF was a mistake because it's obvious when you give very limited services to one percent of the [refugee] population, everyone else would want to be there as well and they have the right to," a former UNHCR staff member told me. "The UN never did any contingency planning," said another aid worker who attended a lot of UN-run meetings about the Libya response. "The UN is inefficient in Libya—they acquire money. They talk. They don't care. They only care about how to get more funding."

Now a new, drastic roadmap was put forward. Three days after the IOM assessment, on November 26, UNHCR circulated a document called "Plan for new modalities of engagement by UNHCR/UN in the GDF."[24] It said that around one thousand people now in the GDF were not eligible for evacuation or were not being considered for it while they stayed in the center. They had been offered a small amount of money to leave and go out on the streets, but were refusing to take it (refugees told me they were worried about being attacked and kidnapped or detained at checkpoints and asked for documents they did not have). As a result, food provision would be completely halted beginning December 31 until the remaining refugees left. Cleaning would continue, the document said, partly "to prevent the reputational risk of having deficient/broken toilets and showers in an inhabited GDF." It also suggested five possible scenarios that could come next, including Libyan authorities "mov[ing] in and forcibly remov[ing] all the migrants/asylum seekers still in the GDF, and plac[ing] them in detention centers," or Libyan authorities turning the GDF into a detention center.

"Living in the city is just like playing hide and seek."

I was forwarded the email and attached document by an alarmed aid worker. "They are starving the population inside the [facility]. They're just trying to starve them to motivate them to leave," the person told me. "It's deliberately withholding aid to put people under pressure."

That same day, I again contacted UNHCR staff saying I was writing a report alleging that they were deliberately starving refugees to get them to leave, and inviting them to comment. Once again, they did not reply.[25]

"They are forcing us to the outside. We know nothing outside so how can we get out of this? This is the death penalty for us. We do not know what to do."

My report was published in *The Guardian* newspaper on November 28.[26] Shortly afterwards, UNHCR released a statement saying it would be expanding support for refugees in a Tripoli community day center, but it was "reassessing the role and function of the GDF."[27] UNHCR high commissioner Filippo Grandi then responded to my report. "I find that accusation offensive," he told reporters in Athens.[28] "Us, starving refugees and migrants in Libya? When my colleagues, day in, day out, risk their lives to access people that are often detained by criminal gangs?"

Grandi's dismissal of what refugees were going through contrasted with his public appreciation for the EU. The next day, on November 29, he tweeted a "farewell to the outgoing EU Commission and to its leadership—with appreciation for having stood for refugees in difficult times." He thanked European Commission president Jean-Claude Juncker, EU foreign affairs chief Federica Mogherini, EU commissioner for migration Dimitris Avramopoulos, and colleagues, "for your support and friendship."[29]

"As you know, they kicked us out of [the] GDF . . . They swore and beat me and threw me like a bag [of] garbage because I refused to go out."

On November 30, Dimitris Avramopoulos tweeted his own congratu-latory message to UNHCR.[30] "Meeting in Athens with my good friend Filippo Grandi, UN High Commissioner for Refugees," he wrote. "Thanks for our cordial and constructive cooperation during the last four years." In an accompanying photo, the two gray-haired men stood in their suits, one with a blue tie, one navy. Avramopoulos, almost laughing, had one arm around smiling, ruddy-cheeked Grandi, both of them in front of a shelf stacked with leather-bound books. The resemblance between the two men was notable.

In the GDF, Libya's EU-funded "alternative to detention," starvation, continued.

———

Two more things posted to social media stuck out to me in the following weeks, even as I continued to get messages from refugees desperate for food.

On December 3, 2019, UN Secretary General António Guterres an-nounced that Federica Mogherini, the former EU foreign affairs chief who had overseen the Libyan coastguard deal, would co-chair a new High-Level UN Panel on Internal Displacement.[31]

Three days later, on Friday, December 6, UNHCR was awarded "best communications team" by the Geneva press corps.[32] Photos showed their spokespeople jubilant at a celebration, one man with his two thumbs up, an-other leaping forward, three of the seven clasping glasses of wine.[33] "Very proud to work alongside such great colleagues. Recognized as the best UN agency news team for the second year in a row. They're all superstars," wrote Yaxley, the same spokesperson who ignored my emails about refugees starving.[34]

———

A wall was built. It separated the four hundred Abu Salim refugees from the rest of the compound; now others living in the GDF could not even throw them scraps of food. Four who tried to walk out the front gates to buy bread were taken away by Libyan guards and detained.[35] Friends said they were told that these four would only be released if everyone else agreed to go out on the streets.[36] Instead, they spent New Year's Day 2020 protesting, huddled together, surrounded by the newly built brick wall. "No food, no life," read a poster. "Our life is at risk. We need evacuation to any safe place." "Starvation is our New Year gift, but why this happen?" Those infected with tuberculosis stopped taking medication because it was too difficult to hold it down on an empty stomach.[37]

> *"Four peoples taken by the police . . . We don't know where are they now . . . Their phone is not working. We inform to the guards but they didn't care and they said 'we have not responsibility of you until you leave the center.'"*

> *"There is water but very, very hungry. No food at all. We have finished our biscuits weeks ago."*

A few Eritreans did eventually agree to go out into Tripoli. Two of them were killed within a fortnight, seemingly by Libyans who were trying to rob them.[38]

> *"They came here, then after they were denied food and water they left the GDF, that is the reality. UNHCR were taking people to the urban areas and said it is safe and with protection, so where is the safety and their protection? The truth is UNHCR is trying to cover their fault . . . They don't want to admit that these people went to the city because of a lack of food."*[39]

Again, the Abu Salim boys and men protested, this time with candles. "We have lost our brothers, who is responsible for this casualty?" one wrote on a white sign, their heads lowered as they wielded it.

Vincent Cochetel, the UN Special Envoy for the Central Mediterranean, was later questioned about the deaths and the group of Abu Salim detainees who were going without food. He claimed most of them wanted to return to their home countries. "If a refugee gets shot, it's not just because they leave what you call a UNHCR center, which is no longer a UNHCR center," he told a crowd of activists in Berlin. "We are a protection agency, and I'm telling you we don't provide protection to people in Libya. We cannot. We cannot provide protection to people in Libya."[40]

Aid workers told me they were distressed about what was happening, but they could not see the UN shifting its position. They expected Libyan guards to come in and force the remaining people out at any time.

"No matter if they kill us. It is a solution. We don't fear death but painful life."

Ultimately, the refugees agreed to leave. In the months after, they complained that it became almost impossible to get appointments with UNHCR, and calls to a hotline for help went largely unanswered.

"We told them we are leaving because we have no other option . . .
Starvation and stress have gone over our ability so all the Abu Salim
group have decided to go out. We know we are going to death ourselves,
it's not our choice. Destiny can't be changed, you have only to accept it."[41]

Dozens paid smugglers to try and cross the sea another time. The others rented rooms in run-down areas with dwindling finances, cramming in small spaces together, so afraid to go outside that there was little difference between the life there and in a detention center. Militants and even armed landlords would come to rob and extort them, or would sporadically evict them. A 15-year-old from the group was killed during an attack by an unknown shooter.[42] Tuberculosis continued to spread, and refugees who could not get medical care died in those rooms, their bodies thrown out on the streets by landlords if friends could not deliver them to a medical clinic.

The remaining Tajoura bombing survivors—including Sudanese, Er-itreans, Yemenis, Nigerians, Syrians, and a Nigerien, children, and a five-month-old baby—left the GDF, too. First, they held a protest to mark the six-month anniversary of the bombing, but were shocked when three mortar shells hit close by that same day.[43]

> *"It's too hard, there's bombing of the mortars and rockets, they're shooting around us in the gate of the GDF . . . How in the world, how this can happen? . . . This is a civilian place, GDF is the center of civilians so most people here are civilians. That's why we need this place as safe from others."*

> *"The people are afraid to sleep tonight inside the buildings. But the weather is very cool and rain is falling."*

On January 30, 2020, UNHCR announced it had suspended all opera-tional work at the GDF "after learning that training exercises, involving police and military personnel, are taking place just a few meters away from units housing asylum seekers and refugees," said Jean-Paul Cavalieri, the agency's head.[44] The dream of an "alternative to detention" in Libya was dead.

"There's still no viable alternative to detention in Tripoli," said one ob-server who sat in on meetings in Tunis after the closure of the GDF. "The urban response just basically doesn't exist. It's astonishing."

> *"I don't have much hope now but tell me what you have, my sister."*

The money promised by UNHCR was not paid to many of those who left the GDF—spokespeople said they were facing "liquidity" issues that made it difficult to fulfil the promise on time. Refugees waited to be called for interviews or to hear who was being considered for evacuation, while struggling to stay safe and get by in whatever way they could. Their phones were stolen regularly, eliminating the only way UNHCR staff were likely to get in touch. Crowds gathered outside UNHCR's community day center, but most were not allowed in. The stress was relentless.

"I went there and did an interview," described one refugee, who then waited nine months for a follow-up call. "They asked me [questions] for two hours, and I answered all the questions with integrity. At the end of the interview they said wait for a call from us to tell you the result of this interview. Since that time, it became like a nightmare. Every ringing in my phone I think is UNHCR calling. When I sleep, I wake up too quickly in order to not miss the UNHCR phone call and miss my chance to change my miserable life. So I'm destroyed physically and mentally thinking about when they will call me, what the result will be, and how can I stay strong until that time."

This state of uncertainty continued, endless suffering interspersed with occasional events deemed worthy of international attention. In October 2021, one such incident came when refugees forced out of the GDF—as well as those "released" from detention centers like Khoms Souq al Khamis— were among more than 5,000 refugees and migrants violently rounded up during days of raids by Libyan authorities in Tripoli, in what authorities said was a security operation ahead of the still pending election. Some victims were shot dead. Around 600 women, 30 of whom were pregnant and roughly 250 children, including babies, were among those threatened, tied and locked up, or sexually abused. The number of detainees in centers across the city increased threefold.[45] The fact that some had documents given to them by UNHCR, saying they were recognised as asylum seekers, made no difference.[46]

"More than 90% of all the migrants are arrested. It's like we are playing hide-and-seek with the police or other forces now."

This time, hundreds of men, women and children, who managed to avoid the initial arrests, gathered at the UNHCR community day center. Staff briefly emerged, offering a small amount of money and toiletries, but refused to let anyone in. Two days after the raids began, UNHCR announced it was suspending activities there too.[47]

> *"We asked them where should we take [the toiletries], we don't have homes. They said, 'Just take it and stay outside.' Life is paining us. There is no mercy in this world. It's become survival of the fittest."*

When thousands were either released or escaped from one of the newer detention centers the following week, Al Mabani, at least six—and potentially dozens of people—were shot dead by guards, with IOM staff saying they saw bodies in a pool of blood.[48]

> *"We don't have anywhere to go. We don't know what to do and where to run. What do they want us to do? They catch us at sea, they catch us in our homes. What do they need us to be? What's our fault in this life?"*

CHAPTER 21

THE MEDITERRANEAN SEA: FORTRESS EUROPE

"Whoever saves a life, it is considered as if he saved an entire world."
–A VERSION OF A QUOTE INCLUDED IN BOTH THE TALMUD,[1] THE HOLY BOOK OF JUDAISM, AND THE QUR'AN,[2] THE HOLY TEXT OF ISLAM

"The sea has swallowed many great men and boys."
–THE MOTHER OF AN ETHIOPIAN TEENAGER WHO DIED TRYING TO REACH EUROPE

I landed in Palermo, the capital of the southern Italian island of Sicily, in December, 2019—right in the run-up to Christmas. My first view of the *Alan Kurdi* rescue ship came the following afternoon, from the passenger seat of a rented car driven by Matthias Wiedenlübbert. The 52-year-old was a kilt-wearing coach driver and paramedic who had been volunteering with refugees in Greece and Serbia since 2015. This would be his second mission on a rescue ship, and he was happy to be there. "For me, borders are institutional racism. I don't like borders, I think everybody has to have the possibility to be free," Wiedenlübbert told me. "Us whites, with a European passport, we can do what we want, and they are not allowed to do what they want, and I think our European industrial system for the last some hundred years . . ." he trailed off. "There's a reason for this situation now."

We met at the entrance to the port. It was a run-down block of a building, an underwhelming threshold to the exciting new world that lay beyond. I showed my passport to an official with a pointy black beard who grunted when I failed to understand his Italian.

The Port of Palermo was long and winding, ending in a series of concrete projections jutting out into the water. We passed offices, workshops, cranes, cargo ships, and rusting piles of metal before turning a final corner to find the *Alan Kurdi* before us. I recognized it from its shape, the white and black paint familiar from news reports, though smaller than I expected. On one side shone a small Christmas tree, flashing green and red lights—a reminder that others were already on holidays. This ship would be our home for the next month.

The *Alan Kurdi* was operated by German charity Sea-Eye. It took its name from a Syrian boy who drowned seeking safety in 2015. The image of the lifeless three-year-old—lying on his front on the Turkish coast, arms by his sides—made headlines around the world, provoking an outpouring of sympathy and anger.[3]

This ship was scheduled to be out at sea into the 2020 new year, with the goal of patrolling off the Libyan coast to save lives. Between 2014 and 2019, more than 19,000 men, women, and children had drowned in the Mediterranean.[4] The Central Mediterranean route, between Libya and Malta or Italy, was the deadliest migration route in the world.[5]

The *Alan Kurdi* was just 300 tons, much smaller than other refugee rescue ships, such as the 2,000-ton MSF and SOS Méditerranée-operated *Ocean Viking*. It was 38.6 meters long, 7.2 meters wide, and traveled at 7.6 knots (less than nine miles per hour). On board was a volunteer crew of around a dozen people, who had paid for their own flights to get to Sicily, and a professional crew who would work alongside them. The sum total was a motley group from countries as far spaced as Norway, Spain, and Ghana. A few said they had never even met a refugee before.

I ended up on the *Alan Kurdi* by chance. At that stage, I had spent more than a year investigating what was happening in Libya, on top of previous reporting across Africa and the Middle East. The Mediterranean seemed almost like a distraction, a symptom of many, less understood crises, yet the part that garnered the most headlines. I wanted to believe this attention was due to the scale of the death toll, but I suspected it was also because white Europeans could be positioned as the heroes.

I knew refugee boats kept going missing, and the public estimates of deaths at sea were likely much lower than the reality. Big charities had largely stopped doing sea rescues after coming under extreme pressure from authorities, and it was mainly smaller organizations—with varying levels of experience and professionalism—continuing patrols. They clearly had noble intentions, and life-saving efforts were desperately needed.

The charity ships were operating in an increasingly hostile environment. Anti-immigration politicians had decried the ships as a "taxi service" for smugglers, saying they acted as a "pull factor"—something which incentivized people to make dangerous journeys. When I interviewed Libyan coastguard commander Reda Essa, he accused the charities of encouraging refugees to take to the sea. Italian prosecutors had leveled charges against some of the crews, while putting undercover agents on ships to spy on operations, wiretapping the phones of journalists who reported on migration to gather information, and even geotracking the journalists themselves.[6] Ships had been seized, and rescuers who worked with Save the Children, MSF, and on the *Iuventa*—which was bought by volunteers through a crowdfunding campaign—were facing up to twenty years in prison for complicity in people smuggling.[7]

The time had come to see that side of the story.

———

I began contacting rescue organizations in September 2019. Sea-Eye's chief spokesperson, Gorden Isler, was the first person to reply and say I could join a mission.

"Dear Sally,

I know exactly who you are. I've been following you on Twitter for some time
now . . . You can board without reservations from my side. Can you? :)

Kindly,

Gorden"

After this, things became more complicated. Gorden said the charity
was "financially strained," but confirmed I could go on a December mission as long as "nothing unexpected" happened. Then he stopped responding. Apart from one confusing email on November 2, I received no
updates. I ended up privately messaging Sea-Eye's Twitter account in late
November, asking what to do. That was how I was instructed to come to
Italy.

Upon arrival, it turned out I was not the only one confused by my experience so far. From the beginning, the *Alan Kurdi* mission was chaotic. The
volunteers' arrival was delayed one week, but—even when everyone arrived—no second officer had been hired for the mission, and the ship could
not leave without one. It was difficult finding someone at Christmas. The
ship's engine was also missing parts. In the meantime, the crew, volunteers,
and I lived on the docked *Alan Kurdi*, getting used to the close quarters and
the gentle rock of the waves.[8] Volunteers did training, arranged a schedule
for chores, and got to know each other. They practiced first aid, simulating
rescues and what to do if an unconscious person was brought on board. I
grew accustomed to words like galley (kitchen), mess (the room for meals
and general socializing), stern (the back of the ship), and starboard (the right
side as you look ahead).

Each month-long sea mission by the *Alan Kurdi* cost roughly 60,000
euro. A lot of that money came from German Protestant churches, but donations were also raised online. A volunteer was instructed to constantly
create content that could be posted on social media and used to raise dona-

tions. I knew, from talking to sources in Libya before embarking on this mission, that they sometimes saw this content too.

From the beginning, there seemed to be some confusion about my role on board, with the mission head trying to make me wear branded clothing and pose for photos. I told him I was a journalist so could not fundraise for them and would not actively take part in rescues unless it was a life-or-death situation. I was there to document, not to participate. We eventually agreed that I would help with general chores, like cleaning and preparing meals, but would stay independent apart from that.

On Thursday, December 19, 2019, as we remained in port, Pope Francis publicly called for the closure of Libyan detention centers. He unveiled a cross made from a lifejacket taken from a Mediterranean rescue ship, while praising rescue organizations. "How can we not hear the desperate cry of so many brothers and sisters who prefer to risk the stormy seas rather than die slowly in Libyan detention camps, places of ignoble torture and slavery?" asked the pontiff.[9] "We have to seriously commit to emptying the detention camps in Libya, with all possible solutions." (Eight months later, Pope Francis would compare Libyan detention centers to concentration camps.[10] "You cannot imagine the hell that people live there in those *lagers* of detention," he said, using an abbreviation of the German word *Konzentrationslager*. "All these people had was hope as they were crossing the sea.")

I asked Kaleb how he recommended acting if we did find people at sea. "You should first say congratulations," Kaleb replied. "And we Eritreans, once we are out of Libya we start thinking about the future, not the past."

———

"Unfortunately, we drowned for about ten hours. I was swimming, I saw death hundreds [of] times until the fishermen rescued us."

———

Not knowing the first time the *Alan Kurdi* left would be a false start, the mayor of Palermo came to see us off. Leoluca Orlando was a 72-year-old with broad, exaggerated, Italian features. He was famous for fighting the mafia, but his latest battle was against European migration policy.[11] "Do you remember the first process of Nuremberg was against the Italians and Germans for genocide?" he asked me as we stood beside the docked ship. "At this moment there is another genocide in Libya and in the Mediterranean Sea . . . We will not be able to say to our grandson or granddaughter that we did not know."

He told me he expected a Nuremberg-style mass trial in the future, similar to what happened after the Second World War. "To let these people stay in concentration camps means to finance criminality . . . I think what happens in Libya is a shame for the Italian government, it's a shame for the European Union, it's a shame for all European states. They are paying the criminals, giving them the right of life, of death, of thousands and thousands of people."

I asked if he worried about how many refugees and migrants would come to Italy if everyone was allowed to enter Europe. "One million, two million, three million, four million?" Orlando replied. "Do you think that Europe is not big enough to welcome everybody? I say that we need them, we are dying, Europe is dying . . . We need to send the message the European Union is not only a union of banks, it's also a union of human rights. I am completely against the European Union if the European Union does not respect human rights."

We boarded, and he waved as the ship pulled away.

It was time to secure everything. Cabinet doors were locked together with loops of string. Sticky table mats kept crockery in place. Belongings went in boxes. In the cabins, we put anything heavy on the floor. Climbing up to the monkey deck, the highest point on the ship, I watched the port retreat behind us. It was beautiful—the light, the sky, the waves. Yet that evening, there was seemingly an electrical fault; the crew was woken by alarms and the smell of burning. We were far from the search-and-rescue zone. The ship returned to port again.

———

On our way back to Italy, on December 21, I got a message. By this stage my phone number was publicly available online.

"I am a photographer living in France as a refugee . . . are you still at ALAN KURDI ship? Because there is a boat that left the Libyan city of Zuwara today, with thirty people on board, among [them are] women, children and youth . . . I want to ask if the ship will be close to the Libyan coast or not . . . to help those people. I had contact with one of them. Thank you."

I told him I could not help and sent the number of AlarmPhone—a crisis hotline—which anyone at sea could call if they were in trouble. I knew already that this was legally acceptable to do.

"The boat returned to land after they found no help . . . I think they will try again soon. Thank you again."

———

The next time we set sail was early on Christmas Day. Hours later, the seasickness began. It was a rumble in my stomach, a lightness in my head. I slept for twenty of the next twenty-four hours. When I was not asleep, I lay in my cabin, listening.

I thought about which words I could use to describe the sound of the sea. Countless others, with much more intimate knowledge, have written about it better than I can. I wondered if I could detail the ebb and flow of a human body, lying in a cramped cabin bed, hemmed in on all sides by wooden paneling to avoid falling out during a rowdy storm. I could describe flows of nausea, the stomping feet of seasick volunteers trying to complete small tasks like fetching water to drink or walking to the bathroom. The sounds of the insides of a ship: gurgles, roars, surges, thumps, hums, and meek rumbles. The contents of a cabinet stirring. The furniture creaking. Everything is taped up, stuck down, or roped together, yet nothing can withstand the sea's effects completely.

Out on the sea, away from this ship, people were taking to the water without the protection of our 70-year-old research vessel. If not on that day, on most days over the previous six years. They would be crammed together, cold, their faces exposed, praying they would survive the night. It could be dark when they drew near, and we had no advanced technology, just binoculars. We might not see them.

The next morning, I woke up and felt better.

———

Captain Uwe Doll used to play with toy ships as a child. We were sitting in the bridge, where the ship's steering wheel was, when he told me about it. The 51-year-old, who came from Saarbrücken, Germany, had been blasting out "Dirty Old Town" by The Pogues while leaning back on his captain's chair and watching water rush by. The sun was shining, and the waves shimmered.

"I've liked ships since I was a boy," he told me. "My first very favorite toy was a sailing ship from Playmobil. I never stopped playing with ships. *Treasure Island* and *Robinson Crusoe*, books like that were my favorite."

For nine years, Doll worked on container ships, tugboats, crew tender vessels, and ferry boats. He knew the Mediterranean Sea well, and offered up a long list of moments that inspired him to become a rescue captain. One was the German movie *Styx*, which he encouraged his crew to watch at the beginning of the mission.[12] It dramatizes how a woman steps up to the challenge after, sailing alone in West Africa, she comes across a boat full of dead and dying migrants.

"It's inside of me, so I have to follow this call," the captain said. He was unmarried, without children. This was only his second mission. On the first, they rescued eighty-four people. "This kind of work makes me happy. Last time, I felt emotions I've never had before in this life. We can help them," he said. "I never had this feeling before."

Doll had not been to Libya, but the descriptions he heard were always the same. "[During the] last mission, somebody [whom we rescued] said it's not a country, it's a hell," Uwe told me. "They tell horrible stories about Libya. This is never an option, going back to Libya."

In his previous life working on merchant ships, if they came across refugees Doll was expected to do nothing, despite that contravening international law. "[We] had a lot of pressure from companies," he explained. "You can also lose your job, and these days it's not so easy to find a job anywhere. So it's a very difficult decision for a captain to make [a] rescue."

———

On Thursday, December 26, around 4:00 p.m., we finally entered the Libyan search-and-rescue zone. On deck, as we watched the sunset—an expanse of purple and orange across the black-tipped waves—two of the volunteers asked me if I thought anyone was setting off from Libya right then. It was clear that they were already imagining refugees in front of them, worrying about missing anyone through the decidedly low-tech binoculars that they used to scan the horizon.

Before I got on the *Alan Kurdi*, I discussed what I could and could not do on board with Sea-Eye's spokespeople. I wanted to be as careful as possible, given how easily authorities seemed to accuse refugee charities of working with smugglers. They told me as long as I did not message refugees in Libya from the search-and-rescue zone, there should be no legal risk. I had further concerns: that my reports or posts online might motivate people to take to sea—a dangerous journey that came with no guarantees, no matter who was patrolling. When I told Sea-Eye spokespeople I was considering waiting until after the mission to publish or post anything, their media head said all journalists publish reports and post updates on Twitter while they are on board—that is the whole point. If migrants or smugglers want to track the rescue ships, that information is publicly available anyway, they don't need to follow social media accounts to find it out.

In the coming days, I expected to meet people who had fled detention centers, but I was to be surprised. It was not refugees from the rest of Africa who would eventually come on board, but Libyan citizens.

———

Dozens of miles away, the Libyans had packed two big boxes of croissants inside an eight-meter fiberglass boat. There were dates, Nescafe, and cigarettes, too—enough for four days. They were scared, "but that's normal," one man told me later. For some, it was their first time at sea.

They searched for rescue ships on MarineTraffic, a phone application that allows anyone to see vessels at sea and their locations. With the *Alan Kurdi*, they were in luck; they saw we were coming. This was their chance.

Khaled, a broad, baby-faced twenty-something from Tripoli, had been perusing Twitter. He scrolled through the pages of MSF Sea, Open Arms, and Sea-Eye before finding my feed. He saw the Christmas dinner the *Alan Kurdi*'s crew ate on December 24, the night before we set out, and a video I took of dolphins jumping. He knew what the ship looked like and was confident he could recognize the big spinning radar on its mast. As the *Alan Kurdi* moved south, they readied themselves. After dark, around 8:00 p.m., they set sail.

Each person on board had paid 10,000 dinars, or around $2,000 on the black market rate, with no discount for babies and children. Around 150,000 dinars went towards the boat, and the rest towards the smuggler. Some of the thirty-two people crammed together were friends already—they had grown tired of Libya together, debating how to find salvation. Others met in the weeks prior to departure.

One year before, Khaled had posted his laptop and Sony camera to France, where his mother and two siblings lived. He tried to cross the sea from Tunisia but was caught. When his father died that May, it increased the feeling of urgency: he needed to be reunited with what was left of his family. As they took to the water this time, he pictured their faces.

The men took turns steering, sitting exposed at the top. Women stayed inside with the children. It was quiet, except for the occasional sounds of vomiting. In the still of night, they crossed twenty miles within five or six hours, making sure they were clear of Libyan waters before they called AlarmPhone, the charity-run phone line for refugee boats in distress. Tareq did not even know the call had been made. He had his headphones on, convinced they would all die.

The first time they called, the person on the other end said he could not guarantee any help, but he would phone back to check on them every fifteen minutes or half hour. The second time, he had better news for them: the *Alan Kurdi* was on its way.

———

22.37 rescue boat reported by Alarm Phone, inside Tunisian SAR zone

00.24 light spotted, giving signals

00.35 second light spotted

00.57 launching rubber boat *Charlotti*

———

The *Alan Kurdi*'s crew went to sleep early on that first night in the search-and-rescue zone, with only a single person keeping watch. Then came the long blaring bursts, rousing everyone. Bleary-eyed, the crew and volunteers gathered in the mess. There was a refugee boat, we were instructed. We were sailing towards it.

I climbed up to the monkey deck. Lights blinked in the distance, shining bright, then dimming. A sign of life. As the *Alan Kurdi* turned to aim for its target, still half a nautical mile away, the flashing became more regular. It looked like a small white powerboat with a red stripe on the side. And suddenly, noise broke through: cries, appeals for help, their voices.

All this time, seagulls, the original long-distance migrators, flew beside us. The *Alan Kurdi*'s crew were donning protective orange suits with helmets and lifejackets secured around their torsos and between their legs, should they fall in the water themselves. Lifeboats were deployed with a crane. The volunteers assigned to operate them were getting in position. A rescue operation is both fast and slow. Fast because everyone's heart is pumping, but slow because it is important to do everything calmly. Panic costs lives.

I waited on deck until the first lifeboat came back. Inside were four children, a woman, and a man. Volunteers hoisted them up, child after child. Once on board, the father held his baby to his face, breathing in the smell, until he burst into tears. He hugged an older boy who came up next, started crying, and then began to vomit. The lifeboat returned again.

"Thank you, thank you," said a woman wearing skinny jeans and a headscarf, who stumbled on. "No problem," replied one of the rescue crew.

"Mama, mama," came the cries of a toddler. Those on the deck already looked confused until a pregnant mother, lifted up behind, clasped the child to her. The lifeboat came back another time, new arrivals greeting each other with shock, fear, and clear relief. "*Salam*," they said to each other, smiling. One made a peace sign from under the blanket that had been wrapped around her shoulders. They sat, huddling against the cold night. Sick bags were handed out.

Younger men were the last to be brought over on the rubber lifeboats. They bent their backs as they climbed the ladder and walked down small wooden steps, some with a measure of attempted swagger, others clearly exhausted, or maybe resigned to the momentous change that was coming. I sat, observing them and taking some photos. A young man in an orange pullover sat in front of me. He looked closely. "Are you Sally?" he asked. "I follow you on Twitter." I would later learn this was Khaled. In fact, his brother was the one who messaged me on WhatsApp the previous week—the first time this group of Libyans tried to cross the sea.

Volunteers directed the young men to the top deck, by the bow. They sat on life vests for warmth. One lit up a cigarette, apologizing if the smoking bothered me. I said it was fine.

We watched as the boat they had been crammed into exploded in flames in the distance—European instructions were that any rescuing crew should destroy vessels they found so they could not be reused by smugglers. "I love that boat, mate," said Tareq, the most outgoing of the lot. "I'm just joking with you," he added, laughing at my surprise.

There was a heavy wind and spray, and I apologized that they had to stay exposed while the cranes and lifeboats were organized. "Let them do their thing, they rescued us," Tareq said.

———

At 4:30 a.m., the *Alan Kurdi*'s head of mission, Rene Stein, ordered the crew to gather. He said they had made the decision that the ship would immediately turn north, sailing out of the search-and-rescue zone and back towards Italy. "We have people on board, guests on board we have rescued. We must bring these people to a safe shore, any shore," he told us. He suggested the Libyan coastguard could try and take them back otherwise. The lookout for other boats in distress was to be called off immediately. "The probability is not very high," he said later, when questioned on this decision.

It was hard not to think about refugees the *Alan Kurdi* could be leaving behind—those who might be sailing without a GPS, satellite phone, or savvy passengers with Twitter accounts and ship-tracking apps who could figure out where to be picked up. There could be gray or blue rubber boats out there, impossible for volunteers to spot at night.

"I'm tired, really tired. I can't really describe that feeling," one of the volunteer paramedics told me afterwards. "I don't see why we couldn't stay out there one more day."

———

The following morning—Friday, December 28—three of the Libyan men pulled chairs onto the deck, and we talked. They wore matching navy tracksuits handed out by the ship's crew.

First was Tareq, the outgoing 27-year-old from Tripoli. He leaned back on his chair and looked at me. "There are civilians dying in the street, young boys dying in the street, boys my age holding guns," he said, when I asked that most basic but paramount question: why he decided to leave Libya. "I have no idea about politics. Who has what, who's supplying who? When people start supplying others with guns, everyone is armed, it's hard to get it stable. What I see is people sleeping in empty buildings with no doors, no windows. People sleep in gardens, packed together at night because they have nowhere to go." He said the militias were targeting teenagers for recruitment, plying them with drugs and alcohol. "They play with them, give them money, get them involved. All I see is people with guns. Some people are killed in the street. Who supplies who I don't know. You can't talk to them . . . They are everywhere. If you have a nice car they will kidnap you, they will take it as well. Killing people, it's all like a game."

In his small bag, he had packed clothes, a vape, and a flimsy book of Sherlock Holmes short stories. Earlier, he had been reading it, but the text got soaked by the waves and the pages were stuck together.

In Libya, he said, "you need to keep your head down, be really careful. Before you go you need to think about where you're going, plan what you're doing. It's really hard to work there. Lots of people my age work in the militias, so it's really hard to find a normal job. It's difficult to study. Many schools are closing now because it's a war." He did not know what his chances of getting asylum in Europe were. "All I know is that I'm never going back," he said.

As Tareq spoke, another Libyan man vomited and a second crouched, dry heaving. Sick bags were regularly hurled into the ocean behind us.

Khaled, who was twenty-four, had similar reasoning to Tareq. "The war, every day, it's worse than before." He had been trying to leave Libya for six years, but his visa applications kept getting rejected.

Eman, a 23-year-old with a narrow face and wide eyes, agreed. "When Gaddafi [was in power] we never saw children die. There is no humanity. They're all corrupt. It's like living with monsters, the militias. There is no love."

———

In what was known as the guests' kitchen (Sea-Eye's crew called rescued people "guests" once they were on board the ship), Muftah had taken over as chef. He was a round 28-year-old who came from a well-known Tripoli family. He used to work in a legal office, where he had a front-row seat to the breakdown of law in Libya, he told me. "There's laws of militias now. There's no hope in this shitty country," he said. "When you wake up in the morning you hear bomb, bomb. I saw with my eyes bombs fall down from the sky. I saw houses blown up from this war. My nephew was killed. They wanted to steal his car, they shot him with one shot in the back." He turned around, pointing at his own back, indicating where the bullet had torn through flesh, bones and organs.

"You have a right to safety. I am talking about security. Freedom. I am not talking about money. I have money," he said. "You can't live in Libya like you live." He indicated towards me. "I need to live like other people. It's been eight years in Libya, war after war, war after war. You go inside yourself. I decided to make a big move to Europe. I applied for a visa. They rejected me. I decided to cross the sea. There was no choice, just cross the sea. It is not easy. It is not a short move, it's a big move."

"I hope to live a good life," continued Muftah, now distracted from his cooking. "Everybody on this planet has a right to do whatever he wants as long as he doesn't hurt anyone else. This is my life, that's your life. I don't hurt you, don't hurt me."

Many fighters had died in Libya now, he told me, so militias were offering poor people 1,000 dinars a week to replace them. This influx meant their behavior was becoming more erratic. "For the moment there is no way to stop the militias because they have a lot of guns. When you have guns you do anything you want. There's a gun here, gun here, gun here, you can't live like this," Muftah gestured around, his fingers pointed together to resemble a weapon. "Maybe I take it one day and put it to my head."

A lot more Libyans would come after him, Muftah then predicted. They would search out smugglers like he had through whispers and word of mouth and cross that dangerous sea.

———

Inside the ship's so-called "hospital," a cramped room with medical equipment, Eisha lay on a narrow examination bed. The mother of three, currently in the later stages of another pregnancy, wanted to go to Switzerland. Her biggest fear was not being able to integrate in Europe, she told me.

"I'm frightened and happy," explained Halima, a 27-year-old with strikingly dark eyes who sat nearby. "I'm worried about the next step. This will be a different country, a different language, a different culture." In Tripoli, where "the war is beside my house," her child was always crying, she said. "You can't imagine the situation [in Libya]." She was relieved now. They all were.

———

The authorities granted the *Alan Kurdi* permission to sail to Pozzallo, in Sicily. We were invited to dock at 8:30 a.m. on December 29, after everything was prepared for the Libyans' arrival.

When they heard the news, the Libyan men began to sing "Bella Ciao," the Italian protest song resurrected by the Netflix show *La Casa de Papel*, or "Money Heist"—the only words of Italian they knew. The women held their children close.

Sicily glittered. "We see the lights, we see the life," said one of the young men. The Libyans offered dinars to the crew. They kept pulling bank notes out of their pockets and looking at them, saying they were useless now. One volunteer lodged a few in a plastic food container marked "beer."

———

Khaled asked me to take a photo of him with the Italian shore visible behind. We could see individual buildings, mountains, and trees, everything bleached under a bright sun and cloud-free sky. "Caption this 'Finally,'" he said, smiling, as a breeze rushed by us. Our hands were stained with salt from climbing the ladder to get to the bow.

A boat from the Guardia Costiera, the Italian coastguard, with the EU stars on the side, flanked the *Alan Kurdi* as it entered the harbor. The men driving it wore dark jackets, sunglasses, and hats. They drew closer, revving their engines, peering at the people on board. "It's about power," said a Libyan father, who leaned on the side of the ship with his baby in his arms, facing away from them.

At the Port of Pozzallo, a collection of people had gathered. The Red Cross, IOM, police, and the military were there. Two medics wearing white hazmat suits and masks came on board. The man had a skullcap of the type that anesthesiologists normally wear, but it had flamingos on it, like he was poking fun at his otherwise ridiculous attire. He was looking for "mama pregnant." The Libyan woman would be taken to a hospital without her husband, but could bring "piccolo," the youngest of her three boys, he said. This was not counting the fourth in her stomach. "Papa, papa," the medic shouted when he realized the children were all male, making everyone laugh.

The families were invited to disembark first, then the single men. They walked one by one down the gang bridge and climbed the steps into a bus with the logo "Autolinee Cipolla" on it. It had dark windows, but there was enough of an outline that we saw their silhouettes waving goodbye as they were driven away to reception centers. I wished the best for them. What a strange few days to share.

Captain Doll and Caterina Ciufegni, the ship's doctor, walked towards Italian journalists who had been cordoned onto one side, TV cameras at the ready.

"What do they run away from?" asked the first journalist, politely.

"Who are they?" growled a man from La7, a bit louder.

"Families?" encouraged a TGR reporter.

My photos of the rescue were picked up by the Associated Press, and they ran in newspapers all over the world. I posted some on Facebook, as well, including one of Khaled holding up his Libyan passport against the sea. In response, there was an outpouring of both sympathy and rage. Other Libyans messaged me by the minute, telling me they wanted to get away, too. Some were angry. "Home is not a shoe we throw when it hurts," read one comment.

A young woman called Asma sent a message, saying her family home was on the front lines of Tripoli's fighting. "I wish I had the courage to do like the families you found in the sea," she wrote. "At least I would feel fear once, not every single day. My dream for these days is just to have a future. The atmosphere is filled with sadness and the smell of blood. This morning, instead of the sounds of birds, there are the sounds of bombings."

––––––

Of the month that Sea-Eye had anticipated the rescue mission might take, the *Alan Kurdi* spent a mere twelve hours in the search-and-rescue zone, all of them in darkness. Thirty-two new people had come to Italy. The amount German donors paid to fund the mission roughly matched the amount the Libyans paid their smuggler.

Some of those on board were not happy. On January 2, the night before I departed, one crew member complained loudly to Stein, the Sea-Eye mission head. He accused the charity of operating to give unskilled Europeans an "experience," with refugee rescues the entertainment rather than the goal.

"It seems organized to maximize the number of people getting to experience this, when it should be organized to maximize the number of lives we can save," the crew member said, slamming a can of beer on the ground in frustration. Others nodded in agreement or looked uncomfortable as he continued. "People are dying because of these decisions."

––––––

Just over a month later, I received an email from Sea-Eye telling me I was banned from the *Alan Kurdi*. Despite having no plans to go back, I was flummoxed. Soon afterwards, I was tipped off that Sea-Eye had made a report to German criminal authorities saying I was complicit in people smuggling. I was never contacted by them again or asked to provide any kind of statement, but I hired a lawyer in Germany to find out what was going on (she kindly worked for a reduced fee). It took more than a year for the investigation to be closed due to a lack of evidence, during which I was uncertain what the specifics were or whether I could be arrested at an airport if I did go to Europe (I was based in Africa for most of this time).

It was only when the investigation was shut down that I learned the full allegations, which were given to my lawyer. A Sea-Eye crew member told prosecutors that I had sent the Libyans the coordinates and course of the rescue ship (despite me knowing nothing about sailing or what the coordinates or course would be). The crew member said I told her I was in touch with refugees in Libya (something that was obvious anyway from my published work) and was motivated by the fee I would get from media outlets for reporting on a successful rescue (I earned less from those reports and photographs than I spent on traveling to Italy and back). In their statement closing the case, German prosecutors said the fact that one of the Libyans had recognized me—"which was disclosed by the accused without need—is an unlikely coincidence, but it is not readily suitable to support the hypothesis of the crime."

What did all this mean? Even now, I am not clear on Sea-Eye's full motivation for reporting me. Could it be related to the disquiet on board about the disorganized mission, the way the Libyans had looked up the *Alan Kurdi* online before leaving shore, or Sea-Eye's financial difficulties and what it would cost them to have their ship seized by authorities? Was this another sign of the paranoia that had built up among these rescue charities, due to the increasing criminalization of what they were doing? Italian authorities impounded the *Alan Kurdi* for much of the following year anyway for unrelated reasons.[13] In mid-2021, the charity sold the *Alan Kurdi* for 400,000 euro, by which time they were operating another rescue ship.[14]

A journalist friend half joked that maybe Sea-Eye targeted me because I was freelance, without a big media organization behind me, and looked like I "couldn't afford a lawyer."

Making criminal allegations against a journalist showed "how amateur-ish" Sea-Eye was, a lawyer reassured me. "You're the perfect scapegoat. I think it's reasonable for them to think that when the Libyans were interviewed they would say they had contact with someone on the ship. They could have told them that was true and you were separate to them but you are innocent. What they've done is more dangerous. They're making them look like they can be used to orchestrate rescues."

The whole debacle felt like another strange distraction from the mass horrors that continued every day in Libya. I was loathe to even include it in this account, except that if it was made public through other means, it would seem like I deliberately left it out to hide something.

———

That was my last involvement with Mediterranean search-and-rescue missions, apart from half a day spent in the Moonbird, a four-person search-and-rescue plane operated by German charity Sea-Watch, in early 2020. We flew for hours over the blue expanse of the Central Mediterranean, getting close enough to Tripoli that we could see its buildings outlined through the cloud, using binoculars or our eyes to scan the sea for rubber boats in distress. The crew were committed activists; some even wore adult diapers to enable them to stay in the sky for long stretches—there was no toilet, and they would not want to leave the site of a shipwreck if the plane came across one in progress. There were caffeine pills for when they started to tire. The sea was choppy, and we found nothing.

The area this small plane was trying to cover was so vast, and the charity did not have the capacity to fly every day, the pilot told me. When possible, its crew spotted refugee boats, contacting authorities and rescue ships if an intervention was needed. Increasingly a key part of their work was staying around to monitor interceptions and wrongdoing by the Libyan coastguard—there was little else they could do when no other ship was nearby to help.

CHAPTER 22

ADDIS ABABA: SMUGGLERS ON TRIAL

"Saving lives is an international obligation. But we also have to stop
criminal smugglers profiting on people's hope."[1]
**—EU COMMISSIONER FOR HOME AFFAIRS, YLVA JOHANSSON, AFTER AN
APRIL 2021 SHIPWRECK IN WHICH 130 PEOPLE DIED**

"Hi, how are you? Listen to me, everybody has paid and got out . . .
I'm left alone and suffering alone. Please do your absolute best to make the
deposit in a week, even in two days if possible. They beat me up every
single day, they punish us with food and a lot of other things, I don't think I
can take it anymore, they punish us in a lot of ways. The situation I am
in right now is between life and death. Please get me out, do whatever you
can to do it in the next two days. I can't handle any more."
**—AN AUDIO MESSAGE SENT FROM ETHIOPIAN SMUGGLING VICTIM DANIEL
TILAHUN TO HIS SISTER IN MID-2018**

In October 2020, I sat in a courtroom in Addis Ababa, trying not to turn
around and stare at the large, glaring man sitting behind me. It was Kidane
Zekarias Habtemariam, the smuggler notorious for how much he seemed to
relish beatings he inflicted in his Bani Walid compound. This time, he was
not the one in control. Kidane had been led into the room by armed guards
wearing handcuffs, an orange prisoner's uniform, and a matching mask (this
being the time of coronavirus).

His arrest, eight months before, came about completely by chance. One
of his victims, 24-year-old Fuad Bedru, recognized Kidane in a street in his
own neighborhood, Bethel, in the Ethiopian capital's northwest. Fuad could
not believe his luck. Thinking quickly, he ran up to police patrolling nearby

and told them the person standing by the electronics stall was one of the world's most-wanted human smugglers. As a police officer attempted to apprehend him, Kidane pulled $500 cash from his pocket, saying the man could use it to purchase "coffee" instead. During testimony in court, the police officer detailed how Kidane tried to run away but fell to the ground. Next, Kidane claimed he was diabetic and needed to buy something sugary, throwing his phone behind a shop counter as he approached (the phone was retrieved). Fuad refused all offers of money, too, despite being more than $10,000 in debt from his time in Libya, including nearly $6,000 he had paid to Kidane himself ("I'll give you whatever you want," he remembers Kidane telling him). "The moral side, the human side of me couldn't do that," Fuad told me months later as we drank soft drinks in a city center bar. "He is a criminal."

So the arrest went ahead, and the previously unthinkable happened. Kidane—who had acted like an invincible king, lording over thousands of captives in Libya—was detained in prison while evidence was gathered and charges leveled.

———

Two days after seeing Kidane, I came face to face with his former associate Welid—the short, balding Bani Walid smuggler, infamous for the number of women he raped. On that morning, Welid sat outside the courtroom, handcuffed to Shishay Godefay Demoz, a fellow Eritrean who victims say arrived in Libya as a refugee but quickly became one of the *capos*, beating, raping, and extorting captives under Welid's direction.

I had flown to Ethiopia, using funding from a journalism grant, after realizing the trials were not being covered by either local or international media. At that stage, I had spoken to many of Welid and Kidane's victims. I kept searching online for updates, but there was almost no publicly available information explaining how the cases were progressing, so I applied for a month-long media visa and went there myself.

In total, I attended seven hearings, sitting behind Kidane, Welid, and Shishay, as witnesses gave testimony in front of a three-judge panel. Young men described being promised quick passage to Europe, driving across the Sahara Desert, and then crossing the Libyan border, where it became clear all promises would be broken. Locked up with hundreds of others, they were forced to call relatives as they were tortured, while the sum of money demanded got higher and higher. A few witnesses tried to avoid turning and looking at the accused men, even when prosecutors requested they identify them—the memories were too painful. Outside the courtroom, an elevated train track ran over a bustling street. Air blew through an ajar window, rustling the blinds and letting in the din of beeping cars, the sounds of life, to permeate proceedings.

Between them, Kidane and Welid were responsible for bringing as many as thirty thousand refugees and migrants into Libya, sending some onto the sea and letting others die in captivity, victims told me. Yet remote testifying was not allowed, which cut off the large majority of potential witnesses, who were scattered across Europe and Africa. Kidane's charges related to his treatment of just eight victims,[2] and Welid only five.[3] They were all Ethiopians who had returned to their home country.

I grew used to the routine. Proceedings often started an hour late. Armed guards led the prisoners in, and I scanned their faces as their expressions shifted between obvious discomfort and bravado. These two men, responsible for extreme abuse, starvation, and sexual violence, were now behind bars. But there seemed to be no international interest in the trials, apart from an extradition request from the Netherlands that had no legal basis, and an informal query about the same from Italy, which went nowhere, according to the Ethiopian Federal Attorney General's Office. Italy refused to share information they had gathered on Kidane, prosecutors told me, because Ethiopia theoretically can inflict the death penalty. Prosecutors also said they had no other communications with human rights groups, embassies, or the International Criminal Court, which had previously said it was moving to investigate crimes against refugees and migrants inside Libya.

Throughout the hearings in Addis Ababa, I kept thinking about all the anti-smuggling rhetoric spewed out by European politicians over the previous few years. Yet when two of the most significant smugglers in North Africa were apprehended, through the bravery of a victim, we were left with this: a quiet courtroom and a handful of witnesses. Apart from the Ethiopian journalist translating for me, I was the only independent observer.

I asked diplomats, UN workers, and staff with human rights organizations why these cases were not getting the attention they deserved. Some referred to the last high-profile European smuggling trial. Farmworker Medhanie Tesfamariam Berhe spent three years locked up in Italy after he was extradited from Sudan in 2016 on charges of smuggling people through Libya. But this was a mistake: Berhe was confused for Medhanie Yehdego Mered, a man accused of overseeing the travel of 13,000 people to Europe.[4] One of the reasons for the mix-up was that Berhe once messaged the real smuggler's wife on Facebook, whom he had never met, saying he found her attractive in photos.[5] Even after journalists exposed the truth, Italian prosecutors doubled down, insisting they had the right person. Berhe was only released in 2019.

The case was shameful for Italian prosecutors. Quietly, it became more usual for them to target refugees and migrants themselves, rather than going after big smugglers. Investigators would scour pictures and interview survivors of boat journeys looking for the *scafisti*—the people who steered the boats to Italy—despite the fact that they were usually innocent asylum seekers asked to take this on at the last moment.[6] Migrants described Italian coastguard officers promising them residency permits if they divulged information that would implicate others who had been on board.[7] The real kingpins, the men who directed operations across North Africa and the Middle East and would never risk their lives in those rubber boats, carried on undisturbed.

———

"It's a very big case," said Temesgen Lapiso, Addis Ababa's director general for organized and transnational crime, sitting behind his desk in the Attorney General's building one afternoon. Still, he expected the two smugglers to get less than ten years in prison, even if more charges were brought following the current trials. There would be no extradition, even when any prison sentence finished, he told me—it seemed like a matter of national pride. "We have the evidence, we can handle them, and we are handling it right now. There is no sound reason to hand them over to another country."

Lapiso said his team was working with Interpol to try and recover money the smugglers stashed away so it could then be given back to victims, but finding it was very unlikely. Ransoms were deposited in many countries, from the United Arab Emirates and Israel to the UK, Ethiopia, and Sudan. Funds were moved on to states, including Canada and Sweden, through a network of the smugglers' relatives and associates. Even if compensation did happen, most victims would never benefit, especially those who did not live to see the trials.

There were irregularities in the way the cases had been put together. Welid, whose real name was Tewelde Goitom, was being charged under what victims said was an alias: Amanuel Yirga Damte. When I asked about this, prosecutors told me it was the name he gave police when he was arrested. Kidane's age was listed as fifty-one. Victims—including one who went to school with Kidane in Eritrea—said that was at least a decade too high. "It's really corruption," said the former classmate, who eventually reached Europe. "They are playing a big game."

Both smugglers had private lawyers while witnesses just had the prosecutors, who often only talked them through the process right before they gave evidence. Independent Ethiopian legal researchers read the charge sheets for me, describing them as confusing and poorly drafted. And there seemed to be clear omissions. Fuad, the young man whose quick thinking secured Kidane's arrest, was not called to testify or included in the cases.

In the run-up to their appearances in court, witnesses came under serious pressure not to participate. They described receiving phone calls from unknown men offering them rewards for keeping details deliberately vague. Before one hearing, the first I was present at, victims told me they were approached outside the courtroom by men carrying cash, and Welid— who was waiting for the judges to arrive—directly urged them to take it (prosecutors confirmed this was the reason why three of Welid's contacts were forced to leave the federal court that day). The attempts at bribery concerned everyone. "In Ethiopia there is a proverb: '*Genzeb kale bezemay menged ale.*' This means 'If there is money, there is a way through the sky,'" one victim worried, anxious that the smugglers would manage to pay people off to avoid punishment.

As the cases drew on, I approached lawyers for both Kidane and Welid, asking for interviews, but neither of the accused men, nor their lawyers, agreed.

––––––

Before they gave evidence in court, I avoided witnesses for fear of being accused of interfering, but afterwards we spoke readily. Standing outside the court building, they pulled up trouser legs and t-shirts to show me their scars, beseeching me to understand what they had been through. "Seeing him again in this condition made me happy, even if I never made it to Europe," said Salih, a 32-year-old father of three who still had head injuries from beatings in Welid's warehouse. "He used to haunt me in my dreams." Still, Salih would have preferred if the cases were prosecuted outside the country. "[Welid] has money. If he manages to get out of prison even after ten or twenty years, he will not have mercy on us. He won't let us live."

Like the others, Salih was impoverished and in debt. It took a lot of willpower to turn down the offers of bribes, but they all wanted justice done. When the trials were over, Salih planned to hit the road again, taking an illegal route to Saudi Arabia, where he hoped he could earn enough to support his young family.

All of the victims testifying in the trials had returned to Ethiopia with help from IOM's voluntary return program (like other returnees, they argued that "voluntary" was the wrong word—they had run out of choices in Libya). Since 2017, IOM—which was getting around $45 million funding annually from the EU for its Ethiopia operation[8]—had brought back 316 people to the Horn of Africa country. This was a relatively low number, demonstrating how few Ethiopians were willing to take up the offer. Upon arrival, returnees were given just $60. IOM spokespeople said a number got training or assistance setting up a business, too, though no one I interviewed said they received that.

———

Before and after proceedings, I used my phone to update victims elsewhere in the world. I was their eyes and ears in the Addis Ababa courtroom, their assurance that bad people do sometimes get punished for their actions. "Everything has its own time," said Aaron, who had been a victim of Kidane's. At this stage, he was twenty-two and living a half life in Tunisia, unable to claim proper asylum rights and enduring ever-increasing hostility from locals. He called the smugglers "savages" and could barely believe the arrests had happened.

"Many lives passed due to them and many have suffered in Libya for more than three years, so my idea is after three years punishment they have to be thrown into the Mediterranean Sea. These kinds of human beings should totally disappear from the Earth and should not [be] buried after death if everyone is going [to] live in peace," he messaged me.

———

On one of my last days in Ethiopia, I took a taxi to Cherkos, an impoverished neighborhood in central Addis Ababa, to meet the family of a teenager called Daniel Tilahun. His mother, Yestihareg Tefera, and brother, Temesgen, testified in court and attended many of the hearings afterwards, gazing wordlessly at Kidane. In a small sitting room, they sat beside each other, facing me. Music videos played silently on the TV, which was almost equaled in size by a big framed photo of Daniel. He was smiling, wearing a white t-shirt, his hands in his pockets and a backpack over one shoulder. "Daniel was just a kid," Temesgen said regretfully, looking at the photo.

Daniel was a quiet 18-year-old who kept things to himself, but his family knew something was up when he lost interest in his business. He would sit in their small, dark sitting room, watching National Geographic on the TV like he was studying it, trying to learn about other countries and how to survive in them. Daniel had been installing TV satellites with another older brother, saving up to start his own electronics shop. They would find out later that, as his earnings grew, he had been targeted by a local woman, a "hustler" and "spiritualist" known as Rainbow, who worked as an agent for smugglers. She looked for young men with a little money and big dreams.

Thousands of people from this neighborhood had made the journey west. The area even birthed a group of Ethiopian Christians who were publicly beheaded by ISIS in Libya in 2015, but that did not deter locals from traveling.[9]

Daniel saved up a whopping 100,000 birr ($2,628). He believed it would be enough for the full trip, which should be over in a few weeks. He only told his family he was leaving on the very day he said goodbye: May 6, 2017. "It takes a strong heart to attempt that journey," his mother said. She was constantly on the verge of tears.

In Bani Walid, the teenager ended up in the hands of Kidane and was told to pay another $5,500. "The deal changed from crossing the sea to buying your life," Temesgen remembered. They would never see Daniel again.

He stayed under the control of smugglers for at least two years, even after Kidane was reported to have left Libya for the last time. In an audio message Daniel sent his sister, he mournfully said that his friends had finally been released and begged her to send more money. In October 2018, Daniel's family made a final payment of 180,000 birr ($4,731), with funding raised through public radio appeals, contributions from neighbors and friends, and begging in a city market. They were promised Daniel would cross the sea shortly, but he did not.

Daniel's last message to his sister, sent through a messaging app on July 30, 2019, read: "Don't worry about my absence, just pray for me." Eventually, word reached his family that Daniel had died, but the information was garbled, and they still do not know the cause. It could have been the result of drowning at sea or years of abuse and torture in a Libyan warehouse. Temesgen said it did not really matter, as "it won't bring him back."

The family were risking their safety to give evidence. They said it was worth it. "I want the whole [smuggling] chain from top to bottom torn apart, every level held responsible," Temesgen said.

"We dearly hope that with God's help, justice will be served," his mother added, her voice shaking. She was praying Kidane would be convicted and given a lengthy sentence. In the end, her prayers came to nothing.

———

Four months later, Kidane escaped from custody.[10] On Thursday, February 18, 2021, he entered a toilet block on the edge of the Addis Ababa federal court complex, changed his clothes, and simply walked away. The police officers charged with guarding him were arrested and questioned, suspected of facilitating the getaway. How did one of North Africa's most notorious smugglers disappear so easily? There was local corruption, but human rights organizations, European diplomats, and UN agencies also bore responsibility. They had failed to monitor the trial or send any clear message that these cases were significant.

It fell on me to tell victims, who were both heartbroken and unsurprised. "You know there's nothing that can be amended for us by him being imprisoned, but we could have felt mental relief at least," messaged Aaron, from Tunisia. "It's Africa. I was sure he would do that," said my contact who had gone to school with Kidane when they were young.

The trial was still ongoing. Kidane was found guilty of all eight trafficking charges against him in absentia and sentenced to life in prison without parole. Welid was convicted on five (his eyes teared up when he heard the verdict; he then kicked a chair at the prosecution lawyer). Security was beefed up after Kidane's escape, and around twenty police officers were present as Welid stood, distant and looking confused, during his subsequent sentencing. He was given eighteen years in prison.

> *"It's too easy. It is very short. How many people are dead in Libya because of him? How much money has he collected? He should be in a very bad place."*

I was not in Ethiopia for Welid's sentencing, but I coincidentally spent the day with one of his victims, whom I was visiting in Sweden at the time. I asked whether he wanted to do something to mark the announcement. His response was muted. Eighteen years was nothing compared to the atrocities that had been committed, the victim said. Kidane was already gone, and he had little faith that Welid would stay in prison, either. Others echoed the same: justice had not been done.

After Kidane's escape, witnesses were afraid for their lives. They had forgone massive bribes, money that could have given them security going forward, and Kidane's victims, in particular, had nothing to show for it.

CHAPTER 23

PARIS AND BERLIN: EUROPE ON THE DOCK

"I am deeply alarmed by reports that thousands of vulnerable
migrants, including women and children, are being held in detention centers
across Libya in often inhumane conditions. Crimes, including killings,
rapes, and torture, are alleged to be commonplace . . . I am similarly dismayed
by credible accounts that Libya has become a marketplace for
the trafficking of human beings . . . We must act."

**–FATOU BENSOUDA, INTERNATIONAL CRIMINAL COURT PROSECUTOR,
IN A STATEMENT TO THE UN SECURITY COUNCIL, MAY 9, 2017[1]**

It had long been clear to me that human rights were not red lines, and no
one was forced to take notice when they were crossed. The world was not
governed by the noble ideals I believed in as a young law student. Instead,
human rights were a concept superimposed on a situation after the fact,
usually by people far away who had little experience of suffering themselves.
They chose what to focus on based on a range of considerations, not least
where they could get funding.

Still, in June 2019, I heard news that surprised me. Two lawyers in
Paris, Omer Shatz and Juan Branco, had filed a submission to the International Criminal Court calling for the EU to be charged with crimes against
humanity. Over 245 pages, it alleged that the EU had intended to sacrifice

the lives of migrants in distress at sea, with the sole objective of "dissuad[ing]" others in a similar situation "from seeking safe haven in Europe" and stopping migration from Libya "at all costs." On top of that, the EU is orchestrating "a policy of forced transfer to detention facilities, where crimes were (and still are committed)," it read.[2]

The ICC was set up under the 1998 Rome Statute, with a mandate to try crimes of interest to the international community, including war crimes and crimes against humanity. It received an average of around eight hundred submissions a year, only 5 percent of which moved forward, so the chances of this progressing were low.[3]

The UN Security Council referred Libya to the ICC in 2011, meaning its investigators had been looking for people whom they should prosecute for a long time before Shatz and Branco's submission. I had even been contacted by ICC investigators directly, and I met two of them in a drab office in north London in early 2019. While they were courteous and seemed enthusiastic, they said they were only interested in the possibility of taking charges against individuals working in Libya, particularly smugglers and traffickers. When I asked about accountability for the broader situation and the migration policies exacerbating it, they said the actions of European states did not fall under their jurisdiction.

In February 2020, I received an email directly from Shatz inviting me to speak at a day-long conference he was hosting in Sciences Po, the university in Paris. I took the opportunity, buying a flight and accepting an offer of free accommodation with the mother of a friend, who lived a bit outside the city. Valentine's Day was approaching, and Paris's cold streets were lit up with red fairy lights hanging in shop windows.

I asked Shatz and Branco for an interview, and they directed me to an office in the upscale sixth arrondissement, about a fifteen minutes' walk from the Seine River and the Louvre Museum. Shatz was a thin, harried-looking Israeli, a migrants' rights activist and lecturer; Branco, a younger, suave, Spain-born Frenchman who had represented Julian Assange, WikiLeaks, and France's Yellow Vest movement, as well as working for the French foreign ministry and for the ICC itself.[4] In 2018, Branco said he was fired by the UN during an assignment in central Africa after he accused Rwandan peacekeepers of massacring civilians.[5] He told me the UN had paid him eight thousand euro a week: a rate so high it was a "scandal."

We walked upstairs and across creaky wooden floors before sitting at a big black table in an airy room. I laid out my recorders and asked them to tell me how the submission came about.

The lawyers began their research in 2016, after they became acquainted with members of a London-based research group called Forensic Oceanography, which uses architectural techniques to investigate human rights abuses around the world. The organization had studied evidence of sinking and capsized boats in the Mediterranean and were interested in what could be done legally to hold people accountable for not rescuing the refugees on board.[6] Shatz and Branco enlisted a class of Sciences Po students to assist them.

Branco said he quickly became convinced that he was witnessing crimes against humanity, a view that had been strengthened by the way European migration policy developed in the ensuing years. "I want people in prison," he told me, his face animated.

The suffering in Libya deserved to be framed as an international crime, said Shatz. "This is serious stuff. We are witnessing the worst humanitarian crisis since World War Two." It is hard for anyone to comprehend that the EU is responsible for atrocities during peacetime, he said, but the number of people drowning was "more or less a genocide in terms of gravity of casualties," while tens of thousands had been returned to Libyan detention centers where every crime against humanity apart from apartheid was being committed: "enslavement, rape, torture, execution, deportation, imprisonment . . . murder."

They explained another key part of their argument: that migrants should be defined as a persecuted group for the purposes of international criminal law. While those trying to reach Europe may have no common ethnicity, they argued, if "tourists" got into trouble at sea, there would unquestionably be attempts to save them, whereas the same would not happen for "migrants."

"We target a specific group and dehumanize it and criminalize it and reject it at borders, and ultimately we exterminate it, this is the slippery road towards [genocide]," Shatz said. "It doesn't [happen] in one slice. It goes slowly, slowly."

Branco said "migrants" had been increasingly lumped together and demonized in public discourse. This created an artificial separation between them and the rest of society that authorities could then use to justify violence. "It doesn't come from nowhere that suddenly 'migrants' appeared in the public sphere as a word. It was a tool to create this separation," he charged.

They accused the EU of using stalling tactics, avoiding public scrutiny, and manipulating discourse "at all points." That included the jargon used in EU communications, which effectively distance the public from the human impact of migration policy. With crimes against humanity, Branco said, controlling language is a necessary enabling tactic because most civilians would not condone what was going on otherwise. "We always wonder how this thing happened, how the Second World War happened . . . We're living it. We're in the middle of one of those things happening," he said.

Branco was also highly critical of the broader human rights and legal community, whom he accused of sitting around, having conversations about refugees and what was happening at sea without creating real change, while collecting grants and earning money "basically on the bodies of these people."

"This migrant crisis feeds so many," Branco emphasized, and that "creates an inertia in which everyone wants to preserve their capital." Both men said they knew people who worked for aid agencies and NGOs, as lawyers, in academia, or for the UN, who were reluctant to take a stand because of how it might affect their future job prospects.

I had already asked other lawyers for opinions on their ICC submission. Most dismissed it as a publicity stunt aimed at career advancement with no legal basis because only individuals can be prosecuted under international criminal law, not a behemoth like the EU, and they had not named anyone specific.

"What do they think, that we are first-year law school?" Shatz asked me, becoming agitated when I told him. Branco said their work was a call for the ICC to launch its own investigation, gathering more evidence and pinning down guilty individuals. Naming people would have been "irresponsible" at this stage of a long process that should involve studying EU institutional structures (including understanding at what exact point any particular decision was made), which was difficult to do from the outside. In the absence of further action from the ICC, the two men said they were continuing the investigation alone: building a list of suspects and gathering evidence against them.

"In my opinion, we won't go for flashy names," Branco told me. Those targeted were more likely to be civil servants, anonymous to the general public and even to the media, because of the way decision-making works in Europe.

The two lawyers started discussing the prospect of another Nuremberg, where European civil servants and politicians would all be tried in public, before Shatz came back down to earth. The ICC is a political organization, and the likelihood of it going after the EU is slim, he said. "If the ICC does nothing, it sacrifices its own legitimacy for the EU. And if it's going after the EU as it should be, it . . . there would be an earthquake in terms of international relations."

While the ICC submission did not appear to progress, Shatz later co-founded a legal hub called Front-Lex with the aim of taking European border agency Frontex to court. It filed various cases, including one at the European Court of Justice ("This is not really a legal case. It's an activist agenda pretending to be a legal case, whose aim is to undermine the EU's resolve to protect its borders,"[7] Frontex spokesperson Chris Borowski told journalists in response to the filing). On its website, Front-Lex said it planned to hold a civil society tribunal in Brussels, where refugees and activists would testify about their experiences and possible charges against the EU including "failure to help, accessory to murder, violation of sea rescue regulations, human rights abuse[s], etc.," could be examined.[8] It would be modeled on a 2016 event in The Hague where victims, experts, and lawyers gathered to give evidence about human rights abuses caused by multinational giant the Monsanto Company.[9] Listening were five judges, led by former European Court of Human Rights judge Françoise Tulkens, who eventually delivered a ruling asking for the term "ecocide," or destruction of the natural environment, to be recognized under international law.[10] It was not legally binding, but the organizers said they hoped it would move the international law process along.

───────

I contacted Forensic Oceanography, the initiative that first inspired Branco and Shatz. On the phone from London, where he works in Goldsmiths University, Italian architect Lorenzo Pezzani described how they use techniques like 3D modeling, fluid dynamics, and remote sensing to produce maps, videos, installations, and human rights reports that recreate the scenes of drownings and shipwrecks. Their aim is to make what is happening in the Central Mediterranean less "opaque," he said.[11] Over the past decade, he had come to see this work as a "daily struggle," fighting for "what some people call mobility justice, others call freedom to move."

"I don't think there is any ending in sight. The only way in which the situation could radically change was one in which there was a complete rethinking of migration policies," Pezzani told me. "It's a very long struggle, and a distant goal. We are rethinking the role that borders have in our societies, which also means interrogating colonialism, imperialism, a huge change for the society we're currently living in. But this is the challenge that all progres-

sive and emancipatory movements face: Black Lives Matter, the climate justice movement, and so on and so forth." Despite everything, he said, he is not
a pessimist. "Things do change, and change is surprisingly fast sometimes."

———

Three months after I met Shatz and Branco, in the summer of 2020, one of
those moments took place where the world suddenly seems to tilt a little.
Global protests erupted, fueled by the death of George Floyd, a 46-year-old
black man murdered by American police officers. Suddenly, statues of colonialists and slave traders were being toppled and white supremacy discussed
by people who had never given much thought to racial inequality before. The
European Parliament even passed a resolution denouncing racism. "EU Parliament declares 'Black Lives Matter,'" ran the headlines.[12]

But for everyone who followed what was happening in the Central
Mediterranean and Libya, this was clearly posturing. "It's kind of hypocrit-
ical to support Black Lives Matter initiatives in the United States and then
engage in racial persecution as enslavement at the external borders of Europe," noted war crimes lawyer Alexandra Lily Kather, with characteristic
understatement, when I met her in Berlin that year.

It was a chilly autumn afternoon, and restaurants were closed because of
the coronavirus pandemic, so we bought coffees and sat in a park, surrounded by autumn leaves. Kather, a small, polite woman, worked for the
European Center for Constitutional and Human Rights, a nonprofit organization founded by international human rights lawyers that described itself
as "dedicated to enforcing civil and human rights worldwide."[13] She explained that they were also preparing a submission to the ICC, this time in
conjunction with the International Federation for Human Rights, the sec-
ond-oldest human rights organization worldwide, and Lawyers for Justice in
Libya, which operates between London and Tripoli. They wanted to connect their submission to the Black Lives Matter movement.

The first challenge was figuring out how the situation in Libya fitted into existing, prosecutable crimes against humanity. They honed in on enslavement.[14] To bolster their case, they were looking for witnesses who could be relied upon to provide evidence and remain engaged during a process that might last years—something she knew was asking a lot. "All parties, investigators, prosecutors, judges, lawyers, and most of all, the survivors, need to be really committed for it to work," Kather said.

We were a stone's throw from a playground where small children laughed, cried, and were cajoled by their parents. The scene contrasted sharply with the atrocities we were talking about. It made me question again the relationship between Europe and North Africa, between comfort and learned ignorance, and how a system can be crafted over many decades to ensure that the most powerful never answer for their wrongdoing. Unlike Shatz and Branco, but like the ICC investigators I had met, Kather said she could not see European institutions or politicians ever being held accountable. That is why European states should make a greater effort when it comes to investigating and prosecuting others, she argued.

"I think it's really important to underline that crimes in Libya are really being committed in the name and for the benefit and the privileges of the European Union," Kather told me, after I explained my thoughts to her. "That, at the same time, there's no mechanism available to hold the EU—as an actor and as an active supporter of crimes against humanity committed against black Sub-Saharan migrants—accountable. And that I think it's in the responsibility of people living here to fight for justice."

———

Across Europe, there were many more lawyers examining what could be done domestically, regionally, and internationally: taking cases, making submissions and complaints. Some of them contacted me, too. They usually wanted to hear testimony from victims who were already in safe countries, ideally in Europe, because they had a "duty of care" and could not take responsibility if a witness was retaliated against.

"There's a lot of creativity being put into finding new legal angles to find accountability. We are really trying to expand the scope of legal tools and instruments that are applied," said Itamar Mann, an international human rights lawyer working with the Global Legal Action Network (GLAN), a nonprofit organization.[15] He spoke on the phone from Haifa in Israel, in mid-2021, and called the treatment of migrants and refugees "the central human rights issue of our time." As an Israeli, Mann said he had a personal interest, because his country's attacks on Gaza were forcing Palestinians to attempt to seek safety in similar ways. The tens of thousands of deaths in the Mediterranean "boggles the mind," he said. "The fact that it's kind of at the doorstep of the European Union and Europe also generates additional irony because in the public imagination Europe is still perceived as the birthplace of this idea of human rights."

Legally, Mann said there have been small wins, but none for almost a decade. In 2012, the European Court of Human Rights ruled that Italy could not return people to Libya itself in what became known as the "Hirsi" case.[16] When we spoke, Mann was waiting for progress in a new European Court of Human Rights case, S.S. and others v. Italy, which GLAN filed. It argued that Italy was responsible for the fates of intercepted people because of its financial, material, and operational support for the Libyan coastguard.[17] "If the case is ultimately successful . . . it will be very, very impactful," Mann told me. "It will require governments to rethink the entire scheme of involvement with Libya." But he was also worried about what could be legitimized if it failed.

One of the words I was intrigued to hear Mann bring up was "apartheid." While he accepted that the strict legal definition of apartheid involves a government or regime creating a racial hierarchy among its own people, in a less formal way he said it could also describe European migration policy. The treatment of refugees relates directly to "systematic racial discrimination, apartheid, and colonial violence as well," Mann said. In the relationship between European and African governments, there are clear "colonial patterns of domination" where African leaders are still expected to, in some way, oppress their own population.

GLAN filed another case with partner organizations.[18] This time, it went to the European Court of Auditors, which is responsible for making sure that the EU's budget is properly spent. The case accused the EU of misusing and mismanaging funds and said further payments should be suspended until certain criteria are met, including refugees and migrants being released from detention centers and a functioning asylum system being created in Libya.[19]

A complaint was also filed with the UN Human Rights Committee about a Panamanian-flagged merchant ship, the Nivin, which brought ninety-three refugees and migrants back to Libya, against their will, in November 2018.[20] The group—which had already spent eighteen hours at sea when they came upon the Nivin—were in touch with me through phone calls and WhatsApp messages, and I wrote reports for Al Jazeera and CNN detailing their pleas.[21] They locked themselves in the ship's hold, saying they would rather die than go back to detention. Ten days later, they were forced out with tear gas and bullets. We lost contact, though one of their phones was later answered by a Libyan coastguard member. "Everything is ok," he told me, though he refused to give details on how the refugees were being treated, or where they had been taken. "I will chuck this phone. For now, I can't tell you any more," he said.

> *"Today, I hate everything. Where is our place in this world? No end to this life, just waiting."*

Months later, one of the young refugees managed to contact me again. He would go on to spend two years in detention before trying and failing to cross the sea another time. Lawyers contacted me looking for survivors from the boat, but then said they could probably not use that contact because he was still in Libya.

> *"What I need is to be out of this hell. It's been five years, entering the sixth year in this country. But my destiny was like this. I am still in their hands."*

All of these processes could take years, and even if a consequential verdict were reached, it might come at a time when EU migration policy had shifted again to another loophole. A negative verdict could have terrible consequences. "How do you get that solid case that can be presented with a one hundred percent win?" asked Marwa Mohamed, the head of advocacy at Lawyers for Justice in Libya. "If you get a ruling that's not in favor of the victim, then you've also set a very, very dangerous precedent . . . It has to be a very, very, very strong case."

Like so many other people I spoke to, she was despondent about how everything had developed. Still, Mohamed thought any change in policy was more likely to come through the international legal system rather than "talking or publishing or showing videos," which she believed had little impact. Without a clear ruling by a significant international court, the interpretation of laws aimed at protecting people in need had become diluted, she argued. "The reality is asylum and refugee protection mean nothing [now]. Laws of the sea have been discarded and disrespected and breached on many occasions."

At the same time, Mohamed was also advocating for justice for Libyans themselves. "We're talking about nearly half a century of atrocities that have been unaddressed from the Gaddafi period to date. That's almost fifty years of crimes committed against people with no justice and no accountability, no reconciliation or reparations for the victims, and so I think it really is time to for the international community to take this seriously," Mohamed said.

Mohamed had long been appealing for a delayed independent fact-finding mission, appointed by the UN Human Rights Council, to publish its reporting. In October, 2021, it did. Among other things, its report said there were "reasonable grounds to believe that acts of murder, enslavement, torture, imprisonment, rape, persecution and other inhumane acts committed against migrants form part of a systematic and widespread attack directed at this population, in furtherance of a state policy," something which "may amount to crimes against humanity."[22]

The report said migrants were "an identifiable group of individual civilians defined by their vulnerability and absence of legal status within Libya." This aligned with the argument Shatz and Branco made, that migrants should be defined as a persecuted group for the purposes of international criminal law.

The report pointed specifically to the Libyan coastguard, saying it carried out interceptions that were "violent" or "reckless", before returning refugees and migrants to detention centers "where they face intolerable conditions calculated to cause suffering and the desire to utilize any means of escape, including by paying large sums of money to militias, criminal gangs, traffickers and smugglers who have links to the state and profit from this practice."

"All migrants—men and women, boys and girls—are kept in harsh conditions, some of whom die . . . Torture (such as electric shocks) and sexual violence (including rape and forced prostitution) are prevalent."

It spoke about the cycle migrants and refugees found themselves trapped in. "Several interviewees [said] they endured the same cycle of violence, in some cases up to 10 times, of paying guards to secure release, sea crossing attempt[s], an interception and subsequent return to detention in harsh and violent conditions, all while under the absolute control of the authorities, militias and/or criminal networks."

Here was a direct link between the Libyan coastguard and allegations of crimes against humanity. But once again, what was most notable in this new report was what was left out of it: the role of the EU.

———

Aside from the lawyers and their quest for accountability, there were activists and volunteers who devoted their free time to helping in more immediate ways. There was Lidiya, an Eritrean 21-year-old based in Canada who raised tens of thousands of dollars to send directly to refugee families in need of aid in Tripoli. There was Giulia Tranchina, a kind Italian solicitor based in the UK who collected testimonies from detainees, appealed to aid organizations, and cried on the phone with refugees as they recounted their latest challenges.[23] There was Abrham Fa, an Eritrean in Bologna who amassed nearly fifty thousand Facebook followers posting Tigrinya-language updates about conditions along North African migration routes while staying in touch with people at all stages of their journeys. There were the European AlarmPhone activists, who took on shifts when their personal phones become the receiver of distress calls, speaking calmly to panicked people on boats in the Mediterranean at all times of the day and night, before forwarding their details to authorities and charity rescue ships.[24]

Countless protests were organized in Europe, but most seemed to attract few people and provoke little reaction. Some were arranged by refugees, like a May 2019 bike ride from Frankfurt to Brussels that ended with speeches in front of the European Commission.[25]

One event that did spark a significant backlash was the arrest of Carola Rackete, the 31-year-old captain of the *Sea-Watch 3* rescue ship who went against orders from authorities and docked in Lampedusa in June 2019 with forty migrants and refugees on board. Thousands of people took to streets across Europe, marching under the slogan "Free Carola."[26] In the aftermath, even Rackete pointed out that the reason she got so much support was because she was a white European (the charges against her were quickly thrown out). Portraying a German woman as a hero deprived rescued people of the limelight, she argued. "It is not necessary for a white woman to take the stage as the supposed 'voice of the voiceless,'" Rackete said on the first anniversary of her arrest.[27] But the truth was that the majority of the European public rarely engaged otherwise.

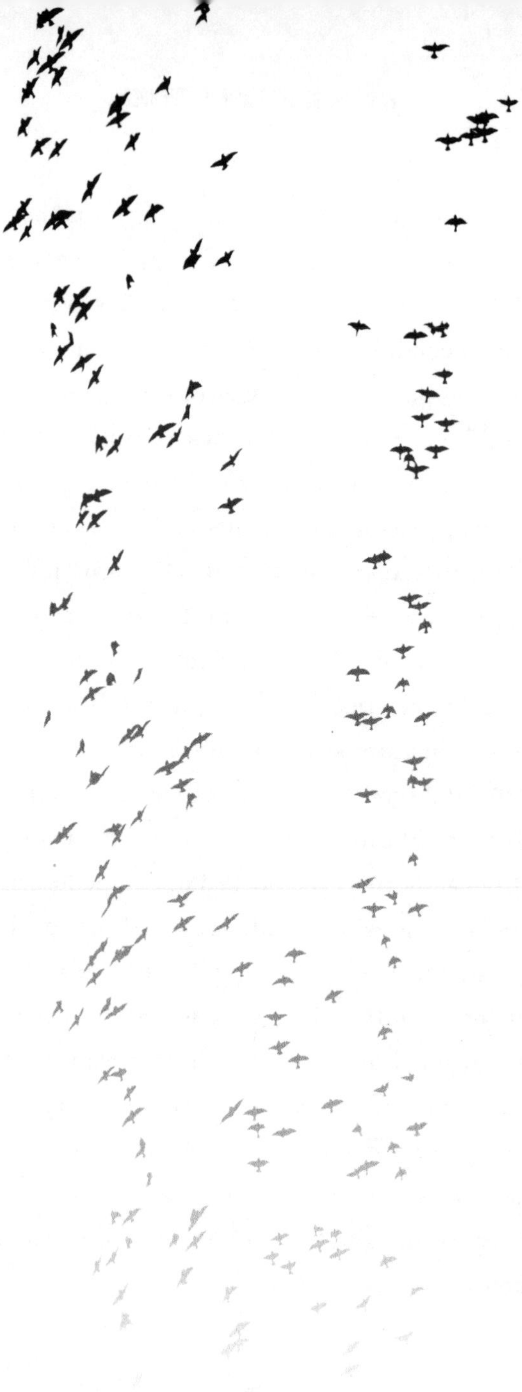

CHAPTER 24

EUROPE: HOME SWEET HOME

"Nothing can be taken for granted. Our individual liberties are
not givens. Democracy is not something we can take for granted, neither
is peace, neither is prosperity."

**—GERMAN CHANCELLOR ANGELA MERKEL, ADDRESSING HARVARD
UNIVERSITY, MAY 30, 2019**[1]

"Whoever was tortured, stays tortured."

—AUSCHWITZ SURVIVOR JEAN AMERY

When refugees make it to a safe country, there is usually a period of time
during which they are uncontactable. They have no access to phones in reception centers, camp, or quarantine sites. Their families worry they are
dead. I often worried, too. But they would resurface, praising God or Allah
and reassuring relatives that everything was going to be better from then on,
even if niggling doubts already bubbled within them.

I had been in touch with hundreds of refugees from a broad range of
backgrounds. Some fell out of contact, while others sent updates about their
new lives in Europe. Whether they had crossed the Mediterranean in a boat
or been evacuated and resettled through the UN, the initial relief and ensuing shock of a new existence was the same. Where I could, I resolved to

travel and meet the people who had risked their lives to send me information from inside Libya's detention centers.

———

One of the first I found was Aaden, a gay Somali teenager who left home after hearing family members say it is necessary to torture LGBT+ people until they turn straight. Aaden tried to cross the sea twice. When he was registered by UN staff in Libya, he lied about his reasons for fleeing Somalia, afraid the interviewers would disclose his sexuality to homophobic Libyan authorities, who, he imagined, might shoot him. In detention, he became terrified that other refugees would discover he was gay, so he used the chaos during one of Tripoli's conflicts to escape. He found work in the city, but every day was dangerous. Two of his friends were shot, one in the street and one in the room they rented.

In 2019, Aaden sailed all the way to Malta in a wooden boat with 229 others. It was Ramadan, so he went without food and water while at sea. "What was there to eat anyway? I was fasting for my future, my survival," he told me. A Maltese helicopter flew overhead, in what they interpreted as a greeting, when they approached the Mediterranean island's shore.

Upon arrival in Malta, Aaden stayed three months in a detention center before he was moved on to another camp, Hal Far. That is when he contacted me again.

> "They took me to an open camp that's far from the city. Also they told me I
> have to go and work by any means, search for a job, after that save my
> money. When one year ends I have to rent a house in the city. As you
> know, I came to Europe first to get protection, secondly to study. If I don't
> know any skills how can I find a job and work? I have to get some skills
> or knowledge to work. Can you give me any LGBT rights movement
> organization in Malta so I can contact them? Because I'm a stranger in
> Malta and I don't know things well, so I need outside help."

The day I arrived in Valletta, Malta's capital city, there was a protest outside the Court of Justice in memory of independent journalist Daphne Caruana Galizia, who reported doggedly on corruption for decades, before she was murdered with a car bomb in 2017. One of her investigations, which looked into Malta's government's "golden passport" plans to effectively sell Maltese, and thus EU, citizenship, to wealthy foreigners who could pay 650,000 euro into a national development fund, was continued by a consortium of journalists after her death.[2]

Not too far from the protest, at the Triton Fountain, I saw Aaden. He was slender, like he had suddenly grown tall but not yet filled out. He had the same young features and tired eyes I noticed on other refugees who escaped Libya, and sat hunched in a red hoodie and an Adidas cap, surveying the scene, only responding when I approached him. We had been in contact for more than a year by then.

The sun was down, and there was a chill wind by the time we reached Hal Far. "This is it. This is where we stay," he said with a wry smile. The rooms looked like shipping containers in a long row, surrounded by a fence topped with barbed wire. I read online that it used to be a British army barracks.[3] People leaned out of windows. They could leave, though they had to sign out and in again. Residents of this camp barely spoke to each other, Aaden said. He never learned the names of the others who slept in his room.

Some Eritreans who arrived in Malta, on the same boat as Aaden, stood outside the gates. They had just returned from a job hunt, but speaking only Tigrinya made finding employment all but impossible. "We don't want to be here anymore, we want to go forward," said Grimai, who owed $10,000 for the journey to Europe. "The container is too cold, no good," said Guesh. He was in his early twenties and wanted to be a mechanic.

With his fluent English, Aaden got work in an Irish pub full of dark wood and steel beer barrels, where signed hurling sticks hung above the bar and the Wi-Fi password was "Guinness." Blur's "Parklife" was playing when I entered the next day, smiling at the few elderly men drinking in a corner.

Aaden earned five euro an hour; he later proudly showed me a wad of fifty-euro notes he had saved up and carried everywhere with him. Once he had enough, he planned to spend 450 euro on a fake travel document and buy a flight to Brussels. From there, he heard a smuggler could put him in the back of a truck to the UK. In London, he wanted to befriend a community of LGBT people and study to become an eye doctor.

The other staff in the bar were all English and Irish. Aaden had not spoken to any Maltese people, apart from camp guards and officials, since he arrived on the island eight months before. "They don't want us here," he said.

His bus ride to work weaved along the coast. It passed the Libyan embassy, its Arabic signage reflecting in the bus's window, alongside crêperies, nail salons, and pizzerias, an aquamarine diving shop, a store with yachting supplies, and a sandstone church with a nativity scene set up in front of it. Men on electric scooters whizzed by moored, bobbing speedboats and beach towels hanging from balconies. The refugees were the underclass here, Aaden told me. They ignored the leisure activities taking place around them and thought about how they could earn money. "If you're underage or overage, it's the same, you have to go to work. No school, no study, no nothing," said Aaden. "Everyone is trying to survive, chasing money, how could they make a community?"

In 2021, the EU Parliament would vote 492 to 141 in favor of making the EU an "LGBTIQ freedom zone" in a motion which took a stand against attacks and discrimination against LGBT+ people in Poland and Hungary.[4] "LGBTIQ rights are human rights," it declared. When I heard that, I wondered how many LGBT+ refugees who tried to reach Europe had been pushed back to Libya through EU policy? And what about those, like Aaden, who felt they were living a half life even after they reached the continent: treated as second-class citizens because of their background and race, even fearful of the other refugees they had been arbitrarily grouped together with, who may hold homophobic views or come from conservative societies unaccustomed to accepting LGBT+ people?

———

"How are you, Sally? Thank you so much. I am ok. As you know it, I am
here in Italy. The situation is, I mean from my arrival, not suitable. There
is no work, I am forced to learn a new language, there is discrimination
here and there, loneliness, health problems . . . but I am trying my best.
How are you doing? You still in Africa? How is your work? I follow your
updates and you are doing good. I wish you all the best in life. Stay safe."

———

In 2020, the coronavirus pandemic spread around the world. Once again, we
could not meet in person, but refugee contacts who reached Europe sent me
updates. Eyob, who left Triq al Sikka via Rwanda, sent pictures of himself
feeding ducks at the edge of a lake in Norway and a video in which he bounced
a football on one knee, surrounded by thick snow. Filmon, who had served on
the organizing committee with Kaleb during his year in Abu Salim, was evacuated to Niger and arrived in Manchester before the pandemic. "I am feeling
very happy because my dreams came true," he messaged. When the first lockdown started, he followed the example of his British neighbors and stockpiled
food—something he never had the chance to do in detention. "Most super-
markets are empty, people started storing everything at home. Even me, I
started collecting everything like any person," he told me. This time, he was
not afraid. His wife, whom he met in Libya, gave birth to their second child
the following year. The baby boy would be a British citizen and was unlikely
to ever struggle like his parents had, though he would also probably never
appreciate what they went through to secure his future, either.

———

"I am great, I am living in France and everything is going well for me. I
have been here eight months. I love it. Djion is a beautiful city, friendly
people, everything is very nice here. Hopefully one day you visit us."

———

The pandemic rolled on, and rich countries bought up the newly created COVID-19 vaccines. In mid-2021, the new Delta variant of COVID-19 caused a surge in cases across the African continent, where poor, under-resourced healthcare systems, incapable of caring for an influx of patients, quickly ran out of oxygen.[5] Lockdowns, in countries where the majority of people lived hand to mouth with no social security net, were simultaneously causing widespread starvation. By October 2021, three-quarters of Europeans would be fully vaccinated, compared to less than 4.5 per cent of Africans.[6]

This coincided with an increase in Libyan coastguard interceptions. On June 12, the Libyan coastguard caught and returned a thousand people trying to cross to Europe in a single day: a new record.[7] By mid August, more people had been intercepted in the Central Mediterranean in 2020 than any other full year since EU support for the coastguard began.[8]

It was against this backdrop that I traveled to Sweden to meet more of my former sources.

———

"I'm in Davos. You know, where they hold the economic forum every year? It's so busy in winter. It's sunny and hot now. It's really breathtaking. I went to school, even in June, finished a level in the German language, it's easy for English speakers."

———

Sweden had committed to resettling five thousand refugees a year, meaning many of the people evacuated from Libya to Rwanda or Niger ended up there.[9] In Gothenburg, a city in the country's southwest, I met David, the former Tajoura detainee who now worked in a retirement home. He handed me a big bunch of roses. We were joined by his friend, a middle-aged man with a lined face whom David had last seen in the Libyan desert. As we squeezed inside a lift in one of the many identical apartment blocks, the men joked that the space reminded them of shift-sleeping in the detention centers, where several people stood so one could lie down. Exactly two years before, David recalled, he had messaged me from the UNHCR "Hotel" saying they were starving and asking if I could let humanitarian organizations know (he said a truck of food arrived shortly afterwards). Now, David was about to be reunited with his wife and child, who would fly to Sweden on family reunification visas. He had not seen them in six years.

In the same city, in a fifth-floor apartment block, Teklia was finding it hard to sleep. He was a kind man in his early thirties with a ready laugh and a keen respect for discipline, gleaned from almost a decade as a schoolteacher in Eritrea. Teklia and his sister came to Sweden from Rwanda in March 2020 on one of the last evacuation flights before the pandemic shut the world down. They lived in separate apartments, thirty minutes apart, where their rent was covered for the first four years. Teklia's apartment was small. There was a bathroom, a closet, and a kitchen with an eating area. His bed was neatly made at one end of the biggest room, which also fit two yellow couches decorated with flowers and birds. On the floor by the entrance was a Swedish-language copy of Donna Tartt's *The Goldfinch*.

Teklia's three children remained in Eritrea with his wife, a childhood sweetheart he fell in love with at school. He applied for family reunification, but the process was slow: forty more cases were still scheduled ahead of his, fourteen months on. When I arrived in Sweden, I bore precious cargo: documents proving his children's relationship to him that I was given by Teklia's friend in Uganda. He needed the documents to win his case, but nothing could make it be heard faster, and when he contacted his state-assigned lawyers, they gave him no assurance that things were moving along.

Each month, Teklia transferred half his monthly allowance of 4,000 Swedish krona to his family. He called them in front of me, on a phone with a screensaver of his wife in a white dress. The line was squeaky and unclear, as each of Teklia's children took turns talking. They sounded shy. The youngest was just eleven months old when Teklia left the country, five years before.

With free time and a desire to improve the world, Teklia volunteered to spend hours on video calls with lawyers in Berlin, who were gathering evidence to bring prosecutions against smugglers in Libya. During one session, he despairingly complained he was considering returning to Eritrea out of an aching desire to see his family again—after all, they were the ones he made this journey for. If he went to prison, maybe he would be released after a few years. His children would still be young.

Teklia had passed more than a year in Triq al Sikka detention center in Tripoli, where he contracted tuberculosis. His symptoms went untreated for months, until his sister, incarcerated, too, begged for him to be examined. This led to a distressing hospital stay during which he called his wife to say his final goodbyes. Back in detention, Teklia fastidiously took prescribed pills at the same time every morning. He was finally clear of the disease, but, in Sweden, he was thankful for regular medical checkups.

Because of the pandemic, his daily Swedish language classes went online. Only once had he encountered his next-door neighbors, who had two small children: they said "hey" and left it at that. "In Eritrea, your neighbors are the same as your family. Lunch, dinner, everything we share. We are social in our country," Teklia explained. The lack of human interaction made him depressed. "Swedish life is being alone. You can eat, you can drink, but you can't sleep." Late at night, unable to calm his mind, he paced through the nearby park to tire himself out.

After seven months, he asked to be transferred to in-person language lessons. On weekdays, Teklia traveled for forty-five minutes to attend two hours of classes that were like the "World Cup," with students from across Africa, Asia, and the Middle East. One afternoon, we walked around Gothenburg's botanical gardens with his classmates and two cheery teachers—

one Swedish, one French—admiring rhododendrons of every shade of orange, purple, and pink; camassia "blue candle" flowers; and a Chinese handkerchief tree. Meeting people face to face made him happier, but it was not enough.

I stayed with Teklia for two weeks. We passed afternoons strolling through Gothenburg, drinking spiced coffee and eating Eritrean food like injera, lentils called "Addis," and *gat*—a fattening porridge traditionally given to honeymooning couples. Teklia made egg sandwiches for breakfast. We watched countless Eritrean music videos on YouTube, many of which focused on the themes of migration, suffering at sea and in the desert, and the general abandonment of the Eritrean people. We also watched the European Football Championships, and Teklia pointed out Alexander Isak, a player of Eritrean origin on the Swedish team.

"I like it here. It has human rights. I can live like a Swedish citizen," said his friend, whose name translated into English as Wave, when he called by the apartment one afternoon. Wave crossed the sea in May 2017. He showed me a video, taken ahead of his boat trip, where refugees danced alongside trucks and fighters with guns. "We didn't know what would happen, so we had to enjoy that day," Wave said. All they had eaten for a week was dry macaroni soaked in cold water. He indicated a woman dancing beside him in the footage wearing a bright blue hijab. She was one of the fifty who died during the subsequent crossing.

———

"Yesterday, I arrived in Toronto. Canada is a big country and it's peaceful and you can easily get a job. One day I hope you will visit me."

———

In the Swedish capital Stockholm, former Zintan detainees kept seeing reminders of death. At the front of the subways, *"mot"* flashed up on an illuminated sign that showed where the train was traveling to. It is the Swedish for "towards," but in Tigrinya it means death. "*Resa*" is "travel" in Swedish, but in Tigrinya it means a dead body, explained Fesseha, a polite man wearing a wooden cross tied around his neck with black string.

I met him with Teo. Both were Eritreans who contracted tuberculosis in Zintan, the remote detention center in the mountains. Miraculously, they made it out alive. One afternoon, just after midsummer, they brought me to an airy restaurant that served Eritrean food. As injera, meat, and vegetables were placed in front of us, they explained starvation. Fesseha was now 72 kilograms, up from the 47 kilograms his weight dropped to in the detention center nicknamed "Guantanamo." He pulled out his phone to show me a photo of his skeletal face then, which was barely recognizable. When it was taken, he remembered trying to smile; his friends said he should be happy because he was going to be evacuated. I saw a grimace, a baring of teeth. Shortly afterwards, UNHCR staff told Fesseha he would need to wait another year for evacuation, until he was fully recovered from tuberculosis. He spent that year in detention, too, wondering if he would die before the flight took off.

"When I got TB I could not stand erect, I just shivered."

Teo's weight dropped to 42 kilograms from around 67 kilograms. During a full year in Zintan he remembered his skin "turning white" due to the lack of sunshine. It was such a contrast with the man I saw before me, wearing jeans and a short-sleeved shirt decorated with watermelons and sipping a beer as I struggled to eat, given what they were describing.

Fesseha looked around, calculating how many people would sleep inside this Stockholm restaurant if it was a Libyan detention center: around four hundred in three lines, he guessed. Sometimes detainees shared mattresses. "We are sleeping crowded. It's not good for the spreading of microorganisms."

We spoke about Zintan's many dead: Fatima, whose son and husband died of medical neglect; Haftom, the dentist who loved to joke; Teddy, whose brother found out his fate through Facebook. Fesseha's eyes welled up; he said thinking about Libya made him "crazy." I apologized and said we could talk about something else, but he countered that it was good for him, in a strange way. He had grown used to staying quiet about his past because Swedish people had no understanding of it. "People like them, they see the glass only, they don't look beyond," he tried to explain to me, gesturing at a water glass on the wooden table between us. "All my friends, they are in Libya still. It is not just my history, it is the history of refugees. I am lucky because I am . . ." Fesseha trailed off and gestured at the food in front of us. "Still now they are detained in the very dark jails of Libya. Even in Europe, it would not be easy to stay four years in one house. Being in Libya is like being in a morgue, sleeping beside *mot* because you are ready to die."

———

"Norway is cold, Sally. Too cold. But it's fine. Here in Norway you have to wait seven years to get citizenship. Norway is a good country, Sally, but all their systems are in their mother language. Even school. Hvordan har du det. That's how you greet in Norwegian."

———

Mustafa, the lovesick Sudanese-Eritrean from Abu Salim whose fiancé had broken off their engagement while he was in detention, ended up in Umeå, northern Sweden. There, the sun never fully set in summer and seemed to barely rise in winter, when snow was thick on the ground. He was now twenty-six, and as handsome in real life as he had been in the selfies he sent me. I spied him waiting at a bus stop with a bunch of pink carnations; on the bus, he later told me, he had plucked one out and presented it to an older lady he got talking to; I imagined she was charmed.

Mustafa spent long days studying in the largest library in the city center, where he was amazed at the idea that he could borrow books for free. He took me there, and we walked through sections dedicated to Farsi, Arabic, Somali, and other languages now spoken in Umeå. In one corner was an exhibition celebrating women throughout history, which Mustafa was enthralled by. Sweden had opened him to new ways of thinking, he told me. He was even considering becoming a vegetarian.

When Mustafa first arrived in Sweden, traveling from the refugee transit camp in Niger, he spent a week in a hospital with malaria. The staff were so nice there, he decided in the future he wanted to train as a nurse.

Now he was healthy again. Three times a week, he ran eleven kilometers through woods by the river that bisected the city. He took me along, and I managed three kilometers before we stopped to walk and talk. "Sometimes miracles are just good people with kind hearts," he posted on Facebook afterwards, along with pictures of us smiling. "Feeling blissful" was the tag.

Like Teklia, Mustafa wandered his neighborhood at night. "I don't have a sleeping problem, I have a thinking problem," he told me. We walked a lot: through forests of tall pine trees; by a lake lined with picnic tables, playgrounds, and fishers. Mustafa wanted a girlfriend, but he was anxious about having his heart broken again. Once, Mustafa told me he knew he was a different person now because he could not dance anymore. In Sudan, in Abu Salim detention center in Libya, and in the transit camp in Niger, he had danced with friends as they celebrated news about evacuations or distracted themselves from worrying about what they were going through. In Sweden, his body felt too heavy when he tried.

While incarcerated in Libya, Mustafa stayed quiet and learned how to make snap judgements about people—a skill necessary for survival. In Europe, this led to him quickly cutting off potential friends. He began seeing a psychologist, paid for by the government, who helped him develop techniques for managing situations where he felt uncomfortable or anxious. He was also relearning how important it is to give people a second chance ("They might have a bad day," he explained).

On a central street, lit by the summer sun, Mustafa ran into another Eritrean from Abu Salim. They had not known each other's names in detention, but they exchanged numbers and spoke about meeting up. It seemed like an extraordinary coincidence that they would end up in the same Swedish city, restarting their lives—but this kind of chance encounter was common among refugees, who spent so long on the move and met so many people, and became attuned to spotting each other in any environment.

Sweden seemed welcoming, but there were signs of disquiet. In Mustafa's language school, an imposing building in the city center, we chatted with his teacher, who was worried the far-right would gain ground in an election scheduled for the next year.[10] Immigration, like usual, was being used as a political football. "Not everyone wants refugees here," he said. Later the same day, at a bus stop, I got talking to a local politician, a gray-haired man originally from Somalia who had similar concerns.

Many Swedish people mentioned neighboring Denmark, where parliament had just passed a law to send asylum seekers out of the country to have their asylum claims processed—most likely in Africa.[11] UNHCR called this a "frightening race to the bottom," and the African Union would eventually come out and condemn it, too, saying "such attempts to stem out migration from Africa to Europe [are] xenophobic and completely unacceptable."[12] Denmark's immigration and integration minister, Mattias Tesfaye, himself the son of an Ethiopian, justified what his government was attempting by saying they were trying to tackle smuggling, while the country's prime minister, Mette Frederiksen, said she wanted to see "zero asylum seekers" in the future.[13]

Denmark was far from the only European country strengthening systems designed to be hostile and keep refugees away. When the Taliban took over Afghanistan in August 2021, anti-refugee discourse became even more prevalent. As images went viral across social media showing Afghans dropping to their deaths from the wheels of military planes they had clung to, propelled by a reckless desperation to be lifted to safety, French president Emmanuel Macron spoke about the need to "anticipate and protect [France] from a wave of migrants."[14] The next day, EU home affairs commissioner Ylva Johansson said while she encouraged states to increase their refugee resettlement quotas, it was important to "prevent people from heading towards the European Union through unsafe, irregular, and uncontrolled routes run by smugglers."[15] Poorer countries were asked to step in again. The US even asked Uganda to host two thousand Afghans on their behalf.[16]

The UK pushed ahead with a bill that would make arriving there without permission a criminal offense and a deciding factor in whether an asylum claim was successful.[17] Human rights groups accused other Western countries of following Australia's example, where refugees have long been indefinitely housed in inhospitable offshore detention facilities.[18] (Australia has a history of racist immigration law. The so-called "White Australia policy," which aimed to keep people from non-European ethnic backgrounds out of the country, was only ended in 1973.[19])

———

"I have resettled to Finland four months ago. Ohh, it is so cold, dear, but I am trying to adapt to it. At the beginning, I passed a tough time. Even I was not able to sleep due to climatic change."

———

On Bachelor's Walk in central Dublin, I sat on a wooden bench with Hibaq and her eight-month-old baby, Maida, who gurgled happily in a black pram, wearing a striped baby onesie and a head covering with pearls at the front. To our right was the Ha'penny Bridge—the famous footbridge that appears on so many Irish postcards. Men in orange kayaks passed in a line down the River Liffey in front of us. The sun was beating down.

Hibaq spent two years in Libya after fleeing Al Shabaab in Somalia. She survived the Tajoura detention center bombing, taking part in the great march to UNHCR's GDF before she was rejected for evacuation. Another charity ship rescued Hibaq and her husband in late 2019, while I was on board the *Alan Kurdi*. It was their third time trying to cross the sea. The following year, unusually, they were resettled to Ireland from Italy.

By August 2021, they were living in a single room in a hostel, close to where we met. The hostel was spread across a few buildings. She estimated that two hundred people lived there—making it particularly difficult at the height of the coronavirus pandemic, when they were instructed to limit their exposure to other residents. The family's legal refugee status was recently confirmed, and they wanted to search for new accommodation, but the city's housing crisis meant it was nearly impossible to find anywhere suitable. Hibaq—who painted her nails red and wore a mask that read "dance every-day"—had small goals. She wanted to start English language classes; join a gym to get fitter; and maybe, in the future, train to help women during pregnancy and childbirth. Several times, she brought up the pain of losing her first baby, who was stillborn in Libya. Healthcare was almost nonexistent for pregnant women in detention, she told me. Despite all she had been through, Hibaq had a long life in front of her now. She was only twenty-two.

————

As I met former Libya detainees, they would fill me in on the fate of others whose stories I had come across. Helen and Birhan—the couple whose daughter, Ikram, was born in Abu Salim detention center as war raged in 2018—were eventually resettled to Canada. Their baby had grown into a healthy toddler with a wide smile who loved dancing in front of the TV. I was passed Birhan's number, and we spoke on the phone. "She changed my life," he said with pride, as Ikram babbled in the background. "She's smarter than average. She's playing with me all the time . . . I love you honey," he added, the last part directed to his daughter. When she was older, he told me, they would tell Ikram where she came into the world, how brave her mother was, and how many people prayed for her survival.

For every uplifting development, there was a tragic one. I was reminded of the trials of a woman detained in Abu Salim who complained of extreme pain from being electrocuted on one breast when she resisted a smuggler's rape attempt. She drowned in 2020, on yet another attempt to cross the sea.

"She is not lucky, she dead last year."

I was told at least two of the twenty-two people imprisoned underground in Triq al Sikka detention center following the February 2019 protest there were also dead.

Like the journeys themselves, arrival was not simple, either. There were trends I began to notice. Refugees who reached Europe often felt crushingly lonely and struggled with depression. They described days when they never left their beds, and it took a real effort to begin engaging with the unfamiliar societies they were now a part of.

Many only maintained minimal contact with friends still in Libya—it was painful and made them feel debilitated to hear about the abuse continuing, survivors told me. Social media added to this strain. Occasionally, refugees who reached Europe deleted their accounts completely or changed their names so no one could search for them. While some did not seem able to engage with people from their past, others felt compelled to post pictures showing how good their new life was, to reassure the family members who sacrificed so much to get them there. A few people worried to me that they were becoming obsessed with looking at social media updates from the places they had left behind.

"So many people spend their time watching TikTok, YouTube, Facebook, so they can't manage their time properly and they don't get enough time to sleep."

Everyone I met in person said they found it hard to relate to the citizens in the country they had arrived in, whom they perceived as having no real experience of hardship. Several refugees in Sweden told me of their amazement at how well dogs were treated there, how sharply this compared to the lack of consideration for humans on Europe's borders. "Step by step," Mustafa said he kept reminding himself about fitting into his new country.

———

I read more about trauma and the lasting impacts of it. Trauma experts say survivors can find it difficult to live in the present, as their energy is focused on suppressing inner turmoil. This is especially likely if they were unable to take decisive action to protect themselves at the time they experienced disaster[20]— for example, because they were locked up in a detention center like Libya's refugees and migrants, or being herded around like animals by gunmen. Trauma affects the brain's ability to function. Memories are impaired, as is the capacity for imagination. Those badly affected can feel like the link between their mind and bodies is completely severed. Life is not easy for people who have been through so much. That was clear for everyone I spent time with.

"Nothing is worse than the past."

The most obvious manifestation of trauma was in sleeping problems. I do not know any refugees who sleep well. Across Europe, there are restless nights, nightmares, red eyes, and stress. Compounding trauma is the shift in culture. African societies are focused around community. Libya's survivors may never have eaten a meal alone or lived without family before. Even the climate can be a shock: most are used to sunshine and can be badly affected by seasonal affective disorder during European winter. Stories of suicides are common but usually go unreported. In one particularly devastating series of deaths in the UK, four Eritrean friends, all teenagers, killed themselves within sixteen months after arrival, between 2017 and 2019.[21]

During long journeys to safety, refugees had to maintain an optimism, even a fantasy, that life would be easier when they reach their final destination. Yet the reality, after arrival, is undoubtedly different.

Refugees can wait years to get their permission to stay in Europe granted. An asylum process is grinding. It firmly positions the applicant as a victim, forcing them to recount all the bad things that have happened in their lives, the challenges and struggles, the violence and abuse. They relive it during evaluations and appeals, facing disbelief and probing questions, when they would rather move on. The word "refugee" itself is one that many people who reach safety do not like. British barrister Simon Cox has suggested that international instruments should have initially called refugees "people in a refugee situation."[22] No one should have to be defined forever by the worst thing that has happened to them.

Outside the legal process, there is racism and xenophobia, confusion about customs, and language problems—even those fluent in the tongue of their new country grapple with subtext and slang. Alongside all of this, they contend with constant reminders—both real and presumed—that everything can be taken away from them at any minute.

For those who do build lives in Europe, there is the question of how their experiences will affect their offspring. To what extent trauma can be passed down through generations is still being studied, but research suggests that crisis coping mechanisms and mental health problems—including difficulty trusting people, low self-worth, anxiety, issues concentrating, and fears about the future—can be seen at higher levels than usual in the children and grandchildren of refugees.[23] History also shows us that people who migrate after surviving something horrible often keep quiet about the past. It is necessary to assimilate, to integrate, and to forget.

LUXEMBOURG: KALEB

"There is no point in taking shelter in a cave after the rain."
—ERITREAN PROVERB

Kaleb's arrival in Italy was uneasy. He began to worry whether it was the right place for him. Several times, he asked me what he should do, and each time I replied saying I am not allowed to give advice; these decisions are his. In messages, other refugees told him they had seen immigrants and black people sleeping on Italian streets—Kaleb did not want that to become his life, too. After a few days spent completing medical checks, he simply walked out of the house he had been accommodated in.

He spent a few days in Rome in an abandoned building that had been taken over by Eritreans. They all recommended different journeys based on whatever ultimate destination they pictured for themselves: the UK, Germany, Scandinavia.

Kaleb fixed on France. He got a bus to Geneva, then a train to Paris, where he stayed with a friend's friend. Then he changed his mind and decided to go to Luxembourg after hearing refugees were treated well there.

"You ask everyone you meet 'where is life better?' How is life here, should I ask for asylum here?"

When Kaleb arrived in Luxembourg, he approached a group of people standing near the train station and asked where he could go to claim asylum. Two men directed him to the bus, naming the stop to get off at and a building to enter where he could declare his presence and request international protection.

————

Shortly after that, in July 2019, I got on a Ryanair flight from Dublin. My takeoff was slightly delayed, and I messaged Kaleb from the plane. He sent me a photo showing him smiling, arms outstretched, in a green field with what looked like a castle behind him. He warned me it was hot there—"like Libya." At least 36 degrees Celsius (or 96.8 degrees Fahrenheit), someone on the flight said.

We talked about what we should do when I arrived, and he said he could go anywhere, as long as he was back by midnight. He asked if I had other friends in Luxembourg so I could visit landmarks with them. "There are many tourists in this country. But me, I am not a tourist. I am a refugee, I can't do such things," he said.

Children down the back of the plane screamed as I took off over Ireland's fields, bleached yellow by an unusually warm summer. We propelled forward, across the Irish Sea. I thought, as I always do, how lucky are those of us who have freedom of movement by the chance of our birth.

As the plane lifted into the air, Boris Johnson was confirmed as the UK's new prime minister, after vowing to be harder on immigrants who "abused" the UK's "hospitality."[1] In the days that followed, he was praised by anti-immigration leaders around the world, with then-US President Donald Trump calling him a "tough and smart . . . Britain Trump" who would "do a great job."[2]

I thought about what Kaleb had told me before. Though he was now in Europe, his mind was still preoccupied with dead friends and their delusions. The horrors he had seen would stay with him for life. He felt those deaths were unnecessary; he did not understand why European policy was contributing to this level of suffering, when Europe was supposed to stand for human rights. He did not know why the UN could not access detention centers at critical moments, when it was supposed to be protecting refugees.

Instead, he attributed his escape from Libya to God and his mother's good wishes. "Mama told me she saw a dream for me," he messaged one day. "You know most of the time when something good or bad happens to me she sees it in her dream. And last time when she saw this dream she went to the church and prayed for me hard. She saw it before I got out. And now she is very happy."

———

I saw him outside my hotel, pressing the buzzer to be let inside.

That first time we met in person, we talked for more than ten hours. Kaleb was slim, with dark, curly hair he was growing out. He had a calm presence and a slow but broad smile. We walked around Luxembourg, through a cavernous green park surrounded by cliffs and ancient castles. We sat on a bench watching children play on a giant wooden ship wedged deep in sand, locals in swimsuits sunbathing nearby. We moved back to the hotel's reception, where there was air conditioning, then to the shelter where he was staying. As evening drew closer, we ordered a small beer each and sat at a table in the street below two graying men who leaned on a balcony railing casually observing life.

I watched Kaleb's face, sometimes so childish it caught you off guard, quick to smile but with eyes that turned sharp in an instant. He had the manner of someone who was capable of becoming invisible at will. Kaleb was clearly a peacemaker, though he told me he had a temper. He already knew his way around Luxembourg City, mastering the system of buses, free Wi-Fi, and street maps.

Kaleb did not like being in cars anymore. He walked in the park so he could feel open spaces. Being locked up for so many years did that to him. When he heard the sound of a slamming door or a dog barking, he jumped. A few days before we met there were fireworks, part of some festival, and he ran outside, thinking the sound was heavy weapons and trying to estimate how far off the rocket might be.

Kaleb did not eat a lot. He missed piling in with others in Abu Salim, one bowl between six, everyone grabbing as much food as they could fit in their mouths before it ran out.

He would not tell friends, still in detention centers, how his life had turned out. They would become depressed wondering why they were still suffering, why their chance had not come. "They are humans, they have feelings. We came together, we are the same citizens, the same age. One got lucky," he said.

The same week we met, an Eritrean refugee killed himself in Luxembourg, with contacts speculating that he became depressed after his wife left him. Walking around, Kaleb seemed to know many people. Everywhere, there were friends and potential friends. In Libya, Kaleb had stopped talking to new people because he found it too painful when they left or disappeared. Now, he was becoming social again, though life remained difficult. He had even made friends with a Libyan neighbor, who he said baked nice biscuit cake. "I have many friends who are Libyans," he said. "I don't want to blame them for everything. Even my friend [jokes] I'm Libyan because I speak Arabic with a Libyan accent."

On my last day, Kaleb accompanied me back to the airport and helped me check in. An hour later, while boarding the plane home, I read that another 150 people had drowned in a shipwreck off Libya.

I learned something new on that journey to Luxembourg: that even though the very first messages I got from Libya were sent on behalf of someone else, it was Kaleb composing them. He helped Tigrinya-speaking friends write in English, and he guarded the phone and checked for responses. Messaging me on one of the anniversaries of the first day they contacted me, Kaleb was reflective. "It is not a bad memory," he said. "Everything, when it passes, it is just a good story that teaches you many things. Maybe I will try to write something today about that day and send [it] for you later. Because that was the first day we started our fight and getting hope."

———

Human consciousness is full of epic tales of travel. Today, we are witnessing heroism, bravery, and sacrifice on as great a level as ever. But what happens next? In the Bible, Moses died within sight of the Promised Land, a place his people could finally feel safe.

For months or years, bodies are pressed against bodies, lives dependent on other lives. You become cargo, a piece of meat, a being that loses humanity when you can no longer recognize the humanity of others around you. At the end of that traumatic, all-encompassing experience, everyone scatters— some to safe countries, some to refugee camps or prisons, some to wars, some back to the countries they had tried to escape from, and some to their graves. This leads to a particular, unimaginable type of isolation.

"There is no place as sweet as home," Kaleb said. "For me, home is not only a place, it is the society, family, friends. In the migration life you meet every day new people with new behaviors, so you can't have true friends. You meet people, and you will not continue together. I don't feel lonely because I know many people, but the problem is separation. Some of us are in Europe. Some Niger, USA, Libya, and some, like Meri, are buried in the ground. I told you, sister, before, I was going to die in Libya. Thanks to my friends who were with me, I am now here alive. When we talk about the past it is very funny. We talk twice or three times a week. Even me, I am free, but my mind has not yet reached its destination."

One day, through Facebook messenger, Kaleb sent me a picture of Heath Ledger as the Joker, the Batman villain, with the caption: "Smile. You are alive. You have options." The picture looked frightening. "The life was also scary," Kaleb responded, when I said this. "Do you know how much I thank God that I made it out alive? This is my quote these days."

––––––––

History is written by the victors. Victims who survive often do not have the strength to stand up and rewrite the narrative, or the power to make sure their voices are counted. Will there ever be a museum commemorating those who died in the Mediterranean Sea or in Libya? And where will it be—in Europe? In Africa?

Stories are a powerful thing. Some injustices are amplified and used to legitimize future directions, to account for a world view. Others are suppressed. If refugees need to integrate into Europe, they can't continually voice resentment, they have to hide it inside themselves. What kind of falsehoods are we forcing people to tell themselves to keep living? What does that mean for the future of our societies?

––––––––

For a time, it seemed like fewer refugees were going to Libya and risking their lives there. Then came the war in Tigray, in late 2020. From Luxembourg, Kaleb scrolled on his phone in horror as conflict erupted in northern Ethiopia, after Nobel Peace Prize-winning Prime Minister Abiy Ahmed announced a military offensive against the region's leadership. Eritrea got involved, too; the country's leaders ordering conscripted soldiers to stream across the border. Eritrean and Ethiopian soldiers were accused of mass rapes, massacres, and other war crimes, as were the rebels they were fighting against.[3] Tens of thousands of Ethiopian civilians fled to eastern Sudan. Eritrean refugee camps in Tigray were looted and destroyed. They had been an insecure home to those who fled slavery-like conscription, and almost 100,000 refugees were captured or displaced again.[4] Seven months after the crisis began, at least 350,000 Ethiopians were experiencing famine.[5] Smugglers said more people than ever before were heading towards Libya—so many that Libya would barely have space for them all.[6]

Kaleb was now the one monitoring human rights abuses from a comfortable distance. "Before I was living it, now I'm observing," he told me. It was his turn to realize the stark extent of the chasm between the obliviously privileged and the set-upon, the gap separating those who pay attention and those who do not have to.

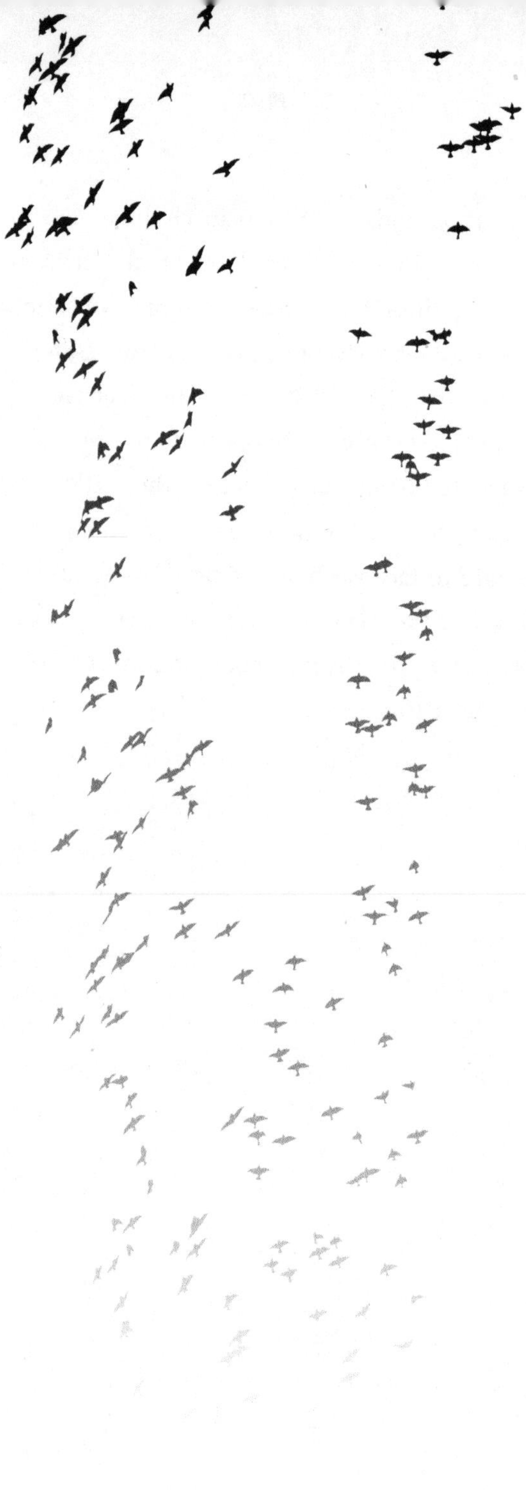

AUTHOR'S NOTE

When I was a student, I visited the site of Auschwitz concentration camp in Poland. Walking between the piles of combs, shoes, hair, and other reminders of those who had been brutally killed,[1] I asked the guide if he found it difficult coming face to face with the cruelty of humans day after day. The difficult thing is not seeing evidence of suffering, he responded. It's making sure you don't become immune to it.

In Europe, we hear constant reports of drownings in the Mediterranean, of torture and abuse along the rich world's borders. How often have you clicked away, closed the tab, switched the channel? How immune have we all grown to the destruction of life and the ongoing failure of humanity when it comes to responding to it?

I think I always wanted to be a journalist. Growing up, I was interested in stories of countries far away. Historically, the Irish are emigrants, and when I graduated, in 2013, I became one, too. The global economic downturn hit Ireland badly, and I moved to London—which to me seemed like an alien city in an unknown country—in the hopes of finding work.

At the time, I did not understand that there were classifications of foreigners. There were economic migrants (like me), refugees, asylum seekers, and "expats" (a word I heard living in various African countries, where the term invariably refers to white people). The difference is usually in the level of unearned privilege. I cannot relate to what it is like to emigrate on top of extreme, communal trauma, or how it feels to leave the place your family has always lived in, at a moment's notice, knowing you may never return.

I began earnestly reporting on migration and refugee issues in 2015, the year more than one million people crossed the Mediterranean Sea to Europe.[2] My then-editor in London suggested I travel to Calais, northern

France, after we heard UK Prime Minister David Cameron saying "swarms" of migrants were gathering there, "seeking a better life, wanting to come to Britain."[3] Who were these people, we wondered aloud. When I got to Calais, I found men, women, and children who had already made incomprehensible sacrifices and had understandable reasons for needing to continue their journeys. One man, whose image sticks with me, had a terminal illness. His relatives were in Manchester, and he knew he would need the daily care they could provide for him. He was not traveling for social security benefits, he was traveling to reach the community he needed so desperately—those who could keep him from being a "burden" on the state.

Forced migration is extremely lonely. Families can be separated by accident, or split deliberately after doing a risk-and-cost analysis. They want to increase their chances of collectively reaching a safe place, but are hindered by what they can afford and which legal chances of reunification may be open to them afterwards. Those who travel alone need to constantly make hard decisions while knowing that, in the end, everything in this world comes down to luck and money. They travel under extreme pressure, aware that their success could reset the course of their families' lives, and failure could destroy them.

The privilege of having a certain passport means that I travel with a freedom most people I interview cannot comprehend. When I first started writing this book, I had just moved from the UK to Uganda. Even traveling around Africa, the Middle East, and Asia, a European often has more ease of access than someone from the region. I have been able to visit families who were torn apart by war or persecution, spending time in different countries with relatives who may not have seen each other in person for years. I am always struck by their graciousness. There was the mother who made me a feast of *fatoush* and *warak enab* in Damascus while we chatted to her son in London on Skype; the brother of an Eritrean man in a Libyan detention center who bought me a beer in Kampala; the sisters in Addis Ababa who handed over sweets and gifts. I was amazed by the kindness and warmth they showed when I know they would have given anything to have their relative in the room instead.

There has also been resentment. As months stretched into years, some of the people sending me evidence from Libyan detention centers rightly noted that I was receiving awards, or being invited to speak at conferences, or accruing other honors. As my career progressed, they were stuck in the same place getting little benefit. That is something I have struggled with, too. I have written many articles but also helped detained refugees publish their own. I hope many more will have the opportunity to tell their stories in the coming years.

On occasion, I have been uncomfortable with the relationship between journalists and people in need. Back in 2015, after a multi-hour stakeout on a bridge in Calais, a British photographer asked me to throw sweets at refugees hiding on the train tracks below, hoping they would rush out so he could get a photo of them (I refused). During the same conversation, another man described being one of the first foreign journalists in West Africa during the 2014 Ebola outbreak. I remember recoiling as he told me how he "feasted" on the story.

I remember reading *The Bang-Bang Club*, which describes the ethical problems faced by photojournalists during South Africa's apartheid regime, and the fate of Kevin Carter, who killed himself shortly after winning the Pulitzer Prize for a photo he took of a starving Sudanese child being stalked by a vulture.[4] Journalists can be vultures. I truly believe in my profession and in the importance of factual information being made public, but I still constantly second-guess myself. I try to tread carefully and be respectful to those I speak to, but there is a power imbalance there, too.

There were stories I wanted to include in this book but was not able to, and there were people never mentioned who deserve to be remembered. In some cases, they were left out at the request of family members who are hiding the truth from other relatives. Across East and West Africa, there are mothers and fathers who will never know the babies they birthed, raised, and loved have died; grandparents being falsely reassured that their grand-children are living a fulfilling and happy life far away, and are simply too busy to call.

Even when interviewees were willing, speaking to people who have been through such a harrowing process is complicated. There are some things they feel unable to tell you because they do not want to relive them. There are some things they do not want to tell you because they feel shame about them. And there are some things they did not understand themselves, at the time or even years afterwards.

On my side, there was pressure to make the reporting digestible for a Western reader with a short attention span. When I first started talking to literary agents, their responses were disheartening. They either said I needed to write a polemic, declaring myself in favor of open borders in the first few paragraphs, or they wanted me to fictionalize what had happened to make it easier to follow. One agent told me there was no "killer narrative," and this book could never compete with Netflix and the bestselling novel-turned-film *Gone Girl*, while suggesting I create a "composite character" and focus only on one, unnamed, detention center in Libya, or an audience would be unwilling to read it. I wanted to write a work of journalism, making sure that this period of time, and this episode of European shame, was documented.

One of the greatest challenges to humanity in the twenty-first century will be how it deals with migration. Much of that is less about capacity and more about human greed. As it stands, developing countries shelter around 87 percent of the world's refugees.[5] More than half a century after most African countries gained independence, the world is still divided, and the specter of colonialism lives on. The daily scramble to get food by people in large portions of the world contrasts grotesquely with the living standards in others.

Why is it that Europeans care so little when black children die in the Mediterranean Sea? How much suffering must a human go through to be seen as equal? While European history texts gloss over the legacy of colonialism, many Africans grow up hearing how their former colonizers have stolen their wealth.

In the twentieth century, the world's population ballooned from 1.6 billion to 6 billion—the biggest increase in known history. Western countries are now aging as residents have fewer children. This has led to a slew of dramatic media coverage, like a 2021 *New York Times* article that predicted maternity wards shutting down, universities unable to find students, and "first-birthday parties [becoming] a rarer sight than funerals."[6] The population of Africa is expected to double by 2050. Yet rich-world discussions around fertility rates usually treat Africa as a sidenote, even suggesting that Western governments should be introducing incentives for childbearing, rather than reexamining migration policies to give more young Africans access to the opportunities they crave.

Climate change will also push people to migrate. By 2070, if populations stay where they are currently, between one and three billion people could be living outside the temperatures humanity is used to, according to a 2020 study by an international team of scientists.[7] One third of the planet would have a mean annual temperature of more than 84 degrees Fahrenheit, a number currently found on less than one percent of land—mostly in the Sahara Desert. Hundreds of millions of people may start searching for a better place to live for that reason. Who could blame them?

———

Despite my privilege, there was one place I could not travel while writing this book.

For the first year that I reported on what was happening to refugees in Libya, from August 2018 to 2019, I did not try to go there for safety reasons. I received death threats online; detained refugees told me my work was well known, and I was warned by security agencies not to go to North Africa at all.

In late 2019, thinking things had calmed down, I applied for a journalist visa to visit Libya. Over the following months, the coronavirus pandemic put a stop to all approvals. In March 2021, a new official took over as head of the Tripoli-based Libyan government's Foreign Media Department and he said my visa would be sent shortly. Then it was delayed again, with no solid explanation as to why. At the time of writing, it still has not been issued.

In January 2020, I spoke at an event with Vincent Cochetel, UNHCR's Special Envoy for the Central Mediterranean. He challenged me in public, saying that I should fly to Libya and witness the challenges that exist on the ground—even offering to bring me himself ("Sally, just go to Libya. Come with me tomorrow").[8] Offstage, when I approached him to say I would like to take up the offer; he responded that he could not even get a visa to go there himself.

Of course, it is always better to see everything with your own eyes, but there were massive limitations to what journalists could do even if they jumped every bureaucratic and security hurdle, procured rare permissions, and made it inside Libya's migrant detention centers. Several times, detainees messaged me directly after visits by journalists.[9] They listed off things they could not say in person for fear of punishment and described improvements that had been made to the center in the hours before the journalists arrived. I watched the important reports that were broadcast and knew I had something many visiting journalists did not—unfiltered, direct contact with detainees.

––––––––

I procrastinated far too much while writing this book, because I found it upsetting to reflect on what happened over those years. I look back and think I never pushed hard enough. You can begin to accept anything as normal. As time wore on, and little changed, I also became slow to respond, and therefore complicit. Journalism can harden you, and if you are not careful, it tears away at your empathy. I hate to think of all the people I have been rude to. And I hate the hubris that can accompany this work, the feeling that you are important simply because you are aware of what is happening. I have certainly made mistakes. I also became frightened by death threats, legal threats, aggressive emails, and everything else that accompanies working on a story like this.

As a freelancer, it is also impossible to get reports published immediately, which was why I originally started posting refugees' messages on Twitter. Still, there were many times that it took too long for something to become public, and I am sorry for them. Covering the smuggling trials in Addis Ababa was one example. I traveled to Ethiopia in October 2020. An editor at an internationally renowned newspaper said he was interested in publishing a report and then did not reply to emails for the next two months. Another editor took weeks to reply. By the time my story finally came out, in February 2021, Kidane Zekarias Habtemariam had escaped from prison. Would there have been more attention on him, more pressure, if my story had been published earlier? Could justice have been seen through to the end? Probably not, but it is painful to contemplate.

Journalists are supposed to observe and not interfere, but there is no doubt that shining a light can lead to small changes, even if there are no structural shifts. I was grateful for any minor impact I made while remaining full of guilt for much that I did and did not do over this period.

———

When I speak publicly about European migration policy and the suffering of refugees at the continent's borders, I am always asked the same question by audience members. "How do you take care of your own mental health in the middle of all this?" they say. "It must be very difficult."

I mostly deflect and mumble something incoherent. My feelings are nothing compared to what my interviewees are going through. In reality, I can't help feeling that this question is another way for people to avoid engaging with the bigger issues. People will focus on me, other Western journalists, individual aid workers, or activists because they find it hard to comprehend the scale of the atrocities taking place. But everyone privileged should be paying attention.

Having said that, it has been upsetting. I had nightmares and trouble sleeping. I noticed that I was becoming angry and irritable. "Nothing changes," my sources would challenge, and at some point, I began to agree.

An important question that I am never asked is this: How can we avoid growing immune to inequality across the world and make sure we are hearing pleas for help? There have been moments when I am too disconnected, dispassionately asking an interviewee about the death of a friend or a relative. One time that attitude was jolted was in January 2019, five months after I began receiving messages from people in Libya, when one of my own friends died back in Ireland. I remember my body hurting, how I felt unable to breathe, the sudden reminders of him that would cloud my mind and my thinking for a long time afterwards. It gave me a renewed empathy for my sources and what they were going through. Even when death and disappearances were happening all around them, they would answer my questions. Each person lost is a new tragedy, another heartbreak.

Journalists all over the world should be aware that my experience is one many more will have in the coming decades. It is not just me grappling with the constant vibrating of a phone, calls for help, and ultraconnectivity to a crisis far away. Increasingly, all of us will be contacted by people desperate for assistance. Growing global access to smartphones means you could receive a message from anyone, anywhere, at any moment. How will you deal with it?

In the meantime, this much is clear: it is getting harder to silence people. The impact of colonization is often left out of Western history books. In the same way, our present is constantly being shaped and refashioned by the powerful and wealthy, but the internet has given those traditionally excluded from these narratives a new way to fight back. I hope the world will start to listen to them.

A NOTE ON TERMINOLOGY

There is a lot of debate over which words we use to describe those on the move. Of course, "people" is better than anything: that's what we all are, first and foremost.

An "asylum seeker" is someone seeking refuge, while a "refugee" is someone who has fled their own country because of war, violence, or persecution.[10] According to the UN Refugee Agency's emergency handbook, if they fulfill this definition, people should be regarded as refugees until it is determined otherwise,[11] though in practice, the agency often only counts someone as a refugee after its staff has assessed and confirmed their claim and may call them an "asylum seeker" before that.[12] Whether to grant refugee status is often decided based on ambiguous UN criteria that is open to interpretation, or even subject to corruption.

I tend to use "refugee" to describe anyone in Libya who has already gone through a process of claiming asylum and been granted refugee status in another country: Eritreans, for example, often procure refugee status from the UN in Sudan but cannot stay there for a myriad of reasons, including that they continue to be persecuted. But I also use "refugee" where a person could reasonably be expected to be granted refugee status, as many others with the same background as them have, but have been denied the chance to claim this for an unusually long time, which commonly happens in Libyan detention centers. I use "migrants" more generally to describe people who are on the move, who may or may not try and claim asylum.

Legally, the terms "trafficking" and "smuggling" mean different things: people smuggling is when someone is illegally brought into another country. Generally that person is paying for a service and being smuggled with their consent. Trafficking describes a situation in which a person has not agreed to travel or they are enticed under false promises into a situation where they are exploited for profit. In Libya, this distinction is not clear cut; both can be interchangeable or one can quickly turn into the other.

Some of this book's vocabulary runs counter to how legislation, politicians, or global organizations use it, but this is a story about how internationally granted rights are being eroded while victims' voices are silenced. I want to make sure we do not allow terminology to shift responsibility, enabling us to avoid the reality of what is happening. As always, with language, we have to question who is shaping it and why. Without this, it is impossible to comprehend the scale of the failure of humanity taking place on Europe's borders. It matters when we call this a "European migrant crisis" instead of emphasizing that this is a crisis—a life or death situation—for the people who need protection. Whether we say detainees "protested" or "rioted," whether we call them "refugees" or "migrants," and whether we suggest that anything that happens to people in a situation where they are powerless, malnourished, hearing traumatic news, and witnessing ongoing violence could ever be their fault makes a difference to how this story is understood.

ACRONYMS

UN	The United Nations
UNSMIL	The UN Support Mission in Libya

UN AGENCIES

UNHCR	The United Nations Refugee Agency
IOM	The International Organization for Migration
WHO	World Health Organization
WFP	World Food Programme
UNICEF	the UN Children's Fund
UNFPA	the UN Population Fund

OTHER AID AGENCIES WORKING IN LIBYA (NOT EXHAUSTIVE)

IRC	The International Rescue Committee
MSF	Médecins Sans Frontières/Doctors Without Borders
IMC	The International Medical Corps

THE TRIPOLI-BASED LIBYAN GOVERNMENT

GNA	The Government of National Accord (the Tripoli-based, UN-backed Libyan government)
DCIM	Department for Combatting Illegal Migration,

which is under the Interior Ministry and is responsible for the management of so-called "official" detention centers

IN SUDAN

RSF　　The Rapid Support Forces (formerly the Janjaweed) were were tasked with guarding Sudan's western border with Libya.

OTHERS

LNA　　The Libyan National Army (aligned with eastern general Khalifa Haftar)

EU　　The European Union

EUBAM　　EU Integrated Border Management Assistance Mission in Libya

NATO　　The North Atlantic Treaty Organization / the North Atlantic Alliance

ICC　　The International Criminal Court (based in The Hague, Netherlands; was set up to try individuals charged with the gravest crimes of concern to the international community: genocide, war crimes, crimes against humanity, and the crime of aggression)

GLAN　　The Global Legal Action Network (a nonprofit organization of lawyers, investigative journalists, and academics)

NGO　　A nongovernmental organization

RPF　　Rwandan Patriotic Front (former rebel group, now Rwanda's ruling political party)

ENDNOTES

PROLOGUE

1   "Support to integrated border and migration management in Libya" under Action Fiches T05-EUTF-NOA-LY-04 for phase one was worth 46.3 million euro: European Union. Action fiche of the EU Trust Fund to be used for the decisions of the Operational Committee. Annex IV to the Agreement establishing the European Union Emergency Trust Fund for stability and addressing root causes of irregular migration and displaced persons in Africa and its internal rules. 1. Accessed August 15, 2021. https://ec.europa.eu/trustfundforafrica/sites/default/files/t05-eutf-noa-ly-04_fin_5.pdf; and T05-EUTF-NOA-LY-07 for phase two. In 2020, the second phase was restructured and revised down to 15 million euro from 45 million euro (this was confirmed to the author by EU spokespeople): European Union. Action Document: The European Union Emergency Trust Fund for Stability and Addressing the Root Causes of Irregular Migration and Displaced Persons in Africa. Accessed August 15, 2021. https://ec.europa.eu/trustfundforafrica/sites/default/files/t05-eutf-noa-ly-07.pdf.

2   Hayden, Sally. Twitter post. August 27, 2018, 2:31 p.m. https://twitter.com/sallyhayd/status/1034070998734331904.

TIMELINE OF IMPORTANT EVENTS AND RELEVANT STATISTICS

1   European Commission. "A European Union Emergency Trust Fund for Africa." Last Modified November 12, 2015.

2   "Support to integrated border and migration management in Libya" under Action Fiches T05-EUTF-NOA-LY-04 for phase one was worth 46.3 million euro: European Union. Action fiche of the EU Trust Fund to be used for the decisions of the Operational Committee. Annex IV to the Agreement establishing the European Union Emergency Trust Fund for stability and addressing root causes of irregular migration and displaced persons in Africa and its internal rules. 1. Accessed August 15, 2021. https://ec.europa.eu/trustfundforafrica/sites/default/files/t05-eutf-noa-ly-04_fin_5.pdf; "Italy-Libya sign agreement to curb flow of migrants to Europe." Euronews, February 2, 2017. Accessed August 26, 2021. https://www.euronews.com/2017/02/02/italy-libya-sign-agreement-to-curb-flow-of-migrants-to-europe.

3   "Shipwreck Off Coast of Libya Pushes Migrant Deaths on the Mediterranean Past 20,000 Mark." International Organization for Migration. Last Modified March 5, 2020. https://www.iom.int/news/shipwreck-coast-libya-pushes-migrant-deaths-mediterranean-past-20000-mark.

4   "Pope compares Libya's detention centers with concentration camps." Al Jazeera, July 8, 2020. Accessed August 26, 2021. https://www.aljazeera.com/news/2020/7/8/pope-compares-libyas-detention-centers-with-concentration-camps.

IMMIGRATION STATISTICS

1   "Mediterranean Situation: Italy." Operational Data Portal: Refugee Situations. Accessed November 13, 2021. https://data2.unhcr.org/en/situations/mediterranean/location/5205.

2   "Libya: European governments complicit in horrific abuse of refugees and migrants." Amnesty International. Last Modified December 12, 2017. https://www.amnesty.org/en/latest/press-release/2017/12/libya-european-governments-complicit-in-horrific-abuse-of-refugees-and-migrants/.

3   UNHCR. Overview 2018: Libya. Accessed August 26, 2021. file:///D:/UNHCR%20Libya%20Activities%20in%202018.pdf.

4   UNHCR. Libya: Activities at Disembarkation, monthly update. Accessed August 26, 2021. file:///D:/2019_12_LBY_UNHCR_Disembarkation.pdf.

5   IOM Libya. Twitter post. August 16, 2021, 4:08 p.m. https://twitter.com/IOM_Libya/status/1427286189246226433.

6   IOM Libya. Twitter post, November 29, 2021, 3:22 p.m. https://twitter.com/IOM_Libya/status/1465340518318153729.

7   See page 7 of: Office of the United Nations High Commissioner for Human Rights. "Lethal Disregard": Search and rescue and the protection of migrants in the central Mediterranean Sea. 2021. Accessed August 26, 2021. https://www.ohchr.org/Documents/Issues/Migration/OHCHR-thematic-report-SAR-protection-at-sea.pdf.

8   "Central Mediterranean." Missing Migrants. Accessed November 29, 2021. https://missingmigrants.iom.int/region/mediterranean?migrant_route%5B%5D=1376.

CHAPTER 1

1   Yeats, William Butler. "Aedh Wishes for the Cloths of Heaven." In *The Wind Among the Reeds*, edited by William Butler Yeats, 60. Project Gutenberg, 2010. Accessed August 6, 2021. https://www.gutenberg.org/files/32233/32233-h/32233-h.htm#Page_60.

2   "The Central Mediterranean route: Migrant Fatalities January 2014—July 2017." ReliefWeb. Last Modified September 2, 2017. https://reliefweb.int/report/world/central-mediterranean-route-migrant-fatalities-january-2014-july-2017.

3   Harter, Fred. "Dissenters tortured in 'North Korea of Africa.'" *The Times*, June 12, 2021. Accessed August 6, 2021. https://www.thetimes.co.uk/article/dissenters-tortured-in-north-korea-of-africa-dpvm7wpc8.

4   "2021 World Press Freedom Index." Reporters Without Borders (RSF). Accessed August 6, 2021. https://rsf.org/en/ranking.

5   Wrong, Michaela. *I Didn't Do It For You: How the World Betrayed a Small African Nation*. London: HarperCollins Publishers Ltd. 2005, 198.

6   Ghebhrehiwet, Samuel. "Eritrea viewpoint: I fought for independence but I'm still waiting for freedom." BBC News, May 24, 2021. Accessed August 6, 2021. https://www.bbc.com/news/world-africa-57187736.amp.

7   Hill, Justin. "Dateline Eritrea: Ciao Asmara." *The Globalist*, August 25, 2005. Accessed August 6, 2021. https://web.archive.org/web/20070625120615/http:/theglobalist.com/storyid.aspx?StoryId=4668.

8   UNHCR. Europe Refugees & Migrants Emergency Response Nationality of Arrivals to Greece, Italy and Spain January–December 2015. 2. Accessed August 6, 2021. https://reliefweb.int/sites/reliefweb.int/files/resources/MonthlyTrendsofNationalities-ArrivalstoGreeceItalyandSpain-31December2015.pdf.

9   Sahan Foundation and IGAD Security Sector Program (ISSP). Human Trafficking and Smuggling on the Horn of Africa-Central Mediterranean Route. February, 2016, 12. Accessed August 6, 2021. https://igad.int/attachments/1284_ISSP%20Sahan%20HST%20Re-

port%20%2018ii2016%20FINAL%20FINAL.pdf.

10 FRONTLINE PBS. "Escaping Eritrea (full documentary)." YouTube Video, 53:16. May 5, 2021. https://www.youtube.com/watch?v=jquCbpLYw7Q; UNHCR. A/HRC/29/CRP.1, Report of the detailed findings of the commission of inquiry on human rights in Eritrea. 29th session 2015. 239. Accessed August 6, 2021. https://www.ohchr.org/Documents/HRBodies/HRCouncil/CoIEritrea/A_HRC_29_CRP-1.pdf.

11 "UN Inquiry finds crimes against humanity in Eritrea." UNHCR. Last Modified June 8, 2016. https://www.ohchr.org/EN/NewsEvents/Pages/DisplayNews.aspx?NewsID=20067&LangID=E.

12 UNHCR, "UN Inquiry."

13 Katlic, Tim. "Understanding Eritrea's Exceptionally Limited Internet Access." ICTworks, August 1, 2014. Accessed August 6, 2021. https://www.ictworks.org/understanding-eritreas-exceptionally-limited-internet-access/#.YQ1YWohKhPY; Winter, Caroline. "Eritrea's Communications Disconnect." *Bloomberg*, June 26, 2014. Accessed August 6, 2021. https://www.bloomberg.com/news/articles/2014-06-26/eritrea-worlds-least-connected-country-tech-wise.

14 Berihun Tessema, Tiru, Michael Jungmeier, and Michael Huber. "The relocation of the village of Arkwasiye in the Simien Mountain National Park in Ethiopia: an intervention towards sustainable development?" *eco.mont* 4, no. 2 (2012): 13-20. Accessed August 6, 2021. doi: 10.1553/eco.mont-4-2s13.

15 "Refugees and Asylum Seekers from Eritrea in Ethiopia." UNHCR. Accessed August 6, 2021. https://reporting.unhcr.org/node/15848.

CHAPTER 2

1 "Eritrea: Events of 2019." Human Rights Watch. Accessed August 12, 2021. https://www.hrw.org/world-report/2020/country-chapters/eritrea.

2 Allison, Simon. "Africa's most authoritarian school." *Mail & Guardian*, August 16, 2019. Accessed August 12, 2021. https://mg.co.za/article/2019-08-16-00-africas-most-authoritarian-school/.

3 Human Rights Watch. "They Are Making Us into Slaves, Not Educating Us." August 8, 2019. Accessed August 27, 2021. https://www.hrw.org/report/2019/08/08/they-are-making-us-slaves-not-educating-us/how-indefinite-conscription-restricts#_ftn51; "Sexual violence against women and girls is widespread and indeed notorious in military training camps. Furthermore, the enforced domestic service of women and girls who are also sexually abused in these camps amounts to sexual slavery. The commission considers that these violations of the rights of women and girls also amount to torture. They are also committed to a lesser extent within the military and are a further example of the Government's failure to fulfil its due diligence obligations to protect, prevent, punish and remedy acts of violence against women." The United Nations Commission of Inquiry into Human Rights in Eritrea, June 4, 2015.

4 "Sudan." European Commission: EU Emergency Trust Fund for Africa. Accessed August 12, 2021. https://ec.europa.eu/trustfundforafrica/region/horn-africa/sudan_en; European Commission. Declaration of the Ministerial Conference of the Khartoum Process (EU-Horn of Africa Migration Route Initiative). Rome, 2014. Accessed August 12, 2021. http://italia2014.eu/media/3785/declaration-of-the-ministerial-conference-of-the-khartoum-process.pdf; Clingendael. Multilateral Damage: The impact of EU migration policies on central Saharan routes, by Jérôme Tubiana, Clotilde Warin, and Gaffar Mohammud Saeneen. CRU Report. 2018. Accessed August 12, 2021. https://www.clingendael.org/sites/default/files/2018-09/multilateral-damage.pdf; "The European Union's cooperation with Africa on migration." European Commission. Last Modified April 22, 2015. https://ec.europa.eu/commission/presscorner/detail/en/MEMO_15_4832.

5 Giacomo, Carol. "U.S. Imposes New Sanctions on Sudan." *Reuters*, November 4, 1997. Accessed September 1, 2021. https://reliefweb.int/report/sudan/us-imposes-new-sanctions-sudan.

6   "Sudan women in trousers: No indecency charges." BBC News. December 10, 2017. Accessed September 1, 2021. https://www.bbc.co.uk/news/world-africa-42300218.

7   See also the chapter on Shagarab refugee camp beginning at p228 in: Neab, Yikealo, and Kenneth James Howe. *I Will Not Grow Downward—Memoir Of An Eritrean Refugee: My Long And Perilous Flight From Africa's Hermit Kingdom.* Brinestone Press, 2018.

8   Shah, Vivek. "EU funds for Sudan may worsen fate of refugees." *EU Observer,* April 10, 2017. Accessed August 12, 2021. https://euobserver.com/migration/137489; Chandler, Caitlin L. "Inside the EU's flawed $200 million migration deal with Sudan." *The New Humanitarian,* January 30, 2018. Accessed August 12, 2021. https://www.thenewhumanitarian.org/special-report/2018/01/30/inside-eu-s-flawed-200-million-migration-deal-sudan; Morgan, Hiba. "Sudan's RSF unit accused of abuses against migrants." *Al Jazeera,* November 17, 2017. Accessed August 12, 2021. https://www.aljazeera.com/features/2017/11/17/sudans-rsf-unit-accused-of-abuses-against-migrants/; Burke, Jason. "Hemedti: the feared commander pulling the strings in Sudan." *The Guardian,* May 29, 2019. Accessed August 12, 2021. https://www.theguardian.com/world/2019/may/29/hemedti-the-feared-commander-pulling-the-strings-in-sudan.

9   Alnour, Aziz, Klaas van Dijken, Heiner Hoffmann, Maximilian Popp, and Nouska du Saar. "Pact with the devils." *Der Spiegel,* November 14, 2020. Accessed August 12, 2021. https://www.spiegel.de/ausland/eu-plaene-fuer-sudan-pakt-mit-den-teufeln-a-997a76d8-fbee-4806-ab46-a410805c9327.

10   Wills, Tom. "EU suspends migration control projects in Sudan amid repression fears." *Deutsche Welle News,* July 22, 2019. Accessed August 12, 2021. https://www.dw.com/en/eu-suspends-migration-control-projects-in-sudan-amid-repression-fears/a-49701408.

CHAPTER 3

1   "International Criminal Court may investigate migrant-related crimes in Libya, Security Council told." United Nations. Last Modified May 8, 2017. https://news.un.org/en/story/2017/05/556872-international-criminal-court-may-investigate-migrant-related-crimes-libya.

2   "Migrants being sold as slaves." CNN video 06:49. Accessed August 12, 2021. https://edition.cnn.com/videos/world/2017/11/13/libya-migrant-slave-auction-lon-orig-md-ejk.cnn; See also: Mark, Monica. "Inside The Country Where You Can Buy A Black Man For $400." BuzzFeed News, December 15, 2018. Accessed August 12, 2021. https://www.buzzfeednews.com/article/monicamark/slavery-nigeria-libya.

3   Konrad Adenaur Stiftung (KAS). Migration in North Africa: An Uncomfortable Position between Sub-Saharan Africa and Europe?, edited by Hassen Boubakri. 2021. Accessed August 12, 2021. https://www.kas.de/documents/282499/282548/Migration+in+North+Africa+-+KAS+PolDiMed+Study.pdf/a6f89474-078a-80f6-0230-75fcadddf341?t=1623168963317; "France calls UN Security Council emergency meeting over Libya slave-trading." *Deutsche Welle News,* November 22, 2017. Accessed August 12, 2021. https://www.dw.com/en/france-calls-un-security-council-emergency-meeting-over-libya-slave-trading/a-41491723.

4   Karim, Naimul. "After Libyan bombing, Bangladeshis wait for injured migrants' return." *Reuters,* July 18, 2019. Accessed August 12, 2021. https://www.reuters.com/article/us-bangladesh-trafficking-libya-idUSKCN1UD2HM.

5   *This American Life.* "This Call May Be Recorded . . . To Save Your Life." August 9, 2013. https://www.thisamericanlife.org/502/this-call-may-be-recorded-to-save-your-life.

6   From interviews with victims.

7   Walsh, Declan, and Suliman Ali Zway. "A Facebook War: Libyans Battle on the Streets and on Screens." *The New York Times,* September 4, 2018. Accessed August 12, 2021. https://www.nytimes.com/2018/09/04/world/middleeast/libya-facebook.html.

8   Facebook statement given in email to the author, January 21, 2019; for more see: Hayden, Sally. "The Families of Migrants Held Hostage Are Using Facebook to Raise Money for Smug-

glers' Ransoms." *TIME* Magazine, February 5, 2019. Accessed August 12, 2021. https://time.com/5510517/facebook-smuggling-libya-ransoms/.

9 "'Abducted, locked up, sometimes even murdered': An MSF head of mission on the abuses faced by migrant detainees in Libya." Doctors Without Borders. Last Modified July 23, 2021. https://www.doctorswithoutborders.ca/article/abducted-locked-sometimes-even-murdered-msf-head-mission-abuses-faced-migrant-detainees.

10 "Truck smuggling migrants crashes leaving 19 dead in Libya." The Migrant Project. Last Modified February 27, 2018. https://www.themigrantproject.org/truck-smuggling/.

CHAPTER 4

1 For more, read: Hilsum, Lindsey. *Sandstorm: Libya in the Time of Revolution.* New York: Penguin Press, 2012.

2 Matar, Hisham. *The Return: Fathers, Sons, and the Land in Between.* New York: Random House Trade Paperbacks, 2016, 10.

3 Lewis, Aidan, and Ahmed Elumami. "Clashes shatter illusion of security in Libyan capital." *Reuters,* August 29, 2018. Accessed August 12, 2021. https://www.reuters.com/article/us-libya-security-idUSKCN1LE1JU.

4 "UNHCR moves detained refugees out of harm's way in volatile Libyan capital." UNHCR. Last Modified August 30, 2018. https://www.unhcr.org/news/press/2018/8/5b8815fa4/unhcr-moves-detained-refugees-harms-way-volatile-libyan-capital.html.

5 "Evacuation of refugees and migrants out of Libya is urgently needed." Médecins Sans Frontières. Last Modified September 7, 2018, https://www.msf.org/evacuation-refugees-and-migrants-out-libya-urgently-needed.

6 Raghavan, Sudarsan. "Thousands of African migrants trapped in the crossfire of clashes between Libyan militias." *The Washington Post,* August 31, 2018. Accessed August 12, 2021. https://www.washingtonpost.com/world/thousands-of-african-migrants-trapped-in-the-crossfire-of-clashes-between-libyan-militias/2018/08/31/defc77ea-ad1b-11e8-9a7d-cd30504ff902_story.html; Musa, Rami. "Aid group warns of militia fighting in Libya's Tripoli." Associated Press News, August 31, 2018. Accessed August 12, 2021. https://apnews.com/article/7c048c9b690347239e14c3011445c8d8; "UNHCR Says Tripoli Facility Ready to Help Refugees." Voice of America (VOA) News, September 8, 2018. Accessed August 12, 2021. https://www.voanews.com/world-news/middle-east-dont-use/unhcr-says-tripoli-facility-ready-help-refugees.

7 Hayden, Sally. Twitter Post, September 3, 2018. 6.27 p.m. https://twitter.com/sallyhayd/status/1036651869542789120?s=20.

8 Hayden, Sally. Twitter post. September 16, 2018, 12:55 p.m. https://twitter.com/sallyhayd/status/1041294408405184512; Hayden, Sally. Twitter post. September 18, 2018, 8:23 a.m. https://twitter.com/sallyhayd/status/1041950816251330560.

9 Hayden, Sally. Twitter post. September 21, 2018, 11:05 a.m. https://twitter.com/sallyhayd/status/1043078877369786368.

10 Hayden, Sally. Twitter post. September 1, 2018, 9:14 a.m. https://twitter.com/sallyhayd/status/1035803092497915904.

11 Hayden, Sally. "'Live free or die trying on the sea': Limbo in Libya for unregistered refugees." *The Irish Times,* September 12, 2018. Accessed August 12, 2021. https://www.irishtimes.com/news/world/africa/live-free-or-die-trying-on-the-sea-limbo-in-libya-for-unregistered-refugees-1.3626006.

12 Grandi, Filippo. Twitter post. September 2, 2018, 4:26 p.m. https://twitter.com/FilippoGrandi/status/1036274136555970560.

13 Hayden, Sally. Twitter post. September 16, 2018, 6:51 a.m. https://twitter.com/sallyhayd/status/1041202854537637888.

14   Hayden, Sally. Twitter post. October 6, 2018, 5:48 p.m. https://twitter.com/sallyhayd/status/
      1048615985069133825.

15   Hayden, Sally. Twitter post. September 6, 2018, 6:29 p.m. https://twitter.com/sallyhayd/status/
      1037754734801809408.

16   Hayden, Sally. Twitter post. September 6, 2018, 12:30 p.m. https://twitter.com/sallyhayd/status/
      1037664425250041858.

17   Elumami, Ahmed. "Tripoli clashes leave 115 dead, 383 injured- health ministry." *Reuters*,
      September 23, 2018. Accessed August 12, 2021. https://www.reuters.com/article/us-libya-se-
      curity-idUSKCN1M30PO; Musa, Rami. "Libyan police say 400 prisoners escape amid Trip-
      oli clashes." Associated Press News, September 3, 2018. Accessed August 12, 2021. https://
      apnews.com/article/7304196eaf584840b187108d0ed3a492.

18   Hayden, Sally. "Migrants deaths in Mediterranean reach record percentage." *The Irish Times*,
      October 4, 2018. Accessed September 1, 2021. https://www.irishtimes.com/news/world/mi-
      grants-deaths-in-mediterranean-reach-record-percentage-1.3652139.

CHAPTER 5

1   Altai Consulting. Learning Lessons from the EUTF—Phase 2—Paving the way for future
      programming on migration, mobility and forced displacement, by Eric Davin and Justine Ru-
      bira. Report written as a consultation for the European Union. 2021, 22. Accessed August 10,
      2021. https://ec.europa.eu/trustfundforafrica/sites/default/files/learning_lessons_from_the_
      eutf_final_0.pdf.

2   "UN human rights chief: Suffering of migrants in Libya outrage to conscience of humanity."
      UNHCR. Accessed August 10, 2021. https://www.ohchr.org/en/NewsEvents/Pages/Dis-
      playNews.aspx?NewsID=22393.

3   As detailed in: Crawford, Alex. *Colonel Gaddafi's Hat*. London: HarperCollins Publishers Ltd.,
      2012.

4   Black, Ian. "Gaddafi's Libyan rule exposed in lost picture archive." *The Guardian*, July 18, 2011.
      Accessed August 10, 2021. https://www.theguardian.com/world/2011/jul/18/gaddafi-bru-
      tal-regime-exposed-lost-archive.

5   From Lindsey Hilsum's book, as well as author interviews with Libyans about their recollec-
      tions of school, see: Hilsum, Lindsey. *Sandstorm: Libya in the Time of Revolution*. New York,
      Penguin Press, 2012.

6   "Living under Gaddafi." BBC. Last Modified September 10, 2018, https://www.bbc.co.uk/
      programmes/w3cswqlz; "Burn Western Musical Instruments That Distort Culture." As-
      sociated Press, June 3, 1985. Accessed August 10, 2021. https://apnews.com/article/
      81d834722e5c10f0e62eea52929b4b4e; Abbas, Mohammed. "Books Gaddafi banned sell well
      in rebel-held Libya." *Reuters*, May 11, 2011. Accessed August 10, 2021. https://www.reu-
      ters.com/article/us-libya-books/books-gaddafi-banned-sell-well-in-rebel-held-libya-idUS-
      TRE74A29Y20110511.

7   See: Cojean, Annick. *Gaddafi's Harem: The Story of a Young Woman and the Abuses of Power in
      Libya*, translated from French by Marjolijn de Jager. New York: Grove Press, 2013.

8   Video available at: SLOBoe. "Muammar Gaddafi speech TRANSLATED (2011 Feb 22)."
      YouTube video, 3:56. February 24, 2011. http://www.youtube.com/watch?v=69wBG6UL-
      NzQ&feature=related.

9   Al-Kekly, Ayman, and Alice Fordham. "Gaddafi's son Saif al-Islam faces uncertain future."
      The Washington Post, November 19, 2011. Accessed August 10, 2021. https://www.wash-
      ingtonpost.com/world/middle_east/saif-al-islam-gaddafis-son-arrested-libyan-command-
      er-says/2011/11/19/gIQA7fs6aN_story.html.

10   Kim, Kyle. Gaddafi's body "packed in shopping center freezer." *Global Post*, October
      21, 2011. Accessed September 1, 2021. https://www.pri.org/stories/2011-10-21/gaddaf-

is-body-packed-shopping-center-freezer-video-graphic.

11 CBS. "Clinton on Qaddafi: We came, we saw, he died." YouTube video, 0:11. October 20, 2011. https://www.youtube.com/watch?v=mlz3-OzcExI.

12 Goldberg, Jeffrey. "The Obama doctrine." *The Atlantic*, April 2016 issue. Accessed August 10, 2021. https://www.theatlantic.com/magazine/archive/2016/04/the-obama-doctrine/471525/.

13 See: Wehrey, Frederic. *The Burning Shores: Inside the Battle for the New Libya*. New York: Farrar, Straus and Giroux, 2018.

14 Wehrey, *The Burning Shores*, 100.

15 Wehrey, *The Burning Shores*, 86.

16 Laessing, Ulf. *Understanding Libya Since Gaddafi*. London: Hurst Publishers, 2020, loc 224.

17 Wehrey, *The Burning Shores*, 69.

18 Hilsum, *Sandstorm*, 63.

19 Hookham, Mark. "MI6 warns Libyan arms dumps are 'Tesco for world terrorists.'" *The Times of London*, June 16, 2013. Accessed August 10, 2021. https://www.thetimes.co.uk/article/mi6-warns-libyan-arms-dumps-are-tesco-for-world-terrorists-ndtnqcczc05.

20 See: Shibani, Heba. "Fight or Flight." In *Our Women on the Ground: Essays by Arab Women Reporting from the Arab World*, edited by Zahra Hankir, 184-195. New York: Penguin Books, 2019.

21 Gadaffi, Muammar. *Escape to Hell and Other Stories: foreword by Pierre Salinger*. London: Blake Publishing, 2011.

22 "Libya PM Zeidan's brief kidnap was 'attempted coup.'" BBC News, October 11, 2013. Accessed August 10, 2021. https://www.bbc.com/news/world-africa-24496357.

23 Amanpour, Christiane. "Libya's power struggle." CNN International video, 05:47. March 25, 2014. https://edition.cnn.com/videos/world/2014/03/25/libya-ali-zeidan-amanpour.cnn.

24 *Reuters* Staff. "Former Libyan prime minister freed after abduction in Tripoli." *Reuters*, August 23, 2017. https://www.reuters.com/article/us-libya-security-abduction-idUSKCN1B325F.

25 Hall, Richard. "Libya now has three governments, none of which can actually govern." *The World*, March 31, 2016. Accessed August 10, 2021. https://www.pri.org/stories/2016-03-31/libya-now-has-three-governments-none-which-can-actually-govern.

26 "High Representative/Vice-President Federica Mogherini's remarks at the UN Security Council, New York." European Union External Action. Last Modified May 11, 2015. https://eeas.europa.eu/headquarters/headquarters-homepage/5570_fr.

27 "Libya's UN-backed government sails into Tripoli." *Al Jazeera*, March 31, 2016. Accessed August 10, 2021. https://www.aljazeera.com/news/2016/3/31/libyas-un-backed-government-sails-into-tripoli.

28 "Gaddafi wants EU cash to stop African migrants." BBC News, August 31, 2010. Accessed August 10, 2021. https://www.bbc.com/news/world-europe-11139345.

29 Traynor, Ian. "EU keen to strike deal with Muammar Gaddafi on immigration." *The Guardian*, September 1, 2010. Accessed August 10, 2021. https://www.theguardian.com/world/2010/sep/01/eu-muammar-gaddafi-immigration.

30 Squires, Nick. "Italians attack Muammar Gaddafi over Islam comments." *The Telegraph*, August 30, 2010. Accessed August 20, 2021. https://www.telegraph.co.uk/news/worldnews/europe/italy/7971883/Italians-attack-Muammar-Gaddafi-over-Islam-comments.html.

31 Boubakri, Hassan. "Migration in North Africa: An Uncomfortable Position Between Sub-Saharan Africa and Europe," 54-55. Accessed August 27, 2021. https://www.kas.de/documents/282499/282548/Migration+in+North+Africa+-+KAS+PolDiMed+Study.pdf/a6f89474-078a-80f6-0230-75fcadddf341?t=1623168963317.

32 E.g. an account from Thursday August 25, 2011 in: Crawford, *Colonel Gaddafi's Hat*, 267.

33 Watt, Nicholas. "Libya 'point of decision' nears as Cameron aims to secure UN resolution." *The Guardian*, March 14, 2011. Accessed August 10, 2021. https://www.theguardian.com/politics/2011/mar/14/cameron-gaddafi-france-lebanon-libya.

34 Laessing, *Understanding Libya Since Gaddafi*, 159-167.

35　Fadel, Leila. "Tripoli Zoo Sees Different Kind Of Cage—One With Migrants." NPR, November 12, 2013. Accessed August 10, 2021. https://www.npr.org/sections/parallels/2013/11/12/244550320/tripoli-zoo-sees-different-kind-of-cage-one-with-migrants?t=1623066624222.

36　Sengupta, Somini. "E.U. Is Prepared to Combat Migrant Smugglers, Official Says." *The New York Times*, May 11, 2015. Accessed August 10, 2021. https://www.nytimes.com/2015/05/12/world/europe/eu-prepared-to-combat-migrant-smugglers-diplomat-says.html.

37　"High Representative/Vice-President Federica Mogherini's remarks at the UN Security Council, New York." European Union External Action. Last Modified May 11, 2015. https://eeas.europa.eu/headquarters/headquarters-homepage/5570_fr.

38　EU External Action, "High Representative/Vice-President Federica Mogherini's remarks."

39　European Court of Auditors. Special Report: European Union Emergency Trust Fund for Africa: Flexible but lacking focus, by Bettina Jakobsen, Katja Mattfolk, Kim Storup, Beatrix Lesiewicz, Emmanuel-Douglas Hellinakis, Laura Gores, Jiri Lang, and Piotr Zych. Pursuant to Article 287(4), second subparagraph, TFEU. Luxembourg, 2018, 4, 9, 20. Accessed August 10, 2021. doi:10.2865/426644.

40　European Court of Auditors, Special Report, 24-28.

41　Altai Consulting, Learning Lessons from the EUTF, 5.

42　Other funding instruments included The European Neighborhood Instrument (ENI), the European Civil Protection and Humanitarian Aid Operations (ECHO), and the Instrument contributing to Stability and Peace (IcSP): The European Union. EU Support on Migration in Libya: EU Emergency Trust Fund for Africa. 2018. Accessed August 10, 2021. https://ec.europa.eu/trustfundforafrica/sites/default/files/eutf_libya_en.pdf.

43　Vermeulen, Maite, Giacomo Zandonini, and Ajibola Amzat. "How the EU created a crisis in Africa—and started a migration cartel." *The Correspondent*, December 11, 2019. Accessed August 10, 2021. https://thecorrespondent.com/166/how-the-eu-created-a-crisis-in-africa-and-started-a-migration-cartel/21953207342-46c48098.

44　Stevis-Gridneff, Matina. "How Forced Labor in Eritrea Is Linked to E.U.-Funded Projects." *The New York Times*, January 8, 2020. Accessed August 10, 2021. https://www.nytimes.com/2020/01/08/world/europe/conscription-eritrea-eu.html.

45　"EU aid increasingly taken hostage by migration politics." Oxfam International. Last Modified January 29, 2020. https://reliefweb.int/report/world/eu-trust-fund-africa-trapped-between-aid-policy-and-migration-politics.

46　Oxfam, "EU aid."

47　Rankin, Jennifer. "$2bn EU-Africa 'anti-migration' fund too opaque, say critics." *The Guardian*, October 31, 2017. Accessed August 10, 2021. https://www.theguardian.com/global-development/2017/oct/31/2bn-eu-africa-anti-migration-fund-too-opaque-say-critics.

48　"Migration Route: Central Mediterranean." Missing Migrants. Last Modified August 10, 2021. https://missingmigrants.iom.int/region/mediterranean?migrant_route%5B%5D=1376.

49　ECtHR—Hirsi Jamaa and Others v Italy [GC], Application No. 27765/09, February 23, 2012. Accessed August 10, 2021. https://www.asylumlawdatabase.eu/en/content/ecthr-hirsi-jamaa-and-others-v-italy-gc-application-no-2776509; Creta, Sara, Bashar Deeb, Klaas van Dijken, Emmanuel Freudenthal, Steffen Lüdke, and Maximilian Popp. "How Frontex Helps Haul Migrants Back to Libyan Torture Camps." Spiegel International, April 29, 2021. Accessed August 10, 2021. https://www.spiegel.de/international/europe/libya-how-frontex-helps-haul-migrants-back-to-libyan-torture-camps-a-d62c3960-ece2-499b-8a3f-1ede2eaefb83.

50　Bewarder, Manuel, and Lisa Walter. "Rescue operations off Libya must be put to the test." WELT, February 27, 2017. Accessed August 10, 2021. https://www.welt.de/politik/deutschland/article162394787/Rettungseinsaetze-vor-Libyen-muessen-auf-den-Pruefstand.html.

51　"Remarks by President Donald Tusk After His Meeting with Prime Minister of Libya Fayez Al-Sarraj." The European Union. Last Modified February 2, 2017. https://europa.eu/newsroom/node/26915_en.

52 Cook, Lorne. "Migrant shooting highlights concern about Libyan coast guard." Associated Press News, September 20, 2019. Accessed August 10, 2021. https://apnews.com/article/europe-shootings-ap-top-news-international-news-libya-de0fc5f0d27f4559bf36f3cbd8e29c7b.

53 Varvelli, Arturo, and Matteo Villa. "Italy's Libyan conundrum: The risks of short-term thinking." European Council on Foreign Relations, November 26, 2019. Accessed August 10, 2021. https://ecfr.eu/article/commentary_italys_libyan_conundrum_the_risks_of_short_term_thinking/.; Global Initiative Against Transnational Organized Crime. The Political Economy of Migrant Detention in Libya: Understanding the players and the business models, by Arezo Malakooti. Produced with the financial support of the European Union. 2019, 5. Accessed August 10, 2021. https://globalinitiative.net/wp-content/uploads/2019/11/Final-Report-Detention-Libya.pdf.

54 Horowitz, Jason. "Italy's 'Lord of the Spies' Takes On a Migration Crisis." *The New York Times*, August 4, 2017. Accessed August 10, 2021. https://www.nytimes.com/2017/08/04/world/europe/italy-marco-minniti-migration.html.

55 Wintour, Patrick. "Italian minister defends methods that led to 87% drop in migrants from Libya." *The Guardian*, September 7, 2017. Accessed August 10, 2021. https://www.theguardian.com/world/2017/sep/07/italian-minister-migrants-libya-marco-minniti.

56 "Mediterranean: As the fiction of a Libyan search and rescue zone begins to crumble, EU states use the coronavirus pandemic to declare themselves unsafe." Statewatch. Last Modified May 4, 2020. https://www.statewatch.org/analyses/2020/mediterranean-as-the-fiction-of-a-libyan-search-and-rescue-zone-begins-to-crumble-eu-states-use-the-coronavirus-pandemic-to-declare-themselves-unsafe/; Cuddy, Alice. "Prompted by EU, Libya quietly claims right to order rescuers to return fleeing migrants." Euronews, August 7, 2018. Accessed August 10, 2021. https://www.euronews.com/2018/07/06/prompted-by-eu-libya-quietly-claims-right-to-order-rescuers-to-return-fleeing-migrants; Altai Consulting. Learning Lessons from the EUTF, 39.

57 European Union. Action fiche of the EU Trust Fund to be used for the decisions of the Operational Committee. Annex IV to the Agreement establishing the European Union Emergency Trust Fund for stability and addressing root causes of irregular migration and displaced persons in Africa and its internal rules. 1. Accessed August 10, 2021. https://ec.europa.eu/trustfundforafrica/sites/default/files/t05-eutf-noa-ly-04_fin_5.pdf.; In an email to the author on August 6, 2021, an EU spokesman said "The existing Border Management programme was reviewed in 2020 to adapt our support to the capacity building of Libyan coastguards to the changing security context of Libya. As part of this revision and in light of the new needs arising, €30 million were reallocated to fund a Covid-19 response in Libya and to contribute to stabilisation in the South. New programmes were also adopted to improve the resilience of Libyans and migrants for the health challenges arising, adding €45.2 million fresh funding to the EUTF Africa portfolio for Libya. The new programmes covered activities related to protection, community stabilisation, including coronavirus specific actions." For more, see: "EU Emergency Trust Fund for Africa: New assistance package to support vulnerable groups and address COVID-19 in North Africa." European Union. Last Modified July 2, 2020. https://ec.europa.eu/commission/presscorner/detail/en/IP_20_1244.; European Union. Action Document: The European Union Emergency Trust Fund for Stability and Addressing the Root Causes of Irregular Migration and Displaced Persons in Africa. 16. Accessed August 10, 2021. https://ec.europa.eu/trustfundforafrica/sites/default/files/t05-eutf-noa-ly-07.pdf.

58 Jolly, Jasper. "Airbus to operate drones searching for migrants crossing the Mediterranean." *The Guardian*, October 20, 2020. Accessed August 10, 2021. https://www.theguardian.com/business/2020/oct/20/airbus-to-operate-drones-searching-for-migrants-crossing-the-mediterranean.

59 See: Creta, Sara, Bashar Deeb, Emmanuel Freudenthal, Steffen Lüdke, Shafagh Laghai, Lara Straatmann, Tomas Statius, Filippos Feizidis, Klaas van Dijken, and Daniel Howden. "Frontex in the Central Mediterranean." Lighthouse Reports. Accessed August 10, 2021. https://

www.lighthousereports.nl/investigation/frontex-in-the-central-mediterranean/; Creta et al., "How Frontex Helps Haul Migrants Back to Libyan Torture Camps." Spiegel.

60 Office of the United Nations High Commissioner for Human Rights. "Lethal Disregard." Search and rescue and the protection of migrants in the central Mediterranean Sea. 2021, 14. Accessed August 10, 2021. https://www.ohchr.org/Documents/Issues/Migration/OHCHR-thematic-report-SAR-protection-at-sea.pdf.

61 Tondo, Lorenzo. "Separated at sea: a Sierra Leonean father's desperate fear for his boy." The Guardian, December 4, 2018. Accessed November 13, 2021. https://www.theguardian.com/world/2018/dec/04/separated-at-sea-fathers-desperate-fear-for-boy-held-in-libyan-camp.

62 UNHCR. The Central Mediterranean Route: Working on The Alternatives to Dangerous Journeys. Geneva, 2017, 62. Accessed August 10, 2021. https://www.unhcr.org/596f4c4a7.pdf.; UNHCR. Expanded Response in Libya: 2017. Supplementary Appeal. Geneva, 2017, 19. Accessed August 11, 2021. https://reporting.unhcr.org/sites/default/files/UNHCR%20Expanded%20Response%20in%20Libya%20Supplementary%20Appeal%20-%20Jan-Dec%202017%20--%20May%202017_1.pdf.

63 Wintour, Patrick. "German report details Libya abuses amid pressure to stem migrant flows." The Guardian, January 30, 2017. Accessed August 10, 2021. https://www.theguardian.com/world/2017/jan/30/german-report-libya-abuses-pressure-migrant-flows.

64 "UNHCR Flash Update Libya (16 November—1 December 2017)." UNHCR, December 1, 2017. Accessed September 1, 2021. https://reliefweb.int/report/libya/unhcr-flash-update-libya-16-november-1-december-2017

65 From 12:29 p.m.: "Committee on Civil Liberties, Justice and Home Affairs Ordinary meeting." European Parliament. Last Modified November 27, 2018. https://multimedia.europarl.europa.eu/en/committee-on-civil-liberties-justice-and-home-affairs-ordinary-meeting_20181127-0900-COMMITTEE-LIBE_vd.

66 Global Initiative Against Transnational Organized Crime, The Political Economy of Migrant Detention in Libya, 6.

67 Carabott, Sarah. "How Libya's human smuggling industry evolved to cash in on captivity." Times of Malta, May 23, 2021. Accessed August 10, 2021. https://timesofmalta.com/articles/view/how-libyas-human-smuggling-industry-evolved-to-cash-in-on-captivity.873859.

68 Altai Consulting. Learning Lessons from the EUTF, 19.

69 "'World's deadliest sea crossing' claimed six lives a day in 2018: UN refugee agency." United Nations. Last Modified January 30, 2019. https://news.un.org/en/story/2019/01/1031582.

70 Seminara, Mauro. "Libyan coastguard flees after training in an Italian base, wanted." Mediterraneo Cronaca, December 31, 2020. Accessed August 10, 2021. https://www.mediterraneocronaca.it/2020/12/31/guardacoste-libico-fugge-dopo-addestramento-in-base-italiana-ricercato/.

71 Miles, Tom, and Stephanie Nebehay. "Migrant deaths in the Sahara likely twice Mediterranean toll: U.N." Reuters, October 12, 2017. Accessed August 10, 2021. https://www.reuters.com/article/us-europe-migrants-sahara-idUSKBN1CH21Y.

72 "Libya conflict: 'Stressed' Ghassan Salame resigns as UN envoy." BBC News, March 2, 2020. Accessed August 10, 2021. https://www.bbc.com/news/world-africa-51713683.

73 From 31:00 onwards: International Crisis Group. "Session III: Can the EU do more to help end the Libyan conflict?" YouTube video, 1:05:30. November 26, 2020. https://www.youtube.com/watch?v=eCSWpejMolE&feature=youtu.be.

CHAPTER 6

1   Global Initiative Against Transnational Organized Crime. The Political Economy of Migrant Detention in Libya: Understanding the players and the business models, by Arezo Malakooti. Produced with the financial support of the European Union. 2019. Figure 9: Detention centers

to which migrants were transferred, 2017–March 2019, 34. Accessed August 12, 2021. https://globalinitiative.net/wp-content/uploads/2019/11/Final-Report-Detention-Libya.pdf.

2   Facebook post. IOM Libya. January 25 2017. https://www.facebook.com/IOMLibya/posts/yesterday-together-with-the-german-ambassador-christian-buck-iom-visited-triq-al/701068440054116/. "Italy stresses strengthening action to combat illegal migration." March 21, 2018. Arraed LG+. Accessed August 14, 2021. https://www.arraedlg.com/italy-stresses-strengthening-action-to-combat-illegal-migration/.

3   "As Libya crisis deepens, UNHCR chief steps up assistance." UNHCR. Last Modified May 22, 2017. https://www.unhcr.org/news/latest/2017/5/5922a4df4/libya-crisis-deepens-unhcr-chief-steps-assistance.html.

4   "Vulnerable refugees evacuated from Libya during visit of UNHCR head." UNHCR. Last Modified June 19, 2018. https://www.unhcr.org/news/latest/2018/6/5b294cb64/vulnerable-refugees-evacuated-libya-during-visit-unhcr-head.html.

5   "Albert Einstein and the birth of the International Rescue Committee." International Rescue Committee. Last Modified June 20, 2017. https://www.rescue.org/article/albert-einstein-and-birth-international-rescue-committee.

6   Mitib, Ali. "David Miliband charity offers unpaid internships." The Times of London, May 15, 2021. Accessed August 12, 2021. https://www.thetimes.co.uk/article/david-miliband-charity-offers-unpaid-internships-hwbpvzl6b.

7   "Global Epidemiology of Tuberculosis and Progress Toward Meeting Global Targets—Worldwide, 2018." Centers for Disease Control and Prevention. Last Modified March 20, 2020. https://www.cdc.gov/mmwr/volumes/69/wr/mm6911a2.htm.

8   "Tuberculosis (TB)." WebMD. Last Modified June 27, 2020. https://www.webmd.com/lung/understanding-tuberculosis-basics.

9   Hayden, Sally. "The migrants plucked from the sea, only to face TB in Libyan detention centers." The Telegraph, March 25, 2019. Accessed August 12, 2021. https://www.telegraph.co.uk/global-health/climate-and-people/migrants-plucked-sea-face-tb-libyan-detention-centers/.

10   Felter, Claire, Jonathan Masters, and Mohammed Aly Sergie. "Backgrounder: Al-Shabab." Council on Foreign Relations, May 19, 2021. Accessed August 12, 2021. https://www.cfr.org/backgrounder/al-shabab.

11   Hayden, Sally. "Somali returned to Libya under Italian policy sets himself on fire." The Irish Times, October 25, 2018. Accessed August 12, 2021. https://www.irishtimes.com/news/world/africa/somali-returned-to-libya-under-italian-policy-sets-himself-on-fire-1.3675942; One year later, the BBC interviewed Abdulaziz's wife: BBC News. "'Tortured and abused': One Somali woman's ordeal in Libya." YouTube video, 13:52. November 11 2019. https://www.youtube.com/watch?v=CB8Cyt-K0dY.

12   Millman, Joel. Email message to the author, October 25, 2018.

13   Argaz, Tarik. Email message to the author, November 9, 2018.

14   Millman, Joel. Email message to the author, October 25, 2018.

15   "UNHCR in Libya Part 2: Migrants in detention centers: 'Why does UNHCR want to keep us in prison?'" Euronews, October 7, 2019. Accessed August 28, 2021. https://www.euronews.com/2019/10/02/unhcr-in-libya-part-2-migrants-in-detention-centres-why-does-unhcr-want-to-keep-us-in-pris.

16   "'Tortured and abused': One Somali woman's ordeal in Libya." YouTube video, 13:52. November 11 2019. https://www.youtube.com/watch?v=CB8Cyt-K0dY.

17   "75 years working for peace." United Nations. Accessed August 12, 2021. https://www.un.org/en/observances/un-day.

18   "Celebrating UN Day on 24 October! #UN70." United Nations: Academic Impact. Accessed November 13, 2021. https://www.un.org/en/academic-impact/celebrating-un-day-24-october-un70.

CHAPTER 7

1   "Fridtjof Nansen Nobel Lecture: The Suffering People of Europe." The Nobel Prize. Accessed August 8, 2021. https://www.nobelprize.org/prizes/peace/1922/nansen/lecture/.

2   Hayden, Sally. "'It's a Form of Torture': UNHCR Launches Campaign to Eradicate Statelessness." VICE News, November 4, 2014. Accessed November 13, 2021. https://www.vice.com/en/article/zm55d4/its-a-form-of-torture-unhcr-launches-campaign-to-eradicate-statelessness.

3   "Uganda GDP Per Capita 1960-2021." MacroTrends. Accessed August 6, 2021. https://www.macrotrends.net/countries/UGA/uganda/gdp-per-capita.

4   UNHCR: The UN Refugee Agency. Global Trends: Forced Displacement in 2017. Geneva, 2018. 3, 29. Accessed August 8, 2021. https://www.unhcr.org/5b27be547.pdf.

5   International Organization for Migration (IOM): The UN Migration Agency. Migration Crisis Operational Framework (MCOF) Sudan 2017-2019. Khartoum, 2017. 9. Accessed August 8, 2021. https://www.iom.int/sites/default/files/our_work/DOE/MCOF/MCOF-SUDAN-2017-2019_5.5mb.pdf.

6   Hayden, Sally. "For refugees in Sudan, fears surround probe into UN resettlement fraud." The New Humanitarian, July 23, 2018. Accessed August 8, 2021. https://www.thenewhumanitarian.org/news/2018/07/23/refugees-sudan-fears-surround-probe-un-resettlement-fraud.

7   Parker, Ben. "Emergency aid funding fell in 2017, even as Syria/Yemen wars drove needs higher." The New Humanitarian, May 15, 2018. Accessed August 8, 2021. https://www.thenewhumanitarian.org/analysis/2018/05/15/emergency-aid-funding-fell-2017-even-syriayemen-wars-drove-needs-higher.

8   "Figures at a Glance." UNHCR. Accessed August 8, 2021. https://www.unhcr.org/en-ie/figures-at-a-glance.html. "Financials." UNHCR. Accessed August 28, 2021. https://reporting.unhcr.org/financial.

9   "Figures at a Glance." UNHCR.

10 Crisp, Jeff. "UNHCR at 70: An Uncertain Future for the International Refugee Regime." Global Governance: A Review of Multilateralism and International Organizations 26, no. 3 (2020): 359-368. Accessed August 8, 2021. doi: https://doi.org/10.1163/19426720-02603004.

11 "UN Shared Rohingya Data Without Informed Consent." Human Rights Watch, June 15, 2021. Accessed August 8, 2021. https://www.hrw.org/news/2021/06/15/un-shared-rohingya-data-without-informed-consent.

12 "Der Deal, die Hölle und der Tod: Internierungslager in Libyen." Facebook, January 16, 2020. 02.20.00 in. Accessed August 20, 2021. https://www.facebook.com/SeebrueckeSchafftsichereHaefen/videos/2148616925241972/?__xts__[0]=68.ARALP7kS-OD-6Me9sMQfPbsnra6cenCchs7WG5Tg2J3TvSLVT0X-kkh4Wz1DBw_tBqkp8J-ucvtd-0J6vna5y-weiKlIh7zr08QE0A-TadZpjBN7GUNGl1sKO9GeWlRt_Mjfj2DUlq1ePxg6E-FeotQazmF9fseDjda0ZfCbLFPVo1NIO_a-awXUdRDDORKBGoHDdJrjGJRkBVF-SajTfQJ3_1L20lQmAwJ-lPYLN9MU3l01vf5tqo6AcZInXFeV7r0Gf6dX-DqE8KbEe-bXAJAP3Z5Z-Yjb5P5oefeGhgkmLPwmltmjLbLRuaoxqaeH08nDa_qXJGgCijlNuQ9c_Sz6K25WnKcCqWPDNKDxpLJgQrUTRBz1l-cs-&__tn__=HH-R.

13 "Un Internal Oversight Opens New Investigations Office in Vienna." United Nations. Last Modified September 15, 2003. https://www.un.org/press/en/2003/org1395.doc.htm.

14 United Nations General Assembly. A/56/733, Investigation into allegations of refugee smuggling at the Nairobi Branch Office of the Office of the United Nations High Commissioner for Refugees. 56th session agenda item 130. December 21, 2001.

15 Hayden, Sally. "EXCLUSIVE: Refugees in Sudan allege chronic corruption in UN resettlement process." The New Humanitarian, May 15, 2018. Accessed August 8, 2021. https://www.thenewhumanitarian.org/investigations/2018/05/15/exclusive-refugees-sudan-allege-chronic-corruption-un-resettlement-process.

16 "UNHCR suspends resettlement programme from Sudan as fraud probe gathers steam." UN-

HCR. Last Modified May 17, 2018. https://www.unhcr.org/news/press/2018/5/5afdb0064/unhcr-suspends-resettlement-programme-sudan-fraud-probe-gathers-steam.html.

17 Dismissal confirmed by email with UNHCR spokeswoman Cecile Pouilly in August 2021; she said the staff member's case is now pending appeal with the UN Appeals Tribunal.

18 UNHCR. UNHCR Brand Book. This brand book provides guidelines for correctly communicating the brand identity of the UNHCR, the UN Refugee Agency. 2016. 4, 9, 41. Accessed August 8, 2021. https://docplayer.net/62483307-Unhcr-brand-book-this-brand-book-provides-guidelines-for-correctly-communicating-the-brand-identity-of-unhcr-the-un-refugee-agency.html.

19 "Goodwill Ambassadors." UNHCR. Accessed August 8, 2021. https://www.unhcr.org/goodwill-ambassadors.html.

20 "Global Social Media Manager, UNOPS IICA-2, London." LinkedIn. Accessed August 8, 2021. https://www.linkedin.com/jobs/view/2654380101/.

21 UNHCR, The UN Refugee Agency. Twitter account. Accessed August 8, 2021. https://twitter.com/Refugees.

22 Morelli, Alessandra. Twitter account. Accessed August 8, 2021. https://twitter.com/UNHCR_Morelli.

23 "Cate Blanchett rewarded for her humanitarian work with the UNHCR." UNHCR. Last Modified June 25, 2020. https://www.unhcr.org/fr/news/stories/2020/6/5ef6f943a/cate-blanchett-recompensee-action-humanitaire-aupres-hcr.html.

24 Morelli, Alessandra, interview with Sally Hayden, August 6, 2020.

CHAPTER 8

1 E.g. see the two phases of EU Trust Fund funding towards the Libyan coastguard: 'Complementarity will be first of all ensured with the organisations active under the protection pillar of this programme, notably the International Organization for Migration (IOM) and the United Nations High Commission for Refugees (UNHCR), whose aim is to expand the protection space in Libya for migrants and refugees and improve the capacity of the competent Libyan authorities in managing mixed migratory flows' p 6, & 'The Italian MoI, DG NEAR, the EU Delegation to Libya, and the Italian Embassy in Tripoli will be the main actors in ensuring that consultation and coordination with these stakeholders is ensured. Close cooperation and permanent operational links will be established with the main European and International stakeholders in Libya, particularly EUBAM Libya, FRONTEX, EUNAVFORMED- Sophia, SEAHORSE MED project, UNHCR, IOM any EU Member States concerned' p 15, T05-EUTF-NOA-LY-04 in: European Union. 'Action fiche of the EU Trust Fund to be used for the decisions of the Operational Committee'. Annex IV to the Agreement establishing the European Union Emergency Trust Fund for stability and addressing root causes of irregular migration and displaced persons in Africa and its internal rules. 6, 15. Accessed 11 August 2021. https://ec.europa.eu/trustfundforafrica/sites/default/files/t05-eutf-noa-ly-04_fin_5.pdf; 'The ongoing project implementation of the first phase has shown that it is important to share information and work together with the main EU and international stakeholders in Libya, such as EUBAM Libya, EUNAVFORMED-Op. Irini, Frontex, IOM and UNHCR.': European Union. 'Action Document: The European Union Emergency Trust Fund for Stability and Addressing the Root Causes of Irregular Migration and Displaced Persons in Africa'. 16. Accessed 11 August 2021. https://ec.europa.eu/trustfundforafrica/sites/default/files/t05-eutf-noa-ly-07.pdf.

2 Wintour, Patrick. "Italian minister defends methods that led to 87% drop in migrants from Libya." The Guardian, September 7, 2017. Accessed August 11, 2021. https://www.theguardian.com/world/2017/sep/07/italian-minister-migrants-libya-marco-minniti.

3 Reynolds, James. 'Marco Minniti: The man who cut the migrant flow to Italy.' BBC News,

20 September 2018. Accessed 11 August 2021. https://www.bbc.com/news/world-europe-45575763.

4   "IOM joins the United Nations." September 19, 2016. Accessed August 24, 2021. https://www.iom.int/video/iom-joins-united-nations.

5   "A rating of 'unsatisfactory' means that one or more critical and/or pervasive important deficiencies exist in governance, risk management or control processes, such that reasonable assurance cannot be provided with regard to the achievement of control and/or business objectives under review" in: United Nations Office of Internal Oversight Services: Internal Audit Division. AR2015/131/02, Audit of the Operations in Libya for the Office of the United Nations High Commissioner for Refugees. Report 2016/031. April 14, 2016.

6   Budgets and annual expenditure available at "Libya." UNHCR. Accessed August 20, 2021. https://reporting.unhcr.org/node/12003.

7   FROM 13:02: "Committee on Civil Liberties, Justice and Home Affairs Ordinary meeting." European Parliament. Last Modified November 27, 2018. https://multimedia.europarl.europa.eu/en/committee-on-civil-liberties-justice-and-home-affairs-ordinary-meeting_20181127-0900-COMMITTEE-LIBE_vd.

8   Oxfam. The EU Trust Fund for Africa: Trapped between aid policy and migration politics. EUTF for Africa project NOA-LY-06. Oxford, 2020, 24. Accessed August 11, 2021. https://oxfamilibrary.openrepository.com/bitstream/handle/10546/620936/bp-eu-trust-fund-africa-migration-politics-300120-en.pdf.

9   UNHCR Libya. Twitter post, 30 July 2019, 3:46 p.m. https://twitter.com/UNHCRLibya/status/1156214363948277761.

10   E.g. UNHCR Libya. Twitter post. October 26, 2018. 10.13 p.m. https://twitter.com/UNHCRLibya/status/1055930455898374145?s=20.

11   "Overview 2018." UNHCR Libya. Accessed September 1, 2021. Arabic-language version: https://reliefweb.int/sites/reliefweb.int/files/resources/67473.pdf. English-language version: https://reliefweb.int/sites/reliefweb.int/files/resources/67474.pdf.

12   "Press point by Ylva Johansson, European Commissioner, and Filippo Grandi, United Nations High Commissioner for Refugees." European Commission. Last Modified May 10, 2021. https://audiovisual.ec.europa.eu/en/video/I-205316.

13   "Libya: 'Registration is a right for asylum seekers and refugees wherever they are.'" UNHCR. Last Modified November 9, 2018. https://www.unhcr.org/blogs/registration-is-a-right-for-refugees/.

14   'Less than 5 per cent of global refugee resettlement needs met last year.' UNHCR. Last Modified 19 February 2019. https://www.unhcr.org/news/briefing/2019/2/5c6bc9704/5-cent-global-refugee-resettlement-needs-met-year.html.

15   Hayden, Sally. "Libya: coronavirus has deadly impact on life-saving evacuations." The Irish Times. January 1, 2021. Accessed November 13, 2021. https://www.irishtimes.com/news/world/africa/libya-coronavirus-has-deadly-impact-on-life-saving-evacuations-1.4448263.

16   "Inaccurate reporting of achievements was a recurring weakness and was rated as a critical recommendation by OIOS in its previous audit report on UNHCR operations in Libya (Report 2016/031), issued in April 2016" in: United Nations Office of Internal Oversight Services: Internal Audit Division. AR2018/131/04, Audit of the Operations in Libya for the Office of the United Nations High Commissioner for Refugees. Report 2019/007. March 1, 2019, 3.

17   The operation was "managed remotely with limited movement of national staff present in Tripoli and Benghazi, supported by occasional missions by international staff from Tunis" between July 2014 and February 2018. As of 31 May 2018, the Mission, headed by a Chief of Mission at the D-1 level, had 40 posts for international staff and 99 posts for national staff. Two international staff and 84 national staff were based in Tripoli, with the rest in Tunis. In addition, the Mission had 22 affiliate staff located in Tunis: United Nations Office of Internal Oversight Services: Internal Audit Division. AR2018/131/04, Audit of the Operations in Libya for the Office of the United Nations High Commissioner for Refugees. Report 2019/007. March 1, 2019, 1.

International staff were again evacuated in August-September 2018, when conflict broke out.

18 From 12:26: "Committee on Civil Liberties, Justice and Home Affairs Ordinary meeting." European Parliament. Last Modified November 27, 2018. https://multimedia.europarl.europa.eu/en/committee-on-civil-liberties-justice-and-home-affairs-ordinary-meeting_20181127-0900-COMMITTEE-LIBE_vd.

19 "Pay and benefits." United Nations Careers. Accessed August 11, 2021. https://careers.un.org/lbw/home.aspx?viewtype=sal.

20 Figures calculated on the basis of a P4 position through https://icsc.un.org/# and https://www.unjobnet.org/jobs/detail/24452354 / https://commonsystem.org/cp/calc.asp.

21 "Tunisia: Monthly minimum wage raised by 6.5 per cent." *The North Africa Post*, December 31, 2020. Accessed August 11, 2021. https://northafricapost.com/46508-tunisia-monthly-minimum-wage-raised-by-6-5-per-cent.html.

22 "Palm City Residences." Palm City Residences. Accessed August 11, 2021. https://www.palmcityresidences.com/#.

23 Wehrey, Frederic. "A Libyan Revenant." *Newlines Magazine*, July 14, 2021. Accessed August 11, 2021. https://newlinesmag.com/first-person/a-libyan-revenant/.

24 European Union External Action. Common Security and Defence Policy: EU Integrated Border Assistance Mission in Libya (EUBAM Libya). 2015. Accessed August 11, 2021. https://eeas.europa.eu/archives/docs/csdp/missions-and-operations/eubam-libya/pdf/factsheet_eubam_libya_en.pdf.

25 From document leaked to author which cannot be referenced to protect the source.

26 Altai Consulting. Learning Lessons from the EUTF - Phase 2 - Paving the way for future programming on migration, mobility and forced displacement, by Eric Davin and Justine Rubira. Report written as a consultation for the European Union. 2021, 24. Accessed August 11, 2021. https://ec.europa.eu/trustfundforafrica/sites/default/files/learning_lessons_from_the_eutf_final_0.pdf.

27 United Nations Office of Internal Oversight Services: Internal Audit Division. AR2018/131/04, Audit of the Operations in Libya for the Office of the United Nations High Commissioner for Refugees. Report 2019/007. March 1, 2019.

28 Molotsky, Irvin. "Red Cross Admits Knowing of the Holocaust During the War." *The New York Times*, December 19, 1996. Accessed August 11, 2021. https://www.nytimes.com/1996/12/19/us/red-cross-admits-knowing-of-the-holocaust-during-the-war.html.

29 Opinion. "Red Cross Inspected One Concentration Camp." *The New York Times*, May 29, 1987. Accessed August 11, 2021. https://www.nytimes.com/1987/05/29/opinion/l-red-cross-inspected-one-concentration-camp-824887.html.

30 "Theresienstadt: Red Cross Visit." *Holocaust Encyclopedia*. Accessed August 11, 2021. https://encyclopedia.ushmm.org/content/en/article/theresienstadt-red-cross-visit.

31 "Five years on, EU and Turkey griping over refugee deal." *France 24 News*, March 17, 2021. Accessed August 11, 2021. https://www.france24.com/en/live-news/20210317-five-years-on-eu-and-turkey-griping-over-refugee-deal.

32 European Commission. EU-Turkey Statement: Four Years On. 2020. Accessed August 11, 2021. https://ec.europa.eu/home-affairs/sites/default/files/what-we-do/policies/european-agenda-migration/20200318_managing-migration-eu-turkey-statement-4-years-on_en.pdf; "Turkey: Nearly 100,000 unregistered Syrians removed from Istanbul." *Deutsche Welle News*, January 4, 2020. Accessed August 11, 2021. https://www.dw.com/en/turkey-nearly-100000-unregistered-syrians-removed-from-istanbul/a-51888092.; "UNHCR Turkey Operational Update October 2020." UNHCR. Last Modified October 2020. https://data2.unhcr.org/en/documents/details/82980; Kirişci, Kemal. "As EU-Turkey migration agreement reaches the five-year mark, add a job creation element." Brookings, March 17, 2021. Accessed August 11, 2021. https://www.brookings.edu/blog/order-from-chaos/2021/03/17/as-eu-turkey-migration-agreement-reaches-the-five-year-mark-add-a-job-creation-element/.

33   "MSF rejects EU funding over 'shameful' migrant pact with Turkey." *Deutsche Welle News*, June 17, 2016. Accessed August 11, 2021. https://www.dw.com/en/msf-rejects-eu-funding-over-shameful-migrant-pact-with-turkey/a-19338001.

34   "Medical care resumes in Tripoli detention centres." Médecins Sans Frontières. Accessed October 5, 2021. https://www.msf.org/medical-care-resumes-libya-detention-centres.

CHAPTER 9

1   "African migrants seek work in Tripoli—in pictures." *The National News*, May 23, 2021. Accessed August 16, 2021. https://www.thenationalnews.com/mena/african-migrants-seek-work-in-tripoli-in-pictures-1.1228028#5.

2   UNHCR. Libya: Mixed Migration Routes and Dynamics in Libya in 2018. 2019, 3. Accessed August 16, 2021. https://reliefweb.int/sites/reliefweb.int/files/resources/impact_lby_report_mixed_migration_routes_and_dynamics_in_2018_june_2019.pdf.

3   Figures given to the author by refugee interviewees who went out to work at this time.

4   For a video of Abu Salim's front gate, see: Creta, Sara. Twitter post. June 22, 2021, 6:19 p.m. https://twitter.com/saracreta/status/1407387690912321549.

5   Hayden, Sally. Twitter post. October 22, 2018, 3:37 p.m. https://twitter.com/sallyhayd/status/1054381295986458624.

6   In an interview in November 2018, UNHCR Special Envoy for the Central Mediterranean Situation, Vincent Cochetel said, "Due to staff safety concerns, we have temporarily suspended registration outside detention centers."; "Libya: 'Registration is a right for asylum seekers and refugees wherever they are.'" UNHCR. Last Modified November 9, 2018. https://www.unhcr.org/blogs/registration-is-a-right-for-refugees/.

7   Hayden, Sally. Twitter post. December 31, 2018, 12:13 p.m. https://twitter.com/sallyhayd/status/1079712194214924288.

8   United Nations Support Mission in Libya/Office of the High Commissioner for Human Rights. "Desperate and Dangerous: Report on the human rights situation of migrants and refugees in Libya," 32. Accessed August 30, 2021. https://unsmil.unmissions.org/sites/default/files/libya-migration-report-18dec2018.pdf.

9   Hayden, Sally. Twitter post. December 28, 2018, 9:13 p.m. https://twitter.com/sallyhayd/status/1078760883420053504.

10   Creta, Sara. "Driven to suicide in Tunisia's UNHCR refugee shelter." *Al Jazeera*, March 20, 2019. Accessed August 16, 2021. https://www.aljazeera.com/features/2019/3/20/driven-to-suicide-in-tunisias-unhcr-refugee-shelter.

11   A video of this speech was provided to the author.

12   Wapner, Jessica. "Do Walls Change How We Think?" *The New Yorker*, March 28, 2019. Accessed August 16, 2021. https://www.newyorker.com/culture/annals-of-inquiry/do-walls-change-how-we-think.

CHAPTER 10

1   Hayden, Sally. Twitter post. August 22, 2019, 4:08 p.m. https://twitter.com/sallyhayd/status/1164554961943957505.

2   Photos sent to the author, see also: Hayden, Sally. "Libya migrants scribble on prison wall: 'People were sold here.'" *Al Jazeera*, December 22, 2018. Accessed August 15, 2021. https://www.aljazeera.com/features/2018/12/22/libya-migrants-scribble-on-prison-wall-people-were-sold-here.

3   Hayden, Sally. "Bodies wash up on Libyan shore a month after shipwreck." *The Irish Times*, August 22, 2019. Accessed August 15, 2021. https://www.irishtimes.com/news/world/africa/

bodies-wash-up-on-libyan-shore-a-month-after-shipwreck-1.3994462.

4   Hayden, Sally. Twitter post. December 7, 2018, 10:43 p.m. https://twitter.com/sallyhayd/status/1071173258622451714.

5   Hayden, Sally. "Protest at Khoms Souq al Khamis detention center." YouTube video, 1:08. December 10, 2018. https://www.youtube.com/watch?v=EF0ssuH9DvU.

6   Hayden, Sally. Twitter post. January 11, 2019, 12:07 p.m. https://twitter.com/sallyhayd/status/1083696953278513152.

7   Hayden, Sally. Twitter post. January 7, 2019, 11:59 a.m. https://twitter.com/sallyhayd/status/1082245430598082565; Hayden, Sally. Twitter post. January 7, 2019, 12:22 p.m. https://twitter.com/sallyhayd/status/1082245430598082565.

8   Hayden, Sally. Twitter post. January 7, 2019, 12:25 p.m. https://twitter.com/sallyhayd/status/1082251998349668353.

9   Full statement from UNHCR, sent in email to author, January 14, 2019: "Having visited the Khoms Souq al-Khamis (KSK) detention center, we are aware that a number of people who were previously been rescued by the Libyan Coastguard and documented as having disembarked in Libya and taken (KSK) are currently unaccounted for. UNHCR is continuing to look in to the situation and we remain concerned for their safety and well-being.

     UNHCR does not have access to locations where refugees are being kept captive by smugglers and traffickers. Grave abuses are being committed against refugees and migrants by traffickers who prey on the desperation of the vulnerable. This cannot be ignored. It is vital that more efforts are undertaken to dismantle smuggling and trafficking networks, and to hold those involved to account, by freezing assets, travel bans, disrupting supply chains and revenues and robust prosecutions.

     UNHCR reiterates that no one rescued on the Central Mediterranean should be returned to Libya, in part due to the volatile security situation, routine use of detention centers and widespread reports of human rights violations. UNHCR reiterates its call to resettlement countries to accelerate additional resettlement places to evacuate refugees out of Libyan detention centers as a matter of urgency.

     Addressing the situation inside Libya and the deaths on the Mediterranean Sea requires a broad approach that involves countries of origin, transit and destination. Support to Libyan border management authorities cannot solve the problem alone but instead requires a comprehensive set of investments that encompasses the full range of political, security, human rights and development needs.

     UNHCR works to ensure all persons of concern held in detention centers are registered through regular visits. These visits are sometimes dependent on circumstances, particularly in regard to security." Yaxley, Charlie. Email message to the author, January 14, 2019.

10   UNHCR Libya. Twitter post. October 27, 2020, 4:11 p.m. https://twitter.com/UNHCRLibya/status/1321122347005452294.

CHAPTER 11

1   Whitelaw, Ben. "Saved for history, the British island fort that sent 50,000 slaves to a life of misery." *The Times of London*, November 14, 2020. Accessed August 12, 2021. https://www.thetimes.co.uk/article/saved-for-history-the-british-island-fort-that-sent-50-000-slaves-to-a-life-of-misery-wrf9tgx0t?t=ie.

2   Figures taken from 2013. World Bank data. Accessed November 13, 2021. https://data.worldbank.org/indicator/SE.ADT.LITR.ZS?end=2018&locations=SL&start=2008.

3   "Sierra Leone: Nonformal Education." State University. Accessed August 12, 2021. https://education.stateuniversity.com/pages/1339/Sierra-Leone-NONFORMAL-EDUCATION.html.

4   Chothia, Farouk. "Ebola drains already weak West African health systems." BBC News,

September 24, 2014. Accessed August 12, 2021. https://www.bbc.com/news/world-africa-29324595.

5   Gbandia, Silas. "Sierra Leone Ebola Burial Teams Struggle as Bodies Decompose." *Bloomberg*, September 18, 2014. Accessed August 12, 2021. https://web.archive.org/web/20141015171734/http:/www.businessweek.com/news/2014-09-17/sierra-leone-s-ebola-burial-teams-struggle-as-bodies-decompose.

6   "Statement on the end of the Ebola outbreak in Sierra Leone." World Health Organization. Last Modified November 7, 2015. https://www.afro.who.int/news/statement-end-ebola-outbreak-sierra-leone. ; "2014-2016 Ebola Outbreak in West Africa." Centers for Disease Control and Prevention. Accessed August 12, 2021. https://www.cdc.gov/vhf/ebola/history/2014-2016-outbreak/index.html.

7   Trenchard, Tommy. "Life Doesn't Go On After The Mudslides In Sierra Leone." NPR, April 8, 2018. Accessed August 11, 2021. https://www.npr.org/sections/goatsandsoda/2018/04/08/599526907/life-doesnt-go-on-after-the-mudslides-in-sierra-leone.

8   "GNI per capita, Atlas method - Sierra Leone." World Bank: Data. Accessed November 23, 2021. https://data.worldbank.org/indicator/NY.GNP.PCAP.CD?locations=SL.

9   Duval Smith, Alex. "Inside Mali's human-trafficking underworld in Gao." BBC News, April 21, 2015. Accessed August 11, 2021. https://www.bbc.com/news/world-africa-32359142.

10   "Spaghetti smugglers of the Sahara." *The Economist*, March 17, 2018. Accessed August 12, 2021. https://www.economist.com/middle-east-and-africa/2018/03/17/spaghetti-smugglers-of-the-sahara.

11   "6,000 Migrant Deaths Recorded in 2017, 'Only a Fraction of the Real Number' Worldwide: GMDAC." International Organization for Migration (IOM). Last Modified February 23, 2018. https://www.iom.int/news/6000-migrant-deaths-recorded-2017-only-fraction-real-number-worldwide-gmdac.

12   E.g. see: Spaggiari, Ottavia. "When a migrant drowns, a whole community feels the loss." *The New Humanitarian*, March 23, 2021. Accessed August 12, 2021. https://www.thenewhumanitarian.org/news-feature/2021/3/23/When-a-migrant-drowns-a-whole-community-feels-the-loss; Davlashyan, Naira, and Makembe Bamba. "From hero to outcast: The grim fate of migrants returning to Guinea empty-handed." *Euronews*, April 15, 2021. Accessed August 12, 2021. https://www.euronews.com/2021/04/15/from-hero-to-outcast-the-grim-fate-of-migrants-returning-to-guinea-empty-handed.

13   "More than 50,000 Migrants Benefited from Voluntary Humanitarian Return Assistance from Libya since 2015." European Commission. Last Modified February 28, 2020. https://ec.europa.eu/trustfundforafrica/all-news-and-stories/more-50000-migrants-benefited-voluntary-humanitarian-return-assistance-libya_en.

14   Global Initiative Against Transnational Organized Crime. The Political Economy of Migrant Detention in Libya: Understanding the players and the business models, by Arezo Malakooti. Produced with the financial support of the European Union. 2019, 35. Accessed August 12, 2021. https://globalinitiative.net/wp-content/uploads/2019/11/Final-Report-Detention-Libya.pdf.

15   Meskel, Yemane G. Twitter post. April 30, 2019. 10:00 a.m. https://twitter.com/hawelti/status/1123150115114557440.

16   IOM—UN Migration. "Assisted Voluntary Return and Reintegration (AVRR)." YouTube playlist. Last Modified May 20, 2021. https://www.youtube.com/playlist?list=PLE0C69EF8DB3A2891.

17   IOM—UN Migration. "Nigerians stuck in Libya return home with a song." YouTube video. March 28, 2017, 0:31. https://www.youtube.com/watch?v=JYVpEwow9Xc.

18   Garrett, Tenley. "What I learned from working for the UN." Medium, January 5, 2018. Accessed August 12, 2021. https://medium.com/@atenleymae/what-i-learned-from-working-for-the-un-38fc1644a600.

19   Vermeulen, Maite. "War of the words: how Europe is exporting its migration philosophy." The Correspondent, January 22, 2020. Accessed November 13, 2021. https://thecorre-

spondent.com/240/war-of-the-words-how-europe-is-exporting-its-migration-philoso-phy/31739576880-b506ad0d.

20 Montalto Monella, Lillo, and Sara Creta. "Paying for migrants to go back home: how the EU's Voluntary Return scheme is failing the desperate." *Euronews*, June 22, 2020. Accessed August 12, 2021. https://www.euronews.com/2020/06/19/paying-for-migrants-to-go-back-home-how-the-eu-s-voluntary-return-scheme-is-failing-the-de.

21 European Union statement, IOM 110th Session of the Council 26 to 29 November 2019. Accessed August 25, 2021. https://governingbodies.iom.int/system/files/en/council/110/State-ments/EU%20coordinated%20statement%20-%20Point%2013%20-%20final%20IOM%20Council%202019%20-.pdf

22 European Union, IOM 110th session.

23 Harvard Center for Health and Human Rights. *Returning Home? The Reintegration Challenges Facing Child and Youth Returnees from Libya to Nigeria*, by Vasileia Digidiki and Jacqueline Bhabha. Boston, 2019, 31. https://cdn1.sph.harvard.edu/wp-content/uploads/sites/2464/2019/11/Harvard-FXB-Center-Returning-Home-FINAL.pdf.

24 "Sierra Leone: Daily Subsistence Allowance." International Civil Service Commission. Accessed August 12, 2021. https://icsc.un.org/#.

25 Rankin, Jennifer. "$2bn EU-Africa 'anti-migration' fund too opaque, say critics." *The Guardian*, October 31, 2017. Accessed August 12, 2021. https://www.theguardian.com/global-development/2017/oct/31/2bn-eu-africa-anti-migration-fund-too-opaque-say-critics.

26 Only 38.4% of applications to Germany were accepted in 2020: "Asylum applications and refugees from Sierra Leone." World Data. Accessed August 12, 2021. https://www.worlddata.info/africa/sierra-leone/asylum.php.

27 "Billionaire fortunes grew by $2.5 billion a day last year as poorest saw their wealth fall." Oxfam International. Last Modified January 21, 2019. https://www.oxfam.org/en/press-releases/billionaire-fortunes-grew-25-billion-day-last-year-poorest-saw-their-wealth-fall.

28 Elliott, Larry. "World's 26 richest people own as much as poorest 50%, says Oxfam." *The Guardian*, January 21, 2019. Accessed August 12, 2021. https://www.theguardian.com/business/2019/jan/21/world-26-richest-people-own-as-much-as-poorest-50-per-cent-oxfam-report.

29 Whitelaw, Ben. "Saved for history, the British island fort that sent 50,000 slaves to a life of misery." *The Times of London*, November 14, 2020. Accessed August 12, 2021. https://www.thetimes.co.uk/article/saved-for-history-the-british-island-fort-that-sent-50-000-slaves-to-a-life-of-misery-wrf9tgx0t?t=ie.

30 Aitken, Jonathan. *John Newton: From Disgrace to Amazing Grace*. London: Continuum Publishing, 2008.

31 "Sierra Leone country profile." BBC News, April 5, 2018. Accessed August 12, 2021. https://www.bbc.com/news/world-africa-14094194.

32 Whitelaw, Ben. "Saved for history, the British island fort that sent 50,000 slaves to a life of misery." *The Times of London*, November 14, 2020. Accessed August 12, 2021. https://www.thetimes.co.uk/article/saved-for-history-the-british-island-fort-that-sent-50-000-slaves-to-a-life-of-misery-wrf9tgx0t?t=ie; Glass, Andrew. "Freed slaves depart for Africa, Feb. 6, 1820." Politico, May 2, 2017. Accessed August 12, 2021. https://www.politico.com/story/2017/02/freed-slaves-depart-for-africa-feb-6-1820-234555.

33 Beverton, Alys. "Recaptives." BlackPast, May 23, 2009. Accessed August 12, 2021. https://www.blackpast.org/global-african-history/recaptives/.

34 Whitelaw, Ben. "Saved for history."

35 Liddell, Marcus. "Christian Cole: Oxford University's first black student." BBC News, October 18, 2017. Accessed August 12, 2021. https://www.bbc.com/news/uk-england-oxford-shire-40429917.

36 Farfán, Abraham, and María del Pilar López-Uribe. "The British founding of Sierra Leone was never a 'Province of Freedom.'" LSE, June 27, 2020. Accessed August 12, 2021. https://blogs.lse.ac.uk/africaatlse/2020/06/27/british-founding-sierra-leone-slave-trade/.

37   "Human Development Report 2020: Sierra Leone" UNDP. Accessed October 8, 2021. http://hdr.undp.org/sites/default/files/Country-Profiles/SLE.pdf.

38   Campbell, Greg. *Blood Diamonds: Tracing the Deadly Path of the World's Most Precious Stones.* New York: Basic Books, 2004. 9.

39   Campbell, *Blood Diamonds*, 60.

40   DeVries, Nina. "Sierra Leoneans Share Memories of Civil War on Anniversary." VOA News, January 6, 2018. Accessed August 12, 2021. https://www.voanews.com/africa/sierra-leoneans-share-memories-civil-war-anniversary.

41   Barnes, Edward. "The Heart Of Darkness." *TIME* Magazine, January 25, 1999. Accessed August 12, 2021. http://content.time.com/time/magazine/article/0,9171,18721-2,00.html.

42   Campbell, *Blood Diamonds*, 16.

43   Médecins Sans Frontières. Assessing Trauma in Sierra Leone: Psycho-Social Questionnaire Freetown Survey Outcomes, by Kaz de Jong, Maureen Mulhern, and Saskia van der Kam. Amsterdam, 2000. 3, 10. Accessed August 12, 2021. https://www.msf.org/sites/msf.org/files/2018-08/assessing-trauma-in-sierra-leone.pdf.

44   Tendayi Achiume, E. "Migration as Decolonization." *Stanford Law Review* 71 (2019): 1510, 1537, 1552. Accessed August 12, 2021. SSRN: https://ssrn.com/abstract=3330353.

45   "Life expectancy at birth, total (years) - Sierra Leone." The World Bank. Accessed August 12, 2021. https://data.worldbank.org/indicator/SP.DYN.LE00.IN?locations=SL.

46   "Sierra Leone country profile." BBC News, April 5, 2018. Accessed August 12, 2021. https://www.bbc.com/news/world-africa-14094194.

47   Mason, Harriet. "Making strides to improve maternal health in Sierra Leone." UNICEF, May 26, 2016. Accessed August 12, 2021. https://www.unicef.org/stories/making-strides-maternal-health-worst-place-to-be-mother.

48   World Health Organization. Sierra Leone Annual Report: A Year in Focus 2017. Freetown, 2017. 13. Accessed August 12, 2021. https://www.afro.who.int/sites/default/files/2018-03/World%20Health%20Organization%20Sierra%20Leone%20Annual%20Report%202017.pdf.

49   Hayden, Sally. "People dying for lack of oxygen during Sierra Leone's third Covid wave." *The Irish Times*, July 31, 2021. Accessed October 8, 2021. https://www.irishtimes.com/news/world/africa/people-dying-for-lack-of-oxygen-during-sierra-leone-s-third-covid-wave-1.4634918.

50   "IOM hails historic first human trafficking convictions in Sierra Leone." United Nations Africa Renewal. Last Modified March 5, 2020. https://www.un.org/africarenewal/news/iom-hails-historic-first-human-trafficking-convictions-sierra-leone.

CHAPTER 12

1   Plunkett, John. "Katie Hopkins: Sun migrants article petition passes 200,000 mark." *The Guardian*, April 20, 2015. Accessed August 6, 2021. https://www.theguardian.com/media/2015/apr/20/katie-hopkins-sun-migrants-article-petition-nears-180000-mark.

2   "Italy migrants: Matteo Salvini calls for end to Sicily 'refugee camp.'" BBC News, June 3, 2018. Accessed November 13, 2021. https://www.bbc.co.uk/news/world-europe-44346084.

3   Engert, Marcus. "The European Union Is Worried That 300,000 People Could Flee Libya If Things Get Any Worse." Buzzfeed News, August 21, 2019. Accessed August 5, 2021. https://www.buzzfeednews.com/article/marcusengert/operation-sophia-report-migrants-libya-warning.

4   Nelson, Zed. "Lampedusa boat tragedy: a survivor's story." *The Guardian*, March 22, 2014. Accessed August 5, 2021. https://www.theguardian.com/world/2014/mar/22/lampedusa-boat-tragedy-migrants-africa.

5   Davies, Lizzy. "Lampedusa victims include mother and baby attached by umbilical cord." *The Guardian*, October 10, 2013. Accessed August 5, 2021. https://www.theguardian.com/world/2013/oct/10/lampedusa-victims-mother-baby-umbilical-cord; Nelson, "Lampedusa

boat tragedy." *The Guardian*; "Survivors of capsized migrant boat brought ashore." *The Irish Examiner*, October 12, 2013. Accessed August 5, 2021. https://www.irishexaminer.com/world/arid-30609936.html.

6   Davies, Lizzy. "Lampedusa boat tragedy is 'slaughter of innocents' says Italian president." *The Guardian*, October 3, 2013. Accessed August 5, 2021. https://www.theguardian.com/world/2013/oct/03/lampedusa-boat-tragedy-italy-migrants; Davies, "Lampedusa victims." *The Guardian*; Nelson, "Lampedusa boat tragedy." *The Guardian*.

7   Scherer, Steve, and Ilaria Polleschi, "Italy in talks with EU to share responsibility for boat migrants." *Reuters* (Milan), July 8, 2014. Accessed August 5, 2021. https://www.reuters.com/article/us-eu-italy-migrants/italy-in-talks-with-eu-to-share-responsibility-for-boat-migrants-idUSKBN0FD1YL20140708; "UNHCR concerned over ending of rescue operation in the Mediterranean." UNHCR: The UN Refugee Agency. Last Modified October 17, 2014. https://www.unhcr.org/en-ie/news/briefing/2014/10/5440ffa16/unhcr-concerned-ending-rescue-operation-mediterranean.html.

8   "Amnesty International protests against abuses at Europe's borders in surprise Sofia action." Amnesty International. Last Modified July 17, 2014. https://www.amnesty.eu/news/amnesty-international-protests-against-abuses-at-europe-s-borders-in-surprise-sofia-action-0773/.

9   The United Nations High Commissioner for Refugees. Convention and Protocol Relating to the Status of Refugees. Geneva. Accessed August 5, 2021. https://www.unhcr.org/en-ie/3b-66c2aa10; "MareNostrum to end—New Frontex operation will not ensure rescue of migrants in international waters." ECRE: European Council on Refugees and Exiles. Last Modified October 17, 2014. https://ecre.org/operation-mare-nostrum-to-end-frontex-triton-operation-will-not-ensure-rescue-at-sea-of-migrants-in-international-waters/; "The worst yet?" *The Economist*, April 19, 2015. Accessed August 5, 2021. https://www.economist.com/europe/2015/04/19/the-worst-yet.

10 "Migration policies in the Mediterranean and Libya: Roundtables on Crimes, Victims and the rule of International Law." Sciences Po, February 12, 2020 (listed the EU Commission's 'Horizon 2020 EU Funding for Research and Innovation' as one of its partners). Last Modified February 12, 2020. https://www.sciencespo.fr/agenda/ceri/fr/event/Migration+policies+in+the+Mediterranean+and+Libya?event=1916.

11 "The Mediterranean's Deadliest Shipwreck Just Got Deadlier." Voice of America, December 20, 2018. Accessed August 5, 2021. https://www.voanews.com/europe/mediterraneans-deadliest-shipwreck-just-got-deadlier.

12 Hayden, Sally. "More Migrant Deaths Reported a Day After 700 Are Feared Drowned in Mediterranean 'Mass Cemetery.'" VICE News, April 20, 2015. Accessed August 5, 2021. https://www.vice.com/en/article/3kexvw/more-migrant-deaths-reported-a-day-after-700-are-feared-drowned-in-mediterranean-mass-cemetery;

    Hayden, Sally. "A Teenage Survivor of the Mediterranean's Worst Migrant Disaster Speaks of His Traumatic Ordeal." VICE News, April 22, 2015. Accessed August 5, 2021. https://www.vice.com/en/article/kz9env/a-teenage-survivor-of-the-mediterraneans-worst-migrant-disaster-speaks-of-his-traumatic-ordeal.

13 "About Us." Operation Sophia. Accessed August 5, 2021. https://www.operationsophia.eu/about-us/.

14 European Union External Action. European Union Naval Force—Mediterranean Operation Sophia. Rome, 2016. Accessed August 5, 2021. https://eeas.europa.eu/archives/docs/csdp/missions-and-operations/eunavfor-med/pdf/factsheet_eunavfor_med_en.pdf.

15 Vassileva, Radosveta. "Bulgaria's dangerous flirtation with the far-right." *New Eastern Europe*, May 21, 2019. Accessed August 5, 2021. https://neweasterneurope.eu/2019/05/21/bulgarias-dangerous-flirtation-with-the-far-right/; Walt, Vivienne. "Why Italy's Matteo Salvini Is the Most Feared Man in Europe." *TIME* Magazine, September 13, 2018. Accessed August 5, 2021. https://time.com/5394448/matteo-salvini/; Aisch, Gregor, Adam Pierce, and Bryant Rousseau. "How Far is Europe Swinging to the Right?" *The New York Times*, October 23, 2017.

Accessed August 5, 2021. https://www.nytimes.com/interactive/2016/05/22/world/europe/europe-right-wing-austria-hungary.html.

16 "France: Marine Le Pen goes on trial over Muslim remarks." BBC News, October 20, 2015. Accessed August 5, 2021; Chrisafis, Angelique. "Marine Le Pen emerges from father's shadow." *The Guardian*, March 21, 2011. Accessed August 5, 2021. https://www.theguardian.com/world/2011/mar/21/marine-lepen-defends-republic; "Résultats de l'élection présidentielle 2017." Ministère de l'Intérieur. Last Modified May 7, 2017. https://www.interieur.gouv.fr/Elections/Les-resultats/Presidentielles/elecresult__presidentielle-2017/(path)/presidentielle-2017/FE.html; Onishu, Norimitsu. "On the Scrappy Fringes of French Politics, Marine Le Pen Tries to Rebrand." *The New York Times*, May 16, 2021. Accessed August 5, 2021. https://www.nytimes.com/2021/05/16/world/europe/france-le-pen-election.html.

17 Bremmer, Ian. "These 5 Countries Show How the European Far-Right Is Growing in Power." *TIME* Magazine, September 13, 2018. Accessed August 5, 2021. https://time.com/5395444/europe-far-right-italy-salvini-sweden-france-germany/.

18 Dam, Philippe. "Hungary's Authoritarian Takeover Puts European Union at Risk: COVID-19 Is Not an Opportunity to Shelve Democracy." Human Rights Watch, April 1, 2020. Accessed August 5, 2021. https://www.hrw.org/news/2020/04/01/hungarys-authoritarian-takeover-puts-european-union-risk; Dunai, Marton. "Hungarian PM vows to resist EU's 'misguided' migrant policy." *Reuters*, February 28, 2016. Accessed August 05, 2021. https://www.reuters.com/article/us-europe-migrants-hungary-orban-idUSKCN0W10UV; "Hungary's Orban proposes to ban migrants for two years." InfoMigrants, June 11, 2021. Accessed August 5, 2021. https://www.infomigrants.net/en/post/32900/hungary-s-orban-proposes-to-ban-migrants-for-two-years.

19 European Union Commission. State of the Union 2018: The Hour of European Sovereignty, by Jean-Claude Juncker. Authorized version of the State of the Union Address, 2018. Accessed August 05, 2021. https://ec.europa.eu/info/sites/default/files/soteu2018-speech_en_0.pdf.

20 Walt, "Matteo Salvini."

21 Giuffrida, Angela. "'Merde alors!': Salvini draws fury with reference to African 'slaves.'" *The Guardian*, September 14, 2018. Accessed August 5, 2021. https://www.theguardian.com/world/2018/sep/14/merde-alors-matteo-salvini-african-slaves-remarks-draw-angry-outburst, last accessed August 4, 2021.

22 Jones, Tobias, and Ayo Awokoya. "Are your tinned tomatoes picked by slave labour?" *The Guardian*, June 20, 2019. Accessed August 5, 2021. https://www.theguardian.com/world/2019/jun/20/tomatoes-italy-mafia-migrant-labour-modern-slavery.

23 Creta, Sara, Bashar Deeb, Klaas van Dijken, Emmanuel Freudenthal, Steffen Lüdke, and Maximilian Popp. "How Frontex Helps Haul Migrants Back to Libyan Torture Camps." Spiegel International, April 29, 2021. Accessed August 5, 2021. https://www.spiegel.de/international/europe/libya-how-frontex-helps-haul-migrants-back-to-libyan-torture-camps-a-d62c3960-ece2-499b-8a3f-1ede2eaefb83; Rankin, Jennifer. "EU to stop Mediterranean migrant rescue boat patrols." *The Guardian*, March 27, 2019. Accessed August 5, 2021. https://www.theguardian.com/world/2019/mar/27/eu-to-stop-mediterranean-migrant-rescue-boat-patrols.

24 Engert, "European Union."

25 Rankin, Jennifer. "EU declares migration crisis over as it hits out at 'fake news'." *The Guardian*, March 6, 2019. Accessed August 5, 2021. https://www.theguardian.com/world/2019/mar/06/eu-declares-migration-crisis-over-hits-out-fake-news-european-commission; Walker, Shaun. "European elections: far-right 'surge' ends in a ripple." *The Guardian*, May 27, 2019. Accessed August 5, 2021. https://www.theguardian.com/world/2019/may/27/european-elections-far-right-surge-ends-in-a-ripple.

26 Schumacher, Elizabeth. "EU post to 'protect European way of life' called 'disgusting,' 'reprehensible.'" *Deutsche Welle News*, September 11, 2019. Accessed August 5, 2021. https://www.dw.com/en/eu-post-to-protect-european-way-of-life-called-disgusting-reprehensible/a-50378215; Stevis-Gridneff, Matina. "'Protecting Our European Way of Life'? Outrage

Follows New E. U. Role." *The New York Times*, September 12, 2019. Accessed August 5, 2021. https://www.nytimes.com/2019/09/12/world/europe/eu-ursula-von-der-leyen-migration.html; Trilling, Daniel. "How rescuing drowning migrants became a crime." *The Guardian*, September 22, 2020. Accessed August 5, 2021. https://www.theguardian.com/news/2020/sep/22/how-rescuing-drowning-migrants-became-a-crime-iuventa-salvini-italy.

27   "Shipwreck Off Coast of Libya Pushes Migrant Deaths on the Mediterranean Past 20,000 Mark." International Organization for Migration (IOM). Last Modified May 3, 2020. https://www.iom.int/news/shipwreck-coast-libya-pushes-migrant-deaths-mediterranean-past-20000-mark.

28   "Most of the cases . . . occurred in just seven countries: Italy, Greece, France, the UK, Germany, Denmark and Spain." Archer, Nandini, Claudia Torrisi, Claire Provost, Alexander Nabert, and Belen Lobos. "Hundreds of Europeans 'criminalised' for helping migrants – as far right aims to win big in European elections." Open Democracy, May 18, 2019. Accessed August 5, 2021. https://www.opendemocracy.net/en/5050/hundreds-of-europeans-criminalised-for-helping-migrants-new-data-shows-as-far-right-aims-to-win-big-in-european-elections/.

29   McGregor, Marion. "Frontex hiring 700 border guards." Open Democracy, November 5, 2019. Accessed August 5, 2021. https://www.infomigrants.net/en/post/20590/frontex-hiring-700-border-guards; "Living in the EU." European Union. Accessed August 5 2021. https://europa.eu/european-union/about-eu/figures/living_en.

30   "Values." Mosaiikki: Information Campaign of the European Parliament. Accessed August 5, 2021. https://europarlamentti.info/en/values-and-objectives/values/.

31   For more information see: "Building walls: Fear and securitization in the European Union." The Transnational Institute (TNI). Last Modified November 9, 2018. https://www.tni.org/en/publication/building-walls; Dempsey, Judy. "Judy Asks: Is Post-1989 Europe Building Walls?" *Carnegie Europe*, November 7, 2019. Accessed August 5, 2021. https://carnegieeurope.eu/strategiceurope/80292; Ferrer-Gallardo, Xavier, and Abel Albet-Mas. "EU-Limboscapes: Ceuta and the proliferation of migrant detention spaces across the European Union." *European Urban and Regional Studies* 23, no. 3 (2016): 527-530.

32   Christides, Giorgos, Klaas van Dijken, Steffen Lüdke, and Maximilian Popp. "Missteps and Mismanagement at Frontex: Scandals Plunge Europe's Border Agency into Turmoil." Spiegel International, February 05, 2021. Accessed August 5, 2021. https://www.spiegel.de/international/europe/missteps-and-mismanagement-at-frontex-scandals-plunge-europe-s-border-agency-into-turmoil-a-d11ae404-5fd4-41a7-b127-eca47a00753f; "FAQ: Key Facts." Frontex. Accessed August 5, 2021. https://frontex.europa.eu/about-frontex/faq/key-facts/; "Frontex is recruiting Border Guards." European Commission. Last Modified October 29, 2019. https://ec.europa.eu/home-affairs/news/20191029_frontex-recruiting-border-guards_en.   Ferrer-Gallardo, Xavier, and Abel Albet-Mas.

33   Allison, Natalie, Bashar Deeb, Giorgos Christides, Klaas van Dijken, Katy Fallon, Ana França, Emmanuel Freudenthal, Heiner Hoffmann, Daniel Howden, Steffen Lüdke, Mitra Nasar, Maximilian Popp, Nick Waters, and Logan Williams. "Frontex Chapter II: Complicit in Pushbacks." *Lighthouse Reports*. Accessed August 5, 2021. https://www.lighthousereports.nl/investigation/frontex-chapter-ii-complicit-in-pushbacks/.

34   Bautista, José, and Ana Rojas. "Frontex turning 'blind eye' to human rights violations, says former deputy." *The Guardian*, June 11, 2021. Accessed August 5, 2021. https://amp.theguardian.com/global-development/2021/jun/11/frontex-turning-blind-eye-to-human-rights-violations-says-former-deputy.

35   "Update: Top 10 Most Influential UK's MEPs (September 2017)." VoteWatch Europe. Last Modified September 11, 2017. https://www.votewatch.eu/blog/update-top-10-most-influential-uks-meps-september-2017/.

36   Hayden, Sally. "Somali returned to Libya under Italian policy sets himself on fire." *The Irish Times*, October 25, 2018. Accessed August 5, 2021. https://www.irishtimes.com/news/world/africa/somali-returned-to-libya-under-italian-policy-sets-himself-on-fire-1.3675942; Hayden,

Sally. "Inside Libyan detention 'hell' where refugee burned himself alive." *Al Jazeera*, November 12, 2018. Accessed August 5, 2021. https://www.aljazeera.com/news/2018/11/libyan-detention-hell-refugee-burned-alive-181110102329706.html.

37   "Libya: situation of migrants and rescue operations up for discussion." European Parliament. Last Modified November 27, 2018. https://www.europarl.europa.eu/news/en/pressroom/20181126IPR20127/libya-situation-of-migrants-and-rescue-operations-up-for-discussion.

38   "Ceremony in memory of Jozsef Antall." European Parliament. Last Modified February 1, 2011. https://www.europarl.europa.eu/former_ep_presidents/president-buzek/en/press/speeches/sp-2011/sp-2011-February/speeches-2011-February-1.html.

39   At 11:47:30: "Committee on Civil Liberties, Justice and Home Affairs Ordinary meeting." European Parliament. Last modified November 27, 2018. https://multimedia.europarl.europa.eu/en/committee-on-civil-liberites-justic-and-home-affairs-ordinary-meeting_20181127-0900-COMMITTEE-LIBE_vd.

40   At 12.03.00: "Committee on Civil Liberties, Justice and Home Affairs Ordinary meeting." European Parliament. Last Modified November 27, 2018. https://multimedia.europarl.europa.eu/en/committee-on-civil-liberites-justic-and-home-affairs-ordinary-meeting_20181127-0900-COMMITTEE-LIBE_vd.

41   At 11:46 a.m.: "Committee on Civil Liberties, Justice and Home Affairs Ordinary meeting." European Parliament. Last Modified November 27, 2018. https://multimedia.europarl.europa.eu/en/committee-on-civil-liberties-justice-and-home-affairs-ordinary-meeting_20181127-0900-COMMITTEE-LIBE_vd; Hayden, Sally. Twitter post. November 28, 2018, 11:24 a.m. https://twitter.com/sallyhayd/status/1067378702969987072.

42   At 12:11 p.m.: "Committee on Civil Liberties", European Parliament.

43   At 12:22 a.m.: "Committee on Civil Liberties", European Parliament.

44   From 13:11 p.m.: "Committee on Civil Liberties", European Parliament.

45   At 12:48 p.m.: "Committee on Civil Liberties", European Parliament.

46   OPEN Media Hub. "Bettina Muscheidt, Head of EU Delegation to Libya." YouTube Video, 4:20. November 29, 2016; "Libya: European Union Ambassador Bugeja presents his credentials to PC President Serraj." EU Neighbors. Last Modified November 5, 2018. https://www.euneighbors.eu/en/south/stay-informed/news/libya-european-union-ambassador-bugeja-presents-his-credentials-pc.

47   Channel 4 News. "Revealed: human rights abuses in Libyan migrant camps." YouTube Video, 10:36. May 10, 2019. https://www.youtube.com/watch?v=MebcasTO0hQ.

48   "Oral update of the United Nations High Commissioner for Human Rights on Libya pursuant to Human Rights Council resolution 37/41; 40th session of the Human Rights Council; Address by Andrew Gilmour; Assistant Secretary General for Human Rights; Geneva, 21 March 2019; Salle XX, Palais des Nations." European Country of Origin Information Network (ECOI). Last Modified March 21, 2019. https://www.ecoi.net/en/document/2005425.html.

49   "Motion for a Resolution further to Questions for Oral Answer B9-0052/2019 and B9-0053/2019 pursuant to Rule 136(5) of the Rules of Procedure on search and rescue in the Mediterranean." European Parliament. Last Modified October 22, 2019. https://www.europarl.europa.eu/doceo/document/B-9-2019-0130_EN.html.; Stone, Jon. "EU parliament votes against improving search and rescue for refugees in Mediterranean." The Independent, October 25, 2019. Accessed August 5, 2021. https://www.independent.co.uk/news/world/europe/eu-parliament-refugees-migrants-deaths-search-rescue-vote-mediterranean-a9171401.html.

50   "Immigration and rights of nationals of non-EU countries." EUR-Lex: EU Law. Accessed August 5, 2021. https://eur-lex.europa.eu/summary/chapter/230106.html.

51   Pitzer, Andrea. "'Some Suburb of Hell': America's New Concentration Camp System." *The New York Review of Books*, June 21, 2019. Accessed August 5, 2021. https://www.nybooks.com/daily/2019/06/21/some-suburb-of-hell-americas-new-concentration-camp-system/.

CHAPTER 13

1   See page 140 in: Guevara, Che. "Interview with *Libération*." In *Che Guevara Speaks*, edited and translated by Pathfinder Press. New York: Pathfinder Press, 1967, 2nd Edition 2000.

2   Thomas, Isaak. "I am a refugee in a Libyan camp. Conditions are so bad, people are dying." *The Guardian*, November 8, 2018. Accessed August 13, 2021. https://www.theguardian.com/commentisfree/2018/nov/08/refugee-libyan-camp-people-dying; Ibrahim, Ali. "As an LGBT refugee, Europe's deal with Libya has left me fearing for my life." *The New Statesman*, December 5, 2018. Accessed August 13, 2021. https://www.newstatesman.com/world/middle-east/2018/12/lgbt-refugee-europe-s-deal-libya-has-left-me-fearing-my-life; Malie, Mario. "As a refugee in one of Libya's dangerous detention centers, I know what it feels like when the world leaves you behind." *The Independent*, July 15, 2019. Accessed August 13, 2021. https://www.independent.co.uk/voices/libya-strike-refugee-unhcr-tripoli-triq-al-sikka-italy-a9004961.html.

3   "Torture and shocking conditions: the human cost of keeping migrants out of Europe." Channel 4 News. Last Modified February 25, 2019. https://www.channel4.com/news/torture-and-shocking-conditions-the-human-cost-of-keeping-migrants-out-of-europe.

4   Channel 4 News. Twitter post. February 25, 2019, 7:06 p.m. https://twitter.com/Channel-4News/status/1100109682444783618.

5   Willan, Philip. "Migrants returned by EU tortured in Libya." *The Times of London*, March 1, 2019. Accessed August 13, 2021. https://www.thetimes.co.uk/article/migrants-returned-by-eu-tortured-in-libya-0bd0t0ffz.

6   E.g. Question from Labour MP Lloyd Russell-Moyle, tabled on March 6, 2019: "To ask the Secretary of State fro Foreign and Commonwealth Affairs, pursuant to the Answer of 5 March 2019 to Question 227143 on Africa: EU aid and with reference to a Channel 4 news report on migrant deaths of 25 February 2019, what information her Department holds on the number of migrant deaths in facilities run by (a) the Directorate for Combating Illegal Migration and (b) other facilities funded by the EU Emergency Trust Fund for Africa." See at: "Africa: Undocumented Migrants Question for Foreign and Commonwealth Office. UK Parliament. Last Modified March 6, 2019. https://questions-statements.parliament.uk/written-questions/detail/2019-03-06/229232; Africa: EU Aid Question for Department for International Development. UK Parliament. Last Modified February 28, 2019. https://questions-statements.parliament.uk/written-questions/detail/2019-02-28/227143.

7   Hayden, Sally. Twitter post. February 26, 2019, 12:53 p.m. https://twitter.com/sallyhayd/status/110037831905540096; This tweet contains photos of the Dutch embassy visit to Triq al Sikka, though the date is listed as one day later than it actually was: Migrant Rescue Watch. Twitter post. February 27, 2019, 10:53 p.m. https://twitter.com/rgowans/status/1100891819271954435.

8   Hayden, Sally. "Refugees in Libya 'tortured' for breaking out of detention center." *Al Jazeera*, March 2, 2019. Accessed August 13, 2021. https://www.aljazeera.com/news/2019/3/2/refugees-in-libya-tortured-for-breaking-out-of-detention-center.

9   "Refugees protest conditions in Libyan detention as resettlement solutions falter." UNHCR. Last Modified March 5, 2019. https://www.unhcr.org/news/briefing/2019/3/5c7e72c14/refugees-protest-conditions-libyan-detention-resettlement-solutions-falter.html.

10   "IOM Condemns Recent Violence in Libyan Detention Center." International Organization for Migration (IOM). March 5, 2021. https://www.iom.int/news/iom-condemns-recent-violence-libyan-detention-center.

11   "In Tarik al-Sikka some access is granted to the international community, but the process is complicated because the center is controlled by the al-Khoja militia, under the command of Naser Hazam." See page 87 in: *Global Initiative Against Transnational Organized Crime. The Political Economy of Migrant Detention in Libya: Understanding the players and the business models*, by Arezo Malakooti. Produced with the financial support of the European Union.

2019. Accessed August 10, 2021. https://globalinitiative.net/wp-content/uploads/2019/11/Final-Report-Detention-Libya.pdf.

12 Hayden, Sally. "The U.N. Is Leaving Migrants to Die in Libya." *Foreign Policy*, October 10, 2019. Accessed August 13, 2021. https://foreignpolicy.com/2019/10/10/libya-migrants-un-iom-refugees-die-detention-center-civil-war/.

13 "Statement By the Special Representative of The Secretary General in Libya, Ghassan Salamé, on the National Conference." United Nations Support Mission in Libya (UNSMIL). Last Modified April 9, 2019. https://unsmil.unmissions.org/statement-special-representative-secretary-general-libya-ghassan-salam%C3%A9-national-conference; "All Parties in Libya Must Seize Critical Chance to Forge Inclusive, Stable Future ahead of National Conference, Special Representative Tells Security Council." United Nations. March 20, 2019. Accessed August 20, 2021. https://www.un.org/press/en/2019/sc13743.doc.htm https://www.un.org/press/en/2019/sc13743.doc.htm.

CHAPTER 14

1 Wintour, Patrick. "UN postpones Libya national conference amid fighting in Tripoli." *The Guardian*, April 9, 2019. Accessed August 16, 2021. https://www.theguardian.com/world/2019/apr/09/un-postpones-libya-national-conference-amid-fighting-tripoli.

2 "Transcript of the Secretary-General's remarks at Press Conference in Tripoli, Libya." United Nations. Last Modified April 4, 2019. https://www.un.org/sg/en/content/sg/press-encounter/2019-04-04/transcript-of-the-secretary-general%E2%80%99s-remarks-press-conference-tripoli-libya.

3 El Gomati, Anas. "Haftar's Rebranded Coups." Carnegie Endowment for International Peace, July 30, 2019. Accessed August 16, 2021. https://carnegieendowment.org/sada/79579.

4 Anderson, Jon Lee. "The Unravelling." *The New Yorker*, February 16, 2015. Accessed August 16, 2021. https://www.newyorker.com/magazine/2015/02/23/unravelling.

5 Barnes, Julian E. "Ex-C.I.A. Asset, Now a Libyan Strongman, Faces Torture Accusations." *The New York Times*, February 18, 2020. Accessed November 14, 2021. https://www.nytimes.com/2020/02/18/us/politics/hifter-torture-lawsuit-libya.html.

6 Al-Warfalli, Ayman. "Libya's eastern commander declares victory in battle for Benghazi." *Reuters*, July 5, 2017. https://www.reuters.com/article/us-libya-security-benghazi-idUSKBN-19Q2SK.

7 Office of the Director of National Intelligence United States of America. Duty to Warn. 2015, 1. Accessed August 16, 2021. https://www.justsecurity.org/wp-content/uploads/2018/10/Intelligence-Community-Directive-ICD-191-duty-to-Warn.pdf.

8 "Tripoli Rapid Situation Overview—Libya, 17 April 2019." ReliefWeb. Last Modified April 18, 2019. https://reliefweb.int/report/libya/tripoli-rapid-situation-overview-libya-17-april-2019.

9 Hayden, Sally. Twitter post. April 11, 2019, 9:25 p.m. https://twitter.com/sallyhayd/status/1116437086276661251.

10 Hayden, Sally. Twitter post. April 12, 2019, 11:36 a.m. https://twitter.com/sallyhayd/status/1116651279160418304.

11 Sky News. "Alex Crawford reports live with rebels as they enter Tripoli." YouTube video, 4:53. August 22, 2011, https://www.youtube.com/watch?v=kwT40TE-pHY; Read also her book: Crawford, Alex. *Colonel Gaddafi's Hat*. London: HarperCollins Publishers Ltd., 2012.

12 Crawford, Alex. "Following the ragtag fighters defending Tripoli." Sky News video, 03:44. April 15, 2019. https://news.sky.com/video/skys-alex-crawford-joins-revolution-fighters-on-libyas-frontline-11694364.

13 UNHCR. Fact Sheet: Libya. 2020, 1. Accessed August 16, 2021. file:///D:/UNHCR%20Libya%20Factsheet%20-%20September%202020.pdf.

14   Crawford, Alex. "Sky News speaks exclusively to Libyan PM." Sky News video, 03:26. April 15, 2019. https://news.sky.com/video/sky-news-speaks-exclusively-to-libyan-pm-11694970.

15   For more on the propaganda wars, see: Assad, Abdulkader. "Libya's UAE-funded AL Marsad newspaper twists Alex Crawford's report on Tripoli war." *The Libya Observer*, April 16, 2019. Accessed August 16, 2021. https://www.libyaobserver.ly/news/libyas-uae-funded-al-marsad-newspaper-twists-alex-crawfords-report-tripoli-war.

16   Denselow, Toby. Email message to the author, April 30, 2019.

17   E.g.: Detsch, Jack. "Libya signs $2 million lobbying deal as Trump warms to rival strongman." Al-Monitor, May 1, 2019. Accessed August 16, 2021. https://www.al-monitor.com/pulse/originals/2019/05/libya-signs-lobbying-deal-trump-warms-rival-hifter.html.

18   Holland, Steve. "White House says Trump spoke to Libyan commander Haftar on Monday." *Reuters*, April 19, 2019. Accessed August 16, 2021. https://www.reuters.com/article/us-libya-security-trump-idUSKCN1RV0WW.

19   Robinson, Kali. "Who's Who in Libya's War?" Council on Foreign Relations, June 18, 2020. Accessed August 16, 2021. https://www.cfr.org/in-brief/whos-who-libyas-war.

20   Badi, Emadeddin. "Russia Isn't the Only One Getting Its Hands Dirty in Libya." *Foreign Policy*, April 21, 2020. Accessed August 16, 2021. https://foreignpolicy.com/2020/04/21/libyan-civil-war-france-uae-khalifa-haftar/.

21   Lardner, Richard. "Libyan National Army hires firm to forge closer ties with US." Associated Press News, May 21, 2019. Accessed August 16, 2021. https://apnews.com/article/eb99fba13d35436f9244cd7ee7e9d698.

22   "Guidance: Secret Recording" BBC. Accessed October 9, 2021. https://www.bbc.com/editorialguidelines/guidance/secret-recording.

23   "About." Mercury. Accessed August 16, 2021. https://www.mercuryllc.com/about/.

24   "International Affairs." Mercury. Accessed August 16, 2021. https://www.mercuryllc.com/capabilities/#27-international-affairs.

25   Charles, Jacqueline. "Cash-strapped Haiti has an image problem. The government is spending thousands to fix it." *The Miami Herald*, April 20, 2021. https://www.miamiherald.com/news/nation-world/world/americas/haiti/article250769074.html; Ordoñez, Franco. "Haiti hires Clinton-linked PR firm to soften image in Washington." McClatchy DC Bureau, March 11, 2018. Accessed August 16, 2021. https://www.mcclatchydc.com/news/nation-world/world/article204613419.html.

26   Harwell, Drew. "How Washington power brokers gained from NSO's spyware ambitions." *The Washington Post*, July 19, 2021. Accessed August 16, 2021. https://www.washingtonpost.com/technology/2021/07/19/nso-business-us/; "Pegasus: Who are the alleged victims of spyware targeting?" BBC News, July 22, 2021. Accessed August 16, 2021. https://www.bbc.com/news/world-57891506.

27   Asthana, Anushka, Sally Hayden, and Jonathan Watts. "Fortress Europe: what happens to the refugees sent back to Libya?" *The Guardian*, May 8, 2019. Accessed August 16, 2021. https://www.theguardian.com/news/audio/2019/may/08/fortress-europe-what-happens-to-the-refugees-sent-back-to-libya.

28   Barry, Sinead, and Anelise Borges. "Libya managing migrants is 'like a sick doctor treating patients.'" *Euronews*, May 21, 2019. Accessed August 16, 2021. https://www.euronews.com/2019/05/21/libya-is-a-sick-doctor-being-asked-to-treat-patients-says-interior-minister.

CHAPTER 15

1   Sallyhayden. "08.04.19 Qasr Bin Ghashir." Soundcloud audio, 0:56, April 8, 2019. https://soundcloud.com/user-60656923/080419-qasr-bin-ghashir.

2   Hayden, Sally. Twitter post. April 8, 2019, 9:16 p.m. https://twitter.com/sallyhayd/status/1115347777993826311.

3   Hayden, Sally. Twitter post. April 9, 2019, 3:53 p.m. https://twitter.com/sallyhayd/status/1115628805975048192.

4   Sallyhayden. "Message from another refugee woman in Qasr bin Ghashir detention center." Soundcloud audio, 0:59, April 10, 2019. https://soundcloud.com/user-60656923/message-from-another-refugee-woman-in-qasr-bin-ghashir-detention-center; sallyhayden. "Message from refugee woman in Qasr bin Ghashir." Soundcloud audio, 0:16, April 10, 2019. https://soundcloud.com/user-60656923/message-from-refugee-woman-in-qasr-bin-ghashir.

5   Hayden, Sally. Twitter post. April 11, 2019, 4:27 p.m. https://twitter.com/sallyhayd/status/1116362209003823105.

6   "UNHCR issues urgent appeal for release and evacuation of detained refugees caught in Libyan crossfire." UNHCR. Last Modified April 12, 2019. https://www.unhcr.org/news/press/2019/4/5cb0b5954/unhcr-issues-urgent-appeal-release-evacuation-detained-refugees-caught.html?fbclid=IwAR3133ZQMaXmgMcT0R0Qx378cXZtQMulk0mENx-AYf-mFmX9Fza17kkttnI4.

7   Hayden, Sally. "'We are in a fire': Libya's detained refugees trapped by conflict." *Al Jazeera*, April 14, 2019. Accessed August 16, 2021. https://www.aljazeera.com/news/2019/4/14/we-are-in-a-fire-libyas-detained-refugees-trapped-by-conflict.

8   Migrace.org. Twitter post. April 15, 2019, 5:29 p.m. https://twitter.com/Migrace_Organiz/status/1117827288303845376.

9   Hayden, Sally. Twitter post. April 14, 2019, 3:15 p.m. https://twitter.com/sallyhayd/status/1117431172001300483.

10   Hayden, Sally. Twitter post. April 24, 2019, 9:37 a.m. https://twitter.com/sallyhayd/status/1120970128760422400.

11   Hayden, Sally. Twitter post. April 23, 2019, 8:52 p.m. https://twitter.com/sallyhayd/status/1120777478874779654; Hayden, Sally. Twitter post. April 23, 2019, 3:04 p.m. https://twitter.com/sallyhayd/status/1120698805912879104.

12   Hayden, Sally. "Libya: Detained refugees shot as clashes near Tripoli continue." *Al Jazeera*, April 23, 2019. Accessed August 16, 2021. https://www.aljazeera.com/news/2019/4/23/libya-detained-refugees-shot-as-clashes-near-tripoli-continue.

13   "UNHCR evacuates hundreds of detained refugees in Libya to safety." UNHCR. Last Modified April 24, 2019. https://www.unhcr.org/news/press/2019/4/5cc09a824/unhcr-evacuates-hundreds-detained-refugees-libya-safety.html.

14   Email to author, April 24, 2019.

15   "Libya: Horrific attack targeting refugees and migrants at detention center must be investigated as a war crime." Amnesty International. Last Modified April 24, 2019. https://www.amnesty.org/en/latest/news/2019/04/libya-horrific-attack-targeting-refugees-and-migrants-at-detention-center-must-be-investigated-as-a-war-crime/.

16   Hayden, Sally. "Calls for Libyan shooting to be investigated as 'war crime.'" *The Irish Times*, April 26, 2019. Accessed August 16, 2021. https://www.irishtimes.com/news/world/africa/calls-for-libyan-shooting-to-be-investigated-as-war-crime-1.3872945.

17   Hayden, Sally. Twitter post. April 24, 2019, 5:51 p.m. https://twitter.com/sallyhayd/status/1121094261368340481.

18   Hayden, Sally. "Refugees detained in Libya are drinking toilet water to survive." *The National News*, September 27, 2018. Accessed August 16, 2021. https://www.thenationalnews.com/world/mena/refugees-detained-in-libya-are-drinking-toilet-water-to-survive-1.774714; Hayden, Sally. "'He died two times': African migrants face death in Libyan detention centers." *The National News*, October 25, 2018. Accessed August 16, 2021. https://www.thenationalnews.com/world/mena/he-died-two-times-african-migrants-face-death-in-libyan-detention-centers-1.783850.

19   Michaelson, Ruth. "Turkey and UAE openly flouting UN arms embargo to fuel war in Libya." *The Guardian*, October 7, 2020. Accessed August 16, 2021. https://www.theguardian.com/

global-development/2020/oct/07/turkey-and-uae-openly-flouting-un-arms-embargo-to-fu-el-war-in-libya.

20   "UNHCR evacuates hundreds of detained refugees in Libya to safety." UNHCR. Last Modified April 24, 2019. https://www.unhcr.org/news/press/2019/4/5cc09a824/unhcr-evacuates-hundreds-of-detained-refugees-libya-safety.html.

21   "Italy accepts migrant families rescued by Sea-Watch ship." *Deutsche Welle News*, May 18, 2019. Accessed August 16, 2021. https://www.dw.com/en/italy-accepts-migrant-families-rescued-by-sea-watch-ship/a-48782847; "Italy's Salvini orders ports to block ship carrying 65 migrants." *Deutsche Welle News*, May 15, 2019. Accessed August 16, 2021. https://www.dw.com/en/italys-salvini-orders-ports-to-block-ship-carrying-65-migrants/a-48754158.

22   Campbell, Zach, and Lorenzo D'Agostino. "Friends of the Traffickers: Italy's Anti-Mafia Directorate and the 'Dirty Campaign' to Criminalize Migration." *The Intercept*, April 30, 2021. Accessed August 16, 2021. https://theintercept.com/2021/04/30/italy-anti-mafia-migrant-rescue-smuggling/; Tondo, Lorenzo. "Arrests made after migrants identify 'torturers' in camp in Sicily." *The Guardian*, September 16, 2019. Accessed August 16, 2021. https://www.theguardian.com/world/2019/sep/16/italy-police-arrest-three-over-and-torture-of-migrants-in-libya.

23   He was referred to 68 times as Ossama and twice as Osama. Prosecutor's report provided directly to the author: N.12809/2019R.G.notiziedireato-DDA, Procuradella Repubblicadi Palermo, Direzione Distrettuale Antimafia.

24   UNHCR. UNHCR Update: Libya 31 May 2019. Accessed August 16, 2021. file:///D:/UNHCR%20Libya%20Update%2031%20May%202019.pdf.

25   Hayden, Sally. Twitter post. June 4, 2019, 10:17 a.m. https://twitter.com/sallyhayd/status/1135837908412313600.

26   Panel of Experts on Libya. Final report of the Panel of Experts on Libya established pursuant to Security Council resolution 1973 (2011), 2019, 169, Annex 21. Accessed August 17, 2021. https://www.securitycouncilreport.org/atf/cf/%7B65BFCF9B-6D27-4E9C-8CD3-CF6E4FF96FF9%7D/S_2019_914.pdf.

27   Panel of Experts on Libya. Final report of the Panel of Experts on Libya established pursuant to Security Council resolution 1973 (2011), 2021, 12-13. Accessed August 17, 2021. https://www.ecoi.net/en/file/local/2047327/S_2021_229_E.pdf.

28   Magdy, Sam. "UN, US sanction Libyan official over human trafficking." Associated Press, October 27, 2021. Accessed November 14, 2021. https://apnews.com/article/middle-east-africa-libya-migration-united-nations-5b5b97d3374dc29a4582a09b26cd4299; US Department of the Treasury. "Treasury Sanctions Libyan Individual for Serious Human Rights Abuse of African Migrants," October 26, 2021. Accessed November 14, 2021. https://home.treasury.gov/news/press-releases/jy0437.

29   Raghavan, Sudarsan. "They are not treated like humans." *The Washington Post*, July 2, 2017. Accessed August 16, 2021. https://www.washingtonpost.com/sf/world/2017/07/02/they-are-not-treated-like-humans-inside-libyas-thriving-migrant-trade/?utm_term=.907978b0ac37.

30   "Mohammed Kachlaf is the head of the Shuhada al Nasr brigade in Zawiya, Western Libya. His militia controls the Zawiya refinery, a central hub of migrant smuggling operations. Kachlaf also controls detention centers, including the Nasr detention center—nominally under the control of the DCIM. As documented in various sources, the network of Kachlaf is one of the most dominant in the field of migrant smuggling and the exploitation of migrants in Libya. Kachlaf has extensive links with the head of the local unit of the coast guard of Zawiya, al-Rahman al-Milad, whose unit intercepts boats with migrants, often of rivalling migrant smuggling networks. Migrants are then brought to detention facilities under the control of the Al Nasr militia, where they are reportedly held in critical conditions. The Panel of Experts for Libya collected evidence of migrants that were frequently beaten, while others, notably women from sub-Saharan countries and Morocco, were sold on the local market as 'sex slaves.' The

Panel has also found that Kachlaf collaborates with other armed groups and has been involved in repeated violent clashes in 2016 and 2017." "Mohammed Kachlaf." United Nations Security Council. Last Modified June 7, 2018. https://www.un.org/securitycouncil/sanctions/1970/materials/summaries/individual/mohammed-kachlaf.

31 Tondo, Lorenzo. "Human trafficker was at meeting in Italy to discuss Libya migration." *The Guardian*, October 4, 2019. Accessed August 16, 2021. https://www.theguardian.com/world/2019/oct/04/human-trafficker-at-meeting-italy-libya-migration-abd-al-rahman-milad.

32 "Abd Al Rahman Al-Milad." United Nations Security Council. Last Modified June 7, 2018. https://www.un.org/securitycouncil/sanctions/1970/materials/summaries/individual/abd-al-rahman-al-milad.

33 Tondo, Lorenzo. "Senior Libyan coastguard commander arrested for alleged human trafficking." *The Guardian*, October 16, 2020. Accessed August 16, 2021. https://www.theguardian.com/global-development/2020/oct/16/senior-libyan-coastguard-commander-arrested-for-alleged-human-trafficking; Magdy, Samy. "Libyan officials say UN-sanctioned human trafficker freed." Associated Press News, April 12, 2021. Accessed August 16, 2021. https://apnews.com/article/libya-middle-east-tripoli-united-nations-83ad345278cc4d6add49ad01f420c3f5.

34 "The EU has always taken very seriously any allegations of criminal activities. Our engagement in Libya aims precisely at limiting any risks of unlawful activities. Our position on the arbitrary detention system is Libya has been and is very clear: it should stop operating and it should be replaced by alternatives that meet international standards.

When it comes to human smuggling and trafficking, the EU worked closely with EU Member States to extend sanctions to traffickers under UN regimes in 2018. In a coordinated effort, several EU Member States contributed and supported the UN Security Council adopting new sanctions to combat human trafficking and migrants smugglers. After its adoption by the UN Security Council, the Council transposed into EU law the sanctions adopted by the United Nations, imposing a travel ban and an asset freeze on six human traffickers and smugglers operating in Libya.

When it comes to the Libyan coastguard, supporting the capacity of Libya to improve Search and Rescue is crucial to save lives at sea and fight trafficking and smuggling as they are responsible for their territorial waters, where we as the EU do not have access. The Libyan Coast Guards are also fully responsible for Search and Rescue activities in the Libyan SAR zone." Email to author, December 19, 2019.

CHAPTER 16

1 A version of this song was uploaded on YouTube: Rediat Tesfasgi. "RTNew Eritrean music 2019 Rediat Tesfasgi (ኤጄ ል) from Libya zinta." YouTube video, 05:09. August 25, 2019. https://www.youtube.com/watch?v=0584FWdGQvc.

2 The author reported from The Gambia the year after Jammeh was ousted from power, traveling around the country to meet victims of his human rights abuses: Hayden, Sally. "Gambia's dictator ordered a witch hunt. This village is still haunted by it." *The Washington Post*, May 28, 2018. Accessed August 18, 2021. https://www.washingtonpost.com/world/africa/gambias-dictator-ordered-a-witch-hunt-this-village-is-still-haunted-by-it/2018/05/27/bb8a4fc2-32a9-11e8-b6bd-0084a1666987_story.html; Hayden, Sally. "After long dictatorship, Gambia's victims step forward." *The Irish Times*, June 22, 2018. Accessed August 18, 2021. https://www.irishtimes.com/news/world/africa/after-long-dictatorship-gambia-s-victims-step-forward-1.3539289.

3 "To understand why a center was established in Zintan and then officialised by the MoI, it is necessary to understand the importance of Zintan to the current power structure in Libya. Zintan is one of the main towns in the western mountains, with a population of 40 000. It

played a quite significant role during the revolution and it has important military power and some stake in the government in Tripoli. For example, the head of the DCIM for the western mountains comes from Zintan, as do Deputy Minister for Illegal Migration under the MoI of the GNA, Mohammed Shibani, and the director of the detention center. This gives the Zintanis considerable power.

"The company in charge of catering the detention centers in the western mountains is owned by a Zintani businessman with connections to the MoI and MoD, another reason why the Zintanis wanted a detention center in their area. The local authorities intend to transform the local airport into an international airport and the presence of a center in Zintan allows them to justify the decision in light of the need to repatriate migrants. Soon after Shibani was appointed, a repatriation flight was organized from Zintan." From page 84: Global Initiative Against Transnational Organized Crime. The Political Economy of Migrant Detention in Libya: Understanding the players and the business models, by Arezo Malakooti. Produced with the financial support of the European Union. 2019, 84. Accessed August 10, 2021. https://globalinitiative.net/wp-content/uploads/2019/11/Final-Report-Detention-Libya.pdf; For footage from the center, see: The New Humanitarian. "Dhar el-Jebel detention center in the town of Zintan, Libya." YouTube video, 01:26. June 24, 2021. https://www.youtube.com/watch?v=n85rQYpA0Sc&t=3s.

4   United Nations Support Mission in Libya and Office of the High Commissioner for Human Rights. "Desperate and Dangerous: Report on the human rights situation of migrants and refugees in Libya," 41. December 18, 2018. Accessed September 1, 2021. https://unsmil.un-missions.org/sites/default/files/libya-migration-report-18dec2018.pdf.

5   "800 migrants moved to safe center in Libya, UNHCR." ANSAmed, September 5, 2018. Accessed August 18, 2021. http://www.ansamed.info/ansamed/en/news/sections/general-news/2018/09/05/800-migrants-moved-to-safe-center-in-libya-unhcr_efce4166-7d1a-475a-bfef-3877f968c2e8.html.

6   Wehrey, Frederic. The Burning Shores: Inside the Battle for the New Libya. New York: Farrar, Straus and Giroux, 2018, 92.

7   Tubiana, Jérôme. "The EU's Shame Is Locked Away in Libya." The Nation, November 13, 2019. Accessed August 18, 2021. https://www.thenation.com/article/archive/libya-refugees-detention/.

8   Mission report, inter-agency mission to Zintan detention center, June 3, 2019 (document in possession of author). Available online at: https://www.humanitarianresponse.info/sites/www.humanitarianresponse.info/files/documents/files/mission_report_-_zintan_dc_3_june_2019.pdf.

9   O'Brien, Paraic. "Starvation, disease and death at Libya migrant detention center." Channel 4 News, June 7, 2019. Accessed August 18, 2021. https://www.channel4.com/news/starvation-disease-and-death-at-libya-migrant-detention-center.

10   Hayden, Sally. Twitter post. May 17, 2019, 9:25 a.m. https://twitter.com/sallyhayd/status/1129301809783349249; For another journalist's reporting on this center, see: Baraaz, Tamara. "Lying on the Floor, Dying of Tuberculosis: Inside the Horrors of Libya's Brutal Migrant Prisons." Haaretz, June 9, 2019. Accessed August 18, 2021. https://www.haaretz.com/middle-east-news/.premium-on-the-lying-floor-dying-of-tuberculosis-inside-libya-s-brutal-migrant-prisons-1.7341017.

11   Hayden, Sally. "'We need urgent help': Refugees perish in Libyan detention center." Al Jazeera, June 7, 2019. Accessed August 18, 2021. https://www.aljazeera.com/features/2019/6/7/we-need-urgent-help-refugees-perish-in-libyan-detention-center.

12   Hayden, Sally. "The EU's deal with Libya is sentencing refugees to death." The Guardian, February 5, 2019. Accessed August 18, 2021. https://www.theguardian.com/commentisfree/2019/feb/05/eu-deal-libya-refugees-libyan-detention-centers.

13   Hayden, Sally. Twitter post. March 17, 2019, 3:41 p.m. https://twitter.com/sallyhayd/status/1107305859967868929.

14 "'Healthwise, it was a disaster' in Libya's Zintan and Gharyan detention centers." Médecins Sans Frontières, June 21, 2019. Accessed August 18, 2021. https://www.msf.org/catastrophic-medical-situation-libyan-detention-centers.

15 Tubiana, Jérôme. "The EU's Shame Is Locked Away in Libya." *The Nation*, November 13, 2019. Accessed August 18, 2021. https://www.thenation.com/article/archive/libya-refugees-detention/.

16 Tubiana, "The EU's Shame."

17 Tubiana, "The EU's Shame."

18 "The establishment of International Medical Corps in 1984 ushered in a new and different kind of relief agency. By providing healthcare through training, International Medical Corps challenged—indeed, changed—the very definition of relief work." in: "Our History." International Medical Corps. Accessed August 18, 2021. https://internationalmedicalcorps.org/who-we-are/our-history/.

19 "In May, IMC had to suspend the referrals to private clinics as a consequence of the overspending of the resources available due to various emergency interventions. Especially, the Sabratah crisis had a significant impact on the increased number of referrals, when hundreds of PoCs (persons of concern), fleeing from conflict areas and smugglers camps, reached our CDCs (community day centres) in need of advanced medical assistance. However, IMC continued to provide referrals to public facilities for admission and investigations. As the public sector has limited resources and capacity in terms of equipment and personnel, most of the time the public structures refuse to receive migrants. The lack of documentation is one of the main issues, and, without at least the UNHCR attestation, PoCs approaching public hospitals always risk to be reported to DCIM authorities and sent to DCs. The lack of options for referrals limited IMC's overall capacity to provide advanced medical care to many PoCs in need." Project performance report delivered to UNHCR by IMC, January 1, 2018 - December 31, 2018. (Document in possession of the author).

20 "On 2nd December 2018, Zintan DC manager refused to let IMC medical team leave the DC at the end of the day unless we were referring 5 sick cases to private clinics. In order to guarantee the safety of our staff, after many negotiations, we decided to take charge of those patients and transferred 2 of them to another DC (Gharyan), and 3 more severe cases to a private clinic in Tripoli." Project performance report delivered to UNHCR by IMC, January 1, 2018 - December 31, 2018. (Document in possession of the author).

21 Figures made public by IMC program director Anil Kangal, who worked for the organization between September 2017 and September 2019: "Anil Kangal." LinkedIn. Accessed August 18, 2021. https://lb.linkedin.com/in/anil-kangal-8985b641.

22 5,685,052.95 USD was the total project budget for "Provision of life-saving assistance to refugees and asylum seekers in Libya." Project performance report delivered to UNHCR by IMC, January 1, 2018 - December 31, 2018; 4,551,432 USD was the total project budget for "Provision of life-saving assistance to refugees and asylum seekers in Libya." Project performance report delivered to UNHCR by IMC, January 1, 2019 - February 29, 2020. (Documents in possession of the author).

23 "Libya." International Medical Corps. Accessed August 18, 2021. https://internationalmedicalcorps.org/country/libya/.

24 Gustafson, Rebecca. Email message to the author, November 15, 2018.

25 Bernhardt, Todd. Email message to the author, February 19, 2019.

26 Bernhardt, Todd. Email message to the author, May 22, 2019.

27 Kangal, Anil. Email in possession of author, May 24, 2019.

28 "Traveller and Humanitarian Anil Kangal talks about how Travelling Changed Her." GoWonder. Accessed August 18, 2021. http://letsgowonder.com/stories-of-wonderers/travellerandhumanitariananil/; "Anil Kangal." LinkedIn. Accessed August 18, 2021. https://lb.linkedin.com/in/anil-kangal-8985b641.

29 Statement emailed to author, September 28, 2019.

30 Hayden, Sally. Twitter post. May 15, 2019, 8:54 a.m. https://twitter.com/sallyhayd/status/1128569206641954816.

31 "UNHCR secures release of 96 detainees from Libya's Zintan detention center." UNHCR. Last Modified June 4, 2019. https://www.unhcr.org/uk/news/briefing/2019/6/5cf61e4e4/unhcr-secures-release-96-detainees-libyas-zintan-detention-center.html.

32 Email sent May 24, 2019, and leaked to the author.

33 Email sent May 24, 2019, and leaked to the author.

34 Mission report, inter-agency mission to Zintan detention center, June 3, 2019 (document in possession of author).

35 Mission report, inter-agency mission to Zintan detention center, June 3, 2019 (document in possession of author); Hayden, Sally. "Deaths pile up in Libyan detention center, leaked UN report shows." *The Irish Times*, June 25, 2019. Accessed August 18, 2021. https://www.irishtimes.com/news/world/africa/deaths-pile-up-in-libyan-detention-center-leaked-un-report-shows-1.3937256.

36 "UNHCR secures release of 96 detainees from Libya's Zintan detention center." UNHCR. Last Modified June 4, 2019. https://www.unhcr.org/news/briefing/2019/6/5cf61e4e4/unhcr-secures-release-96-detainees-libyas-zintan-detention-center.html.

37 "UNHCR has not had access to the Zintan DC since February": Email sent from UNHCR spokesperson Caroline Gluck to author on September 21, 2020.

38 Hayden, Sally. "Man (24) dies in fire in migrant detention center in Libya." *The Irish Times*, March 2, 2020. Accessed August 18, 2021. https://www.irishtimes.com/news/world/africa/man-24-dies-in-fire-in-migrant-detention-center-in-libya-1.4190721; Hayden, Sally. "Migrant (39) who failed to reach Europe dies in Libyan detention center." *The Irish Times*, May 25, 2020. Accessed August 18, 2021. https://www.irishtimes.com/news/world/africa/migrant-39-who-failed-to-reach-europe-dies-in-libyan-detention-center-1.4262356?fbclid=IwAR1FQg3_owrSnpq3yatPkP_GqgIv0NKIjLzf8vzoA96Z0-7v-zzlMLHQ3dA.

CHAPTER 17

1 "First group of refugees evacuated from new departure facility in Libya." UNHCR. Last Modified December 6, 2018. https://www.unhcr.org/news/press/2018/12/5c09033a4/first-group-refugees-evacuated-new-departure-facility-libya.html.

2 "Libya's planned transit center would keep migrants from risky Mediterranean crossing—UN agency." United Nations: Refugees and Migrants. Last Modified November 29, 2017. https://refugeesmigrants.un.org/libya%E2%80%99s-planned-transit-center-would-keep-migrants-risky-mediterranean-crossing-%E2%80%93-un-agency.

3 Creta, Sara. "Anxiety and uncertainty as UN refugee agency halts work at Libya facility." *The New Humanitarian*, January 31, 2020. Accessed August 11, 2021. https://www.thenewhumanitarian.org/news/2020/01/31/Libya-refugees-UNHCR-Tripoli.

4 Figure provided to the author by EU Commission spokesperson.

5 "Libya's planned transit center would keep migrants from risky Mediterranean crossing—UN agency." Refworld. Last Modified November 29, 2017. https://www.refworld.org/docid/5a1ffbe74.html.

6 "First group of refugees evacuated from new departure facility in Libya." UNHCR. Last Modified December 6, 2018. https://www.unhcr.org/news/press/2018/12/5c09033a4/first-group-refugees-evacuated-new-departure-facility-libya.html.

7 "Detained refugees in Libya moved to safety in second UNHCR relocation." UNHCR. Last Modified April 16, 2019. https://www.unhcr.org/news/press/2019/4/5cb60a984/detained-refugees-libya-moved-safety-second-unhcr-relocation.html.

8 "Libya: Evidence of possible war crimes underscores need for international investigation." Amnesty International. Last Modified May 16, 2019. https://www.amnesty.org/en/latest/

news/2019/05/libya-evidence-of-possible-war-crimes-underscores-need-for-international-investigation/.

9 Michael, Maggie, Lori Hinnant, and Renata Brito. "Making misery pay: Libya militias take EU funds for migrants." Associated Press News, December 31, 2019. Accessed August 11, 2021. https://apnews.com/article/9d9e8d668ae4b73a336a636a86bdf27f.

10 "1 John 4: New International Version." BibleGateway. Accessed August 11, 2021. https://www.biblegateway.com/passage/?search=1%20John+4&version=NIV.

11 Jones, Tobias, and Ayo Awokoya. "Are your tinned tomatoes picked by slave labor?" *The Guardian*, June 20, 2019. Accessed August 11, 2021. https://www.theguardian.com/world/2019/jun/20/tomatoes-italy-mafia-migrant-labor-modern-slavery.

CHAPTER 18

1 The Global Initiative Against Transnational Crime. The Human Conveyor Belt Broken—assessing the collapse of the human-smuggling industry in Libya and the central Sahel, by Mark Micallef, Rupert Horsley, and Alexandre Bish. 2019, 27. Accessed August 17, 2021. https://globalinitiative.net/wp-content/uploads/2019/04/Global-Initiative-Human-Conveyor-Belt-Broken_March-2019.pdf; Amnesty International. "No One Will Look for You" Forcibly Returned from Sea to Abusive Detention in Libya. London, 2021, 20. Accessed August 17, 2021. https://www.amnesty.org/download/Documents/MDE1944392021ENGLISH.pdf.

2 Hayden, Sally. Twitter post. December 18, 2018, 10:42 p.m. https://twitter.com/sallyhayd/status/1075159275301937152; / Reenacted shipwreck from 01:28 in: Migrant Rescue Watch. Twitter post. December 19, 2018, 7:11 a.m. https://twitter.com/rgowans/status/1075287463780855808; a list of attendees: Hayden, Sally. Twitter post. December 18, 2018, 11:02 p.m. https://twitter.com/sallyhayd/status/1075164315936849920.

3 Hayden, Sally. Twitter post. December 18, 2018, 11:26 p.m. https://twitter.com/sallyhayd/status/1075170538753024001.

4 Hayden, Sally. Twitter post. December 18, 2018, 11:15 a.m. https://twitter.com/sallyhayd/status/1074986404558573568.

5 Another source on this topic: "we received information concerning the disappearance of between 100 and 150 men from Tajoura detention center between the months of August and October [2018]. Issues at the Tajoura detention center have emerged previously. Earlier in 2018 visiting aid workers at the center discovered a hidden underground storage area in which a group of Eritreans had been held in terrible conditions. When asked, the detention-center management said that the migrants were being punished for trying to escape." The Global Initiative Against Transnational Crime. The Human Conveyor Belt Broken—assessing the collapse of the human-smuggling industry in Libya and the central Sahel, by Mark Micallef, Rupert Horsley, and Alexandre Bish. 2019, 26-27. Accessed August 17, 2021. https://globalinitiative.net/wp-content/uploads/2019/04/Global-Initiative-Human-Conveyor-Belt-Broken_March-2019.pdf

6 Hayden, Sally. "Desperate migrants in Libya detention centers forced to fight on front lines of new civil war." *The Telegraph*, April 28, 2019. Accessed August 17, 2021. https://www.telegraph.co.uk/news/2019/04/28/desperate-migrants-libya-detention-centers-forced-fight-front/.

7 Channel 4 News. "Revealed: human rights abuses in Libyan migrant camps." YouTube video, 10:36. May 10, 2019. https://www.youtube.com/watch?v=MebcasTO0hQ.

8 Channel 4 News. "Revealed: human rights abuses in Libyan migrant camps." YouTube video, 10:36. May 10, 2019. https://www.youtube.com/watch?v=MebcasTO0hQ.

9 Al-Warfalli, Ayman, and Ulf Laessing. "Libya's Haftar orders troops to fight harder during Ramadan." *Reuters*, May 5, 2019. Accessed August 17, 2021. https://www.reuters.com/article/us-libya-security-haftar-idUSKCN1SB0R4.

10 Amru Salahuddien talk at the Frontline Club in London, July 2021: Frontline On-

line Events. "Libya." YouTube video, 1:05:11. July 31, 2021. https://www.youtube.com/watch?v=Tt1-pYGuRQg.

11 "Libya's UN-backed Sarraj seeks European help to stop Haftar assault." France24, May 7, 2019. Accessed November 17, 2021. https://france24.com/en/20190507-libya-sarraj-europe-leaders-help-haftar-assualt-merkel-macron-europe-un.

12 Versi, Anvar. "Haftar's Iron Fist." *New African*, June 16, 2019. Accessed November 17, 2021. https://newafricanmagazine.com/19048/.

13 Hayden, Sally. "Migrants in line of fire as battle to take Tripoli rages on." *The Irish Times*, May 8, 2019. Accessed August 28, 2021. https://www.irishtimes.com/news/world/africa/migrants-in-line-of-fire-as-battle-to-take-tripoli-rages-on-1.3885438.

14 "Article 28 of the 1949 Geneva Convention IV provides: "The presence of a protected person may not be used to render certain points or areas immune from military operations." "Practice Relating to Rule 97. Human Shields." International Humanitarian Law Database. Accessed August 17, 2021. https://ihl-databases.icrc.org/customary-ihl/eng/docs/v2_rul_rule97.

15 A portion of this phone call was played on CNN: CNN Connect the World. "Sally Hayden talks about attack on Libyan migrant center." Facebook, July 3, 2019, 10:48 a.m. https://www.facebook.com/watch/?v=349313772404683; For more of the author's initial reporting on the airstrike, see: Hayden, Sally. "They Hoped to Reach Europe Before They Were Massacred." *The New York Times*, July 3, 2019. Accessed August 17, 2021. https://www.nytimes.com/2019/07/03/opinion/libya-airstrike.html.

16 Hayden, Sally. "'I saw hell': under fire inside Libya's refugee detention centers." *The Guardian*, July 10, 2019. Accessed August 17, 2021. https://www.theguardian.com/global-development/2019/jul/10/under-fire-libya-refugee-detention-centers.

17 "Secretary-General Condemns Killing of Migrants, Refugees in Libya Air Strikes, Noting United Nations Gave Warring Parties Detention Center's Coordinates." United Nations. Last Modified July 3, 2019. https://www.un.org/press/en/2019/sgsm19652.doc.htm.

18 "UNHCR, IOM condemn attack on Tajoura, call for an immediate investigation of those responsible." UNHCR. Last Modified July 3, 2019. https://www.unhcr.org/uk/news/press/2019/7/5d1c836c4/unhcr-iom-condemn-attack-tajoura-call-immediate-investigation-responsible.html.

19 "Libya detention center airstrike could amount to a war crime says UN, as Guterres calls for independent investigation." United Nations. Last Modified July 3, 2019. https://news.un.org/en/story/2019/07/1041792.

20 Hayden, Sally. "Refugee victims of Tajoura bombing still lie in unmarked graves one year on." *The Guardian*, July 3, 2020. Accessed November 17, 2021. https://www.theguardian.com/global-development/2020/jul/03/refugee-victims-of-tajoura-bombing-still-lie-in-unmarked-graves-one-year-on.

21 "Six children among 53 confirmed fatalities after Libya detention center airstrikes: Security Council condemns attack." United Nations. Last Modified July 5, 2019. https://news.un.org/en/story/2019/07/1041911.

22 "Libyan guards shot at fleeing migrants, UN says, as Security Council fails to condemn attack." France 24 News, July 4, 2019. Accessed August 17, 2021. https://www.france24.com/en/20190704-libya-un-security-council-attack-tajoura-libya-migrant-center.

23 "Migrants still detained at site of deadly Libyan air strike." France 24 News, July 4, 2019. Accessed August 17, 2021. https://www.france24.com/en/20190704-migrants-still-detained-site-deadly-libyan-air-strike.

24 "Migrants still detained at site of deadly Libyan air strike." AFP, July 5, 2019. Accessed August 17, 2021. https://www.hurriyetdailynews.com/migrants-still-detained-at-site-of-deadly-libyan-air-strike-144715.

25 Document in author's possession: DSRSDG/RC/HC Ribeiro do Vale Meeting with Mr. Shibani, Deputy Minister and head of the Department for combating illegal migration (DCIM). July 4, 2019, Tripoli.

26 UNHCR, the UN Refugee Agency. Twitter post. July 3, 2019, 7:55 p.m. https://twitter.com/Refugees/status/1146492553920942081; Yaxley, Charlie. Twitter post. July 4, 2019, 7:28 p.m. https://twitter.com/yaxle/status/1146848178559492098.

27 Ganguly, Manisha. "Libya migrant attack: UN investigators suspect foreign jet bombed center." BBC News, November 6, 2019. Accessed August 17, 2021. https://www.bbc.co.uk/news/world-africa-50302602.

28 Hill, Evan, Dmitriy Khavin, Christiaan Triebert, Haley Willis, Malachy Browne, and David Botti. "Europe Shut These Migrants Out, Libyan Rebels Bombed Them." *The New York Times*, July 11, 2019. Accessed August 17, 2021. https://www.nytimes.com/video/world/middleeast/100000006594318/europe-shut-african-migrants-out-libyan-rebels-bombed-them.html.

29 Ganguly, Manisha. "Libya migrant attack: UN investigators suspect foreign jet bombed center." BBC News, November 6, 2019. Accessed August 17, 2021. https://www.bbc.co.uk/news/world-africa-50302602.

30 Hayden, Sally. "Survivors of deadly air attack in Libya demand evacuation." *Al Jazeera*, July 7, 2019. Accessed August 17, 2021. https://www.aljazeera.com/news/2019/7/7/survivors-of-deadly air-attack-in-libya-demand-evacuation.

31 Hayden, Sally. Twitter post. July 9, 2019, 6:04 p.m. https://twitter.com/sallyhayd/status/1148639066063343623.

32 UNHCR Libya. Twitter post. July 9, 2019, 4:01 p.m. https://twitter.com/UNHCRLibya/status/1148608182396305408.

33 UNHCR Libya. Twitter post. July 9, 2019, 11:13 p.m. https://twitter.com/UNHCRLibya/status/1148716806821089281.

34 Yaxley, Charlie. Twitter post. July 15, 2019, 10:05 a.m. https://twitter.com/yaxle/status/1150692752562302976.

35 Cochetel, Vincent. Twitter post. July 11, 2019, 10:18 a.m. https://twitter.com/cochetel/status/1149246642887036928.

36 Cochetel, Vincent. Twitter post. August 18, 2019, 11:10 p.m. https://twitter.com/cochetel/status/1163211553396707329.

37 "Accessed November 17, 2021. Siclari, Alessandro. Twitter post, August 14, 2019. 2:29 p.m. https://twitter.com/alesiclari/status/1163442921951105024.

38 Cochetel, Vincent. Twitter post. August 22, 2019, 10:29 a.m. https://twitter.com/cochetel/status/1164469699578671104.

39 Popowski, Maciej. Status of application for access to documents sent to the author, December 4, 2020.

CHAPTER 19

1 Bellomo, Nicola. Twitter post. April 27, 2021, 7:36 a.m. https://twitter.com/nicolabellomo/status/1386932311208480768.

2 UNHCR. Niger: Emergency Transit Mechanism (ETM). 2019. Accessed August 18, 2021. file:///D:/UNHCR%20Niger%20-%20Factsheet%20ETM%20-%20Update%20December%202019.pdf.

3 Arnold Bergstraesser Institute (ABI). The Political Economy of Migration Governance in Niger, by Leonie Jegen. Funded by Stiftung Mercator. Freiburg, 2019, 35. Accessed August 18, 2021. https://www.medam-migration.eu/fileadmin/Dateiverwaltung/MEDAM-Webseite/Publications/Research_Papers/WAMiG_country_reports/WAMiG_Niger_country_report/WAMiG_Niger_country_report.pdf; Rodrik, Delphine. "Evacuated from Libya, 'indefinite transit' is keeping refugees stuck in limbo." *The New Arab*, April 30, 2021. Accessed August 18, 2021. https://english.alaraby.co.uk/english/comment/2021/4/29/how-indefinite-transit-is-keeping-refugees-stuck-in-limbo.

4   For more on Rwandan genocide see: Dallaire, Romeo. *Shake Hands With The Devil: The Failure of Humanity in Rwanda*. Arrow, 2005; Mamdani, Mahmood. *When Victims Become Killers: Colonialism, Nativism, and the Genocide in Rwanda*. New Jersey: Princeton University Press, 2001; Gourevitch, Philip. *We Wish to Inform You That Tomorrow We Will Be Killed With Our Families*. Farrar, Straus and Giroux, New York, 1998. Hatzfeld, Jean. *Machete Season: The Killers in Rwanda Speak*, translated by Linda Coverdale. New York: Farrar, Straus and Giroux, 2005.

5   "Rwanda agrees to take in hundreds of refugees stuck in Libya." *Al Jazeera*, September 10, 2019. Accessed August 18, 2021. https://www.aljazeera.com/news/2019/9/10/rwanda-agrees-to-take-in-hundreds-of-refugees-stuck-in-libya.

6   "Rwanda Offers to Host African Migrants Stranded in Libya." *The New York Times*, November 23, 2017. Accessed August 18, 2021. https://www.nytimes.com/2017/11/23/world/africa/rwanda-libya-migrants.html

7   Mugisha, Ivan G., and Allan Olingo. "Rwanda offers migrants stuck in Libya, Niger a safe haven." *The East African News*, August 10, 2019. Accessed August 18, 2021. https://www.theeastafrican.co.ke/news/ea/Rwanda-offers-migrants-stuck-in-libya-niger-a-safe-haven/4552908-5230986-dyvo6vz/index.html.

8   "Joint Statement: Government of Rwanda, UNHCR and African Union agree to evacuate refugees out of Libya." UNHCR. Last Modified September 10, 2019. https://www.unhcr.org/uk/news/press/2019/9/5d5d1c9a4/joint-statement-government-rwanda-unhcr-african-union-agree-evacuate-refugees.html.

9   "Rwanda: the EU provides €10.3 million for life-saving refugee support measures." European Commission. Last Modified November 19, 2019. https://ec.europa.eu/commission/presscorner/detail/en/ip_19_6301.

10   Green, Andrew. "Inside Israel's Secret Program to Get Rid of African Refugees." *Foreign Policy*, June 27, 2017. Accessed August 18, 2021. https://foreignpolicy.com/2017/06/27/inside-israels-secret-program-to-get-rid-of-african_refugees_uganda_rwanda/.

11   World Bank figures. Accessed August 30, 2021. https://data.worldbank.org/indicator/NY.GDP.PCAP.CD?locations=KM.

12   Abrahamian, Atossa Araxia. "The Cosmopolites: The Coming of the Global Citizen." Columbia Global Reports. 2015.

13   Melhem, Yaara Bou and Helen Davidson. 'From Nauru to limbo: the anguish of Australia's last asylum seeker in Cambodia.' *The Guardian*. December 28, 2019. https://www.theguardian.com/australia-news/2019/dec/29/from-nauru-to-limbo-the-anguish-of-australias-last-asylum-seeker-in-cambodia.

14   "First group of vulnerable refugees evacuated from Libya to Rwanda." UNHCR. Last Modified September 27, 2019. https://www.unhcr.org/uk/news/briefing/2019/9/5d8dc6e64/first-group-vulnerable-refugees-evacuated-libya-rwanda.html.

15   "Rwanda." UNHCR. Accessed August 18, 2021. https://reporting.unhcr.org/node/12530?y=2019#year.

16   "President Kagame addresses 74th UN General Assembly—General Debate | New York, 24 September 2019." Paul Kagame. Last Modified September 24, 2019. https://www.paulkagame.com/president-kagame-addresses-74th-un-general-assembly-general-debate-new-york-24-september-2019/.

17   "First group of vulnerable refugees evacuated from Libya to Rwanda." UNHCR. Last Modified September 27, 2019. https://www.unhcr.org/news/briefing/2019/9/5d8dc6e64/first-group-vulnerable-refugees-evacuated-libya-rwanda.html.

18   UNHCR. UNHCR Update: Libya 11 October 2019. 2019. Accessed August 18, 2021. https://reliefweb.int/sites/reliefweb.int/files/resources/UNHCR%20Libya%20Update%2011%20October_2019.pdf.

19   Morgan, Richard. "Rwanda is bringing tech buzz to Africa." *Fortune*, December 30, 2019. Accessed August 18, 2021. https://fortune.com/2019/12/30/rwanda-kigali-tech-africa/.

20 Hayden, Sally. "Rwanda remembers: 'It simply should never have happened.'" *The Irish Times*, April 8, 2014. Accessed August 18, 2021. https://www.irishtimes.com/news/world/africa/rwanda-remembers-it-simply should-never-have-happened-1.1753505.

21 "World press freedom index 2014." Reporters Without Borders. Accessed September 1, 2021. https://rsf.org/en/world-press-freedom-index-2014.

22 "Radio station manager missing since genocide anniversary event." Reporters Without Borders, April 9, 2014. Accessed August 18, 2021. https://rsf.org/en/news/radio-station-manager-missing-genocide-anniversary-event.

23 "Kizito Mihigo: The Rwandan gospel singer who died in a police cell." BBC News, February 29, 2020. Accessed August 18, 2021. https://www.bbc.com/news/world-africa-51667168; "Rwanda's Kizito Mihigo and Cassien Ntamuhanga arrested." BBC News, April 14, 2014. https://www.bbc.com/news/world-africa-27028206.

24 See: Wrong, Michaela. *Do Not Disturb: The Story of a Political Murder and an African Regime Gone Bad*. New York: Public Affairs, 2021.

25 Booth, Robert. "Does this picture make you think of Rwanda?" *The Guardian*, August 3, 2010. Accessed August 18, 2021. https://www.theguardian.com/media/2010/aug/03/london-pr-rwanda-saudi-arabia.

26 See: Purdeková, Andrea. "'Even if I am not here, there are so many eyes': surveillance and state reach in Rwanda." *The Journal of Modern African Studies* 49, no. 3 (2011): 475-497. Accessed August 18, 2021. http://www.jstor.org/stable/23018902.

27 See: "Libya: Alarming rates of malnutrition and inhumane conditions in Tripoli detention center." Médecins Sans Frontières (MSF). Last Modified March 20, 2019. https://www.msf.org/alarming-rates-malnutrition-and-inhumane-conditions-tripoli-detention-center-libya; Malie, Mario. "As a refugee in one of Libya's dangerous detention centers, I know what it feels like when the world leaves you behind." *The Independent*, July 15, 2019. Accessed August 18, 2021. https://www.independent.co.uk/voices/libya-strike-refugee-unhcr-tripoli-triq-al-sikka-italy-a9004961.html.

28 Cochetel, Vincent. Twitter post. November 27, 2019, 11:20 a.m. https://twitter.com/cochetel/status/1199649233726558208.

29 Rwandan National Police. Twitter Post. April 18, 2020, 12.13 a.m. Accessed September 1, 2021. https://twitter.com/Rwandapolice/status/1251287660070666246?s=20. "Refugees Protest Under Coronavirus Lockdown in Rwanda." Associated Press via Voice of America, April 17, 2020. Accessed August 30, 2021. https://www.voanews.com/covid-19-pandemic/refugees-protest-under-coronavirus-lockdown-rwanda.

30 Hayden, Sally. "Rwandan police chief accused of sexual assault of child refugee at UN center." *The Guardian*, April 27, 2020. Accessed August 18, 2021. https://www.theguardian.com/global-development/2020/apr/27/rwandan-police-chief-accused-of-sexual-assault-of-child-refugee-at-un-center; Rudatsimburwa, Albert. "The Guardian feeds its readers with refugee porn." *The New Times*, May 1, 2020. Accessed August 18, 2021. https://www.newtimes.co.rw/news/guardian-feeds-its-readers-refugee-porn.

CHAPTER 20

1 "Libya's Relentless Militia War: Civilians Harmed in The Battle for Tripoli, April—August 2019." Amnesty International. Last Modified October 22, 2019. https://www.amnesty.org/en/documents/mde19/1201/2019/en/.

2 Hayden, Sally. Twitter post. September 1, 2019, 1:17 p.m. https://twitter.com/sallyhayd/status/1168135681564119045.

3 Hayden, Sally. Twitter post. September 1, 2019, 1:58 p.m. https://twitter.com/sallyhayd/status/1168146012382347264.

4   Hayden, Sally. Twitter post. September 1, 2019, 5:56 p.m. https://twitter.com/sallyhayd/status/1168206095166386177.

5   "Germany provides 2.24 mln USD to support refugees in Libya." *Xinhua*, July 22, 2029. Accessed August 11, 2021. http://www.xinhuanet.com/english/2019-07/22/c_138245934.htm.

6   "Venezuela, Poland and Sudan amongst 14 new Human Rights Council members." United Nations. Last Modified October 17, 2019. https://news.un.org/en/story/2019/10/1049461.

7   Hayden, Sally. "Vulnerable child and women refugees refused evacuation from Libya." *Al Jazeera*, October 21, 2019. Accessed August 11, 2021. https://www.aljazeera.com/news/2019/10/21/vulnerable-child-and-women-refugees-refused-evacuation-from-libya.

8   Email to the author, October 21, 2019.

9   Hayden, Sally. "'They don't help': refugees condemn UN over failures that drove them to sea." *The Guardian*. January 9, 2020. https://www.theguardian.com/global-development/2020/jan/09/they-dont-help-refugees-condemn-un-over-failures-that-drove-them-to-sea.

10 "U.S. dollar drops to 3.93 against Libyan dinar in black market: media." Xinhua, November 20, 2019. Accessed August 11, 2021. http://www.xinhuanet.com/english/2019-11/20/c_138570387.htm.

11 Michael et al., "Making misery pay."

12 Michael et al., "Making misery pay."

13 Michael et al., "Making misery pay," Associated Press News; A UNHCR-issued document titled 'Plan for new modalities of engagement by UNHCR/UN in the GDF,' written on November 19, 2019, and leaked to the author, also referred to "serious issues related to LibAid contracting procedures."

14 Alkhoja, Mohammed. Facebook page. Accessed August 11, 2021. https://www.facebook.com/mohammed.alkhoja.94.

15 Hayden, Sally. Twitter post. July 1, 2019, 8:19 p.m. https://twitter.com/sallyhayd/status/1145774022547922946.

16 Hayden, Sally. Twitter post. May 14, 2019, 9:51 p.m. https://twitter.com/sallyhayd/status/1128402386135994374.

17 Hayden, Sally. Twitter post. June 11, 2019, 11:19 p.m. https://twitter.com/sallyhayd/status/1138571526238822400.

18 Hayden, Sally. Twitter post. June 13, 2019, 11:05 p.m. https://twitter.com/sallyhayd/status/1139292726921502720.

19 Hayden, Sally. Twitter post. October 10, 2019, 4:59 p.m. https://twitter.com/sallyhayd/status/1182324758978924546.

20 Hayden, Sally. Twitter post. October 29, 2019. 1.04pm. https://twitter.com/sallyhayd/status/1189166117413097472.

21 "200+ people arrived from Abu Salim detention center & urban areas at the Gathering & Departure Facility in Tripoli, asking to be hosted there. Situation is tense as the GDF is already overcrowded. UNHCR fully mobilized to counsel & seek solutions, including via its urban programme." UNHCR Libya.Twitter post. October 29, 2019, 5:18 p.m. https://twitter.com/UNHCRLibya/status/1189230043333120000?s=20.

22 Hayden, Sally. Twitter post. November 1, 2019, 7:14 p.m. https://twitter.com/sallyhayd/status/1190346404218253315.

23 Hayden, Sally. Email message to Charlie Yaxley and Tarik Argaz, November 4, 2019.

24 UNHCR Libya. "Plan for new modalities of engagement by UNHCR/UN in the GDF." UNHCR. November 19, 2019 (leaked to author). On January 6, 2020, UNHCR spokeswoman Cécile Pouilly would finally comment on this in an email to the author, saying "What you have shared is not part of a health sector report, but appears to be an internal early IOM draft input. We do not comment on leaked documents."

25 Hayden, Sally. Twitter post. December 1, 2019, 11:13 a.m. https://twitter.com/sallyhayd/status/1201096998067331075.

26   Hayden, Sally. "Refugees being 'starved out' of UN facility in Tripoli." *The Guardian*, November 28, 2019. Accessed August 11, 2021. https://www.theguardian.com/global-development/2019/nov/28/refugees-being-starved-out-of-un-facility-in-tripoli.

27   "UNHCR expands help to refugees in urban areas in Libya, reassesses role of Gathering and Departure Facility." UNHCR. Accessed October 8, 2021. https://www.unhcr.org/uk/news/press/2019/11/5ddffe994/unhcr-expands-help-refugees-urban-areas-libya-reassesses-role-gathering.html.

28   "UN refugee agency rejects 'starving migrants' claim." Yahoo! News, November 28, 2019. Accessed August 11, 2021. https://ph.news.yahoo.com/un-refugee-agency-rejects-starving-migrants-claim-234040513.html.

29   Grandi, Filippo. Twitter post. November 29, 2019, 10:07 p.m. https://twitter.com/FilippoGrandi/status/1200536909048619009.

30   Avramopoulos, Dimitris. Twitter post. November 30, 2019, 2:43 p.m. https://twitter.com/Avramopoulos/status/1200787439633207299?s=20.

31   "High-Level Panel on Internal Displacement." United Nations. Last Modified December 3, 2019. https://www.un.org/sg/en/content/sg/personnel-appointments/2019-12-03/secretary-general-appoints-members-of-the-high-level-panel-internal-displacement.

32   Yaxley, Charlie. Twitter post. December 6, 2019, 8:39 p.m. https://twitter.com/yaxle/status/1203051483727618048.

33   Lomax, Gisella. Twitter post. January 29, 2020, 10: 37 p.m. https://twitter.com/GisellaLomax/status/1222649929396629507; Licona, Dante. Twitter post. January 29, 2020, 4:27 p.m. https://twitter.com/Dante_Licona/status/1222556844306128896.

34   Yaxley, Charlie. Twitter post. December 6, 2019, 8:39 p.m. https://twitter.com/yaxle/status/1203051483727618048.

35   Hayden, Sally. Twitter post. December 27, 2019, 7:10 p.m. https://twitter.com/sallyhayd/status/1210639117266161666; Hayden, Sally. Twitter post. December 31, 2019, 3:04 p.m. https://twitter.com/sallyhayd/status/1212026795672920069.

36   Hayden, Sally. Twitter post. January 8, 2020, 2:43 p.m. https://twitter.com/sallyhayd/status/1214920463304077313.

37   Hayden, Sally. Twitter post. January 7, 2020, 1:51 p.m. https://twitter.com/sallyhayd/status/1214545181518835712.

38   Hayden, Sally. Twitter post. January 10, 2020, 7;06 p.m. https://twitter.com/sallyhayd/status/1215711535038976000; Magdy, Samy. "Refugees shot dead in Libya were pushed out of UN facility." Associated Press News, January 11, 2020. Accessed August 11, 2021. https://apnews.com/article/afae0d3505300533a5479ff37f254858.

39   Hayden, Sally. Twitter post. January 12, 2020, 11:32 a.m. https://twitter.com/sallyhayd/status/1216322012194492417.

40   Seebrücke. "Der Deal, die Hölle und der Tod: Internierungslager in Libyen." Facebook, January 16, 2020. 01.49.43 in. Accessed August 20, 2021. https://www.facebook.com/SeebrueckeSchafftsichereHaefen/videos/2148616925241972/?__xts__[0]=68.ARALP7kS-OD-6Me9sMQfPbsnra6cenCchs7WG5Tg2J3TvSLVT0X-kkh4Wz1DBw_tBqkp8J-ucvtd-0J6vna5y-weiKlIh7zr08QE0A-TadZpjBN7GUNGl1sKO9GeWlRt_Mjfj2DUlq1ePxg6E-FeotQazmF9fseDjda0ZfCbLFPVo1NIO_a-awXUdRDDORKBGoHDdJrjGJRkBVF-SajTfQJ3_1L20lQmAwJ-lPYLN9MU3l01vf5tqo6AcZInXFeV7r0Gf6dX-DqE8KbEe-bXAJAP3Z5Z-Yjb5P5oefeGhgkmLPwmltmjLbLRuaoxqaeH08nDa_qXJGgCijlNuQ9c_Sz6K25WnKcCqWPDNKDxpLJgQrUTRBzll-cs-&__tn__=HH-R.

41   Hayden, Sally. Twitter post. January 24, 2020, 12:06 p.m. https://twitter.com/sallyhayd/status/1220679349403295745.

42   Hayden, Sally. Twitter post. November 12, 2020, 6:36 p.m. https://twitter.com/sallyhayd/status/1326957059955372032.

43   "UNHCR to suspend operations at GDF in Tripoli amid safety concerns." UNHCR. Last

Modified January 30, 2020. https://www.unhcr.org/news/press/2020/1/5e32c2c04/unhcr-suspend-operations-gdf-tripoli-amid-safety-concerns.html.

44   UNHCR, "UNHCR to suspend."

45   Hayden, Sally. "Reports of physical and sexual violence as Libya arrests 5,000 migrants in a week." *The Guardian*, October 8, 2021. Accessed October 8, 2021. https://www.theguardian.com/global-development/2021/oct/08/reports-of-violence-libya-arrests-5000-migrants.

46   "Libya: Thousands of migrants rounded up and taken to 'inhumane' detention centres." Channel 4 News, October 8, 2021. Accessed October 10, 2021. https://www.channel4.com/news/libya-thousands-of-migrants-rounded-up-and-taken-to-inhumane-detention-centres.

47   UNHCR statement available here: Hayden, Sally. Twitter post. October 8, 2021, 4:34 p.m. https://twitter.com/sallyhayd/status/1446136767313104907.

48   IOM. "IOM Condemns Killing of Six Migrants at Detention Centre in Tripoli." October 9,2021. Accessed October 10, 2021. https://www.iom.int/news/iom-condemns-killing-six-migrants-detention-centre-tripoli.

CHAPTER 21

1   "Mishnah Sanhedrin 4:9; Yerushalmi Talmud, Tractate Sanhedrin 37a." GoodReads. Accessed August 13, 2021. https://www.goodreads.com/quotes/7123194-whoever-destroys-a-soul-it-is-considered-as-if-he;.

2   "Verse (5:32)—English Translation." Qur'an. Accessed August 13, 2021. https://corpus.quran.com/translation.jsp?chapter=5&verse=32.

3   Walsh, Bryan. "Alan Kurdi's Story: Behind The Most Heartbreaking Photo of 2015." *TIME* Magazine, December 29, 2015. Accessed August 13, 2021. https://time.com/4162306/alan-kurdi-syria-drowned-boy-refugee-crisis/.

4   "Migration Route: The Mediterranean." Missing Migrants. Accessed August 13, 2021. https://missingmigrants.iom.int/region/mediterranean.

5   Camilli, Annalisa and Eleanor Paynter. "Death on the Central Mediterranean: 2013-2020." *The New Humanitarian*, January 12, 2021. Accessed August 30, 2021. https://www.thenewhumanitarian.org/news-feature/2021/01/12/migration-central-mediterranean-timeline-rescue.

6   Trilling, Daniel. "How rescuing drowning migrants became a crime." *The Guardian*, September 22, 2020. Accessed August 30, 2021. https://www.theguardian.com/2020/sep/22/how-rescuing-drowning-migrants-became-a-crime-iuventa-salvini-italy. Guardian Staff. "Sicilian prosecutors wiretapped journalists covering refugee crisis." *The Guardian*, April 2, 2021. Accessed August 13, 2021. https://www.theguardian.com/world/2021/apr/02/sicilian-prosecutors-wiretapped-journalists-covering-refugee-crisis.

7   Tondo, Lorenzo. "Refugee rescuers charged in Italy with complicity in people smuggling." *The Guardian*, March 4, 2021. Accessed August 13, 2021. https://www.theguardian.com/global-development/2021/mar/04/refugee-rescuers-charged-in-italy-with-complicity-in-people-smuggling; Trilling, Daniel. "How rescuing drowning migrants became a crime." *The Guardian*, September 22, 2020. Accessed August 13, 2021. https://www.theguardian.com/news/2020/sep/22/how-rescuing-drowning-migrants-became-a-crime-iuventa-salvini-italy.

8   My initial report from the ship: Hayden, Sally. "Christmas on the Mediterranean—a month on a migrant rescue ship." *The Irish Times*, December 14, 2019. Accessed August 13, 2021. https://www.irishtimes.com/news/world/europe/christmas-on-the-mediterranean-a-month-on-a-migrant-rescue-ship-1.4114485 (through a Subject Access Request to the European External Action Service made on May 11, 2021, and responded to on June 11, 2021, I later found out that this report was given to EU foreign policy chief Josep Borrell on December 16, 2019, as part of his daily press review.)

9   "Pope calls for closure of Libyan migrant detention camps." Associated Press News, Decem-

ber 19, 2019. Accessed August 13, 2021. https://apnews.com/article/56e44dab43f81d8b-2411522c2167185b.

10   *Reuters* Staff. "Libyan migrant centers are like concentration camps, pope says." *Reuters*, July 8, 2020. Accessed August 13, 2021. https://www.reuters.com/article/us-europe-migrants-pope-libya-idUSKBN2491JO.

11   For more on his background, see: Van der Zee, Renate. "He fought the mafia and won. Now this mayor is taking on Europe over migrants." *The Guardian*, April 18, 2017. Accessed August 13, 2021. https://www.theguardian.com/global-development-professionals-network/2017/apr/18/he-fought-the-mafia-and-won-now-this-mayor-is-taking-on-europe-over-migrants.

12   "*Styx.*" IMDb. Accessed August 13, 2021. https://www.imdb.com/title/tt5942864/.

13   "Two rescue ships impounded by Italy." *Al Jazeera*, May 7, 2020. Accessed August 30, 2021. https://www.aljazeera.com/news/2020/5/7/two-rescue-ships-impounded-by-italy; "On 10 October, the NGO ship *Alan Kurdi* was detained for the second time in six months in Sicily." MSF, October 23, 2020; "Lives on the line as legal appeal lodged to free the *Sea-Watch 4*." Accessed August 30, 2021. https://www.msf.org/lives-line-legal-appeal-lodged-free-sea-watch-4.

14   "In total, Sea-Eye sent the *Alan Kurdi* on twelve rescue missions and thus saved 927 lives. Around 240 crew members total went on missions on this vessel"; "Sea-Eye ceases to operate the rescue ship *Alan Kurdi*." Sea-Eye, July 19, 2021. https://sea-eye.org/en/sea-eye-ceases-to-operate-the-rescue-ship-alan-kurdi/.

CHAPTER 22

1   Johansson, Ylva. Twitter post. April 23, 2021, 6:44 p.m. https://twitter.com/YlvaJohansson/status/1385650905241071626.

2   English translation from Amharic of Kidane's charges in authors possession: Ethiopia. Addis Ababa. Federal First Instance Court. Plaintiff: The Federal Attorney General. Defendants: 1. Kidane Zekarias Habtemariam. 2. Saba Mendir Hayl. First charge on defendant number 1: Violating article 32(1) (a) of the 2004 FDRE Criminal code, and articles 3(1) and 6 of Proclamation Number 909/2015, Prevention and Suppression of Trafficking in Person and Smuggling of Migrants. Second charge on defendant number 1: Violating article 32(1) (a) of the 2004 FDRE Criminal code, and articles 3(1) and 6 of Proclamation Number 909/2015, Prevention and Suppression of Trafficking in Person and Smuggling of Migrants. Third charge on defendant number 1: Violating article 32(1) (a) of the 2004 FDRE Criminal code, and articles 3(1) and 3(2)(c) of Proclamation Number 909/2015, Prevention and Suppression of Trafficking in Person and Smuggling of Migrants. Fourth charge on defendant number 1: Violating article 32(1) (a) of the 2004 FDRE Criminal code, and articles 3(1) and 3(2)(c) of Proclamation Number 909/2015, Prevention and Suppression of Trafficking in Person and Smuggling of Migrants. Fifth charge on defendant number 1: Violating article 32(1) (a) of the 2004 FDRE Criminal code, and articles 3(1) and 3(2)(c) of Proclamation Number 909/2015, Prevention and Suppression of Trafficking in Person and Smuggling of Migrants. Sixth charge on defendant number 1: Violating article 32(1) (a) of the 2004 FDRE Criminal code, and articles 3(1) and 3(2)(c) of Proclamation Number 909/2015, Prevention and Suppression of Trafficking in Person and Smuggling of Migrants. Seventh charge on defendant number 1: Violating article 32(1) (a) of the 2004 FDRE Criminal code, and articles 3(1) and 3(2)(c) of Proclamation Number 909/2015, Prevention and Suppression of Trafficking in Person and Smuggling of Migrants. Eighth charge on defendant number 1: Violating article 32(1) (a) of the 2004 FDRE Criminal code, and articles 3(1) and 3(2)(c) of Proclamation Number 909/2015, Prevention and Suppression of Trafficking in Person and Smuggling of Migrants. Ninth charge on defendant number 2: Violating article 37 (1) of the 2004 FDRE Criminal code, and articles 3(1) and 6 of Proclamation Number 909/2015, Prevention and Suppression of Trafficking in Person and Smuggling of Migrants.

3   English translation from Amharic of Welid and Shishay's charges in authors possession: Ethiopia. Addis Ababa. Federal First Instance Court. Plaintiff: The Federal Attorney General. Defendants: 1. Amanuel Yirga Damte (Walid). 2. Shishay (Sisay) Godefay Demoz. First charge on defendants number 1 and 2: Violating article 32(1(a)) and 32(1(b)) of the 1996 Criminal Code of the Federal Democratic Ethiopia and article 3(1) and 392(c)) of the Prevention and Suppression of Trafficking in Persons and Smuggling of Migrants Proclamation No. 909/2015. Second charge on defendants number 1 and 2: Violating article 32(1(a)) and 32(1(b)) of the 1996 Criminal Code of the Federal Democratic Ethiopia and article 3(1) and 392(c)) of the Prevention and Suppression of Trafficking in Persons and Smuggling of Migrants Proclamation No. 909/2015. Third charge on defendant number 1: Violating article 32(1(a)) and 32(1(b)) of the 1996 Criminal Code of the Federal Democratic Ethiopia and article 3(1) and 392(c)) of the Prevention and Suppression of Trafficking in Persons and Smuggling of Migrants Proclamation No. 909/2015. Fourth charge on defendant number 1: Violating article 32(1(a)) and 32(1(b)) of the 1996 Criminal Code of the Federal Democratic Ethiopia and article 3(1) and 392(c)) of the Prevention and Suppression of Trafficking in Persons and Smuggling of Migrants Proclamation No. 909/2015. Fifth charge on defendant number 1: Violating article 32(1(a)) and 32(1(b)) of the 1996 Criminal Code of the Federal Democratic Ethiopia and article 3(1) and 392(c)) of the Prevention and Suppression of Trafficking in Persons and Smuggling of Migrants Proclamation No. 909/2015.

4   Tondo, Lorenzo. "Long road to freedom for farmworker accused of being notorious trafficker." *The Guardian*, July 12, 2019. Accessed August 15, 2021. https://www.theguardian.com/world/2019/jul/12/long-road-to-freedom-for-farmworker-accused-of-being-notorious-trafficker; Hayden, Sally. "Eritrean farmer released from Italian prison in mistaken identity case." *The Irish Times*, July 15, 2019. Accessed August 15, 2021. https://www.irishtimes.com/news/world/africa/eritrean-farmer-released-from-italian-prison-in-mistaken-identity-case-1.3957471.

5   Taub, Ben. "How not to solve the refugee crisis." *The New Yorker*, July 24, 2017. Accessed August 15, 2021. https://www.newyorker.com/magazine/2017/07/31/how-not-to-solve-the-refugee-crisis.

6   Tondo, Lorenzo. "Italy using anti-mafia lawas to scapegoat migrant boat drivers, report finds." *The Guardian*, October 15, 2021. Accessed November 17, 2021. https://www.theguardian.com/global-development/2021/oct/15/italy-using-anti-mafia-laws-to-scapegoat-mirant-boat-drivers-report-finds.

7   Campbell, Zach, and Lorenzo D'Agostino. "Friends of the Traffickers: Italy's anti-mafia directorate and the 'dirty campaign' to criminalise migration." *The Intercept*, April 30, 2021. Accessed August 15, 2021. https://theintercept.com/2021/04/30/italy-anti-mafia-migrant-rescue-smuggling/.

8   Figure given to author by IOM spokespeople in November 2020.

9   D. Kirkpatrick, David. "ISIS Video Appears to Show Executions of Ethiopian Christians in Libya." *The New York Times*, April 19, 2015. Accessed August 15, 2021. https://www.nytimes.com/2015/04/20/world/middleeast/isis-video-purports-to-show-killing-of-ethiopian-christians.html.

10   For more on these cases and the background to them, see the author's reports: Hayden, Sally. "Inside the smuggler's warehouse: Africa's 21st-century slave trade." *The Irish Times*, April 11, 2020. Accessed August 15, 2021. https://www.irishtimes.com/news/world/africa/inside-the-smuggler-s-warehouse-africa-s-21st-century-slave-trade-1.4224073; Hayden, Sally. "How Did One of North Africa's Biggest Human Traffickers Escape Prison?" VICE News, February 23, 2021. Accessed August 15, 2021. https://www.vice.com/en/article/m7an4x/how-did-one-of-north-africas-biggest-human-traffickers-escape-prison; Girma, Kaleab, and Sally Hayden. "'Cruel' trafficker accused of torturing refugees found guilty in Ethiopia." *The Guardian*, April 30, 2021. Accessed August 15, 2021. https://www.theguardian.com/global-development/2021/apr/30/cruel-trafficker-accused-of-torturing-refugees-found-guilty-in-ethiopia;

Hayden, Sally. "People trafficking: 'They were killers. They have raped many women.'" *The Irish Times*, March 13, 2021. Accessed August 15, 2021. https://www.irishtimes.com/news/world/africa/people-trafficking-they-were-killers-they-have-raped-many-women-1.4508833.

CHAPTER 23

1   'Statement of ICC Prosecutor to the UNSC on the Situation in Libya.' May 9 2017. https://www.icc-cpi.int/pages/item.aspx?name=170509-otp-stat-lib Accessed August 6, 2021.

2   Shatz, Omer, and Juan Branco. EU Migration Policies in the Central Mediterranean and Libya (2014-2019). Communication to the Office of the Prosecutor of the International Criminal Court: Pursuant to the Article 15 of the Rome Statute, Paris, 2019, 8, 9, 11, 18, 30, 32.

3   "Overall between July 2002–December 2019, the OTP [Office of the Prosecutor] received 14,167 communications, of which 715 were determined to be Warranting Further Analysis (WFA)." Independent Expert Review of the International Criminal Court and the Rome Statute System: Final Report, 207. September 30, 2020. https://asp.icc-cpi.int/iccdocs/asp_docs/ASP19/IER-Final-Report-ENG.pdf.

4   Coker, Demirkan. "Juan Branco on Julian Assange, the Yellow Jackets and the 'Twilight' of Macron." *The Yale Politic*, September 1, 2019. Accessed August 6, 2021. https://thepolitic.org/juan-branco-on-julian-assange-the-yellow-jackets-and-the-twilight-of-macron/.

5   See also: Ross, Aaron. "U.N. fires Central Africa legal adviser who accused peacekeepers of massacre." *Reuters*, May 31, 2018. Accessed August 6, 2021. https://www.reuters.com/article/us-centralafrica-un/un-fires-central-africa-legal-adviser-who-accused-peacekeepers-of-massacre-idUSKCN1IW265.

6   "Death by Rescue: The Lethal Effects of Non-Assistance at Sea." Forensic Architecture. April 18, 2016. Accessed August 23, 2021. https://forensic-architecture.org/investigation/death-by-rescue-the-lethal-effects-of-non-assistance-at-sea.

7   "NGOs file case against Frontex for violating migrants' rights." *Daily Sabah*, May 26, 2021. Accessed August 6, 2021. https://www.dailysabah.com/politics/eu-affairs/ngos-file-case-against-frontex-for-violating-migrants-rights.

8   "A Civil Society Tribunal, Brussels 2022." Front-Lex. Accessed August 6, 2021. https://www.front-lex.eu/front-lex-tribunal/.

9   "International Monsanto Tribunal." Monsanto Tribunal. Accessed August 6, 2021. https://www.monsanto-tribunal.org/.

10 "The Pesticide Generation: Children on the Front Line." France 24. Accessed August 6, 2021. https://webdoc.france24.com/france-pesticide-generation-children-front-line-glyphosate-monsanto/; Sheppard, Christine. "I believe Roundup gave me cancer. The Monsanto settlement is a slap in the face." *The Guardian*, June 30 2020. Accessed August 6, 2021. https://www.theguardian.com/commentisfree/2020/jun/30/monsanto-settlement-roundup-cancer-lawsuits.

11 "Dr. Lorenzo Pezzani." Goldsmiths: University of London. Accessed August 6, 2021. https://www.gold.ac.uk/visual-cultures/staff/pezzani-lorenzo/.

12 E.g.: "EU parliament declares 'Black Lives Matter.'" France 24 (via AFP), June 20, 2020. Accessed August 6, 2021. https://www.france24.com/en/20200619-eu-parliament-declares-black-lives-matter.

13 "Who We Are: With Justice. Against Injustice. Justified." European Center for Constitutional and Human Rights (ECCHR). Last Modified April 28, 2016. https://www.ecchr.eu/en/about-us/.

14 "For the purpose of this Statute, 'crime against humanity' means any of the following acts when committed as part of a widespread or systematic attack directed against any civilian population, with knowledge of the attack: a. Murder; b. Extermination; c. Enslavement; d. Deportation or forcible transfer of population; e. Imprisonment or other severe deprivation of

physical liberty in violation of fundamental rules of international law; f. Torture; g. Rape, sexual slavery, enforced prostitution, forced pregnancy, enforced sterilization, or any other form of sexual violence of comparable gravity; h. Persecution against any identifiable group or collectivity on political, racial, national, ethnic, cultural, religious, gender as defined in paragraph 3, or other grounds that are universally recognized as impermissible under international law, in connection with any act referred to in this paragraph or any crime within the jurisdiction of the Court; i. Enforced disappearance of persons; j. The crime of apartheid; k. Other inhumane acts of a similar character intentionally causing great suffering, or serious injury to body or to mental or physical health." Available at: "Rome Statute of the International Criminal Court Article 7: Crimes Against Humanity." on "Crimes Against Humanity." United Nations Office on Genocide Prevention and the Responsibility to Protect. Accessed August 6, 2021. https://www.un.org/en/genocideprevention/crimes-against-humanity.shtml.

15 "About Us." Global Legal Action Network (GLAN). Accessed August 6, 2021. https://www.glanlaw.org/about-us.

16 ECtHR—Hirsi Jamaa and Others v Italy [GC], Application No. 27765/09. Accessed August 6, 2021. https://www.asylumlawdatabase.eu/en/content/ecthr-hirsi-jamaa-and-others-v-italy-gc-application-no-2776509.

17 Reidy, Eric. "The legal battle to hold the EU to account for Libya migrant abuses." *The New Humanitarian*, August 10, 2020. Accessed August 6, 2021. https://www.thenewhumanitarian.org/analysis/2020/08/10/Libya-migrant-abuses-EU-legal-battle.

18 Global Legal Action Network (GLAN), Association for Juridical Studies on Immigration (ASGI), and Italian Recreational and Cultural Association (ARCI). Complaint to the European Court of Auditors Concerning the Mismanagement of EU Funds by the EU Trust Fund for Africa's "Support to Integrated Border and Migration Management in Libya" (IBM) Programme, June 11, 2020. Accessed August 6, 2021. https://docs.wixstatic.com/ugd/14ee-1a_956dfef570094e7ca67aace2668fc951.pdf.

19 Moreno-Lax, Violeta. "The Architecture of Functional Jurisdiction: Unpacking Contactless Control—On Public Powers, S.S. and Others v. Italy, and the Operational Model.'" German Law Journal 21 (2020): 385–416. Accessed August 6, 2021. doi: https://doi.org/10.1017/glj.2020.25; Reidy, "The legal battle", *The New Humanitarian*.

20 "Privatised Migrant Abuse by Italy and Libya." GLAN. Accessed August 6, 2021. https://www.glanlaw.org/nivincase; GLAN. Communication to the United Nations Human Rights Committee in the case of SDG Against Italy (Anonymized version), by GLAN, Violeta Moreno-Lax, Itamar Mann, and Noemi Magugliani. Submitted for consideration under the Optional Protocol to the International Covenant on Civil and Political Rights to The United Nations Human Rights Committee. Accessed August 6, 2021. https://c5e65ece-003b-4d73-aa76-854664da4e33.filesusr.com/ugd/14ee1a_e0466b7845f941098730900ede1b51cb.pdf.

21 Hayden, Sally. "Barricaded refugees 'ready to die' than return to Libya detention." *Al Jazeera*, November 19, 2018. Accessed August 6, 2021. https://www.aljazeera.com/news/2018/11/19/barricaded-refugees-ready-to-die-than-return-to-libya-detention; Hayden, Sally. "Nearly 80 rescued migrants forced off cargo ship in Libya." CNN, November 20, 2018. Accessed August 6, 2021. https://edition.cnn.com/2018/11/20/africa/libyan-migrants-forced-off-ship-intl/index.html.

22 "Report of the Independent Fact-Finding Mission on Libya", Advance Unedited Version. UN Human Rights Council. October 1, 2021.

23 Ellebrecht, Maximilian. "'This is hypocrisy'—A Q&A with Giulia Tranchina on European migration policy in Libya." *Routed*, October 24, 2020. Accessed August 6, 2021. https://www.routedmagazine.com/hypocrisy-eu-policy-libya.

24 "About." AlarmPhone. Accessed August 6, 2021. https://alarmphone.org/en/about/.

25 "From May 1st to 5th, Eritrean refugees cycled from Frankfurt to Brussels, for 452 kilometers. The 'Ride4Justice' started from Frankfurt, Koblenz, Köln, Aachen from there to Maastricht and finally to Brussels, to raise awareness about the inhumane conditions that refugees and

migrants in Libya are trapped in. Torture, lack of food, water, and other abuse takes place in human trafficking warehouses and official detention centers alike." Available at: Trivellato, M. Paron. "#Ride4Justice—a unique demonstration demands EU action on refugees stuck in Libya." EPA, May 9, 2019. Accessed August 6, 2021. https://www.eepa.be/?p=2844.

26 Le Blond, Josie. "Over €1m raised for migrant rescue ship captain arrested in Italy." *The Irish Times*, July 2, 2019. Accessed August 6, 2021. https://www.irishtimes.com/news/world/europe/over-1m-raised-for-migrant-rescue-ship-captain-arrested-in-italy-1.3944578. Schumacher, Elizabeth. "Germans march in solidarity with Sea-Watch." *Deutsche Welle News*, July 6, 2019. Accessed August 6, 2021. https://www.dw.com/en/germans-march-in-solidarity-with-sea-watch/g-49499396.

27 Quote seen on *World Today News*: "*Sea-Watch* captain Carola Rackete: As a white person, I don't want to be in the spotlight." *World Today News*, June 28, 2020. Accessed August 6, 2021. https://www.world-today-news.com/sea-watch-captain-carola-rackete-as-a-white-person-i-dont-want-to-be-in-the-spotlight/. Confirmed directly with Rackete by author.

CHAPTER 24

1 "Speech by Dr. Angela Merkel, Chancellor of the Federal Republic of Germany, on the occasion of the 368th Harvard University Commencement on May 30, 2019, in Cambridge MA." The Federal Chancellor. Last Modified May 30, 2019. https://www.bundeskanzlerin.de/bkin-en/news/speech-by-dr-angela-merkel-chancellor-of-the-federal-republic-of-germany-on-the-occasion-of-the-368th-harvard-university-commencement-on-may-30-2019-in-cambridge-ma-1634366.

2 "The Passport Papers." The Daphne Caruana Galizia Foundation. Accessed October 11, 2021. https://www.daphne.foundation/passport-papers/

3 *Reuters* Staff. "Rioting migrants torch cars, injure policeman at Maltese holding center." *Reuters*, October 21, 2019. Accessed August 20, 2021. https://www.reuters.com/article/us-europe-migrants-malta-idUSKBN1X00TM.

4 European Parliament. "European Parliament resolution of 11 March 2021 on the declaration of the EU as an LGBTIQ Freedom Zone (2021/2557(RSP))." 2021. Accessed August 20, 2021. https://www.europarl.europa.eu/doceo/document/TA-9-2021-0089_EN.html; press release: "Parliament declares the European Union an 'LGBTIQ Freedom Zone.'" European Parliament. Last Modified March 11, 2021. https://www.europarl.europa.eu/news/en/press-room/20210304IPR99219/parliament-declares-the-european-union-an-lgbtiq-freedom-zone.

5 Beaubien, Jason. "Africa Is Running Out of Oxygen." NPR, June 24, 2021. Last Accessed November 17, 2021. https://www.npr.org/sections/goatsandsoda/2021/06/24/1009475339/africa-is-running-out-of-oxygen.

6 "COVID-19 Vaccine Tracker." European Centre for Disease Prevention and Control, figures for EU vaccine uptake taken on October 11, 2021. https://vaccinetracker.ecdc.europa.eu/public/extensions/COVID-19/vaccine-tracker.html#uptake-tab; Mwai, Peter. 'Covid-19 vaccinations: More than 50 nations have missed a target set by the WHO'. BBC News, October 1, 2021. Accessed October 11, 2021. https://www.bbc.com/news/56100076

7 UNHCR Libya. Twitter post, 12 June 2021, 11:46 p.m. https://twitter.com/UNHCRLibya/status/1403846177158742021.

8 Hayden, Sally. Twitter post, 12 August, 2021, 12:59 p.m. https://twitter.com/sallyhayd/status/1425789124670279684?s=20

9 "The Swedish resettlement programme." Migrationsverket. Accessed August 20, 2021. https://www.migrationsverket.se/English/About-the-Migration-Agency/Our-mission/The-Swedish-resettlement-programme.html.

10 "Sweden's caretaker leader tapped to present new government." Associated Press News, July

5, 2021. Accessed August 20, 2021. https://apnews.com/article/sweden-europe-government-and-politics-3317b10aac56e1807396c6138beae52e.

11 "Danish parliament approves law to deport asylum seekers." *Al Jazeera*, June 3, 2021. Accessed August 20, 2021. aljazeera.com/news/2021/6/3/danish-parliament-approves-law-to-deport-asylum-seekers.

12 "Press Statement On Denmark's Alien Act provision to Externalize Asylum procedures to third countries." African Union. Last Modified August 2, 2021. https://au.int/en/pressreleases/20210802/press-statement-denmarks-alien-act-provision-externalize-asylum-procedures.

13 Specia, Megan. "Denmark Would Push Asylum Seekers Outside Europe for Processing." *The New York Times*, June 3, 2021. Accessed August 20, 2021. https://www.nytimes.com/2021/06/03/world/europe/denmark-asylum-process.html.

14 Willsher, Kim. "Macron accused of pandering to far right over Afghan crisis." *The Guardian*, August 17, 2021. Accessed August 20, 2021. https://www.theguardian.com/world/2021/aug/17/macron-accused-of-pandering-to-far-right-over-afghan-crisis.

15 "Statement by Commissioner Johansson on the situation in Afghanistan at the extraordinary meeting of Interior Ministers." European Commission. Last Modified August 18, 2021. https://ec.europa.eu/commission/presscorner/detail/en/statement_21_4286.

16 Athumani, Halima. "Uganda to Host 2,000 Afghan Refugees at US Request." Voice of America News, August 17, 2021. Accessed August 20, 2021. https://www.voanews.com/africa/uganda-host-2000-afghan-refugees-us-request.

17 Morris, Sophie. "MPs back new immigration bill which makes arriving in UK without permission a criminal offence." Sky News, July 21, 2021. Accessed August 20, 2021. https://news.sky.com/story/mps-back-new-immigration-bill-which-makes-arriving-in-uk-without-permission-a-criminal-offence-12359884.

18 "Australia: 8 Years of Abusive Offshore Asylum Processing." Human Rights Watch. Last Modified July 15, 2021. https://www.hrw.org/news/2021/07/16/australia-8-years-abusive-offshore-asylum-processing.

19 "End of the White Australia policy." National Museum of Australia. Accessed August 20, 2021. https://www.nma.gov.au/defining-moments/resources/end-of-white-australia-policy.

20 E.g.: Van der Kolk, Bessel. *The Body Keeps the Score: Brain, Mind, and Body in the Healing of Trauma*. Penguin Random House: New York, 2015, 53.

21 Taylor, Diane. "Teenage refugee killed himself in UK after mental health care failings." *The Guardian*, April 07, 2021. Accessed August 20, 2021. https://www.theguardian.com/society/2021/apr/07/teenage-refugee-killed-himself-uk-mental-health-care-failings?CMP=Share_AndroidApp_Other.

22 Cox, Simon. Twitter post. August 17, 2021, 10:41 a.m. https://twitter.com/SimonFRCox/status/1427566157670780930.

23 Flanagan, Natalie, Aine Travers, Frederique Vallières, Maj Hansen, Rory Halpin, Greg Sheafe, Nina Rottmann, and Anna Thit Johnsen. "Crossing borders: a systematic review identifying potential mechanisms of intergenerational trauma transmission in asylum-seeking and refugee families." *European Journal of Psychotraumatology* 11 (2020): 1-13. Accessed August 20, 2021. doi: 10.1080/20008198.2020.1790283; Sangalang, Cindy C., and Cindy Vang. "Intergenerational Trauma in Refugee Families: A Systematic Review." *Journal of Immigrant and Minority Health* 19, no. 3 (2017): 745-754. Accessed August 20, 2021. doi: 10.1007/s10903-016-0499-7.

EPILOGUE

1 Elgot, Jessica. "Boris Johnson vows push on immigration points system." *The Guardian*, June 27, 2019. Accessed October 11, 2021. https://www.theguardian.com/politics/2019/jun/27/boris-johnson-vows-push-on-immigration-points-system.

2   Henley, Jon. "Far-right leaders join Trump in welcoming Boris Johnson to No 10." *The Guardian*, July 24, 2019. Accessed October 11, 2021. https://www.theguardian.com/world/2019/jul/24/far-right-leaders-join-trump-in-welcoming-boris-johnson-to-no-10.

3   See: "Ethiopia: Eritrean Forces Massacre Tigray Civilians." Human Rights Watch. Last Modified March 05, 2021. https://www.hrw.org/news/2021/03/05/ethiopia-eritrean-forces-massacre-tigray-civilians; Kassa, Lucy. "'A Tigrayan womb should never give birth': Rape in Tigray." Al Jazeera, April 21, 2021. Accessed August 16, 2021. https://www.aljazeera.com/news/2021/4/21/a-tigrayan-womb-should-never-give-birth-rape-in-ethiopia-tigray; Muhumuza, Rodney. "'Our Season': Eritrean troops kill, rape, loot in Tigray." Associated Press News, May 28, 2021. Accessed August 16, 2021. https://apnews.com/article/only-on-ap-eritrea-africa-religion-9fe9140b76da946e4fa65095a1d5b04f.

4   Schlein, Lisa. "UN Finds Destroyed, Deserted Eritrean Refugee Camps in Northern Tigray." Voice of America News, March 26, 2021. Accessed August 16, 2021. https://www.voanews.com/africa/un-finds-destroyed-deserted-eritrean-refugee-camps-northern-tigray.

5   Gladstone, Rick. "Famine Hits 350,000 in Ethiopia, Worst-Hit Country in a Decade." *The New York Times*, June 10, 2021. Accessed August 16, 2021. https://www.nytimes.com/2021/06/10/world/africa/ethiopia-famine-tigray.html.

6   Hayden, Sally. "How Europe deals with the new wave of refugees is a test of our humanity." *The Irish Times*, June 19, 2021. Accessed August 16, 2021. https://www.irishtimes.com/opinion/how-europe-deals-with-the-new-wave-of-refugees-is-a-test-of-our-humanity-1.4597092.

AUTHOR'S NOTE

1   Ryback, Timothy W. "Evidence of Evil." *The New Yorker*, November 07, 1993. Accessed August 18, 2021. https://www.newyorker.com/magazine/1993/11/15/evidence-of-evil.

2   "Over one million sea arrivals reach Europe in 2015." UNHCR. Last Modified December 30, 2015. https://www.unhcr.org/uk/news/latest/2015/12/5683d0b56/million-sea-arrivals-reach-europe-2015.html.

3   "David Cameron criticised over migrant 'swarm' language." BBC News, July 30, 2015. Accessed August 18, 2021. https://www.bbc.com/news/uk-politics-33716501.

4   See: Marinovich, Greg, and Joao Silva. *The Bang-Bang Club: Snapshots from a Hidden War*. New York: Basic Books, 2001.

5   European Civil Protection and Humanitarian Aid Operations. "Forced displacement: refugees, asylum-seekers and internally displaced people (IDPs)." Last modified July 22, 2021. Accessed August 21, 2021. https://ec.europa.eu/echo/what-we-do/humanitarian-aid/refugees-and-internally-displaced-persons_en#:~:text=87%25%20of%20refugees%20are%20hosted%20in%20developing%20countries.

6   Cave, Damien, Emma Bubola, and Choe Sang-Hun. "Long Slide Looms for World Population, With Sweeping Ramifications." *The New York Times*, May 22, 2021. Accessed August 18, 2021. https://www.nytimes.com/2021/05/22/world/global-population-shrinking.html.

7   Xu, Chi, Timothy A. Kohler, Timothy M. Lenton, Jens-Christian Svenning, and Marten Scheffer. "Future of the human climate niche." *PNAS* 117, no. 21 (2020):11350-11355. Accessed August 18, 2021. doi: 10.1073/pnas.1910114117.

8   Vincent Cochetel: "Sally, just go to Libya. Come with me tomorrow, go to Libya . . . If you have solutions, bravo." "Der Deal, die Hölle und der Tod: Internierungslager in Libyen." Facebook, January 16, 2020. 01.06.18 in. Accessed August 20, 2021. https://www.facebook.com/SeebrueckeSchaf ftsichereHaefen/videos/2148616925241972/?__xts__[0]=68.
ARALP7kS-OD6Me9sMQfPbsnra6cenCchs7WG5Tg2J3TvSLVT0X-kkh4Wz1DBw_
tBqkp8J-ucvtd0J6vna5y-weiKlIh7zr08QE0A-TadZpjBN7GUNGl1sKO9GeWlRt_Mjfj-
2DUlq1ePxg6EFeotQazmF9fseDjda0ZfCbLFPVo1NIO_a-awXUdRDDORKBGoHD-
dJrjGJRkBVFSajTfQ_J3_1L20lQmAwJ-lPYLN9MU3l01vf5tqo6AcZInXFeV7r0Gf-

6dX-DqE8KbEebXAJAP3Z5Z-Yjb5P5oefeGhgkmLPwmltmjLbLRuaoxqaeH08nDa_qX-
JGgCijlNuQ9c_Sz6K25WnKcCqWPDNKDxpLJgQrUTRBz1l-cs-&__tn__=HH-R.

9   Stone, Duncan. "2019 25th April Tripoli, Libya. Migrants stuck in detention center—Orla
    Guerin." Vimeo video, 03:01. April 25, 2019. https://vimeo.com/332546934.

10 "What is a refugee?" UNHCR. Accessed August 15, 2021. https://www.unhcr.org/uk/what-
    is-a-refugee.html.

11 "The refugee definition is declaratory, i.e. a person is a refugee as soon as s/he fulfils the criteria
    contained in the definition. This would necessarily occur prior to a formal determination of
    her/his refugee status. Until such determination is made it must be assumed that those who
    have crossed an international border to escape a risk of serious harm in their country of origin
    are refugees and should be treated as such." UNHCR. "Refugee Definition." In Emergency
    Handbook (4th edition), 1. Accessed August 15, 2021. file:///D:/Emergency%20handbook.
    pdf; "Many [detainees] would fall under the realm of prima facie [refugees]. So you don't even
    need to do the determination of their status. And secondly, unless you determine the status of
    asylum seekers, you should treat them as refugees until you prove otherwise, it's not the other
    way around," a former UNHCR staff member in Libya told the author during an interview in
    2020.

12 For e.g.: see UNHCR Tunisia's Frequently Asked Questions, "A person registering with UN-
    HCR is considered as an asylum seeker until recognized as a refugee by UNHCR once their
    claim has been evaluated." "Frequently Asked Questions." UNHCR. Accessed August 15,
    2021. https://help.unhcr.org/tunisia/faq/.